Library of
Davidson College

Radio Corpse

DANIEL TIFFANY

Radio Corpse

IMAGISM AND THE
CRYPTAESTHETIC
OF EZRA POUND

HARVARD UNIVERSITY PRESS

CAMBRIDGE, MASSACHUSETTS

LONDON, ENGLAND   1995

Copyright © 1995 by the President and Fellows of Harvard College
All rights reserved
Printed in the United States of America

Permission has been kindly granted by New Directions Publishing Corporation to reprint the following material: "Anima Sola," from Ezra Pound, *Collected Early Poems,* copyright © 1976 by the Trustees of the Ezra Pound Literary Property Trust.

Earlier and shorter versions of Chapters 3 and 6 appeared, respectively, in *Paideuma,* vol. 21, no. 3 (Winter 1992), and *SubStance,* no. 61 (1990).

Library of Congress Cataloging-in-Publication Data

Tiffany, Daniel.
Radio corpse: imagism and the cryptaesthetic of Ezra Pound /
  p. cm.
Includes index.
ISBN 0–674–74662–7 (alk. paper)
1. Pound, Ezra, 1885–1972—Criticism and interpretation. 2. Radio broadcasting—Italy—History—20th century. 3. Fascism and literature—United States. 4. Imagist poetry—History and criticism. 5. Modernism (Literature)—United States. 6. Pound, Ezra, 1885–1972—Aesthetics. 7. Aesthetics, Modern—20th century. 8. Death in literature. 9. Dead in literature
I. Title.
PS3531.O82Z865   1995
811'.52—dc20   95-10353
CIP

Designed by Gwen Frankfeldt

For Norman O. Brown

Contents

Abbreviations ix

1 The Mystery of Negation *1*
2 Mortal Images *37*
3 Cryptaesthesia *65*
  Making and Unmaking *65*
  Memory Cells *81*
  Corpse Language *113*
  Hyperaesthetics and the
    Cult of Mourning *129*
4 Anathemata *147*
  The Sad Wit of Pollution *147*
  Plastic Surgery *159*
5 Impossible Effigies *175*
6 Radioactivity *221*
  Radium *221*
  Phantom Transmissions *236*
  Magical Realism *251*
  Erotic Casualties *262*
  Dictation and Oblivion *273*

Acknowledgments 293

Index 295

Abbreviations

ABC	Ezra Pound, *ABC of Reading*. New York: New Directions, 1960; orig. pub. 1934.
C	Ezra Pound, *The Cantos*. Fourth collected edition. New York: New Directions, 1987.
CEP	Ezra Pound, *Collected Early Poems*. New York: New Directions, 1982.
EPVA	*Ezra Pound and the Visual Arts*. Ed. Harriet Zinnes. New York: New Directions, 1980.
GB	Ezra Pound, *Gaudier-Brzeska: A Memoir*. New York: New Directions, 1970; orig. pub. 1916.
GK	Ezra Pound, *Guide to Kulchur*. New York: New Directions, 1970; orig. pub. 1934.
J/M	Ezra Pound, *Jefferson and/or Mussolini*. New York: Liveright, 1935.
L	Ezra Pound, *Selected Letters, 1907–1941*. Ed. D. D. Paige. New York: New Directions, 1971.
LE	*Literary Essays of Ezra Pound*. Ed. T. S. Eliot. New York: New Directions, 1960.
NPL	Ezra Pound, "Postscript." Rémy de Gourmont, *Natural Philosophy of Love*, trans. Ezra Pound. New York: Collier, 1961. Reprint of 1932 edition; trans. orig. pub. 1922.
P	Ezra Pound, *Personae* (1926). New York: New Directions, 1971.
PD	Ezra Pound, *Pavannes and Divagations*. London: Peter Owen, 1960.
P/J	*Pound/Joyce: The Letters of Ezra Pound to James Joyce*. Ed. Forrest Read. New York: New Directions, 1967.

Abbreviations

P/L	*Pound/Lewis: Letters of Ezra Pound and Wyndham Lewis.* Ed. Timothy Materer. New York: New Directions, 1985.
PMN	Ezra Pound, *Plays Modelled on the Noh.* Ed. Donald C. Gallup. Toledo: Friends of University of Toledo Library, 1987.
P/S	*Ezra Pound and Dorothy Shakespear: Their Letters, 1909–1914.* Ed. Omar Pound and A. Walton Litz. New York: New Directions, 1984.
RB	*"Ezra Pound Speaking": Radio Speeches of World War II.* Ed. Leonard W. Doob. Westport, Conn.: Greenwood, 1978.
SC	Humphrey Carpenter, *A Serious Character: The Life of Ezra Pound.* Boston: Houghton Mifflin, 1988.
SP	Ezra Pound, *Selected Prose, 1909–1965.* Ed. William Cookson. New York: New Directions, 1973.
SR	Ezra Pound, *The Spirit of Romance.* New York: New Directions, 1968; orig. pub. 1910.
T	*The Translations of Ezra Pound.* Ed. Hugh Kenner. New York: New Directions, 1963.

> I die in the tears of the morning
> I kiss the wail of the dead . . .
> Exquisite, alone, untrammeled
> I kiss the nameless sign
> And the laws of my inmost being
> Chant to the nameless shrine.
>
> —Ezra Pound, "Anima Sola"

CHAPTER 1

The Mystery of Negation

> The living being is only a species of the dead, and a very rare species.
> —Friedrich Nietzsche, *The Gay Science*

> Man is made in his own image: this is what we learn from the strangeness of cadavers. But this formula should first of all be understood this way: *man is unmade according to his image.*
> —Maurice Blanchot, "Two Versions of the Imaginary"

Few people would dispute the fundamental association between imagery and visuality; the idea of a nonvisual image is paradoxical. Yet pictures of all kinds, including graphic images, frequently resist, contest, or subvert visuality by a variety of formal means. Furthermore, images routinely seek to represent invisible things, or things without a sensible basis in the natural world, and, increasingly, to render objects (and bodies) in a manner that presupposes the dislocation and restructuring of the object according to nonocular principles (such as magnetic resonance imaging). By contesting or simulating the visible, images often reinvent visuality. Thus, although it is tempting to understand images as being defined by their intrinsic visuality, it is probably more accurate to say that "visuality" per se is the contingent term, which depends on the changing discourse and materiality of images for its conceptual coherence. If indeed images provide an index of the historical character of visuality, then we can only conclude that in certain periods the realm of the visible is continually submerged, or defaced, by the invisible and by what does not exist or has never existed. One could argue that *all* images display a general—that is to say, generative—resistance to visuality, yet I think it is essential to regard the fundamental obscurity of images, in any medium, as the residue of historical tensions.[1] History may indeed be frankly visible in a picture, yet it may also make its appearance by confounding the observant eye and by censuring the realm of the visible.

The aggressive visualization of the unseen that characterizes modern culture frequently produces images that are distinguished, paradoxically, by a resistance to visuality and a persistent quotient of the invisible.[2] These qualities, though certainly implicated in the modern fetishizing of means, should not be understood merely as effects of the modern technical media. Rather, the paradox of a nonvisual image must be attributed to a more general "scopic regime" of modernity, in which the desire to see, to possess, is continually frustrated and confounded by the image itself, by an opaque immediacy that forecloses the possibility of resemblance. Opacity and negativity—the power to withhold from the eye the visualization promised by the image—become the salient features of the image. A superb example of this negativity and its effects occurs in one of the opening chapters of Melville's *Moby-Dick*, where the narrator describes a painting that is remarkable for its obscurity:

> On one side hung a very large oil-painting so thoroughly besmoked, and every way defaced, that in the unequal cross-lights by which you viewed it, it was only by diligent study and a series of systematic visits to it, and careful inquiry of the neighbors, that you could anyway arrive at an understanding of its purpose. Such unaccountable masses of shades and shadows, that at first you almost thought some ambitious young artist, in the time of the New England hags, had endeavored to delineate chaos bewitched. But by

---

1. My discussion in this chapter of the problematic visuality of the image owes a large debt to suggestions made to me by W. J. T. Mitchell and, more generally, to his remarkable study *Iconology: Image, Text, Ideology* (Chicago: University of Chicago Press, 1986).

2. More predictably, modern discourse has tended to react against visual culture. Martin Jay finds in modern French theory, for example, "a profound suspicion of vision and its hegemonic role in the modern era." See his recent book *Downcast Eyes: The Denigration of Vision in Twentieth-Century French Thought* (Berkeley: University of California Press, 1993), p. 14. I am suggesting that this discursive negativity is already an integral part of modern visual culture (and a source of its fascination).

dint of much earnest contemplation, and oft repeated ponderings, and especially by throwing open the little window towards the back of the entry, you at last came to the conclusion that such an idea, however wild, might not be altogether unwarranted.[3]

Although the narrator, at once perplexed and fascinated by the image, is eventually able to construct a "final theory" about its significance, I would like to forgo consideration of whatever specific meaning the narrator ascribes to the painting (its "sublimity," its possible evocation of the "great leviathan"), in order to concentrate instead on the formidable negativity of the image and its tantalizing deferral of vision.

Even before we can address the painting as such, however, we must acknowledge that, as readers, we experience the painting only as a verbal description. Thus, as a verbal image, the painting never becomes visible to the reader in any real sense, though the immediacy of Melville's ekphrastic description is likely to produce an impression, or at least the effect, of visualization. We might then suppose that the reader's approximate relation to the painting resembles the narrator's vexed apprehension of it, which, given the bad light, stems as much from "conversation" and "contemplation" as it does from actual looking. From this standpoint, Ishmael's "vision" of the painting is perhaps more akin to reading than it is to looking (though reading, of course, is a kind of looking that entails being sequestered visually from the world of objects—a looking founded on blindness). The experience of visualization for both the spectator/narrator and the reader is highly mediated, though the reader, it seems, is apt to be more credulous than the spectator regarding the painting's visuality. Although Ishmael initially ascribes the image's obscurity to poor light and the accumulation of smoke and grime, he eventually decides that the resistance to visualization, which is "enough to drive a nervous man distracted," is intrinsic to the painting. This material image, which one would assume to be intrinsically visual, is therefore distinguished by its formidable and tantalizing obstruction of visual experience. Compelled by the image's obscurity to mediate (that is, to textualize) its ambiguous visuality, the narrator's vision of the painting can be no more than a "theory," constructed upon the opinions of

3. Herman Melville, *Moby-Dick* (Evanston, Ill.: Northwestern University Press, 1988), p. 12.

others (though we should not forget the unexpected illumination afforded by "the little window towards the back of the entry"). The negativity of the painting further suggests to the narrator that it might be an artifact produced during the time of the Salem witchcraft trials and that the inscrutable subject of the image is "bewitched." This association is confirmed for the reader, if not explicitly for the narrator, by the other objects displayed in the room with the painting: "The opposite wall of this entry was hung all over with a heathenish array of monstrous clubs and spears. Some were thickly set with glittering teeth resembling ivory saws; others were tufted with knots of human hair" (13). We can hardly avoid the conclusion that this wall hung with fetishes is the primitive counterpart of the inscrutable painting.[4]

Writing about images can bring to light only what resists the observant eye, as well as the residual blindness of the picture itself. To write about images, then, is to write about nothing. Yet nothing, as grammatical categories inform us, is always something; and little has been written about images that makes more of nothing than Maurice Blanchot's "Two Versions of the Imaginary." The essay is built around a startling gambit: "At first sight, the image does not resemble a cadaver, but it could be that the strangeness of the cadaver is also the strangeness of the image."[5] The initial shock of this comparison, which suggests, curiously, a latent animism in the artifact, depends on a moment of blindness: a resemblance has "at first sight" been overlooked. Yet the "second sight" that would enable one to grasp this resemblance is deferred, at least initially, by Blanchot's use of the term "resemble" *(ressembler)*. For to resemble a cadaver, an image may be said to be an *image* of a cadaver. Making sense of this comparison

---

4. David Simpson has examined Melville's writing in relation to the discourse of fetishism; see Simpson, *Fetishism and Imagination: Dickens, Melville, Conrad* (Baltimore: Johns Hopkins University Press, 1982). Although the originality and articulation of Simpson's essay are impressive, I find his argument to be less than satisfying for several reasons. First, his emphasis on phallicism and his tendency to define fetishism as a kind of false consciousness (a definition that risks confusing fetishism with the concept of ideology) neglect the crucial problem of materiality in fetish discourse. Second, Simpson rarely views Melville's (or Conrad's) novels as informing or mediating the discourse of fetishism; rather, he sees them as being merely symptomatic or illustrative of a concept that is already somewhat narrowly defined.

5. Maurice Blanchot, "Two Versions of the Imaginary," in *The Gaze of Orpheus*, ed. P. Adams Sitney, trans. Lydia Davis (Barrytown: Station Hill, 1981), p. 81.

The Mystery of Negation

therefore depends on Blanchot's precise conception of the image and, more specifically, on his concern with the duplicity of the image, which is at once material and ideal, opaque and transparent. Are we to understand the correlation of corpse and image in ideal, that is to say primarily visual, terms? Or are we to grasp a more difficult resemblance, dictated by the intransigent materiality of the corpse and somehow resistant to visuality (in spite of the conventional association of imagery and vision)?

For the moment, I'd like to defer this question by posing it in relation to another, more celebrated theory of images, which is captivated by, and indeed founded on, a similar moment of blindness. The section of Marx's *Capital* titled "The Fetishism of Commodities and the Secret Thereof" opens with a statement that serves as one of the founding principles of cultural criticism in the humanities: "A commodity appears at first sight an extremely obvious, trivial thing. But its analysis brings out that it is a very strange thing, abounding in metaphysical subtleties and theological niceties."[6] Overcoming the limitations of the naked eye, the second sight of analysis, decomposing the commodity's "stiff and starchy existence as a body" (*Capital* 144), discovers what Marx calls the "phantom objectivity" (*gespenstige Gegenständlichkeit*) of exchange value (128). Thus, poised on the threshold of sightless vision, the materialist historian discovers a non-visual, metaphysical component of the fetish object, which is the "secret" of its enigmatic power. The second sight of analysis described by Marx may be compared to Ishmael's theoretical "vision" of the inscrutable painting. As an image, then, the commodity resists visuality in an essential manner. Indeed, the "perversity" of the fetish, whether economic, sexual, or aesthetic, consists in the ambiguity of being at once present and absent, visible and invisible.[7]

---

6. Karl Marx, *Capital: A Critique of Political Economy*, vol. 1, introd. Ernest Mandel, trans. Ben Fowkes (Harmondsworth: Penguin, 1976), p. 163.

7. The material instability of the fetish object may be ascribed, in part, to the historical uncertainty of the fetish concept in colonial discourse. In his survey of fetish discourse, William Pietz notes that the fetish is described variously as a decorative object, a form of currency, a demigod, and a verbal charm or oath. Pietz, "The Problem of the Fetish," pts. 1, 2, and 3a, *Res* 9 (Spring 1985): 5–17; 13 (Spring 1987): 23–45; 16 (Autumn 1988): 105–123. On colonial fetish discourse in particular, see pt. 2, pp. 36–45, and pt. 3a, pp. 108–122.

Although Marx does not evince the "strangeness" of the commodity fetish by comparing it to something else (as is the case with Blanchot's revelation of the strangeness of the image), he does repeatedly emphasize the *Doppelcharakter* of the fetish—the fact that commodities are "sensuous things which are at the same time suprasensible" (*sinnliche übersinnliches Ding* 165). In effect, the commodity fetish is a split or double object, with material and phantasmic properties; it is an inert body haunted, or animated, by the specter of human labor. This spectral dimension of the fetish has not been overlooked by critics. Michael Taussig, for example, has observed, "Fetishism elucidates a certain quality of ghostliness in objects in the modern world and an uncertain quality of fluctuation between thinghood and spirit."[8] Marx, indeed, identifies not only the ghostly inference of commodities but his own investment in a rhetoric of death and animation when he refers to "all the magic and *necromancy* that surrounds the products of labor on the basis of commodity production" (169, emphasis added). One should also recall that Freud, in his later reflections on the subject, calls the fetish a "remnant" or "precipitate" of an archaic sexual formation, thus insinuating the corpse into medical definitions of fetishism.[9] Furthermore, the most important twentieth-century theorist of commodity fetishism, Walter Benjamin, argues that the modern fetish, succumbing to "the sex-appeal of the inorganic," represents "the rights of the corpse."[10] It is

---

8. Michael Taussig, "*Maleficium:* State Fetishism," in William Pietz and Emily Apter, eds., *Fetishism as Cultural Discourse* (Ithaca: Cornell University Press, 1993), p. 217. See also Thomas Keenan, who conjures the ghost of "humanity" from Marxian exchange value: "Humanity, the abstraction, is the ghostly residue that names the pragmatic necessity of likeness in exchange. To be alike is to be abstract, which is to say, to be a ghost—to be human, or a commodity." Keenan, "The Point Is to (Ex)Change It: Reading *Capital* Rhetorically," in *Fetishism as Cultural Discourse,* p. 172.

9. Sigmund Freud, *Three Essays on Sexuality* (1905), reprinted in the *Standard Edition of the Complete Psychological Works,* ed. James Strachey (London: Hogarth Press, 1960), vol. 7, p. 154, n. 2. Freud added this footnote in 1920 in a later edition of the *Three Essays.* The idea of the fetish as a "remnant" anticipates the views of the "Fetishism" essay of 1927, where Freud describes the fetish as a "memorial" to a lost object, an abstract *image* of the dead. In the same essay, Freud compares the loss precipitating the fetishistic exchange to an unmournable death—a case of two sons who "disavow" even as they recognize their father's death (*Standard Edition,* vol. 21, pp. 152–157).

10. Walter Benjamin, *Charles Baudelaire: A Lyric Poet in the Era of High Capitalism,* trans. Harry Zohn (London: Verso, 1983), p. 166.

no accident, then, that Blanchot's theory of the image shares this necrophilic dimension with Marx's great philosophy of the animism of the made object. For the most important modern allegories of making, such as sexual or economic fetishism, or formalism, usually exhibit a fascination with death, which finds its limit—and extinguishes itself—by deconstructing "death" in matter (or language), thereby revealing the fundamental animism of things (and words). Similarly, modern cultural fixations on death, as unmaking or decomposition, should be viewed as negative or inverted allegories of the irrationality—the "magic"—of making.

By invoking the strange materiality of the cadaver, Blanchot intends to break the spell of visuality and abstraction that holds the image as well as the observer in thrall, and to emphasize, therefore, the essential duplicity of the image. He observes, for example, "how much the apparent spirituality, the pure formal virginity of the image is fundamentally linked to the elemental strangeness and to the shapeless heaviness of the being that is present in absence" ("Two Versions" 83). Behind the transparency of the image that "helps us to recapture the thing in an ideal way" are the *remains* of the image, its materiality as a thing that refers only to itself—or to nothing at all. We are drawn to this other "image" not by its visuality but by its gravity and its opacity. Hence, for Blanchot, as for Marx, the "strangeness" of the image behind the image remains suspended in a problematic visuality: "When someone who is fascinated sees something, he does not see it, properly speaking, but it touches him in his immediate proximity, it seizes him and monopolizes him, even though it leaves him absolutely at a distance."[11] The object of "fascination," whether commodity fetish or cadaverous image, imposes a kind of "seeing" which is at once visionary and oblivious to any real thing that the image might represent. By abdicating its meaning as a sign—indeed its status as a sign—the fetish becomes indistinguishable from what it represents and thus forecloses the possibility of resemblance (since it has become the object itself).[12] The enigmatic power of the fetish depends entirely,

---

11. Maurice Blanchot, "The Essential Solitude," in *The Gaze of Orpheus*, p. 97. Blanchot's discussion of "fascination" occurs in a section of his essay titled "The Image."

12. Michael Taussig writes, "The fetish has a deep investment in death—the death of the signifying function. Death endows both the fetish and the Nation-State with life,

however, on the possibility of resemblance (albeit inscrutable) and the "phantom" of socially constructed meaning. The "magical" identification of sign and referent results, paradoxically, in the disappearance of the referent as an objective or empirical entity (and, conversely, in the desublimation of the image).

Whereas Marx associates the object of visionary abstraction—somewhat conventionally—with a realm of "phantom" values (which can be grasped only by the second sight of analysis), Blanchot insists upon anchoring this problematic visuality in the least accessible features of materiality: "What we call the mortal remains evades the usual categories: something is there before us that is neither the living person himself nor any sort of reality, neither the same as the one who was alive, nor another, nor another thing" ("Two Versions" 81). For Blanchot, it is not the abstraction, the metaphysicality, of the phantom but the obdurate facticity of the cadaver that destabilizes the "usual categories." The "strangeness" of the cadaver as an image resides, as I have suggested, in its resistance to visuality, imposing "vision that is no longer the possibility of seeing, but the impossibility of not seeing, impossibility that turns into seeing."[13] Yet "the impossibility of not seeing" coincides with an aversion to a representational image that has been stripped of its referent; the cadaver is a picture of no one; there is nothing to "see" but the material license of the image. In certain respects, like a modernist abstract painting, "The cadaver is its own image. He no longer has any relations with this world, in which he still appears, except those of an image" ("Two Versions" 84). Yet the corpse, unlike the abstract painting, retains in the strongest conceivable manner not only the possibility of resemblance, as well as unassailable objectivity, but an organic resistance to meaninglessness.

---

a spectral life, to be sure. The fetish absorbs into itself that which it represents, leaving no trace of the represented." Taussig, *"Maleficium,"* p. 246.

13. Blanchot, "The Essential Solitude," p. 75. For Blanchot, the counterpart of the image as cadaver is a philosophy of vision that is epitomized by what he calls "the gaze of Orpheus." The object of this gaze always escapes visibility, or disappears as it becomes visible: "As we look at the most certain masterpiece, whose beginning dazzles us with its brilliance and decisiveness, we find that we are also faced with something which is fading away, a work that has suddenly become invisible again, is no longer there, and has never been there. This sudden eclipse is the distant memory of Orpheus' gaze." Blanchot, *The Gaze of Orpheus*, p. 103.

Nevertheless, as Blanchot observes, "The image has nothing to do with signification, meaning, as implied by the existence of the world . . . Not only is the *image* of an object not the *meaning* of that object and of no help in comprehending it, but it tends to withdraw it from its meaning by maintaining it in the immobility of resemblance that has nothing to resemble" ("Two Versions" 85).

The melancholy severance of the image from its referent, as well as its paradoxical nonvisuality, produces another kind of "strangeness"—namely, estrangement. In Marxist terms, of course, the subject is profoundly estranged from its "possessions," which accumulate as commodities, seeing only its death as a subject reflected in the "phantom" objectivity of commodities. Similarly, even if a dead person is not transformed into a vengeful ghost, the subject's relation to the corpse is profoundly estranged by the sudden instability of reference and temporal dislocation. As an image, the cadaver, like the fetish, exerts a powerful sense of autonomy; it not only signals its estrangement from its referent by a paradoxical opacity, but it isolates the subject from its possessions (its images), instituting a separation that is nevertheless an encounter. Thus, Marx claims that commodity fetishes "appear as autonomous figures endowed with a life of their own" (*Capital* 165). Furthermore, the strangeness of the image, which is an effect of its complete autonomy, derives from what Blanchot calls "the power of the negative"—a negation of both subject and object which vitalizes the image itself. Hence, the image is not merely a dead thing but a corpse animated by negation, by what Elaine Scarry calls "the nonreferential character of the dead body . . . a nonreferentiality that rather than eliminating all referential activity instead gives it a frightening freedom of referential activity."[14]

Though the idea of an autonomous image, as well as Blanchot's trope of the cadaver, may seem far-fetched and even grotesque, a quick glance at the basic tenets of Kant's *Critique of Judgement* will show that Blanchot has not strayed very far from the origins of modern formalism in his theorization of the image. Or let us say he has *illustrated*—deconstructed—the aesthetic philosophy of modern formalism, by realizing its necrophilic inclination. Pleasure, says Kant, is

14. Elaine Scarry, *The Body in Pain: The Making and Unmaking of the World* (New York: Oxford University Press, 1985), p. 119.

the basis of aesthetic judgment, but a pleasure that is "pure and disinterested"—a *negative* pleasure, if you will. The "strangeness" of Blanchot's image-cadaver, which is an effect of its autonomy, appears in this light as a startling but authentic expression of Kant's theory of aesthetic disinterestedness. The opening sentence of Kant's "Analytic of Aesthetic Judgement" states, "If we wish to discern whether anything is beautiful or not, we do not refer the representation of it to the Object by means of understanding with a view to cognition, but . . . we refer the representation to the Subject and its feeling of pleasure or displeasure."[15] Thus, from the standpoint of aesthetic judgment, the image is severed from its empirical object, which exists not to be known, understood, or defined in relation to a concept but to be pleasurably intuited by the subject through the material form of the work. The disappearance of the object is only the first step, however, in a relentless dissociation of the image from anything real or empirical, including the subject: "The delight which we connect with the representation of the real existence of an object is called interest . . . Now, where the question is whether something is beautiful, we do not want to know, whether we, or anyone else, are, or even could be, concerned with the real existence of the thing . . . One must not be in the least prepossessed in favor of the real existence of the thing, but must preserve complete indifference in this respect" (42–43). Thus, the negative pleasure evoked by the image depends not only on the disappearance of the object but on the mortification of the subject.

In a reading of Kant's third Critique, Derrida claims that "pleasure does not presuppose the pure and simple disappearance, but the neutralization, not simply the death but the entombment of everything which exists insofar as it exists."[16] The distinction made here, as I understand it, is essential in comprehending the necrophilic dimension of both formalism and fetishism, as the essential modern allegories of making. The "death" of subject and object presupposed (and embodied) by the modern, formalist image is emphatically *not* a simple disappearance or elimination of these entities but a suspended ani-

---

15. Immanuel Kant, *The Critique of Judgement*, trans. James Creed Meredith (Oxford: Clarendon, 1952), p. 41.

16. Jacques Derrida, "The Parergon," trans. Craig Owens, *October* 9 (Summer 1979): 11.

mation, a transubstantiation, a mediation of bodies. As the rhetoric of death in Marx and Blanchot indicates, to be entombed or encrypted implies not only reanimation and metamorphosis but the art of cryptology, hermeneutics, and hieroglyphic meaning. Thus, Derrida argues, "Beautiful forms, which signify nothing and have no determined purpose are therefore also, and by that very fact, encrypted signs, a figural writing set down in nature's production. The *without* of pure detachment is in truth a language that nature speaks to us—she who loves to encrypt herself and record her signature on things."[17] Death, in this context—as in every other—is a discursive condition, a mediation of bodies and historical conceptions of the artifact, visuality, pleasure, and subjectivity.

The autonomous image, the image as corpse, should be regarded as a *cryptic* image, not only because of its obscurity and its withdrawal from visuality, but as a reminder of its figurative debts to the topos of death. Furthermore, the negative pleasure afforded by the image should be compared, as Derrida suggests, to the task of mourning: "A pleasure of this sort defines the judgement of taste and the enigmatic relation of mourning—the work of mourning begun beforehand—with beauty."[18] Indeed, the concept of aesthetic disinterest, eventually consumed by the discourse of *objectivity*, may be understood as a form of exquisite but aberrant mourning. Julia Kristeva's conception of the abject, which is founded, she claims, on "the logic of prohibition," renders the image-cadaver as an effect of melancholy.[19] Echoing Blanchot's thoughts on the imaginary, Kristeva writes that "the corpse is the utmost of abjection" and "the most sickening of all wastes"; "It is something rejected from which one does not part . . . Imaginary uncanniness and real threat, it beckons to us and ends up engulfing

---

17. Jacques Derrida, "Economimesis," trans. R. Klein, *Diacritics* 11 (June 1981): 15.

18. "The Parergon," p. 11. Elsewhere, Derrida draws a specific correlation between mourning and visuality. In Kant's aesthetic philosophy, he argues, "the greatest nobility accrues to sight, which achieves the greatest remove from touch and allows itself to be less affected by the object. In this sense, the beautiful has an essential relation with vision insofar as it consumes less. Mourning presupposes sight. *Pulchritudo vaga* [vague beauty] gives itself above all to be seen: and, by suspending consumption on behalf of *theorein*, it forms an object of pure taste in nature." Derrida, "Economimesis," p. 19.

19. Julia Kristeva, *The Powers of Horror: An Essay on Abjection*, trans. Leon S. Roudiez (New York: Columbia University Press, 1982), p. 64.

us" (3–4). The abject withdraws entirely from meaning and intelligibility; it is irremediably lost, foreign. Yet the cryptic features of the dead object, which are an effect of its radical materiality, are also, according to Walter Benjamin, the basis of its allegorical propensity.[20] The cadaverous image can mean almost anything to the modern eye—an eye "engulfed" by melancholy.

Encrypted by the gesture of negation, the image-corpse oscillates, like the fetish, between thing and phantom, but it also becomes a tomb in which subject and object are encrypted. What this means historically, as I have indicated, is not the disappearance of these entities but their transformation. Thus, historically speaking, the formalist image becomes a vault, a crypt, in which not only the concept of the sign, but the social formations of visuality and subjectivity which it assumes, enter a period of decomposition and reanimation. The correspondences between the image, mortification, and the renovation of discursive formations such as visuality and subjectivity emerge most effectively—and unexpectedly—in the concept of scientific and aesthetic objectivity, as it emerges at the end of the nineteenth century and the beginning of the twentieth. Not only is the concept of scientific objectivity, like that of aesthetic disinterestedness, characterized by what Derrida calls "the *without* of detachment," but it institutes a similar encrypting of natural signs, and depends on a nonvisual conception of the image as well as on a new model of material or carnal vision. Indeed, I will argue that the discourse of objectivity, deployed across a spectrum of positivistic disciplines, provides the most important modern examples of the autonomous, cryptological image.

The strange autonomy of the image is, of course, a fiction of almost irresistible potency, signaled by the fact that no living thing can achieve such independence: only a phantom or a corpse is adequate as a figure for the magical "objectivity" of the fetish. In spite of its power to enthrall and to obscure historical recollection, the autonomous image is never more than an empty vault, a crypt on whose walls are inscribed the ciphers of modernity, with its violent transformations of subjec-

20. Benjamin's theory of melancholy is most fully developed, along with his theory of the image, in *The Origin of German Tragic Drama*, trans. John Osborne (London: NLB, 1977).

tivity and perception. Among the most powerful and enigmatic of modern hieroglyphs, of course, is the concept of scientific objectivity. Its obscurity, as well as its remarkable resistance to disenchantment, are due in part to the uniquely powerful sedimentation of empiricism, asceticism, and irrationality embedded in its theoretical and practical expressions. (We should bear in mind that scientific empiricism, which began as a movement against rationalism, can be swayed and even enchanted by the physical magnetism of "nature.") Indeed, the figure of the autonomous image, along with its fetishistic and necrophilic habits, finds a perfect host in the modern discourse of scientific and aesthetic objectivity.

In a recent study, Lorraine Daston and Peter Galison argue that "objectivity is a multifarious, unstable thing, capable of new meanings and new symbols: in both a literal and figurative sense, scientists of the late nineteenth century created a new image of objectivity."[21] Surveying the production of visual "atlases" by physiologists, botanists, and other scientists, the authors emphasize the divergence of seventeenth- and nineteenth-century empirical epistemologies, in their efforts "to pry apart the ideals of verisimilitude and objectivity" (84). Thus, it is not "truth to nature" that modern positivism seeks, but a form of representation characterized by the power of negation—a distinction which is essential in illuminating the otherwise puzzling distinctions that modern poets make, for example, between naturalism and realism, or mimesis and objectivity. Emphasizing "the negative forms of all objectivity" (82), Daston and Galison argue that "objectivity is a morality of prohibitions rather than exhortations . . . Among these prohibitions are bans against projection and anthropomorphism, against the insertion of hopes and fears into images of and facts about nature: these are all subspecies of interpretation, and therefore forbidden" (122). Thus, the concept of objectivity is constructed on a system of taboos that seeks to rid scientific (and aesthetic) representation not only of ambiguity but of all interpretive meaning. (The taboo, of course, only ensures the hypostasis of that which is prohibited, including the phantom of meaning.) Foremost among the taboos of objectivity is subjective intervention (the port through which

21. Lorraine Daston and Peter Galison, "The Image of Objectivity," *Representations* 40 (Fall 1992): 123.

socially constructed meaning surreptitiously enters): "In its negative sense, this ideal of objectivity attempts to eliminate the mediating presence of the observer" (82). The mortification of the subject in the context of science clearly resembles not only the Kantian concept of disinterestedness but, more immediately, the "doctrine of impersonality" in Anglo-American modernism.

Moreover, as the authors indicate, the new "image" of objectivity is not merely a figure of speech. Images—graphic, mechanical, and photochemical—literally become the privileged medium of scientific representation: "The image, as the standard bearer of objectivity, is inextricably tied to a relentless search to replace individual volition and discretion in depiction" (98). As instruments of the negative power of objectivity, images are "talismanic guards" (115) and "protective charms" (82) against not only ambiguity but "interpretation, selection, artistry, and judgement itself" (98). Thus, scientific objectivity seeks to establish its authority by using images as fetishes to ward off the delusional powers of subjective, hermeneutical, and socially constructed meaning. Objectification, in this regard, is equivalent to forgetting, to oblivion.[22] Although images possess a fetishistic power in the discourse of objectivity, it is a dialectical and even antithetical potency, since they are instruments of disenchantment and iconoclasm—images directed against the potency of images.

The image of objectivity is clearly in thrall to what Blanchot terms "the power of the negative"; such an image implies not only the mortification of the subject but its own possible extinction. In a phrase that betrays the inherent conflict with linguistic values and modes of expression, Daston and Galison note the historical tendency to view scientific images as "texts so laconic that they threaten to disappear entirely" (82). The idea of an image hovering on the threshold of disappearance recalls the possibility of an image that is somehow nonvisual but also, more surprisingly, it suggests a trace of resistance to the visuality of the object. Although the discourse of objectivity depends upon the mortification of the subject, and the reduction—

---

22. Theodor Adorno and Max Horkheimer observe that "the loss of memory is a transcendental condition for science. All objectification is a forgetting." *Dialectic of Enlightenment,* trans. John Cumming (New York: Continuum, 1970), p. 230.

even disappearance—of the medium, one does not expect to discover in the modern construction of objectivity a resistance to the object itself.[23] Yet Daston and Galison indicate that "photochemical, mechanical reproduction was not always or even usually the means to make an image that readers would automatically find most similar to a bird, a dissected corpse, or a cell" (117). What, then, is left? Not the subject, or the object precisely, or the medium itself (in the sense that images are "texts so laconic that they threaten to disappear entirely"). An image of a corpse will not resemble a corpse, especially if we view it "automatically," that is to say, naturally. The corpse will appear—somehow—but always at the risk of disappearing. If, in fact, the object disappears—along with everything else—in the image of objectivity, then the image will be no different from the corpse itself, or it will at least possess all of the features of autonomy that Blanchot attributes to his image-cadaver. Yet nothing, as semantic and grammatical categories indicate, is always something. The necrophilic dimension of objectivity teaches us, above all, that nothing disappears; and death is the shrine of nothing.

In his book *Techniques of the Observer,* Jonathan Crary confirms the intuitions of Daston and Galison regarding the disappearance of the object in "objective" modes of representation: "Certain forms of visual experience usually uncritically categorized as 'realism' are in fact bound up in *non-veridical* theories of vision that effectively annihilate the real world."[24] I want to reiterate that the disappearance of the object signals not its nonexistence but rather a peculiar resistance to *appearing,* to visuality, or, perhaps more appropriately, a dislocation

23. From a Marxist perspective, photography, the most "objective" of all media, is characterized by this improbable estrangement from the object: "The relationship between the camera's shot and its target is not the same as that between conscious subject and his world. Any picture represents an act of the camera. Not only does it not identify *with* its object, it does not identify an object at all. It is a human agency that is reflected in the choice of image." Marcus Paul Bullock, *The Violent Eye: Ernst Jünger's Visions and Revisions on the European Right* (Detroit: Wayne State University Press, 1992), p. 109. The discourse of objectivity requires us, of course, to shed as well the deforming influence of "human agency," in order to ensure the complete autonomy and reflexivity of the image.

24. Jonathan Crary, *Techniques of the Observer: On Vision and Modernity in the Nineteenth Century* (Cambridge, Mass.: MIT Press, 1990), p. 14.

or restructuring of the object by nonocular visual practices. Crary's work derives from, but also refashions, the familiar premise that the sense of sight dominates a modern era inaugurated by Descartes and Bacon and permeated by the ideology of science.[25] Crary breathes new life into the equation of modernity and visuality by stressing the issues of spectatorship and corporeality. He argues that "modernization effected a deterritorialization and revaluation of vision" (149), and that the decomposition of vision in the late nineteenth and early twentieth centuries resulted in "practices in which visual images no longer have any reference to the position of an observer in the 'real' optically perceived world" (2).

Crary and others have discerned that the so-called annihilation of the real world is, in fact, a *quantification* of the object, which reappears in contemporary fields of nonvisual imagery (such as ultrasound, positron-emission tomography, and magnetic resonance imaging). The modernists themselves, of course, were exposed to images of the unseen (harbingers of purely quantitative images) through the development of X-ray technology.[26] (We should also bear in mind that X-ray images are *negative* images.) On the problem of "graphic inscriptions that effectively subsume the sense-based perceptions of the autonomous subject," Lisa Cartwright has written: "An overlooked fact of contemporary imaging technologies is that they do not allow the observer to see more clearly either the body or the unseen (or any other entity). In fact, imaging systems usually involve an optical display of properties initially conceived in terms other than optical . . . These images are, essentially, quantitative depictions of properties like density or mass—properties that exceed or confound

---

25. Martin Jay provides a good discussion and bibliography of this topic. See Jay, "Scopic Regimes of Modernity," in Hal Foster, ed., *Vision and Visuality* (Seattle: Bay Press, 1988), pp. 3–23. Jay borrows the phrase "scopic regime" from Christian Metz. A more recent volume of essays on the subject of modernity and vision is David Michael Levin, ed., *Modernity and the Hegemony of Vision* (Berkeley: University of California Press, 1993).

26. Photography is also capable of such nonvisual images. The German artist Sigmar Polke, for example, has produced a series of images by placing a piece of uranium on sheets of photosensitive paper. The resulting "photographs" record the invisible radioactive energy of the stone—each bearing a different "image" of the same object. See the exhibition catalogue *Photography in Contemporary Germany: 1960 to the Present* (Minneapolis: Walker Art Center, 1992).

optical geometry."[27] The idea of visual images of pure quantity has an important bearing on the problem of the fetish, since Marx claims that the "phantom objectivity" of exchange value emerges from the transformation of *quality* into *quantity,* at the moment when the quality of a thing's use value becomes a quantity of abstract human labor (*Capital* 125). Thus, the modernist conception of scientific objectivity (as a precursor to nonvisual images of pure quantity) must be viewed as an essential expression of the logic of fetishism. The problematic visuality of the Marxian fetish coincides historically with the "formalization of vision" that Crary and Cartwright describe.

It should already be evident that Crary (under Foucault's influence) also separates the history of perception from the history of representation. In turn, he distinguishes these two sites of inquiry from (yet sees them as symptomatic of) the more fundamental question of the historical formation of subjectivity. Thus, any speculation regarding the transformation of the modern visual sign, artifact, or apparatus always entails other questions. First, what model of perception can we deduce from the artifact? And second, what type of observer, or subject, is embedded in the artifact and its implied model of visuality? Indeed, as the title of his book *(Techniques of the Observer)* suggests, Crary is less interested in modernist representations than in the artifactuality of physiological vision. He views specific modernist artifacts (whether poems, paintings, or buildings) as *afterimages* of the decomposition of the autonomous subject. Correlating the triumph of objectivity with a specific historical formation of subjectivity, Crary writes, "The achievement then of that kind of optical neutrality, the reduction of the observer to a supposedly rudimentary state, was both an aim of artistic experimentation . . . and a condition for the formation of an observer who would be competent to consume the vast new amounts of visual imagery and information increasingly articulated during this same period" (96). Only by viewing the modernist artifact in relation to the model of vision that it implies, and then by viewing both as symptoms of a larger discursive formation of subjectivity, can we view a modernist poem, for example, as being related to a specific political discourse such as fascism. Cartwright takes this correlation a step fur-

27. Lisa Cartwright, " 'Experiments of Destruction': Cinematic Inscriptions of Physiology," *Representations* 40 (Fall 1992): 134.

ther by linking new configurations of "life" to the articulation of "death" through scientific (and avant-garde) experimentation: "The decline of sensory observation, and of sight in particular, accompanies the development of visual instrumentation not for the production of scientific knowledge *in* the observer, but for the reconfiguration of life *through* the experimented-upon body" (136). We must therefore assume that modernist images in any medium, as well as the artifact of vision, are haunted by afterimages and remnants of archaic visual formations—by the ghosts, for example, of verisimilitude, naturalism, or realism. Still, we must ask—especially in the face of certainty—"Where do the ghosts come (back) from?"[28]

As Crary sees it, the modern reconstruction of optical experience implies that vision is *constitutive*. Modernism entails "a positive reorganization of the senses. The issue was not just how does one know what is real, but that new forms of the real were being fabricated, and a new truth about the capacities of a human subject was being articulated in these terms" (92). Crary attributes this extraordinary reinvention of reality and subjectivity to a single historical development, namely "the insertion of a new term into discourses and practices of vision: the human body, a term whose exclusion was one of the foundations of classical theories of vision and optics."[29] With the emergence of the new discipline of physiology in the nineteenth century and its discovery that light is only one among a variety of stimuli that are capable of producing visual experience, scientists began to develop theories of vision that identified "the physiological makeup of the subject as the site on which the formation of representation occurs" (Crary, *Technique* 77). Furthermore, the study of neurophysiological phenomena such as afterimages led to conceptions of "a new produc-

---

28. Having posed this question, having acknowledged the impossibility of exchange (the impossibility of the fetish), we must resist the temptation to answer it—though it must also be true that a ghostbuster believes in ghosts. See Keenan, "The Point Is to (Ex)Change It," p. 169.

29. Jonathan Crary, "Modernizing Vision," in Foster, ed., *Vision and Visuality*, p. 33. Although Crary argues that the incarnation of vision emerges historically as a result of discoveries made in the nineteenth century, Barbara Stafford has demonstrated that the investigation of this phenomenon must begin earlier, in the context of eighteenth-century theories of art and medicine. See her book *Body Criticism: Imaging the Unseen in Enlightenment Art and Medicine* (Cambridge, Mass.: MIT Press, 1991).

tive observer whose body has a range of capacities to generate visual experience; it is a question of visual experience that does not refer or correspond to anything external to the observing subject" (Crary, "Modernizing Vision" 34).

As I have indicated, there are two primary consequences of what Crary calls "the carnal embodiment of sight." First, people come to understand the visual perception of real external phenomena as a product of neurophysiological and biochemical processes that can be influenced by nonocular sources. The problem of modern spectatorship therefore asks: How do we draw the line between the transparency of visual experience and the opacity of the physiological processes that produce it? We must, in response, begin to acknowledge and to theorize "the palpable opacity and carnal density of vision" (*Technique* 150). Indeed, I would argue, modernist theories of the image struggle to comprehend *opacity* as a crucial and productive component of vision. Furthermore, the incarnation of vision, which anchors the visible in the body's darkness, is precipitated by the visualization of the unseen, by physiology's penetration into the hidden recesses of the body. This complex dialectic of incarnation has its ideological counterpart in the negativity of the modernist image, in the fetishized superimposition of seeing and not seeing, blindness and insight. We can thus say that the modernist image resists visuality in its specifically carnal dimension, which in turn corresponds to the imageric subversion of visibility in modern formalism.

One must also emphasize that the carnal embodiment of sight assumes a conception of the body as a physiologically productive apparatus. Images of the real are not received but *conceived* in the volatile matrix of the body. Though this remarkable new conception of vision emerges in the context of science, Crary reminds us that "what is in question here is the discovery of the 'visionary' capacity of the human body" ("Modernizing Vision" 34). Thus, what Derrida says of the Kantian doctrine of aesthetic disinterestedness could well be said of the scientific discourse of objectivity: "Utterly irreducible heteroaffection inhabits—intrinsically—the most hermetic autoaffection" ("Parergon" 13). Just as the disappearance of the object in the autonomous image depends on its being translated into *quantity,* so the mortification of the subject assumed by the image reveals itself to be a transubstantiation (or translation) of the Cartesian subject into a visionary body. Nothing disappears, and death is the shrine of nothing.

The proper subject of my book is not a general theory of the image or of vision, but a specific historical instance of what Martin Jay calls the "scopic regimes of modernity." The present study examines Ezra Pound's "Doctrine of the Image," which in 1913 inaugurated the poetics of Anglo-American modernism. The Imagist moment is exemplary in the sense that it entails and portrays the conversion of literary Decadence into a formation of the avant-garde—a metamorphosis that is reiterated in countless other manifestations of modernism. In Pound's case, the emergence of Imagism in his career coincides with his repudiation of what he calls the "corpse language" of late Victorian poetry (which includes most of his own early poems). More specifically, the Image (a term that I capitalize when it pertains to Pound's poetic conceptions) is the centerpiece of Pound's efforts to rid his work of an illicit—and obviously Decadent—infatuation with dead bodies and ghosts, which in turn sustains a poetic language exemplified by these figures. My revision of Pound's aesthetic ideology proceeds, therefore, by excavating from the poetics of Imagism (and its immediate prehistory) a preoccupation with death and memory that impedes his formalist agenda. I argue not only that the modern poetics of "objectivity" (exemplified by the Image) is constructed on the basis of Pound's youthful experiments with "death" in poetic language, but that the essential negativity of the Image (its objectivity) is formulated as a cryptology, a poetics of decomposition and reanimation. The crypt aesthetic of the Image survives, moreover, into its political afterlife via Pound's fusion of modernist practice and fascist ideology.

The essential negativity of the modernist Image identifies it, on one hand, as advancing the poetics of "objectivity" and modern positivism, but also, given its cryptic nature, as susceptible to hermeneutical or "mythological" structures of meaning. Thus, the modernist Image, founded on a doctrine of impossibility—the impossible criteria of objectivity—falls prey to a variety of phantasmic effects, also held to be "objective," which extend as far as Pound's fascist radio broadcasts. Indeed, Pound originally conceived of the Image as a "radiant node or cluster"—a radioactive and "mythological" substance, conceived on the analogy of radium and endowed with telegraphic properties. As such, the modernist Image appears in a certain physical and ideological "frequency," yet is continually verging, from its inception, upon radiography (the art of radio images) and the "tribal magic" of radio. Under certain historical circumstances, then, the Image is displaced along a spectrum that is at once material and ideological: the Image conceived as a "radiant" cadaver becomes the voice of fascism, converted by the medium of radio into the ghost of a lost aesthetic (its political afterlife). In terms of aesthetic ideology, this radiological phantom is indistinguishable not only from the "radiant" substance of Image, but from the technical medium of radio, and must therefore be viewed as the deranged fulfillment of Pound's (and modernity's) program of literary and cultural positivism.

In more mundane terms, my speculation concerning a radiological medium that veers between verbal and visual "frequencies" is rooted in the assumption that the modernist poetic image entails a mediation of visuality simply by its displacement of the image concept into a verbal medium. A verbal image is visual only in a complex and rather problematic sense. (On the larger question of what constitutes an image, I would refer the reader to W. J. T. Mitchell's seminal work, *Iconology*.) Yet even if we acknowledge that Pound wished to exploit certain features of the ideology of vision (such as its association with objectivity) by designating modern poetry as imagistic, we must not ignore the subversion of the visible and the empirical that he proposes in the name of the Image. Thus, I will argue that the modernist poetic Image is equivocally, but intentionally, *nonvisual,* insofar as it resists, contests, and mediates the experience of visuality, but also in its preoccupation with the invisible.[30] Second, in its fascination with things characterized by a peculiar resistance to appearing, to visibility, the

---

30. Herbert Schneidau has noted the resistance to visuality in the earliest expressions of Imagism: "Although these poems neither rely on visual images nor conform very well to any 'theory of the Image' as usually understood, we must face the fact that no visualization requirement nor theory of the Image is listed among the points agreed upon by Pound, H.D. and Aldington." Though Schneidau's observation is valuable, it fails to consider that Pound's conception of the Image may be important precisely because it does *not* conform to any "theory of the Image as usually understood." More specifically, Schneidau neglects the possibility that one might retain a notion of the Image

necrophilic dimension of the Image is a fundamental expression of objectivity's inscrutable relation to fetishism. Furthermore, the necrophilic dimension of the Image raises a literary historical question that overlaps yet is distinct from the cultural poetics of vision and imagery. To what degree does Pound's pursuit of objectivity via the Image correspond to the development of a distinctively modern mode of poetic elegy—indebted to Hardy and emerging from the experiences of war and exile? Given the abiding and generative yet also ambivalent concern with death that Pound displays in his work (as poet, translator, and critic), shouldn't we question the conventional wisdom of viewing T. S. Eliot as the exemplar of "elegiac modernism"? Indeed, we should seriously consider whether it is not Eliot's but Pound's work that articulates most suggestively and comprehensively a poetics of aberrant mourning that is specifically modern in its reformulations of loss, pleasure, and visuality for the male poet.

Critical attention to Pound's writings on the subject of the Image almost invariably equates the Image with visuality and the origins of a particular strain of modern poetry dominated by the sense of sight. In addition, this critical history has been for the most part fixated on the nature of the Image as sign or representation, or preoccupied with a vague conception of "immediacy" that falls somewhere between the realms of perception and representation. In a recent work by Vincent Sherry, for example, one finds the claim that "the Vorticists' own program—it foresaw a literature written to the more demanding standards of the visual arts—explains their attraction to the European physiology of the senses, above all the superiority of the eye."[31] Although Sherry offers a valuable survey of the physiological speculations of writers such as Sorel, Benda, and LeBon, he stops short of characterizing physiological vision as an artifact that is in fact shaped by these theorists and by sources such as Pound's writings on the Image. In the case of Imagism, it is not simply that representation (the poetics of the Image) is conditioned by an eccentric "idéologie" of vision (which Sherry holds to be a distortion of the physical neutrality

---

that has "no visualization requirement." Schneidau, *Ezra Pound: The Image and the Real* (Baton Rouge: Louisiana State University Press, 1969), p. 8.

31. Vincent Sherry, *Ezra Pound, Wyndham Lewis, and Radical Modernism* (Oxford: Oxford University Press, 1993), p. 5.

of perception). Rather, "natural" vision and the semiotic properties of the Image are entangled in a series of reciprocal alterations: influence runs in both directions. According to Pound, the telegraphic character of the Image requires alterations in the basic features of perception. Thus, the Image emerges as an instrument to reconstruct not only the medium of poetic representation but the social artifacts of vision and, more obliquely, subjectivity.

Following the methodology I outlined in the previous section, I hope to avoid the misleading equation of Image and visuality—an equation that inhibits recognition of the reciprocal relations between artifactuality, perception, and subjectivity in the discursive formation of the Image. Thus, in my estimation, the influence of the visual arts, which is normally emphasized in discussions of Imagism, is important but not decisive. It is essential to recall that the public declarations of Vorticism take a clear stand *against* the confusion of artistic media—a principle supported and frequently reiterated by Pound. Hence his view that each artistic impulse occurs in a "primary form" (*GB* 81). Although this does not prevent Pound from suggesting correspondences between poetry and sculpture (primarily because of its tactile nature), it should also encourage the student of Imagism to take seriously the analogies drawn from physics, biology, mathematics, and engineering—a mosaic of disciplines that indicates the discursive foundation and ambitions of Imagism. Furthermore, critics rarely acknowledge that the most celebrated figures of the Image (vortex, ideogram, Freudian complex, algebraic equation, and so on) are curiously resistant to conventional notions of visual experience. The idea of the Image as a Chinese ideogram, for example, clearly mediates the experience of visualization in a manner that produces the visible realm as an effect of *reading* rather than looking (insofar as reading is a kind of looking, founded on blindness). Furthermore, conceived as a vortex, the Image is even more remote from any stable or traditional notion of a visual image. Imagism's evocation of the opacity, or uncertainty, of vision, as well as the heterogeneity of Imagist rhetoric, indicates, as Martin Jay suggests, that "the scopic regime of modernity may best be understood as a contested terrain, rather than a harmoniously integrated complex of visual theories and practices" ("Scopic Regimes" 4).

I am concerned, then, not merely with the modernist Image as a sign (as a form of representation) but with the model of perception and the type of observer that its formulation implies. My sometimes elaborate speculations on the nature of the Image as a sign, and its flight from meaning, are always shadowed by a question concerning the observer as one who sees, but also as one who conforms or adheres to, and abides by. What must the observer adhere to, in the act of seeing (or not seeing) the Image? What notion of subjectivity (and subjugation) does Pound's Image theory imply? Ultimately, these questions pertain to the difficult debate concerning the relation between the Image (or, more broadly speaking, visuality) and fascism. Are we to find, with Donald Davie, a line "clear and unbroken" from Imagism to fascism?[32] Or, as Robert von Hallberg argues, is Imagism to be associated with the heyday of "anarchist individualism" prior to World War I, and therefore fundamentally inconsistent with the "state totalitarianism" of fascist Italy?[33]

Generally, there has been a strong tendency to equate visuality and fascism—an echo, perhaps, of the imputed dominance of visuality in the modern era (as if fascism were the essence of modernity). Russell Berman, for example, claims that "the fascist modernist denounces identities constituted by language, while expressing a desire for the image freed of verbal mediation."[34] Sherry takes a similar position: "The modernists' new standard of visual immediacy in words led them to esteem (what they saw as) a superior directness in the political cultures of Nazism and fascism" (7). In my view, aside from whether or not their conclusions are correct, the terms of their arguments are impaired by the same limitations that characterize the critical reception of Imagism generally. Berman depends on an untenable and misleading conception of pure visuality as the index of fascism; whereas Sherry, as I have already indicated, does not sufficiently articulate

32. Donald Davie, *Purity of Diction in English Verse* (New York: Schocken, 1967; orig. pub. 1952), p. 99.
33. Robert von Hallberg, "Notes on Imagism and Politics," paper delivered at the Modern Language Association conference, Chicago, 1990.
34. Russell A. Berman, "Written Right Across Their Faces: Ernst Jünger's Fascist Modernism," in *Modernity and the Text: Revisions of German Modernism,* ed. Andreas Huyssen and David Bathrick (New York: Columbia University Press, 1989), p. 75.

either the discursive character of vision or the incursions of the Image into the histories of perception and subjectivity. Only by distinguishing carefully between these latter two fields and the history of the artifact, and then by establishing their symptomatic correspondences, can we determine what bearing the poetics of Imagism might have on the formations of subjectivity that the politics of fascism engender. Only by formulating, first of all, a sense of the pliability, the blindness, of the observer implied in the rhetoric of the Image, and, second, a notion of the kind of observer required by fascism (that is, state totalitarianism), might we argue that the modernist Image anticipates, or dictates from afar, Pound's speculations on fascist culture. We might then ask whether a theory of autonomous images bears any relation to the rise of state fetishism, to Pound's Rome Radio broadcasts, or to the collapse of subject and artifact into a new medium "half-way between writing and action" (*SP* 217).[35]

Should we begin to think about the radio broadcasts as a culmination of the *radiology* of the Image, a discourse of radio pictures—not darkness visible, but the light of reason made invisible and displaced along the magnetic spectrum? Is the cryptological Image merely dead, or does the strangeness of the cadaver call to mind a thing animated by negation and translated into its political afterlife by a technical medium, by the "tribal magic" of radio? Is the autonomy of the Image therefore an effect of its radioactivity—the incommensurable half-life of an artifact that cannot be neutralized or eliminated?[36] And, finally,

---

35. Writing about Lenin in 1928, Pound observed, "Apart from the social aspect, he was of interest, technically, to serious writers. He never wrote a sentence that had interest in itself, but he evolved almost a new medium, a sort of expression half-way between writing and action." Cited in Tim Redman, *Ezra Pound and Italian Fascism* (Cambridge: Cambridge University Press, 1991), p. 74.

36. Elaine Scarry describes nuclear waste as an "autonomous object" that has severed the reciprocal relation between the artifact and its maker: "An object that refuses to surrender its referentiality will be destroyed; if it both refuses to surrender its referentiality and cannot be destroyed, we then enter the nightmare situation of the sorcerer's apprentice." The autonomy of this type of object does *not* stem primarily from its animism (since all made objects, according to Scarry, are animated); rather, it stems from a refusal to refer back to its maker or to anything other than itself. The modern, formalist Image then begins to resemble the artifactuality of nuclear waste not only in its extreme reflexivity but in its claims to objectivity and universality, which amount to a disavowal of history and its own mortality. Scarry, *The Body in Pain*, p. 365, n. 79.

shouldn't we view the strange materiality of the Image, which is somehow radioactive, as the sign at once of immortality and mortal danger?

P ound began his career as a poet fascinated by scenes of loss, by mournful "spirits" that often refused to appear openly, and by their resistance to visibility. Yet the gradual emergence of the figure of the Image around 1912 signals an estrangement from the realm of the dead, from the veil and compulsion of mediation that governs all contact with the dead. The modern poet would seek to converse *directly* with things. At the same time, the Image becomes the displaced object of sightless vision (the poet's means of apprehending the dead) and of the negative pleasure of mourning. The Image, like the "cadaverous dead," submits to visibility only to withdraw from it. The immediate—though overlooked—context for Pound's ambiguous and still puzzling correlation of death and visuality (which finds death encrypted in the Image) is one of his earliest translation projects, the *Sonnets and Ballate of Guido Cavalcanti,* published in 1912. These translations provide an indispensable key to the necrophilic dimension of the modernist Image. Indeed, I will argue that Pound's conception of the Image cannot be properly understood without reference to his theory of translation and exchange, a debt that further illuminates the contribution of Imagism to fetish discourse. It is through his translation of Cavalcanti's poems that Pound first discovers the Image that blinds and annihilates, as well as the Image as a medium or sign that preserves, even as it conceals, the power of death. Further complicating the translational effect of the Image is the fact that the effects of World War I confuse historically Pound's attempt to break, or to formalize, the elegiac spell of the dead. It is no coincidence that the most comprehensive treatment of the Image occurs in his memoir of the young sculptor Gaudier-Brzeska (who died in battle in 1915), a book of the dead that records not only the poet's grief over the loss of his friend but gruesome descriptions of the battlefield from Gaudier's letters, as well as Pound's repugnance at the destructiveness of the war in general. Indeed, the public act of mourning Gaudier and the anonymous dead must be understood as a perilous restaging of the poetics of Imagism.

The historical tendency to characterize Imagism as a doctrine of impersonality and objectivity must therefore somehow accommodate a submerged economy of loss and mourning. This can be accomplished, however, only by claiming—in complete contradiction to the received wisdom about the nature of Imagism—that Pound's conception of the Image neglects the "real" and even actively seeks to sever itself from the empirical object. At the same time, we must give full consideration to Pound's inclination to align the poetics of Imagism with the scientific discourse of objectivity. Recalling Daston and Galison's comment about "the negative forms of all objectivity," we are struck by the almost entirely negative or prohibitive character of the basic tenets of Imagism, including "a series of about forty cautions to beginners" (*GB* 84). The Imagist poem, which Pound calls an "objective reality" (*GB* 85), is essentially the precipitate or remnant of a regime of prohibitions. The result is a poem composed of "the smallest possible number of words" (*LE* 50), an Image that appears and then returns to obscurity, indeed, appears with the sole aim of enacting its disappearance. By resisting the duplicity of appearance, the objectivity of the poetic Image ultimately veers toward tautology—a crumbling of the distinction between sign and object: "The serious artist is scientific in that he presents the image of his desire, of his hate, of his indifference, as precisely that, precisely the image of his own desire, hate, or indifference" (*LE* 46). Indeed, some of the earliest and most perceptive responses to Imagism noted the tautological character of the Image. In 1915, for example, May Sinclair wrote, "The Image is not a substitute; it does not stand for anything but itself . . . You cannot distinguish between the thing and its image."[37]

It is not a question, therefore, of whether Pound sees the Image as objective; it is a question of what he understands by "science" and what becomes of the object in the discourse of poetic objectivity. An article that Pound published in 1912—around the time he was formulating the poetics of Imagism—suggests that the fate of the object

37. May Sinclair, "Two Notes," *The Egoist* 2 (1915): 88–89.

is not entirely secure in the discourse of poetic "objectivity." Citing a "scientific and satisfactory definition of poetry" from an unnamed author,[38] Pound concurs that in poetry "all animate, inanimate, and intangible things may assume the properties and attributes of tangible, living, thinking, and speaking things, possessing the power of becoming what they seem, or of transfiguration into what they suggest" (*SP* 359). Poetry, then, in its "scientific definition," appears to be equivalent to a form of animism—quite distinct, apparently, from the stutter of tautology. Yet if tautology dictates that the Image is identical to its object, then the object must exhibit the inherent ambiguity of the Image, and thus always points beyond itself to its superfluous other. Naught copulating with naught, tautology produces an open cancellation, an Image that, by its very meaninglessness, its innocence, is continually susceptible to hidden values and significance. Tautology, engulfing the objects of both poetry and science, therefore engenders an art of cryptography, as we learn from Pound's analogy of "a few sheets of paper covered with arbitrary symbols—without which we should have no wireless telegraph" (*SP* 362). Implicitly comparing poetry to the equation on which telegraphy is based (the advance signal of radio), Pound asks, "Is the formula nothing, or is it cabala and the sign of unintelligible magic? The engineer, understanding and translating to the many, builds for the uninitiated bridges and devices. He speaks their language. For the initiated, the signs are a door to eternity and into the boundless ether" (*SP* 362). Following the logic of this analogy, several years later Pound will describe the Image as an algebraic equation whose signs have "variable significance" (*GB* 84).

From the analogy of mathematical formulas, we can begin to understand how the discourse of scientific (and poetic) objectivity can sever itself from the empirical object. As Pound sees it, the "arbitrary symbols" of scientific objectivity (epitomized by mathematics) have a double significance. On one hand, these symbols point to an object in the world and can serve as a set of instructions for building such an

---

38. Ian F. A. Bell has identified the unnamed author as Hudson Maxim, whose book *The Science of Poetry and the Philosophy of Language* (1910) Pound cites. See Bell, "Mauberley's Barrier of Style," in Philip Grover, ed., *Ezra Pound: The London Years, 1908–1920* (New York: AMS Press, 1978), pp. 107–108.

object. Yet, to the "initiated," who are capable of eliciting another meaning from the "formula," these signs point beyond the object. It is this metaphysical reference that Pound associates not only with the more exalted objectivity of science but with the art of poetry. Historically speaking, however, this cryptic dimension of objectivity is not at all metaphysical, but rather a restructuring of the object of perception and of perception itself, in response to the modern proliferation of visual signs.

Although Pound is inclined to draw upon analogies from the visual arts to explain his evolving conception of the Image, a close look at these comparisons reveals that the Image is increasingly resistant to natural vision and acts as an enigmatic "key" to new perceptual orders. In *The Spirit of Romance,* where one often finds frank discussion of dimensions of the Image that later become submerged, Pound claims,

> There are two kinds of beautiful painting and one may perhaps illustrate by the works of Burne-Jones and Whistler; one looks at the first kind of painting and is immediately delighted by its beauty; the second kind of painting, when first seen, puzzles one, but on leaving it, and going from the gallery one finds new beauty in natural things—a Thames fog, to use the hackneyed example. Thus, there are works of art which are beautiful objects and works of art which are keys or pass-words admitting one to a deeper knowledge, to a finer perception of beauty. (*SR* 154)

Although Pound makes the art of Burne-Jones stand for the qualities of his own earliest poetry (which he has not yet entirely relinquished), it is a painting by Whistler, whom Pound once called "the great grammarian of the arts" (*GB* 122), that provides an example of art capable of revising, and even creating, habits of perception. Yet this image is remarkable for its opacity—it even depicts a phenomenon, fog, that inhibits visibility while stimulating certain hallucinatory effects. As in the cases of the Marxian fetish and Blanchot's image-cadaver (as well as the inscrutable painting in *Moby-Dick*), Whistler's painting does not reveal itself "when first seen." The image yields its "puzzling" significance only through the blindness of second sight: only by *not looking* at the image, by leaving the gallery, does the observer finally "see" the image, not so much as a visual phenomenon in itself but as an ideological form, a phantom, that haunts and eventually transforms the habitual forms of nature. We should also note that the idea of the Image as a "password" or "key" evokes a conception of visual perception as something akin to the art of cryptography, and a world that is at once deciphered by, and captive to, certain cryptic images.

It is essential to emphasize Pound's view that the ultimate aim of Imagism is to transform vision or perception itself (and not merely the art or medium of poetry). In his essay on Vorticism, Pound cites approvingly a "Russian correspondent" on the nature of the Vorticist Image: "I see, you wish to give people new eyes, not to make them see some new particular thing" (*GB* 85).[39] In addition, several comments Pound made about the vortoscope, a photographic apparatus that he and Alvin Langdon Coburn invented, convey a similar awareness of the artifactuality of vision. In the catalogue essay for a show of Coburn's vortographs in 1917, Pound writes, "The tool called the vortoscope was invented in late 1916. Mr. Coburn had been long desiring to bring cubism or vorticism into photography. Only with the invention of a suitable instrument was this possible" (*EPVA* 154). It is significant that vortographic images can be produced only with the invention of a new apparatus, a change that is internal to the perceptual mechanism (though this "tool" is, in fact, a technical medium that externalizes the sense of sight). It is not sufficient merely to construct composite images, to use the technique of montage (which is external to the mechanism); rather, vortographs are the integral products of a new perceptual mechanism, one that is incapable of "seeing" realistic images. Furthermore, Pound claims, "Vortography may have, however, very much the same place in the coming aesthetic that the anatomical studies of the Renaissance had in the aesthetics of the academic school" (*EPVA* 156). In a remark that reminds us of Daston and Galison's thesis about the role of nineteenth-century scientific atlases in the construction of the concept of objectivity, Pound sug-

---

39. A book by Nils Ake Nilsson on Russian "Imaginism" reveals the identity of this anonymous correspondent and the surprising legacy of this interview: "The appearance of Russian Imaginism is usually connected with an article in a literary collection, *The Archer (Strelec)*, published in 1915 . . . The article in question was an interview by Zinaida Vengerova with the American poet Ezra Pound under the title *English Futurists (Anglyskie futuristy)*." Nilsson goes on to explain how the Russian Imaginist movement was founded in 1916 after the example of English Vorticism and, to no small degree, following the tenets that Pound prescribed in the interview. See Nilsson, *The Russian Imaginists* (Stockholm: Almquist and Wiksell, 1970), p. 7.

The Mystery of Negation

gests that vortography will provide a similar atlas of "objective" reality (based on the analogy of Renaissance atlases that transformed perception by incorporating new discoveries in anatomy and optical perspective). The atlas of vortography, however, will provide the perceptual standards for a *nonrepresentational* objectivity—a scopic regime of invisibility and the negative image.

Though analogies from the visual arts, such as vortography, can help us determine the nature or status of the object in Imagist poetics, such analogies may be even more effective in enabling us to determine what the Image is *not*, or what escapes the observer implied by the autonomous Image. Pound claims in 1918, for example, that "literature" (characterized presumably by the basic principles of Imagism) does not share with the cinema a common subject matter: "It [cinema] is an excellent medium for news. News is the antipodes of literature ... It should be an excellent medium for instructing children in botany, physics, geography, zoology, the costume of foreign peoples, the appearance of foreign cities, and the process of manufacturing. It makes excellent 'historic' records ... The cinema is the phonograph of appearance" (*EPVA* 79). If we view the cinema as the "antipodes" of the poetic Image, then we could say that the poetic Image, as a medium, is inhospitable to representations of nature, of technology, and of foreign peoples and places (the historical legacy of colonialism). Indeed, as Pound sees it, the Image seems to be estranged from history generally and from all "appearances." The Image does not seek, then, to make the world its object, or to record history or the visibility of things; nor is it an expression of personal feelings, desire, or sentiment. We must bear in mind May Sinclair's observation that the Image "does not stand for anything but itself." The Image is strange, indeed—an autonomous thing.

If we take the vortoscope as a mechanization of Imagist poetics, the severing of the Image from its empirical object is quite unambiguous. In a letter to John Quinn, Pound writes, "Don't know that there is much to report save that Coburn and I invented the vortescope [*sic*], a simple device which frees the camera from reality and lets one take Picasso direct from nature."[40] The idea that "objective" Images should turn away from "reality," from the empirical object, appears

---

40. From a letter to Quinn dated October 13, 1916, several months before Coburn's

again and again in Pound's statements about Imagism: "The image is the poet's pigment . . . He should *depend,* of course, on the creative, not upon the mimetic or representational" (*GB* 86); "The hard stone is not the live coney. Its beauty cannot be the same beauty" (*GB* 107). In a letter to Alice Henderson and Harriet Monroe in 1917, protesting their definition of Imagism in their anthology *The New Poetry* (1917), Pound is emphatic about the nonempirical orientation of Imagism: "I shall never accept the statement that 'poetry, new or otherwise' looks outward rather than inward . . . Imagism of the first book 'Des Imagistes' NEVER, never looking out rather than in."[41] Furthermore, Pound's promotion of nonrepresentational art coincides with his skepticism concerning a purely visual aesthetic. Indeed, he criticizes Ford Madox Ford, who is normally cited as an important influence on Imagism, for being excessively visual in his orientation: "I think Hueffer goes wrong because he bases his criticism on the eye, and almost solely on the eye."[42] If we correlate this observation with Pound's earlier judgment that "Mr. Hueffer is not an imagiste but an impressionist," it is clear that the principles of Imagism depart in some fundamental sense from the realm of the visible.[43] This perspective helps explain Pound's observations concerning Gaudier-Brzeska's "hieratic" sculpture of him: "A kindly journalist 'hopes' that it does not look like me. It does not. It was not intended to" (*GB* 49). The Vorticist Image implies, therefore, that poets do not merely turn a blind eye to what physically exists, but that they represent something invisible, something that lacks a sensible basis in the natural world.

Several letters of Pound's from the Vorticist period offer an index of his anxieties about imagery in general, based on his comments about the capacities of various types of imagery to capture his own likeness.

---

exhibit. *The Selected Letters of Ezra Pound to John Quinn: 1915–1924,* ed. Timothy Materer (Durham: Duke University Press, 1991), p. 88.

41. *The Letters of Ezra Pound to Alice Corbin Henderson,* ed. Ira B. Nadel (Austin: University of Texas Press, 1993), p. 206. Pound's correspondence to Henderson on the subject of Imagism is among the most revealing material available on this period of his career.

42. Pound, "On Criticism in General," *The Criterion* 1, no. 2 (January 1923): 146.

43. Pound's comment about Ford Madox Ford appears in a note that concludes his review of Ford's *Collected Poems,* in *Poetry* 2, no. 3 (June 1914): 120. This phrase does not occur in the essay as it appears in Pound's *Literary Essays* (*LE* 371–377).

The Mystery of Negation

In these letters the tension between the visible and the invisible—a tension that distinguishes Pound's conception of the Image—comes to focus on the problem of resemblance, especially when it is compounded by "distance." In a letter to James Joyce in 1915, for example, Pound goes on at some length about the inadequacy of various images of himself:

> Also I solemnly swear that I will someday send you a photograph; at present I am torn between conflicting claims. I have an excessively youthful and deceptive photograph (very rare edition). I have several copies of a photo of a portrait of me, painted by an amiable jew who substituted a good deal of his own face for the gentile parts of my own. I have the seductive and sinister photograph by Coburn which I expect to have photograved in order to sell my next book of bad poems. It is like a cinque, or quattrocento painting. My father-in-law says "A sinister but very brilliant italian." My old landlady said "It is the only photograph that has ever done you justice," and then as she was sidling out of the door, with increasing embarrassment: "ah, ah. I. I hope you won't be offended, sir, but it is rather like the good man of Nazareth, isn't it sir?"
>
> Dante, you remember at the beginning of the epistle to Can Grande (at least I think it is there) mentions a similar predicament about presenting oneself at a distance. It is my face, so I can not be represented in your mind by that semitic image alone (which I enclose), it is my face as it may have been years ago, or my face greatly beautified, or as I enclose, my face immortalized by vorticist sculpture, which I enclose, this bust is monumental, but it will be no use to the police, it is hieratic, phallic, even, if you will consider the profiles not shown in the photograph.
>
> No, I will either, get a new photo, or send you the photogravure in good time. (*P/J* 35)

On the basis of this letter, there can be little doubt that Pound's intentions (and his ideas about the talismanic powers of photography) are "torn by conflicting claims."[44] All of the images, according to Pound, are "deceptive" in some fashion; each is susceptible to some form of

---

44. Pound expresses similar concerns about a photo of himself sent to Kate Buss in 1916: "It is the most recent, probably the most disagreeable, and slightly resembles Mr. Shaw, which I do not" (*L* 72). Apparently, Pound wishes to send a photo that accurately represents his present appearance ("the most recent"), even at the risk of sending

misrecognition or confused identity, which becomes implicated in the problem of "representing oneself at a distance" (a problem, according to Blanchot, that is characteristic of images in general). Pound's solution, apparently, is to send Joyce *all* of the images.

In his letter to Joyce, Pound mentions four photographs. The first is a picture of him as a youth, which he labels "deceptive" (presumably because he no longer resembles the photograph, but also, perhaps, because of its archaic style). The second is a photograph of a portrait painted by an "amiable jew who substituted a good deal of his own face" for Pound's—an instance of mimetic violence as well as mimetic enchantment. The third image is a "vortograph" by Alvin Coburn, which appeared as the frontispiece to *Lustra*.[45] And the fourth image is a photograph of Gaudier-Brzeska's famous bust of Pound (which manages to "immortalize" Pound's features). It is interesting to note, in view of Pound's concern about distance and mediation, that he tends to favor the more highly mediated images—the ones resistant to visible evidence. The vortograph is a shadowy affair inspired by cubism, and two of the other images are photographs of other works of art. Only the photo taken in his youth is, we assume, "realistic," yet he rejects it as being "deceptive." Pound's dissatisfaction with this portrait suggests that he does not regard the mimetic image as the most authentic or revealing. Indeed, the most reliable image, to his mind, is more likely to be a "vortograph," or a photo of an abstract sculpture. Yet this contradiction also reveals the degree to which Pound views *all* images as unreliable, or inscrutable, in some fashion. The visual image must somehow depict what cannot be seen.

Our characterization of the two images favored by Pound (the vor-

---

one that is "disagreeable." The risk of misrepresentation seems, however, to be unavoidable, since the poet feels compelled to warn the reader that the photo resembles George Bernard Shaw, though he himself does not. Other correspondence from the years 1915 and 1916 confirms Pound's inclination during this period to send photographs of himself to friends, along with an expression of his concern about the reliability of the image. In a letter to Pound in 1916, Alice Henderson reassures him: "I'm awfully glad to have that little picture of you. It looks just like you to me!" (*Letters to Alice Henderson*, p. 149).

45. This photograph is reproduced in Richard Humphrey, *Pound's Artists: Ezra Pound and the Visual Arts in London, Paris, and Italy* (London: Tate Gallery, 1985), p. 70.

tograph and Gaudier's sculpture) should not rely on categories such as abstraction or formalism, unless we understand these concepts as being resistant to the experience or constitution of "natural" vision. Evidently, Pound seeks an Image representing something that does not appear, or that does not make an appearance in the world; yet it is also specifically an Image of something that *cannot be seen*, of something that exceeds the capacity of "natural" vision. In its simplest aspect, this resistance to visuality informs a statement such as, "Don't be descriptive; remember that the painter can describe a landscape much better than you can" (*LE* 6). In a bolder conception, the strange visuality of the Image assumes a material or carnal density. It becomes opaque: "There are two ways of thinking of a man: firstly, you may think of him as that toward which perception moves, as the toy of circumstance, as the plastic substance *receiving* impressions; secondly, you may think of him as directing a certain fluid force against circumstance, as conceiving instead of merely reflecting and observing" (*GB* 89). It is no longer sufficient to argue, as most critics do, that Pound's notion of perception is merely a figure of speech illustrating a poetics of volition or action. Rather, following the work of Crary and others on modern, physiological conceptions of vision, we must view it not as an analogy at all but as a literal description of visual perception. (The "literal" description remains figurative, of course, in its susceptibility to ideologies of gender and political domination.) Thus, the transparency of visual experience, epitomized by reflection and observation, has become a "fluid force," a physiological process that shapes not only perception but "circumstance" and the external object. "Vision" collides with circumstance, engendering the Image from a nonvisual or sightless encounter with the real.

Clearly, we are at the threshold of Crary's conception of the "visionary body" and the "carnal embodiment of sight." In fact, Pound's reference to perception as a "fluid force" suggests that by the date of this essay (1916) he was already aware of Rémy de Gourmont's ideas about physiological style and spermatozoic images.[46] If

---

46. Pound's first review of Gourmont's work appears in 1915: "Rémy de Gourmont: A Distinction," *Fortnightly Review* 98, no. 588 (December 1915): 1161. Moreover, in a letter to his father in 1913, Pound indicates that he hopes to meet Gourmont personally in Paris (*L* 21).

I am correct about Pound's familiarity with Gourmont's *Natural Philosophy of Love* during the Vorticist period, then we can partly explain the peculiar opacity of the modernist Image, as Crary suggests, by a physiological theory of vision. But the question of dates, while significant, is not decisive, since Pound's ideas about poetry betrayed the influence of physiology and biomedical discourse long before he published his translation of *The Natural Philosophy of Love* in 1922.

Pound makes it clear that the physiological model of perception implied by the Image is "creative" or *constitutive:* "Our respect is not for the subject matter, but for the creative power of the artist; for that which he is capable of adding to his subject from himself; or, in fact, his capability to dispense with external subjects altogether, to create from himself" (*GB* 98). In work of this kind, there is no external object to be seen or grasped; the Image derives from experience that is essentially nonvisual. Or, rather, the "objective" or constitutive nature of vision is conceived as *dominating* external things and facts. Invoking once again the analogy of the Image as a mathematical equation, Pound writes, "The statements of 'analytics' are 'lords' over fact. They are thrones and dominations that rule over form and recurrence. And in like manner are great works of art lords over fact" (*GB* 92). The idea that certain abstract forms of representation (or perception) hold absolute power over "facts" suggests that Pound's theories of imagery and visuality aspire to rebuild not only subjective experience (as something impersonal) but the "real" (the factual) itself. Thus, the domination of Images over things and facts actually constitutes a *fabrication* of things and facts—a poetics of revolutionary ideology, which eventually finds a "cause" in fascism. The fetishistic objectivity of the Image coincides therefore with its power to change things, which starts with the entombment of subject *and* object, and which elaborates, poetically, the spectral (and material) negativity of death. The sudden indeterminacy of the cadaver—veering, like the fetish, between mystery and inertia, between image and thing—becomes an emblem of the lability of all things.

CHAPTER 2

Mortal Images

> "He is knowledge's lover," as Glenway Wescott has said, "speaking of it and to it an intimate idiom which is sometimes gibberish," and if his equivalents for that which is "dead" or foreign seem to some not always perspicuous, his contagiously enjoyable enjoyment of and his unpedantic rendering of "dead" language have done as much as have his poems, one feels—to create an atmosphere in which poetry is likely to be written.
>
> —Marianne Moore, " 'New' Poetry since 1912"

Many readers of modern poetry are familiar with the principles of Imagism, or at least with the name of the movement, even if they have never read Ezra Pound's poetry. The general reader associates the figure of the Image in modern poetry with empirical values—direct observation of actual experience—and with a revival of the virtues of a classical style: economy, precision, restraint.[1] This popular formulation, which conveys, while also moderating, the essential negativity of the project that Pound initiated in 1913 with "A Few Don'ts by an Imagiste," serves as an index for literary historians who describe Imagism as "the grammar school of modern poetry, the instruction and drill of basic principles," or as the center of a "revolution in the literature of the English language as momentous as the Romantic one."[2] Stephen Spender makes a comparable claim about Imagism as it cor-

---

1. My decision to capitalize the term "Image" follows Pound's practice—never entirely consistent—of distinguishing between his own conceptions of the Image and general notions of verbal or graphic imagery.

2. The first view is cited by David Perkins in *A History of Modern Poetry: From the*

responds to the major developments of modernism in other artistic media: "The aims of the imagist movement in poetry provide the archetype of a modern creative procedure."[3] Such views, though overstated, are characteristic of inherited notions about the formalist orientation of Anglo-American modernism as it first emerged prior to World War I. The actual conception of the Image, however, has been all but eclipsed, garbled in successive revisions of the antipoetic platform that it helped construct.[4] Reduced to a formulaic, all-too-obvious position in modern poetry, the Image—as it is normally construed—appears vaguely inauthentic, incommensurate with its foundational role. How could a revival of values such as brevity and precision, even if they were not widely appreciated at the time, have triggered a literary revolt? In the course of its historical transmission, the Image seems to have gained in stature what it has lost in substance.

Or perhaps the concept of the modernist Image has gained in substance what it has lost in creative and critical efficacy—in the sense that Pound originally launched Imagism as a movement *against* substance in all of its various implications: gravity, authority, plenitude, excess, intoxication. It is essential to recall that Pound explicitly identified Imagism as a *critical* movement, distinguished by its negativity. In his essay on Vorticism, published in 1914, Pound writes, "As a 'critical' movement, the 'Imagisme' of 1912 to '14 set out 'to bring poetry up to the level of prose' " (*GB* 83). Furthermore, he explains, "Imagisme, in so far as it has been known at all, has been known chiefly as a stylistic movement, as a movement of criticism rather than of creation. This is natural, for, despite all possible celerity of publication, the public is always, and of necessity, years behind the artists' actual thought" (*GB* 82). In the case of Imagism, what remained years ahead of public awareness was not so much specific poetic practice, or even notions of poetic form, but, as Pound explains, critical "thought." In

---

1890s to the High Modernist Mode (Cambridge, Mass.: Harvard University Press, 1976), p. 329. The second opinion is Graham Hough's in *Image as Experience* (Lincoln: University of Nebraska Press, 1960), p. 4.

3. Stephen Spender, *The Struggle of the Modern* (Berkeley: University of California Press, 1963), p. 110.

4. For a discussion of Imagism's influence on the antipoetic thrust of modernism, and on the Objectivist movement in particular, see Robert von Hallberg, *Charles Olson: The Scholar's Art* (Cambridge, Mass.: Harvard University Press, 1978), pp. 116, 171–173.

this regard, we can compare Imagism to manifestations of the historical avant-garde, such as Dada (with which Pound was later involved), whose "works" are less important than the critical perspective that informs the works (though Imagism's critique does not extend to the institution of art as such). Indeed, this is precisely how critics immediately involved in the historical context of Imagism have perceived its significance. In his *Criterion* commentary of July 1937, T. S. Eliot wrote, "The accomplishment of the Imagist movement in verse seems to me, in retrospect, to have been critical rather than creative; and as criticism, very important." It is in this spirit that the concept of the Image must be recovered from its historical substantiation and decline into pure visuality. Though Pound's conception of the Image was constantly evolving, it retained its essential negativity, its resistance to substantiation: what began as a critique of style and poetic language developed into a broader cultural, economic, and political critique. This implies, of course, that we must seek the roots of Pound's fascist cultural critique in the essential negativity of the Image. It also implies that any attempt to reconstruct the antithetical character of the Image—the basis of a movement *without substance*—must proceed by focusing primarily on poetics rather than poems, theory rather than practice (though such a division, in Pound's case, is particularly unstable).

The insubstantial character of the Image troubles critics who are suspicious, understandably, of its status as a virtual icon of twentieth-century poetics. Seeking to correct various distortions, some of Pound's best critics have challenged historical assumptions regarding the importance of Imagism in Pound's career and the development of modern poetics. The skepticism of these critics has often proved more effective—inadvertently—at disclosing the powerful tensions that sustain the figure of the Image than have the standard apologies for Imagism. R. P. Blackmur, for example, calls Imagism "a mere lively heresy of the visual in the verbal," a comment that alludes to historical controversies linking religious and verbal images, even as it dismisses Imagism as nothing more than a witty transgression.[5] In a more polemical context, Hugh Kenner condemns Imagism as a "red her-

5. R. P. Blackmur, cited in Hugh Witemeyer, *The Poetry of Ezra Pound: Forms and Renewal, 1908–1920* (Berkeley: University of California Press, 1969), p. 35.

ring" in the evolution of Pound's ideas about poetry. This charge is later echoed by Ronald Bush, who describes the ideogram (a prominent figure for the Image) as a "red herring" in the search for the genesis of the *Cantos*.[6] In both cases, the analogy of the red herring implies not only that the Image means less than it signifies, but that its appearance is deceptive, misleading. These charges, which attempt to defuse the originary power attributed to the Image, are typical features of the rhetoric of iconoclasm—a strategy that often undermines its own premises by emphasizing, negatively, the potency of the image. For example, Kenner's analogy of the red herring portrays the Image as a kind of bait or decoy (a potentially dangerous kind of image). Indeed, he disparages the Image by stressing its materiality and its powers of deception. In a later work, he corroborates this etymological subtext when he refers to the Image as an "enigmatic stone" that "continues to create its distracting turbulence."[7] Once again, he describes the Image tautologically, as a charm or a fetish, a source of turbulence and distraction. Yet the Image, in this case, seems to mean more, not less, than it signifies; the stone is mute, "enigmatic," yet surrounded by turbulence that it somehow creates. The Image is fundamentally untrustworthy: a red herring lures the critic into irrelevance—it's a dead end, whereas the "enigmatic stone" harbors an inscrutable meaning. The Image, as Kenner has it, always means either more or less than it signifies. This would suggest that the figure of the Image warrants greater scrutiny, yet the resistance of critics such as Kenner and Bush does little to counter or correct the position of those who emphasize the importance of Imagism without registering the turbulence surrounding it.

To exhume the remains of Imagism (and, by implication, of modernist poetics), we must begin by delineating three distinct tiers of Imagist rhetoric. The first, or most prominent, is what Kenner calls "technical hygiene"—the prohibitions enunciated by Pound in "A Few Don'ts by an Imagiste" (the aspect of Imagism that is most

---

6. Hugh Kenner, *The Poetry of Ezra Pound* (New York: New Directions, 1951), p. 58. Ronald Bush, *The Genesis of Ezra Pound's Cantos* (Princeton: Princeton University Press, 1976), pp. 13–15.

7. Hugh Kenner, *The Pound Era* (Berkeley: University of California Press, 1971), p. 173.

familiar to readers). The second tier of Imagism encompasses the ensemble of disparate figures that Pound employs to describe the Image (mask, translation, Freudian complex, algebraic equation, ideogram, vortex, and so on). The heterogeneity of this ensemble has historically resisted a coherent account of the Image, and continues to act as a formidable barrier to understanding the broader implications and affinities of the Image. A third dimension of Pound's conception of the Image, beyond the rules of hygiene and beyond the menagerie of figures, clearly controverts the first tier. This third dimension belongs to the shadowy "Doctrine of the Image," which Pound alludes to, but declines to discuss, in the first public announcement of Imagism in 1913.[8] He is reluctant to speak about it, in part because it undermines the rigorous formalism of the Imagist manifesto. This hidden dimension of the Image is a relic of Pound's earliest poetry, and is associated with visionary experience, dreams, and phantoms. It survives covertly in a trio of cognate terms employed by Pound in his poetry and criticism, which betray the phantasmic origin of the modernist Image: "phanopoeia," "phantastikon," and "phantasmagoria." In broader terms, what I am calling the cryptic dimension of the Image is entangled with the problem of "beauty" in modern art. More provocatively, beauty—from a modernist perspective—becomes associated with *kitsch,* and thus we can view kitsch as a foreign or cryptic body lodged in the discourse of modern formalism.

By situating the three divergent aspects of Imagism (its technique, its figurative emblems, its cryptic "Doctrine") *within* Pound's nascent poetics, we are obliged to regard literary positivism as conserving a remnant of a Decadent interest in the occult, or to regard poetic "technique" as a residual formation of "telepathy." Restored to its syncretic origins, the technological face of the Image is riddled with ghosts, vortices, and ideograms. A certain binarism persists, however, in some of the most important recent scholarship on Imagism—scholarship that concerns the role and significance of H.D. in the founding of poetic modernism. This revisionary work tends to argue that the

---

8. In "A Few Don'ts by an Imagiste" Pound remarks, "They held a certain 'Doctrine of the Image,' which they had not committed to writing; they said that it did not concern the public, and would provoke useless discussion." *Poetry* 1, no. 6 (March 1913): 200–206. When Pound reprinted portions of the Imagist manifesto in 1918, he deleted this passage (*LE* 4–7).

primary (and often divergent) features of Imagism are to be associated *either* with Pound *or* with H.D. This approach has helped clarify or correct certain longstanding obscurities and misrepresentations in the critical history of modern poetry. Cyrena Pondrom, for example, argues persuasively that between Pound's enunciation of the cryptic "Doctrine of the Image" and his subsequent disfiguring of the Image into vortex and ideogram, H.D.'s early poems intervene decisively in the technical dimension of the Image concept.[9] Thus, according to Pondrom, the principles most commonly associated with Imagism (its negativity, its "technical hygiene") are indebted to the model of H.D.'s poems. Although Pondrom's essay accomplishes the important work of restoring H.D. to her rightful place at the portal of Anglo-American modernism, it also perpetuates the monological conception of the Image as solely an instrument of positivism. Pondrom ignores the difficulties posed by the figures of the vortex, the ideogram, or the Freudian "complex," as well as the cryptic dimension of Pound's or H.D.'s conception of the Image. For Pondrom, H.D.'s infatuation with dead languages and cultures, with dreams and hieroglyphs, has little bearing on her fictive identity as an "imagiste."

A very different characterization of H.D.'s significance emerges if we regard her poetic mediation of death as the distinguishing feature of her work with "images." It is possible to construct a cryptic dimension of the Image, as Elizabeth Hirsh does in a recent essay, from H.D.'s fascination with antiquity (especially the Egyptian cult of the dead) and from her engagement with cinema and psychoanalysis.[10] Hirsh integrates these elements admirably into a hermeneutics of seeing (or not seeing), which on one hand accounts for H.D's "veiled" images, yet remains incommensurable (so far as Hirsh is concerned) with their technical aspect. Hirsh makes no mention of the extreme economy of H.D.'s images (the aspect emphasized by Pondrom), an omission that permits her to construct an opposition between two kinds of images (objective and mediumistic), between

---

9. Cyrena N. Pondrom, "H.D. and the Origins of Imagism," in Susan Stanford Friedman and Rachel Blau Duplessis, eds., *Signets: Reading H.D.* (Madison: University of Wisconsin Press, 1990), p. 105.

10. Elizabeth A. Hirsh, "Imaginary Images: 'H.D.,' Modernism, and the Psychoanalysis of Seeing," in *Signets*, pp. 430–451.

Mortal Images

Pound and H.D., between positivism and hermeneutics.[11] The gendering of this opposition derives from Hirsh's claims, equally reductive, that the concepts of the image and of femininity are historically interchangeable, and that we must therefore seek the key to Imagism, both historically and ideologically, in the fictive identity of "H.D." The cult of mourning that attends Pound's conception of the Image does indeed entail a feminization of the poet, but not because of any intrinsic link between imagery and femininity, and not in a manner that displaces a rather volatile procedure performed by Pound on the phantasms of masculine identity. Indeed, the instability of gender associated with the Image serves more importantly in Pound's case to disclose the homoerotic dimension of some of his most influential poetic and political positions.

Taking into account the revisions offered by Pondrom and Hirsh (as well as the pioneering studies of Susan Stanford Friedman and Rachel Blau Duplessis), we face the challenge of reconciling the technical and phantasmic aspects of the Image in both H.D. and Pound (a project that, given the extent of both poets' careers, I must restrict here to the example of Pound). We must in any case preserve the syncretism and the essential heterogeneity of the modernist Image. Assigning one or another of the aspects of Imagism to either Pound or to H.D. not only relieves the critic of a considerable burden, but imputes a false coherence to the modern discourse of images (by isolating its most intractable qualities). In contrast, by acknowledging the reciprocity of poetic effects between Pound and H.D. (the effects, in part, of a teenage love affair), we preserve with greater fidelity the haunting formation of the Image and modern poetry.

Once we move beyond the first tier of Imagism—the "technical hygiene" of "A Few Don'ts by an Imagiste"—it is not at all surprising to find terms such as "enigmatic" and "heresy" applied to the Image, even by critics who wish to defuse its emblematic power. Beyond the

11. Hirsh writes, "For the illusion(ism) of referentiality, the illusion of the presence of something actually absent, Pound sought to substitute the real presence of the Image/ideogram as form, a form incarnate in the text as perfected through the poetic regimen of 'Imagism.' 'H.D.' the living doll, the spitting Image of Imagism, responds with a 'hieroglyphic' text that, on the one hand, reinterprets the Image in light of psychoanalysis, as a mode of hermeneutic veiling that restores the centrality of reading" (p. 448).

simple prohibitions that founded the Imagist movement, we encounter a bewildering ensemble of figures for the Image, which seem to have little to do either with one another or with the technical criteria they are meant to elucidate. The Image, Pound tells us, is the centerpiece of "a revival of the sense of realism" (*GB* 113). This claim apparently supports the familiar emphasis on clarity, precision, and objectivity. What Pound means by "realism," however, begins to recede, or to lose its explanatory value, when we discover that he traces the origins of the Image to his use of literary *masks* in a "search for the real" (*GB* 85). In a related analogy, the exchange that occurs in translation—so important to Pound's understanding of poetry—is said to produce Images of the dead, *memento mori* (a formulation which reminds us that the Image is implicated in a "*revival* of realism"). The association of realism and the Image becomes even more perplexing when Pound asks us to think of the Image as an algebraic equation (with "variable significance"), or as a Freudian "complex" (a moment in which an object or idea is possessed by "subconscious energies"). One of Pound's most celebrated figures for the Image—the Chinese ideogram—removes the composite structure of an equation or a Freudian complex to a more exotic and archaic context. The erosion of the Image as an emblem of realism reaches its most fertile and puzzling extremity in the figure of the Image as a vortex. What is the relation between vortex and mask, vortex and translation, vortex and ideogram, or vortex and Freudian complex? More fundamentally, what sort of "realism" does the figure of a vortex represent?

How are we to make sense of this ensemble of figures and evaluate its bearing on the explicit aims of Imagism? In the first place, Pound's attempts to define the Image violate the basic principles of Imagism (economy, precision, clarity). Not only is he unable to offer a literal definition of the Image, but the figurative analogies multiply with remarkable fecundity and obscurity. Given the irreconcilable nature of the ensemble as a whole, we must ask whether it is susceptible to thematic or inductive analysis. Is it possible to isolate a basic premise from these disparate figures, one that would yield a general understanding of the Image? Given the history of critical response to Imagism, we would have to say that the heterogeneity of these figures presents a considerable obstacle to any rationalized account of *the* Image. To understand what Pound means by the Image, we must adopt a model of discourse that is essentially materialist, or, more appropriately, atomist, following a regressive path toward the "atomic facts" and "symptoms" revered by Pound—approximating, that is, the ensorceled state of the positivist critic, the ethnographer, the philologist.

The rhetoric of the Image establishes what Marcelin Pleynet calls "an intelligible system of productive irrationalities."[12] Pleynet emphasizes the role of historical and biographical materials in constructing a "signifying space" that overcomes the limitations of purely formal analysis. This is particularly relevant to a reading of the Image, which formal analyses have frequently—and inadvertently—reduced to the status of a decorative art. The historical and biographical materials I incorporate into my reading of the Image—especially Pound's relation to Gaudier-Brzeska—should therefore be regarded as elements in an "irrational system" that also includes Pound's views on the formal properties of the Image. Pound's public mourning of Gaudier provides what Jean-François Lyotard calls a "libidinal apparatus"—an empty form or structural matrix for the ideological permutations of the Image. Biographical details in particular should be understood not as causal or motivational but as elements in an expanded textual field, as materials resistant to the political naïveté of Pound's own formalism and that of his major critics. In this sense, certain biographical sources (letters, the radio broadcasts, anecdotal evidence) can be read as historical texts that frequently subvert the explicit aims of Imagism (that is, its emphasis on pure form), as well as a subtext that helps link the disparate figures of the Image. What's more, the political shadow cast by the Image, which extends as far as Pound's fascist radio broadcasts during World War II, becomes visible only if we introduce those biographical and historical materials into the discourse of Imagism.

Evidence of a third dimension of Imagism appears in the first public announcement of Imagism (in the March 1913 issue of *Poetry* magazine). The article is not quite what it appears to be: Pound composed an interview with himself, but asked F. S. Flint to sign it (the article

12. Marcelin Pleynet, *Painting and System,* trans. Sima N. Godfrey (Chicago: University of Chicago Press, 1984), p. 35.

bears Flint's name). The ghost author of the article claims to have "sought out an *imagiste*," an anonymous informant (Pound), who spells out the "rules" of his poetic formula. In addition to the now famous guidelines, the informant alludes to "a certain Doctrine of the Image," which he declines to discuss. A curious allusion to the veiled "Doctrine" survives, however, in the original draft of the interview—a phrase that Pound excised and that refers cryptically to the "penumbral" features of Imagism: "He [Pound] told me later that the school consisted of three poets, one or two affiliated writers, and a . . . penumbra!"[13] Flint's manuscript contains no explanation of this peculiar comment, nor should we seek any particular significance in the reference to a "penumbra." I do want to insist, though, that we not ignore the *suggestion* of secrecy—for that is all it is—enshrouding the principles of Imagism and the anonymous informant of the article. From its inception, therefore, the figure of the Image appears to be implicated in what Nicholas Rand calls a "poetics of hiding," a cryptic enunciation of forbidden values.[14] The secrecy of the Image does not concern any specific meaning it might harbor—the crypt, at this point, is entirely vacant; rather, it concerns a hermeneutical model that will later inform Pound's cultural politics, and the occluded aspect of what has been called an "inaugural moment in modern poetics." Thus, on one hand, the air of secrecy is something more than an illusion if we understand that it refers to Pound's conception of mythological experience, a conception that is, as he explains it, not only visionary but necessarily encrypted—a cultic substance that forms the basis of secret societies (*LE* 431; *SR* 92). Hence, Pound does not fully enunciate the principles of Imagism, because of the "mythological" character of the Image. On the other hand, we must acknowledge that the cryptic dimension of the Image is, at this point, probably empty: the odd comment about the "penumbra" and the allusion to a hermetic "Doctrine" are nothing more than suggestions.

Yet the idea of a vacant crypt reflects the character of the Imagist movement itself, which at its founding was little more than a fiction.

---

13. Flint's original draft of the interview is reproduced in Christopher Middleton, "Documents on Imagism from the Papers of F. S. Flint," *The Review* 15 (April 1965): 34–45.

14. Nicholas T. Rand, *Le cryptage et la vie des oeuvres* (Paris: Aubier, 1989).

Martin Kayman has argued, "The movement sprang into being with the stroke of a pen. Rather than *avant la lettre,* Imagisme is fundamentally—and, I shall argue, definitively—*avant la chose.*"[15] Thus, he claims, "what Pound produced in Imagisme was a *literary history—*or rather, a fiction of a literary history, and hence a history of quasi-mythic character" (63). We must also bear in mind that the fictive origins of the Imagist movement coincide with the construction of a fictional identity—"H.D."—that holds one of the many keys to the marginalization of women's writing in the standard histories of literary modernism.[16] From this perspective, the empty crypt becomes a figure for the avant-garde movement created *ex nihilo,* a peremptory gesture that ensures the phantasmic disruption of its founding principles. Indeed, by constructing the Imagist movement as an empty crypt, Pound wrote into history the return of the phantom inhabiting that empty place. In this regard, there is a fundamental correspondence between the fictional character of the Imagist movement and the phantasmagorical properties of the mythic Image.

James Longenbach traces the secret "Doctrine of the Image" to Pound's association with Yeats at Stone Cottage, where Pound became interested in various occult traditions. Longenbach argues, "From the start, though, Pound maintained a private conception of Imagism, distinct from the publicized goals of 'A Few Don'ts by an Imagiste' "; and further, "while Pound was compiling *Des Imagistes* at Stone Cottage, the visionary 'Doctrine of the Image' was as important as the 'Don'ts.' "[17] Longenbach is right to emphasize an occult theory of the Image (which is not, by any means, restricted to the "supernatural"), but he does not go far enough in exposing this unknown territory. Nor is he correct in assuming that the figure of

---

15. Martin A. Kayman, *The Modernism of Ezra Pound: The Science of Poetry* (London: Macmillan, 1986), p. 53.

16. One is struck by the enigmatic quality of the contributor's note on "H.D." in her first appearance as an "Imagiste" in *Poetry:* " 'H.D. Imagiste' is an American lady resident abroad, whose identity is unknown to the editor. Her sketches from the Greek are not offered as exact translations, or as in any sense finalities, but as experiments in delicate and elusive cadences, which attain sometimes a haunting beauty." *Poetry* (January 1913): 135.

17. James Longenbach, *Stone Cottage: Pound, Yeats, and Modernism* (New York: Oxford University Press, 1988), pp. 31, 54.

the Image mingles with the fetishized realm of the dead for the first time as a result of Pound's research at Stone Cottage.

In my assessment of Imagism, I am particularly concerned with these hidden dimensions of early modernist poetics and with an adulterated figure of the Image—a kind of radiological medium—which later serves as the principle of unrestricted exchange (a vortex) in Pound's vision of fascist, totalitarian culture. For example, Pound, like many writers and artists prior to World War I, was intrigued by the idea of a submerged relation between primitive culture and advanced technological society. This sort of speculation found an important analogue in the contemporary fascination with crowds and mass psychology (epitomized by the popular theories of LeBon, Tarde, and others). Hence, while Pound conceived of the Image as an artifact that linked the archaic and the modern (comparing the vortex to the "horrific energy" of African fetishes), he also cited, as counterparts to Imagism, the Unanimiste movement and the writings of Jules Romains on "crowd feeling." In certain respects, then, Pound's conception of the Image as a vortex is representative of the emerging relation between fetishism and the new "science of crowds." This configuration becomes particularly important when we consider the role of ethnography in Pound's fascist cultural theory during the 1930s. In effect, Pound constructs a prehistory of the future (the archaic dimension of a fascist utopia) on the basis of an epistemological model (the ideogram) and a dynamic emblem (the vortex) that are drawn from the principles of Imagism.

The "enigmatic" character of the modernist Image derives, in part, from mistaken assumptions about its history. These historical distortions, which include the suppression of H.D.'s significance, are symptomatic of a more profound resistance to conceptual anomalies in the rhetoric of the Image. Most critics limit Pound's creative or theoretical interest in the Image to his brief involvement with the Imagist movement. Typically (in Kenner's account, for example), the influence of the Image on Pound's thinking emerges sometime in 1912, and begins to wane prior to his break with Amy Lowell and Imagism in July 1914. Accounts of why Pound suddenly abandons the figure of the Image at this point in his career are generally unsatisfactory (a fact that explains, in part, the "distracting turbulence" generated by the

Image). Pound, I suggest, appears suddenly to abandon the tenets of Imagism (an uncharacteristic decision for him) for reasons that correspond obliquely, yet fatefully, to the traumatic effects of World War I, including the loss of Gaudier-Brzeska. First, the Image is contaminated by the necrophilia of Pound's early poetry—a Decadent countersign, a backwardness, that Gaudier's death threatens to revive. Second, the rules of "technical hygiene" jeopardize, even as they seek to invigorate, the existence of "poetry" as it faces the prospect of catastrophic martial violence in the Great War. The "objectivity" of the Image is so extreme that it threatens to extinguish altogether what passes for "poetry" in the year 1912—a danger that has been thoroughly mediated by the ideology of "formalism" and now stands, inscrutably, as the familiar—and benign—basis of the Imagist movement. Thus, what one may call the traumatic or apocalyptic dimension of the Image—its negativity and its belligerent rhetoric—is arrested by the appearance of its historical counterpart in the martial spectacle of World War I and, more intimately, by the loss of Gaudier-Brzeska.

We could argue, therefore, that the "violence" characterizing Pound's sudden dissociation from the Imagist movement is already implicit in the principles of Imagism.[18] Distilled to a handful of syllables, the Imagist poem derives its power from its resistance to language, from the perilous condition of its own medium—a form that is inherently self-destructive. Thus, the influence of Japanese haiku on Imagism, for example, can be understood as an exotic means of formalizing and dignifying a poetic suicide. The remains of Victorian poetry assume the haiku form as a cipher of ritual death (hence the arduous and protracted deletion of "In a Station of the Metro"— reduced over a period of six months from thirty lines to fourteen words). As a counterpart to the Image, the haiku form permits European (or Anglo-American) poetry to take its own life publicly, in a manner that implicates other dimensions of Western culture but is not fully intelligible (since it is foreign). Though it is articulated through the Imagist movement as a public, discursive event, the suicide of

---

18. The destructive impulse inherent in Imagism is evident in a comment that Pound made to Alice Henderson, the assistant editor of *Poetry:* "I had one brilliant inspiration. I was about to declare the imagist movement *over,* when the first anthology came out. Like a damn fool, I didn't." *Letters to Alice Henderson,* p. 142.

poetry—which is not to be confused with its end—is never acknowledged as such, because that death is encrypted in the legitimizing discourses of objectivity (the sponsor of the Image) and orientalism (the belated fascination with haiku). Thus, Pound's second thoughts about Imagism are not so much disavowal as they are hesitation before an abyss. Indeed, his construction of a poetic form—the Image—that continually verges on silence can best be understood in relation to the problems that Wittgenstein addresses contemporaneously in the picture theory of the *Tractatus*. Furthermore, I would suggest, we cannot isolate this retrenchment on Pound's part from the general suppression of the achievements and significance of positivism in the available histories of modernism.

The historical uncertainty surrounding Imagism is not at all surprising, since there is considerable evidence to indicate that Pound was thinking about the Image as early as 1908, and that it remained a central focus of his poetics long after 1914. By his own admission, his attraction to the Image began at least five years prior to the emergence of the Imagist movement in 1913. In his earliest public reference to Imagism (in an appendix to *Ripostes,* published in October 1912), Pound suggests that the origins of Imagism lie in his earliest writings and ideas about poetry: he calls the Imagist poets "the descendants of the forgotten school of 1909" (*P* 251). He confirms this chronology in a letter to René Taupin in 1926, where he characterizes his literary activities before World War I as "l'inception de l'imagisme à Londres (1908–1914)" (*L* 218). The Image, so far as Pound is concerned, emblematizes not only the movement that bears its name but the period in which he published his first six books of poetry (1908–1912).

The role of the Image in Pound's thinking after he broke with Amy Lowell must be expanded in a similar fashion. In the first place, it is important to recognize that Pound's break with the Imagist movement in July 1914 did not coincide with a rejection of the figure of the Image as such. In fact, he continued to develop his conception of it in new contexts. His famous definition of the Image as a vortex, for example, did not appear until September 1914, in an article titled "Vorticism." As the analogy suggests, Vorticism, from Pound's standpoint, was essentially a revision and expansion of the Image concept;

his articles on Imagism for the "Affirmations" series in *New Age* do not appear until January and February 1915. Moreover, the first public reference to the Image as ideogram comes even later, in an article titled "Imagisme and England," published in *T.P.'s Weekly* on February 20, 1915. During the same period, writing in the *New Age* of February 11, 1915, Pound offers an "Analysis of the Decade," listing the most important figures of the artistic movements with which he has been associated, and the particular "donation" of each of those individuals. When it comes to his own contribution, he identifies "the Image" as his most important creative legacy (*GB* 115).

Another discrepancy emerges regarding the putative influence of the visual arts on Imagist poetry. Most critics proceed from the thesis that developments in painting and sculpture influenced Pound's conception of the Image, and that his interest in the visual arts coincides with a visual orientation in his poetry (defined by Pound as "phanopoeia").[19] Yet his first published review of modern painting did not appear until April 1914 in *The Egoist* (shortly before he dissociated himself from the Imagist movement). He wrote the majority of his art criticism even later, when he was art critic for *New Age*, from 1917 to 1920. The dates of these activities suggest a flaw in the conventional wisdom about the relation of graphic and verbal imagery in Pound's early poetry: either the analogy is misleading from the start, or we must extend its range to a later date in his career—or, as I want to suggest, a revision and combination of both possibilities is necessary. Meanwhile, Pound's most comprehensive treatment of the verbal Image appeared in 1916, in the memoir of Gaudier-Brzeska (two years after his break with Imagism). In addition, "Hugh Selwyn Mauberley," written in 1919 and 1920, offers a summation of Pound's long struggle with divergent conceptions of the Image. Indeed, looking back on his career, Pound identifies the year 1920 as marking the end of a period of "reform" that is clearly associated with the tenets of Imagism: "The poetical reform between 1910 and 1920 coincided with the scrutiny of the word, the cleaning-up of syntax" (*SP* 321).

---

19. Good source materials on Pound's interest in the visual arts can be found in *Ezra Pound and the Visual Arts*, ed. Harriet Zinnes (New York: New Directions, 1980). See also the exhibition catalogue *Pound's Artists: Ezra Pound and the Visual Arts in London, Paris, and Italy* (London: Tate Gallery, 1985).

Finally, there is evidence that the concept of the Image remains crucially important to the earliest versions of the *Cantos*. In a letter of 1917 to James Joyce, Pound writes, "I have begun an endless poem of no known category. Phanopoeia or something or other, all about everything" (*P/J* 102). This revival of Pound's interest in phanopoeia is confirmed by a poem of the same title, which he published in the *Little Review* in November 1918 (*P* 169–170). Moreover, in the March 1918 issue of *Future* magazine, Pound published what he then called "Images from the Second Canto of a Long Poem."

The expanded historical field of the Image extends, therefore, from the publication of Pound's first book of poems in 1908 to the publication of "Hugh Selwyn Mauberley" in 1920. The cohesiveness of this period, viewed as an effect of the Image on Pound's poetry and thought, depends to a large extent on the hidden dimensions of the Image that I mentioned above (and that I will define more clearly in a moment). In other critical respects, the Image exceeds even these historical limitations. Indeed, we can discern a second, distinct phase of Imagist poetics, in which the Image incorporates the hermeneutical dimension of meaning that had originally been the primary target of Imagist poetics. During his engagement with Italian fascism, Pound revived the Image under the guise of the ideogram, translating it into a model of discourse that he called the "ideogrammic method." Yet the ideogram in its "totalitarian" phase is no longer simply a formal paradigm but a hermeneutical instrument, a means of rendering and disclosing "meaning" as if it were a kind of mythological substance. What had been antithetical to the Image during the Vorticist period— meaning, "literary content," substance—becomes its dialectical equivalent under fascism. Indeed, in 1937 Pound goes so far as to suggest that the ideogram should be viewed as the unifying principle for all of his work *since 1905,* culminating in his program of "totalitarian" culture. He writes, "The choice and juxtaposition of items in a given programme is the fruit of the IDEOGRAMMIC method wherein are combined Fenollosa's thought (and thirty years work) and my own since 1905."[20]

Expanding the historical field of the Image is only the first step in

20. Pound, "Totalitarian Scholarship and the New Paideuma," *Germany and You* (April 25, 1937): 96.

Mortal Images

exhuming the Imagistic remains of modern poetics. Revised in the image of mass death dispatched from the battlefields of World War I (including the loss of Gaudier), the modernist Image emerges as an expression of aberrant cultural mourning, a cryptic figure that redefines, as I have indicated, relations between gender, loss, and pleasure for the male poet. The object of mourning shifts historically for Pound, but the figure of the Image remains a consistent focus for the experience of loss—whether personal, creative, or political. The elegiac Image revises, in its earliest manifestations, a fascination with death that permeates the first six books of Pound's poetry. The early poems abound with references to cadavers, tombs, and the accoutrements of death. Occasionally, the poet assumes the voice of a dead person, but more frequently he is visited, or haunted, by *images* of the dead, by ghosts. Thus, Pound's earliest conception of the Image not only emerges from the grave but presupposes a profound state of passivity. (One is visited by phantoms.) The Image, in this respect, is an apparition, a phantom, because it represents the return of a lost or dead object, a moment when the poet is *haunted* by reality. The spectral Image presents life imaged as death, a living death. If we take into account the "prehistory" of the Image in Pound's career, then we must view the formal properties of the Image (the qualities conventionally associated with Imagism) as displacing an earlier spectral figure of the Image—which continues to haunt Pound's formalist agenda. Thus, from the perspective of literary history, I am inclined to view the Imagist movement as a largely unsuccessful attempt by Pound to bury—that is, to modernize—his earlier and more archaic conceptions of the Image.

Though Pound insists that the Image is neither mimetic nor rhetorical, I want to suggest that his conception of the Image embodies certain monstrous properties of these traditional figures; furthermore the mimetic Image becomes a phantom and the rhetorical Image a corpse under the regime of his infatuation with death. Indeed, the Image assumes the uncanny properties of the living dead, thereby serving as a legitimate object for a cryptic meditation on the process of making and the limits of symbolization—a deconstruction of "death" in poetic language. Although Pound attacked the "corpse language" of late Victorian poetry, the Image, in its most uncompromising aspects, comes to embody the idea of language as a corpse. Thus, the figure of the Image is highly ambiguous: it assumes the despicable but alluring properties of "corpse language"—a dead language that is directed against the magical properties of the dead. In a similar fashion, the spectral and homoerotic properties of the mimetic Image are reawakened and held in reserve by the death of the sculptor Gaudier-Brzeska.

Pound relegates to the "underworld" certain dimensions of language that can be revived only in the form of an Image. The idea of a repression carried out against a word that can return to consciousness only as an image is the basis of Nicolas Abraham and Maria Torok's theory of cryptonymy. Their concept of "the crypt" calls to mind an artificial unconscious, constructed according to the Hermetic and atomistic principles of the Renaissance "art of memory."[21] According to Abraham and Torok, what lies in the crypt is "nothing but a word translated into an image" (*Wolf Man* 22). A word (or a language) associated with certain ineffable pleasures is placed in a crypt, never to be acknowledged again. A mechanism evolves, however, that allows the so-called pleasure word, the lost language, to be revived *if* it is disguised as an image. The crypt preserves and conceals "a word that operates only from the Unconscious, that is as a *word-thing*. In conscious life it can be recouped only as a visual image" (*Wolf Man* 46). The object in the crypt is not a word *for* a thing, but a word-thing, a fetish. From this perspective, the history of Imagism should be read as a cryptonymous account of the disappearance (and revival) of a language that is associated with the pleasures of the grave: blindness, passivity, materiality, sentiment. Pound seals in a crypt the "corpse language" of his youth and his illicit infatuation with the dead. Later, the exquisite corpse that is preserved and concealed in the crypt revives in the form of the Image (as an "atomic fact," an apparition of the dead, or a "symptom" of totalitarian culture).

---

21. Nicolas Abraham and Maria Torok, *The Wolf Man's Magic Word: A Cryptonymy*, trans. Nicholas Rand, foreword by Jacques Derrida (Minneapolis: University of Minnesota Press, 1986). Important work on the problem of cryptology can also be found in Giorgio Agamben, *Stanzas: Word and Phantasm in Western Culture*, trans. Ronald L. Martinez (Minneapolis: University of Minnesota Press, 1993). Agamben constructs a "topology of the unreal" that parallels in many respects Derrida's formulation of the crypt.

So far, I have addressed the problem of Imagism only in regard to poetics and the peculiar veiling of the Image concept during the course of its critical history. It is essential, however, to identify the poems written by Pound that pertain specifically to the problem of Imagism and to show precisely how these poems negotiate and embody the cryptic properties of the Image. Any revisionary account of Pound's early work (poems written, for the most part, prior to 1917 and reprinted in *Personae* in 1926) inevitably enters the historical debate over the relative literary merits of the early poetry in contrast to the *Cantos*. ("Hugh Selwyn Mauberley" can be considered a transitional work.) When Marianne Moore, for example, reviews in 1931 *A Draft of XXX Cantos*, she addresses herself partly to "those who object to the Cantos' obscurity—who prefer the earlier poems."[22] Much of Pound's early poetry, which earned him considerable popular success as well as critical esteem, has slipped into obscurity, as a result of academic emphasis on the *Cantos*. Thus, any reappraisal or theoretical revision of the early work bears significantly not only on evaluations of Pound's overall career (including its political dimension) but on the relative achievements of poetic modernism.

As to the relevant texts, the first intimations of Imagism emerge through the medium of translation (a topic that I will discuss at length in Chapter 5). Thus, Pound's translations of Cavalcanti (produced in 1910) and of "The Seafarer" poem (published in 1911) evince for the first time the cryptic properties of the Image, combined with an impulse toward "objectivity." Of Pound's own compositions prior to 1917, we can discern two groupings of poems that pertain directly to the Imagist movement and to the cryptic dimension of Imagist poetics: first, the poems collected in *Ripostes*, which was published in October 1912; and, second, poems published by Pound in *Poetry* magazine (the official "organ" of the Imagist movement) during 1912 and 1913. Many of these poems would later be collected and published in *Lustra* (1916). Finally, among the texts directly pertinent to Imagism, we would have to include Pound's adaptations of Japanese and Chinese sources, drawn from the papers of Fenollosa, which came into his hands near the end of 1913. Pound's celebrated "translations" of Chinese poetry were actually executed *after* he had already finished

---

22. Marianne Moore, "The Cantos," *Poetry* (October 1931); reprinted in *The Complete Prose of Marianne Moore*, ed. Patricia C. Willis (New York: Viking, 1986), p. 273.

work on the Japanese materials, though the Chinese poems were published first in *Cathay* (1915). The Japanese translations appeared in *Certain Noble Plays of Japan* (1916) and *"Noh" or Accomplishment* (1917).

The volume *Ripostes* (1912) contains the first public reference to Imagism (*P* 251), as well as the two poems "Doria" and "The Return," which Pound selected as his contribution to the anthology *Des Imagistes*, published in March 1914.[23] Thus, the poems representing Pound in the first Imagist anthology derive from a period in his career *prior* to the announcement of the Imagist movement in March 1913. Both poems, which Pound reprinted in *Umbra* (1920) and *Personae* (1926), evoke a "dorian" or "crepuscular" mood. In "Doria," the speaker invokes "the eternal moods of the bleak wind" and "the shadowy flowers of Orcus" (*P* 67)—that is, the shades of the underworld. "The Return" is even more significant in the context of Imagism, since Pound describes it in his "Vorticism" essay as "impersonal" and as "an objective reality" (*GB* 85), and compares it to "new sculpture" by Jacob Epstein and Gaudier-Brzeska. A quick glance at the poem, however, indicates that we cannot possibly isolate Pound's grasp of the "impersonal," or "objective reality," from the poem's languid and justly celebrated rhythms, or from its subject matter—the ghostly return of "the souls of blood," who are at once "inviolable" and "half-awakened" (*P* 74). Moreover, as the poem's refrain ("See, they return") indicates, in the "objective reality" of this particular "image," seeing is remembering. The "objectivity" of the poem corresponds to the "impersonality" of the dead, to their somnambulistic quality.

The phantasmic, or cryptological, features of "Doria" and "The Return"—poems that Pound designated as exemplars of Imagism—appear in a number of other poems in the *Ripostes* volume. "Apparuit," for example, one of Pound's most beautiful and sustained apparitional poems, resembles "The Return" in its evocation of a phantom presence. The poet glimpses "Half the graven shoulder" of a ghostly image "casting a-loose the cloak of the body" (*P* 68). At the moment

---

23. Pound's contribution to the first Imagist anthology also included four brief adaptations from an anthology of Chinese literature compiled by H. A. Giles in 1901. His only original compositions, however, were "Doria" and "The Return." Ezra Pound, ed., *Des Imagistes: An Anthology* (New York: Boni, 1914), pp. 41–46.

of apparition, "Life died down in the lamp and flickered, / caught at the wonder," as "the stunned light / faded about thee." The poet describes the apparition as "a portent . . . swift in departing." Another poem, "Sub Mare," evokes more distinctly a tomblike space, an ocean grave, in which two lovers "grope" amid "things older than the names they have" (*P* 69). The poem begins:

> It is, and is not, I am sane enough,
> Since you have come this place has hovered
>   round me,
> This fabrication built of autumn roses. (*P* 69)

The opening phrase, "It is, and is not," immediately establishes the haunting terms of ephemerality, through a chance meeting or tryst ("since you have come"). The ocean grave, with its "Pale slow green surgings of the underwave," becomes the site of ephemerality (and silence), a sepulchral "fabrication built of autumn roses." The themes of chance, ephemerality, loss, and silence—so essential to Pound's crypt poetry and, by inference, to the poetics of Imagism—emerge in a more reflective, or polemical, context in "Silet" ("He is Silent"), the poem that opens *Ripostes:*

> There is enough in what I chance to say. . . .
> It is enough that we once came together. . . .
> Time has seen this, and will not turn again;
> And who are we, who know that last intent,
> To plague tomorrow with a testament! (*P* 59)

This poem, which begins by mocking the "black, immortal ink" and the writer's "deathless pen," not only embraces ephemerality and loss as the basic premises of the "new" poetry, but suggests that it is best *not to speak at all* of such ephemeral moments. Silence, then, is the most appropriate witness to a lover who is "swift in departing." Thus, from its earliest impulses ("Silet" is dated "Verona 1911"), Imagism displays a tendency to curtail language, which is somehow implicated in the experience of loss; a movement, then, toward silence, toward death.

The cryptological dimension of *Ripostes* does not, by any means, vanish from Pound's poetry with the formal announcement of Imagism in *Poetry* magazine in March 1913. Indeed, the first recorded instance of Pound's use of the term "imagist" occurs (in a letter of August 1912 to Harriet Monroe) in relation to one of his most extravagant crypt poems, "Middle-Aged," which appeared in the October 1912 issue of *Poetry* (a poem that I will examine at greater length in Chapter 3). Along with his public pronouncements on Imagism, Pound published in *Poetry* during 1913 a number of poems that would have been viewed by the magazine's readers as representative of the principles of Imagism. (These poems were later collected and published in *Lustra* in 1916.) Among these poems, so closely identified with the "objective reality" of Imagism, one finds work that is clearly cut from the same cloth as the crypt poetry published in *Ripostes*. The poem "Dance Figure," for example (published in *Poetry* in April 1913), originally carried the subtitle "A Thoroughly Sensuous Image." Like "Middle-Aged" and "The Tomb at Akr Çaar" (from *Ripostes*), "Dance Figure" is a crypt poem set in an Egyptian tomb: "Gilt turquoise and silver are in thy place of rest / O Nathat-Ikanaie . . . Thine arms are as a young sapling under the bark; / Thy face as a river with lights" (*P* 91). The apparitional theme emerges more fully in the poem "Surgit Fama" ("There is a Rumor"), published in *Poetry* in November 1913. Like the earlier poems ("The Return" and "Apparuit"), "Surgit Fama" announces a *return* to an archaic dimension of spirit. At the same time, it depicts an apparition that is understood to be expressive of that archaic realm:

> Koré is seen in the North
> skirting the blue-gray sea
> in gilded and russet mantle. (*P* 90)

The poem gives voice (or vision) to a rumor that Koré (Persephone, queen of the underworld), along with "the tricksome Hermes," have been sighted "in the North"—a vision that portends a *return* to antiquity: "Once more are the never abandoned gardens / Full of gossip and old tales" (*P* 90). Gossip, old tales, and rumor become models of artistic expression in an age heralded by apparitional sightings of Persephone and Hermes. The new poetry (Imagism) will be composed under the twin signs of death and hermeticism. The Imagist poem is at once rumorous and precise. Its "objectivity" is guaranteed by its impossibility (by its apparitional subject) and by its mediumistic procedure: the Image always arrives from afar, from the realm of the dead.

Mortal Images

The apparitional and nostalgic features of poems directly associated with Imagism became more elegiac in Pound's adaptations of Japanese Noh dramas (which I will examine more closely in Chapter 6) and in his "translations" of Chinese poetry. The poems in *Cathay* (1915) all deal with the experience of exile, separation, and loss.[24] The speaker in "Song of the Bowman of Shu," for example, observes, "When anyone says 'Return,' the others are full of sorrow" (*P* 127); while the voice in "Lament of the Frontier Guard" speaks of "sorrow, sorrow like rain. / Sorrow to go, and sorrow, sorrow returning" (*P* 133). One of the most affecting sequences, "Four Poems of Departure," bears witness to "leave-taking": "Here we must make separation / And go out through a thousand miles of dead grass" (*P* 137). The elegiac mood extends to the disappearance—always ambiguous—of the "house" of culture:

> The phoenix are at play on the terrace.
> The phoenix are gone, the river flows on alone.
> Flowers and grass
> Cover over the dark path
> where lay the dynastic house of the Go. (*P* 138)

In a number of these poems, we also find the Imagist theme of silence impinging on language, of voices forsaken or eclipsed: "Our mind is full of sorrow, who will know of our grief?" (*P* 127). Another speaker confides, "however we long to speak / He cannot know of our sorrow" (*P* 142). The loss of a beloved person, place, or thing is signaled—indeed embodied—by words that long to return to silence: "What is the use of talking, and there is no end of talking, / There is no end of things in the heart" (*P* 136).

The poetic Image is never far removed from the "end of talking," which signals in turn its proximity to the "things of the heart." Imagism's entanglement with the idea of death portrays allegorically the mortality of poetry itself, as well as the essential negativity of the Image: language is consistently deployed against itself in the name of the Image. More precisely, the Image is implicated in a struggle

---

24. Some recent thoughts on elegy in Pound's *Cathay* can be found in Ming Xie, "Elegy and Personae in Ezra Pound's '*Cathay*,'" *ELH* 60, no. 1 (Spring 1993): 261–281.

between verbal and visual values—usually understood as a correspondence between poetry and the visual arts. We can grasp this struggle more effectively, as I have already indicated, if we view it as occurring between divergent symbolic economies at a given moment in the history of modernism. This epochal moment witnesses a partial eclipse of "the heyday of meaning" by a resurgence of empirical values, under the rubric of positivism, which accompanies the rapid development of new technical media. The modernist Image, an expression of this resurgence of empiricism, is contaminated—and enriched—by the decaying materials of late Romantic poetics and its philosophical counterpart, hermeneutics. Thus, when Pound remarks, "The Image is the word beyond formulated language" (*GB* 88), we should understand the Image as an emblem of positivism that positions itself outside the hermeneutical concept of "meaning" as such. Yet the idea that the Image is a word excluded from language also brings to mind a notion of the image as the "plus of appearance," the apparition of something that does not exist, a phantasm that stands in contrast to the brute fact of positivism. The modernist Image, like the fetish as Marx conceives it, occupies both of these positions at once: a material thing, unmediated by any form of exchange or transference, and a metaphysical thing, imperceptible to the senses, which arises in the act of exchange (or translation) to become the object of collective hallucination. The modernist Image is therefore essentially schismatic, bearing the marks of a struggle between the symbolic economies of positivism and hermeneutics.

To associate Imagism, a theory of poetics, with hermeneutics, a theory of interpretation, may seem improbable, even puzzling at first. Yet the most basic principles of Imagism were entangled with the problem of meaning and its relation to the artifact or sign, a problem that had been the special province, since the early nineteenth century, of the philosophy of hermeneutics. Indeed, as the earliest and most prominent standard of objectivity in Anglo-American poetics, the Image was implicated in a fierce campaign against improper or inauthentic meaning. In addition, Pound's poetics always evolves in relation to new models of discourse or criticism. The "method of the luminous detail" in criticism, for example, becomes the "radiant cluster" of the poetic Image. The direction of this correspondence is later reversed when the poetic ideogram evolves into the "ideogrammic method" of scholarship. Hence, much of Pound's thinking about poetics possesses an implicit epistemological or hermeneutical dimension. His early preoccupation with the nature and limits of symbolism evolves into a general epistemology that reflects the economic determinism governing both his poetry and his criticism in the latter part of his career. This may explain, in part, why recent critical history has treated Pound largely as a poet of ideas—an extremely hazardous, though necessary, departure.

In the specifically literary context of Imagist polemics, Pound addresses (and usually attacks) the problem of hermeneutical meaning under the name "symbolism." Although he usually characterizes the Image as the antithesis of symbolism, there are similarities between the two that tend to undermine their strict opposition. Pound associates the Image, for example, with what he calls "absolute metaphor," which may be understood in the context of his peculiar notion of objectivity as the nonempirical referent of the Vorticist Image, the object of sightless vision. Indeed, Pound makes a rather startling admission about this feature of Imagism: "To hold a like belief in a sort of permanent metaphor is, as I understand it, 'symbolism' in its profoundest sense. It is not necessarily a belief in a permanent world, but it is a belief in that direction" (*GB* 84). One might well ask whether the "permanent world" implied by the symbolist features of the Image does not eventually become the fascist utopia that Pound sought to construct with the help of the ideogram.

Modern hermeneutics is a product of German Romanticism, and, with a few important exceptions, has never fared very well as a discipline outside the German context. Its early associations with "divination" and esoteric meaning, in particular, have not found a receptive audience in American institutions. Yet we might ask whether the elements of mysticism and fanaticism in Pound's poetry, which are essential to its modernity, have proved any less resistant to his Anglo-American audience. Do Pound's efforts to "screen" his belief in visionary experience, esoteric knowledge, and the occult (all aspects of symbolism) imply an effort to mask, but also to preserve, a conception of "meaning" inimical to the constraints of Imagism—a conception that is grounded in the general features of hermeneutics? If so, does the relevance of hermeneutics in Pound's poetry extend beyond the problem of illicit or esoteric meaning? Does the modernist Image, as an instrument of positivism, risk conversion to hermeneutics by insisting that *all* meaning is illicit, excessive, and, hence, fetishistic? Let me suggest, at least provisionally, several points: first, hermeneutics and the poetics of the Image share a fundamental belief in the mortality of the artifact, and this mortality is a linguistic or discursive condition. Second, the positivist reduction of meaning cannot be addressed without reference to the influence of hermeneutics; third, the figure of the Image as an ideogram, in particular, must be restored to the hermeneutic context of nineteenth-century discourse on the nature of hieroglyphic writing.

The figure of the crypt mediates the divergent symbolic economies that lay claim to the modernist Image. On the one hand, the crypt is the symbolic site of modern literary positivism, and the Image is what lies within the crypt: corpse, fact, word-thing, symptom. The irreducible materiality of the Image, in this case, poses a challenge to the hermeneutical concept of meaning itself, which is based on a distinction between surface and depth, the manifest and the latent, history and divination. Yet the Image, like the figure of the crypt, harbors figurative debts to this hermeneutical model, and must therefore also be understood as reviving the phantom of meaning from the dead letter of the crypt. That is, the Image, as an emblem of hermeneutical understanding, is not an inscrutable yet all-too-obvious "thing" in the crypt, but the crypt itself and its spiritual "content." The problem of hermeneutics and its relation to the crypt emerges most prominently, as I have indicated, in Pound's conception of the Image as a Chinese ideogram (which inherits the historical discourse on hieroglyphics).

Historically speaking, and for the purposes of this study, the concept of the fetish divides along lines similar to those fracturing the modernist Image. On one hand, in its most familiar form, the fetish is an object whose value or meaning is incommensurate with its "real" material properties; it is dangerously overvalued and hence the object of an irrational fixation. This conception of a trivial object charged with phantasmic or surplus value, a conception that extends from colonial fetish discourse to Marx and Freud, informs the hermeneutical model of understanding (in which meaning exceeds the letter of the word). On the other hand, from the perspective of the fetishist and, I will argue, from that of the positivist (who subscribes to the discourse of objectivity), the value or meaning of the fetish is indistinguishable from the object itself. Thus, as William Pietz argues, "Marxism's commodity fetish, psychoanalysis's sexual fetish, and modernism's fetish as art object all in an essential way involve the object's untranscended materiality."[25] Insofar as the fetish is characterized by its irreducible materiality, then, it is an emblem of positivism; yet insofar as it is characterized by surplus value and meaning, it is an emblem of hermeneutics. In other words, either the object falls under the spell of meaning (from the standpoint of the "enlightened" critic of fetishism), or meaning falls under the spell of its object (from the standpoint of the fetishist and the positivist). On this account, Pietz observes, "Fetish discourse always posits this double consciousness of absorbed credulity and degraded or distanced incredulity" (14). The practitioner and the observer of fetishism participate together in what he calls a "primary and carnal rhetoric of identification and disavowal" (14). We must bear in mind, however, that the iconoclastic critic of fetishism often subscribes to the empirical values of positivism, thus extolling the magical proximity of the object and initiating a transvaluation of the fetish (which has now become the object of science).

Pound endowed the Image with a redemptive power: he intended it to restore—to poetry, to language in general, and eventually, in the context of fascism, to the "symptoms" of culture—some measure of representational authority. It must be remembered, however, that the Image is the centerpiece of a "*revival* of realism." The objective Image emerges from the realm of the dead as the visual counterpart to the dead languages that attracted Pound's attention as a scholar and translator. Its "scientific" materialism is recovered, in part, from the distant past (from Baroque thinkers such as Bacon and Leibniz) and is therefore troubled not only by the contrary values of the underworld but by the syncretism of the Baroque model. Yet the fascination with death that attends the atavistic prize of the Image is dialectical; for if the Image can also be understood as "youthful language" (as Gaston

---

25. William Pietz, "The Problem of the Fetish: Part 1" *Res* 9 (Spring 1985): 7.

Bachelard observes), then poetry's attempt to revive its own dead past in the Image is not simply anachronistic but an effort to tap the anarchic and revolutionary vigor of the crowd.[26] And indeed, Pound often invokes the Image as a figure of revolutionary power, especially when he associates it with the artistic and sociological project of the avant-garde, or with fascism. In his view, the Image as a vortex marshals the atavistic power of the crowd against "clichés," against the magnetism of dead thoughts anchoring the spell of realism. The Image summons the "horrific energy" of the African fetish to counteract the fetishes of the mind—all in the name of science.

26. Gaston Bachelard, *The Poetics of Space,* trans. Maria Jolas (Boston: Beacon, 1969), p. xv.

CHAPTER 3

Cryptaesthesia

Making and Unmaking

> The imaging of death necessarily involves images not belonging to it.
> —Kenneth Burke, "Thanatopsis"

> In this terror before mass-produced death there is the sadness of the artist who honors well-wrought things, who wants to make a work and make of death his work. Death is thus from the start linked to the movement, so difficult to bring to light, of the artistic experience.
> —Maurice Blanchot, *The Space of Literature*

Death, in Ezra Pound's poetry, is always an event migrating from its immediate physical condition to other provinces of meaning, both near and remote, and evoking, in the process, the problem of "meaning" itself. Before we ask, therefore, *what* death means in the context of Imagism, or modernism in general, we must first ask *how* death means. Images of death always have the power to remind us that death—to the living—can be nothing more than an image, the rendering of an absence, of something that does not exist. Representations of death invariably call into question the nature of representation itself. One critic of modernism, for example, suggests that all representations of death are, by nature, symbolic: " 'Real' death is for all of us rigorously unimaginable: the images and representations by which we seem to have achieved some tangible certainty as to the nature of death must from that standpoint be supposed, a priori, to be so many deflections. But if this is so, then representations of death will always prove, under closer inspection, to be complex displacements of an indirect, symbolic meditation about *something else*."¹ A stronger way of saying this is to claim, with Elisabeth Bronfen and Sarah Goodwin, that "every representation of death is a misrepresentation. Thus the analysis of it must show not only how it claims to represent death, but also what else it in fact represents, however suppressed."² One must further assume, as will be evident in the present study, that the gap between the ostensible meaninglessness of "real" death and its symbolic significance is easily overlooked. Indeed, the confusion in Pound's writing between real death and death as it figures in language produces a death that *is* language—a language captivated by death, in its material and phantasmatic properties. Yet the idea that death's way of knowing (which manufactures, in a literary and sociological sense, our knowledge of death) is necessarily symbolic cannot be helpful to us as a bridge between death and the Image unless we acknowledge, first of all, that Pound's theory of the Image placed this kind of meaning in question. Fredric Jameson, whose views on symbolic representations of death I cited above, assumes that we must look beyond the physical fact of death to find meaning at all: the meaning of death is necessarily latent, metaphysical, discursive. Imagism, however, contested assumptions of this kind, along with the hermeneutical model of understanding implied in Jameson's speculation. Yet we might still retain, at least for the moment, this transitive conception of the meaning of death, which implies an "afterlife" of meaning, by emphasizing not its symbolic but its allegorical properties. Reviewing Walter Benjamin's theory of allegorical criticism, one discovers a comment that illuminates the possibility of death's meaning as a construction, a rebuilding of the fact: "Birth is a 'natural' condition, death is a 'social' one."³ This is not to say, of course, that birth is a "natural" event, unmediated by social ideologies, but that death, since it inaugurates nothing and is in itself nothing (except pure

1. Fredric Jameson, *Fables of Aggression: Wyndham Lewis, the Modernist as Fascist* (Berkeley: University of California Press, 1979), p. 160.
2. Sarah Webster Goodwin and Elisabeth Bronfen, eds., *Death and Representation* (Baltimore: Johns Hopkins University Press, 1993), p. 10.
3. Walter Benjamin, cited in Susan Buck-Morss, *The Dialectics of Seeing: Walter Benjamin and the Arcades Project* (Cambridge, Mass.: MIT Press, 1990), p. 101.

negativity), can be made intelligible, emotionally or otherwise, only as a reconstruction of "life." Hence, any meditation about death must be a register of social and cultural (as well as biographical) history, which would explain Jameson's "something else." In his *Trauerspiel* book, a work that establishes the image as the object of his most influential and original thinking about aesthetics, Benjamin observes, "The greater the meaning, the greater the subjection to death, because death digs out most deeply the jagged line of demarcation between physical nature and meaning."⁴ This statement suggests not merely that death is an especially meaningful event, but that the production of "meaning" is implicated in the "social condition" of death. This idea—that the meaning of death, as a surplus, is symptomatic of all meaning—finds its most powerful expression in the discourse of fetishism (a correspondence that helps explain Benjamin's importance as a theorist of modern fetishism).

It would not be misleading to understand death in Pound's early poetry as an articulation of "the infinitely suggestive word *death*, which disrupts many systematic orders"—that is, as an instrument of change.⁵ Yet it would be more accurate to characterize Pound's use of death as both stemming from and inciting revolutionary change, as both symptomatic and instrumental. The necrophilic features of Pound's early poetry should not be understood, as they usually are, merely as the belated trappings of Decadent literary fashion. Nor should they be circumscribed by the thesis that "a desire for death is perhaps the hidden *telos* of beauty and truth, ascetic ideals that predetermine their own failure."⁶ Rather, as Marx observed, a complex relation to death can be a dialectical feature of revolution:

> The tradition of all the dead generations weighs like a nightmare on the brain of the living. And just when they seem engaged in revolutionizing themselves and objects, in creating something that has never yet existed, precisely in such epochs of revolutionary crisis they anxiously conjure up the spirits of the past to their

4. Walter Benjamin, *The Origin of German Tragic Drama*, trans. John Osborne (London: NLB, 1977), p. 166.

5. Svetlana Boym, *Death in Quotation Marks: Cultural Myths of the Modern Poet* (Cambridge, Mass.: Harvard University Press, 1991), p. 12.

6. Steven Shaviro, *Passion and Excess: Blanchot, Bataille, and Literary Theory* (Tallahassee: Florida State University Press, 1990), p. 11.

> service and borrow from them names, battle slogans, and costumes
> in order to present the new scene of world history in this time-
> honored disguise and this borrowed language.⁷

Pound himself recognizes similar tendencies in the "revolution" of Italian fascism, whose atavistic character he discerns as well in the Imagist and Vorticist movements: "As in a new art movement, I think the vitality shows first in a greater exigence and precision with regard to antiquity" (*J/M* 84). He also notes that one of the first symptoms of fascism in government is a larger budget for the restoration of antiquities.

When critics acknowledge Pound's fascination with death in his early poetry, and throughout his career as a translator and literary critic, they usually see it as an expression of his complex relation to the past, to his literary forebears, and to historical materials in general. A recent critic, referring to the Malatesta cantos (VIII–XI), expands this view to include all of literary modernism:

> While writing the sequence, Pound came to view the church of San Francesco—a sepulchral monument—as a symbol of his own poetic and cultural enterprise. And insofar as the *Cantos* is the major experiment of Anglo-American modernism, a text that embodies all its aspirations and contradictions, the sepulchre can also epitomize the cultural monument of literary modernism—not just its "texts" or works, but the whole field of agents, practices, institutions, and ideological structures that have shaped its critical reception.⁸

Though this claim is far too broad to be viable, its main tenet regarding the sepulchral analogy of Pound's enterprise is essentially correct. One could argue, for example, that Pound's lifelong project of rewriting Dante's *Commedia* never really leaves the *Inferno*. Yet this general conception of Pound's poetry as a medium between present and past, the living and the dead, tends to withdraw, theoretically, from the "pre-

---

7. Karl Marx, *The Eighteenth Brumaire of Louis Bonaparte*, no translator indicated (New York: International Publishers, 1963), p. 15.
8. Lawrence S. Rainey, *Ezra Pound and the Monument of Culture* (Chicago: University of Chicago Press, 1991), p. 2.

supposition of mediality" that it implies.[9] Imagism emerges during a historical period of unprecedented growth in the invention of new technical media, and helps inaugurate for poetry the radical fetishizing of means usually referred to as formalism. Although Pound conceives of the modernist Image as a medium between past and present, the living and the dead, he also presents it as revising not only the verbal medium of poetry but the very concept of the medium itself. Thus, when considering the mediality of the poetic Image, we must begin with Friedrich Kittler's dictum: "A medium is a medium is a medium. As the sentence says, there is no difference between occult and technological media. Their truth is fatality, their field the unconscious."[10]

Pound's necrophilia, quite obviously, has the poet facing backward, staring into the past, conjuring the dead. Yet if we take Marx's observation seriously, the preoccupation with death must also be concerned with something that has "never existed before." Once again, Benjamin is helpful: "For people as they are today, there is only one radical novelty—and that is always the same: Death."[11] Hence, Pound's early poetry, and the Image that emerges from it (which is not far removed, at that point, from a poetics of translation), is a medium that registers not only transmissions from the past but phenomena that are not yet meaningful, because of their novelty. The Image and its latent necrophilia emerge during a transitional period in literary and cultural history: not only the literary artifact and the domain of material culture in general but the very concepts of representation and meaning are in a state of crisis. Marx's linkage of revolution and images of the dead should therefore be focused more specifically on the Image as a force in the development of the avant-garde. In a recent work, Paul Mann has written that the avant-garde "was never distinct from its death, indeed death was always its most abiding force," and furthermore, "the discourse of the avant-garde is its death and in death it continues

---

9. This is David Wellbery's term for one of the basic tenets of Friedrich Kittler's "discourse analysis." See Wellbery's foreword to Friedrich A. Kittler, *Discourse Networks: 1800/1900,* trans. Michael Metteer, with Chris Cullens (Stanford: Stanford University Press, 1990), p. xiii.
10. Kittler, *Discourse Networks,* p. 229.
11. Walter Benjamin, cited in Buck-Morss, *Dialectics of Seeing,* p. 195.

to reproduce itself as a death-discourse."[12] If Mann is right that the postmodern discourse on the death of the avant-garde can be traced to the origin of the avant-garde itself, and that we must therefore "write the whole history of the avant-garde as a death," then the necrophilic dimension of the Image must be regarded as an indication of its role in the formation of the avant-garde. What one hears distantly in the obituaries of the avant-garde are its Decadent foundations.

Insofar as Pound is a poet of the incipient avant-garde, his negotiation with death permits him to reflect obliquely, esoterically, on certain absolutes—on the origins and limits of language, symbolization, and poetry. On one hand, the cryptological dimension of the Image is implicated in the hermeneutical construction of meaning, which emerged with the poetics of Romanticism and has been characterized as "a resuscitation of the living spirit from the tomb of the letter."[13] Yet the necrophilic Image, as I indicated in the previous chapter, is also implicated, by its emphasis on materiality and its efforts to rid poetry of meaning, in the symbolic economy that would supersede hermeneutics: positivism. The attack on meaning carried out in the name of the Image must be viewed as an attack not merely on certain archaic dimensions of poetry but on poetry as such—at least as it survived in the "crepuscular" spirit of Romanticism during the fin-de-siècle period (hence the antipoetic character of Imagism). The Image is therefore what I would like to call a "Janusian" object, looking both forward and backward, a symptom of the turbulent and revolutionary moment in which it was conceived. It is at once a late and barbarous emblem of what Jean-Joseph Goux calls a "cryptophoric" economy of signification (hermeneutics), as well as an early model of an "operative" economy that continually *moves toward* the elimination of meaning, as a realization of the "impossible" correspondence between positivism and fetishism.[14]

12. Paul Mann, *The Theory-Death of the Avant-Garde* (Bloomington: Indiana University Press, 1991), p. 40.

13. Hermeneutics inevitably "stylizes" itself in this manner, according to David Wellbery (foreword to Kittler, *Discourse Networks*, p. x).

14. For the term "cryptophoric economy" and the less satisfactory designation "operative sign," see Jean-Joseph Goux, *Symbolic Economies,* trans. Jennifer Gage (Ithaca: Cornell University Press, 1990), p. 122.

One aspect, in particular, of the modern crisis of representation finds expression in the necrophilic dimension of the Image: the verbal artifact portends a crisis of reciprocation. It is a mistake, given the insistent and graphic nature of his pronouncements about death and literature, not to take Pound at his word when he attacks the "corpse language" of late Victorian poetry. He means, quite literally, that poetic language is no longer animate, sentient, or vital, and that the properties of the Image, as he conceives it, will restore to the literary artifact an archaic and thoroughly mundane vitality. It is difficult *not* to understand such views figuratively, just as it is difficult to assess the animism of object relations in modern culture. Yet we cannot overlook the fact that the rhetoric of the Image is built on the assumption that an artifact fulfills its function only when it is alive in some fashion, and that a useless artifact is described as a corpse. From the perspective of Elaine Scarry's remarkable study of the animism of the made object, we would have to argue that Pound's views reflect broader cultural assumptions about the awareness, the sentience, that is normally ascribed to objects: "Object-awareness is the acceptable, expectable, and uncelebrated condition of civilization, while object-unawareness is the unusual and unacceptable condition."[15]

Although Scarry attributes the usual and expectable sentience of the artifact, in part, to projection—"artifacts are (in spite of their inertness) perhaps most accurately perceived as 'a making sentient of the external world'" (281)—she also attributes it, more importantly, to the obligations that the artifact incurs to its maker: "Made things do incur large responsibilities to their human makers (and their continued existence depends on their ability to fulfill those responsibilities: a useless artifact, whether a failed god or a failed table, will be discarded)" (182). The obligation of the artifact is to alter, enhance, or transform the powers of those who make it or use it, to refashion human beings in order to relieve them of the burden of sentience. Thus, Scarry sees the relation between human maker and artifact as one of "reciprocation," emphasizing "the double consequence of creation, in which simultaneously the body is projected out into artifice and the human

---

15. Elaine Scarry, *The Body in Pain: The Making and Unmaking of the World* (New York: Oxford University Press, 1985), p. 296.

body itself becomes an artifact" (261). Hence, "the act of human creating includes both the creating of the object and the object's recreating of the human being, and it is only because of the second that the first is undertaken" (310).[16] This chiasmic relation between sentience and inertness, between the artifact and its maker, is an essential feature of the discourse of fetishism (though it is usually condemned as a sinister effect of the fetish).

As Scarry suggests, it is when this reciprocative relation breaks down, when the artifact fails to "live up" to its obligation, that the usual and unremarkable animateness of the object is thrown into relief—precisely because that quality (the *caritas* of the artifact) is missing. It is also at this moment of crisis, when the artifact is in need of repair or revision, or when its mechanism must be abandoned entirely, that its human construction, the madeness of the artifact, emerges into prominence, often dominating our perception of it. With the help of Scarry's remarkable insights into animism and artifacts, I think it is difficult not to conclude that Imagism, given its preoccupation with death, emerges as a response to a historical failure of "reciprocation" in the literary artifact. Pound characterizes late Victorian poetry as dead precisely because it fails to reinvent its makers and readers; it fails to enhance their powers or relieve the burden of sentience in a modern world. In an essay written just prior to the emergence of Imagism, Pound writes, "If a book reveals to us something of which we were unconscious, it feeds us with energy; if it reveals to us nothing but the fact that its author knew something which we knew, it draws energy from us" (*SP* 30). This crisis of reciprocation, in turn, places the artifactual quality of the poem in a particularly harsh and critical light. Hence, Pound's emphasis on technique and construction (especially with the ideogram) is an oblique reference to the crisis of the artifact that gives rise to the Image in the first place. The activity of making thus becomes the activity of animating the external world, of restoring the reciprocative capacity of the artifact.

16. Scarry eloquently describes the inscrutable transaction of reciprocation in this brief passage: "The human being, troubled by weight, creates a chair; the chair recreates him to be weightless; and now he projects this new weightless self into new objects, the image of an angel, the design for a flying machine" (*The Body in Pain*, p. 321).

Cryptaesthesia

The main thesis of Scarry's book concerns the inscrutable relation between creation and activities that destroy the world and the human body. In a highly original analysis, she argues that "torture and war are not simply occurrences which incidentally deconstruct the made world but occurrences which deconstruct the structure of making itself" (179). Torture, as a practice of unmaking the human body, provides an inverted, one might even say cryptonymous, account of the act of making. Furthermore, she writes, "physical pain always mimes death and the infliction of physical pain is always a mock execution" (31); hence, "the 'unmaking' of the human being is equally characteristic of dying" (122). Death's discourse, then, like pain, is a hermetic index of creation. The importance of this insight to understanding the necrophilic dimension of the Image cannot be overestimated. Pound's early fascination with death must therefore be understood as an oblique expression of concern for the act of making (hence the Imagistic emphasis on technique and form), a concern that stems from the animistic crisis of reciprocation in the literary artifact. In Pound's case, Decadent poems and theorizing about "death-in-life" bear witness to a catastrophic loss of vitality in poetic language (eventually matched by the specter of mass death in World War I), as well as to the poet's desperate project to revive the corpse of poetry, to reconstruct the artifact. Even the artifact magically invigorated, however, retains its fundamental inertness and can never be more than an emblem of the living dead. Thus, Pound's necrophilic poetics remain captive to the insidious logic that eventually produces the dialectical equation of construction and destruction in the context of fascist ideology.[17] The instability of the distinction between "death"

---

17. The inverted allegorical relation between life and death, making and unmaking, that I am proposing as the basis of Pound's necrophilic poetics corresponds in a historically significant (and perilous) manner to the dialectical equation of "life" and "death" in fascist ideologies. Alice Yaeger Kaplan, for example, citing the observations of Walter Benjamin, notes the influence of Decadent aesthetics on the fascist dialectic of "construction" and "destruction." See her discussion of the "polarity machine" of fascist ideology in *Reproductions of Banality: Fascism, Literature, and French Intellectual Life* (Minneapolis: University of Minnesota Press, 1986), pp. 25–35. From a broader perspective, Marcus Paul Bullock argues that the inversion or "re-creation" of death routinely occurs in the context of political ideology, where death and violence sanctioned by the State are made to signify acts of creation or edification: "An act of formalized or institutionalized violence, in short, becomes a manifestation of something other than

and "life" that initially serves the interests of "life" in poetry ends by serving the interests of "death" in the realm of politics.

Although Scarry does not say as much, her anatomy of the artifact is essentially an account of the role of fetishism in material culture. Hence, her book is sustained at crucial moments by readings and transformations of Marx, whom she regards as "our major philosopher on the nature of material objects" (179). Likewise, my reflections on the fetishistic transactions of the Image will coincide more frequently with the concerns of Marx than with those of Freud (the other major modern theorist of fetishism) for a very simple reason: the Marxian fetish is a made object, whereas the Freudian fetish is essentially a found object (hence the appeal of his theory of fetishism to the Surrealists). Clearly, the Marxian conception is more relevant to the artifactual and technical priorities of Imagism, and to my concern with literary fetishism as an expression of material culture. This configuration of interests will explain my recourse to Marx as a "philosopher on the nature of material objects" rather than as an economist, as well as my decision not to undertake a direct comparison of Pound's poetics and his economic theories.[18] Having identified the special relevance of Marx to my project, I do not wish to imply that Marxian and Freudian conceptions of fetishism can be separated so easily (Freud refers to the sexual fetish as a "token" and a "monument," both made objects), or that Freud is not germane to my interests—he makes an important reference, for example, to verbal fetishism.

---

itself. It stands in a dialectical opposition between building or constituting and destruction. That which it constitutes, this other sphere or stratum to which it refers, endows it with what we have already, in other areas of signification, called an aura." Bullock, *The Violent Eye: Ernst Jünger's Visions and Revisions on the European Right* (Detroit: Wayne State University Press, 1992), p. 61. A particularly chilling instance of this allegorizing of death emerged in the military briefings of the Persian Gulf War, where the inflicting of enemy casualties was described as "making bodies"—hence, to kill is to make bodies. In an entirely different sphere, Pound exploits the allegorical lability of death to signal the creation of poetic bodies (and antibodies) in the form of images.

18. The best account of the relation between economics and poetics in Pound's works is the fifth chapter of Jean-Michel Rabaté, *Language, Sexuality, and Ideology in Ezra Pound's Cantos* (Albany: SUNY Press, 1986), pp. 183–241. See also Peter Nicholls, *Ezra Pound: Politics, Economics, and Writing* (London: Macmillan, 1984); and Richard Sieburth, "In Pound We Trust: The Economy of Poetry / The Poetry of Economics," *Critical Inquiry* 14, no. 1 (Autumn 1987): 142–172.

(The central illustration of Freud's theory in his "Fetishism" essay of 1927 is an instance of verbal fetishism drawn from the Wolf Man case. Recognition of the verbal disposition of Freud's theory, however, has not come easily. The major exception to this historical oversight is Abraham and Torok's theory of cryptonymy, a theory of verbal fetishism, which detonates Freud's veiled reference to the Wolf Man in the "Fetishism" essay.)[19] This verbal disposition is not, as it might first appear, unrelated to Freud's notion of the fetish as a kind of image (token, monument, and so on). Indeed, the theory of cryptonymy (a "word translated into an image") is built upon the tension between the verbal and visual poles of the fetish.

It is the Marxian concept of the fetish, however, in its basic identity as an artifact, that will serve as the context, at least initially, for my thesis regarding the Image as a countersign of literary and cultural fetishism. Yet this easy correspondence of Marxian fetish and modernist Image, this artifactual affinity, masks certain questions concerning the relevance of Marx's theory of commodity fetishism to a literary device that has traditionally been viewed as a paradigm of formalism. From the standpoint of Marx, the theory of commodity fetishism is embedded in a larger analytical project that is committed to social, political, and economic revolution. How, then, are we to justify extending the discourse of fetishism to a literary concept that has, ostensibly, no political aims or values? A question of social and economic transformation risks becoming simply a question of poetic form. Is the link between the Image and the discourse of fetishism no more than a "figurative" resemblance? The answers to these difficult questions are to be found in the rhetorical features of Marx's theory of commodity fetishism—a rhetoric that portrays the modern crisis of representation (and artifactual reciprocation) in terms similar to Pound's theory of the Image. Indeed, Marx conceives of commodity fetishism as a kind of "necromancy," and constructs it according to a chiasmic (and unstable) relation between living and dead matter. The *figurative* correspondence between Pound's and Marx's conceptions is substantial—and perhaps unavoidable—precisely because com-

19. Nicolas Abraham and Maria Torok reveal the identity of the "disguised" patient in Freud's essay. See *The Wolf Man's Magic Word: A Cryptonomy,* trans. Nicholas Rand, foreword by Jacques Derrida (Minneapolis: University of Minnesota Press, 1986), p. 32.

modity fetishism and poetic Imagism are discourses on the nature of *figural* representation. Thus, the peculiar animism of the modernist Image reflects the basic and "enigmatic" condition of the commodity fetish. It is not simply that the Image is fetishistic because it enacts a deconstruction of death in poetic language, but that Marx's analysis of modern fetishism is motivated by a crisis of dead artifacts (which turn out to be animate after all—enchanted by the projection of human labor).

The process of making is characterized by Marx as a revival of dead matter: "Yarn with which we neither weave nor knit is cotton wasted. Living labor must seize on these things, awaken them from the dead."[20] The world populated with artifacts is a place enchanted by things recalled from death. In the context of capitalism and commodity fetishism, however, the animateness of the artifact becomes a perversion or "monster," as Marx explains in a discussion of commodities integrated into the labor process: "By incorporating living labor power into their dead substance, the capitalist transforms value, i.e., past labor in its dead and objectified form, into capital, into self-expanding value, a monster quick with life, which begins to 'work' as if love were breeding in its body" (*Capital* 302). And when it is placed in contrast to the lifelessness of its human maker, the "living" artifact exposes the essential inversion of the fetishistic transaction. W. J. T. Mitchell explains the sources and significance of this chiasmic relation between the living and the dead:

> The "horror" of fetishism was not just that it involved an "illusory," figurative act of treating material objects as if they were people but that this transfer of consciousness to "stocks and stones" seemed to drain the humanity out of the idolater. As stocks and stones come alive, the idolater is seen as falling into a kind of living death . . . in which the idol is more alive than the idolater. Marx's claim that commodity fetishism is a kind of perverse "exchange," producing "material relations between persons and social relations between things" employs precisely the same logic.[21]

20. Karl Marx, *Capital: A Critique of Political Economy,* vol. 1, introd. Ernest Mandel, trans. Ben Fowkes (Harmondsworth: Penguin, 1976), p. 289.
21. W. J. T. Mitchell, *Iconology: Image, Text, Ideology* (Chicago: University of Chicago Press, 1986), p. 190.

Whether we regard the sentience of the artifact as a perversion or a restoration of the object to its proper state, the overriding concern in Marx with the animation of inert matter is closely related to Pound's desire to revive the "corpse language" of poetry.

What Walter Benjamin calls the "rights of the corpse" (the logic of fetishism) actually confuses, then, the distinction between the living and the dead. As Marx conceives it, the appeal of the inorganic pertains as well to divination and the problem of afterimages (or phantoms). In his discussion of commodity fetishism, Marx refers to "all the magic and necromancy that surrounds the products of labor on the basis of commodity production" (*Capital* 169). Necromancy is the art of conjuring the spirits of the dead; Marx's use of this trope suggests that we are not far from the topography of the crypt, though it is not clear from this statement alone what he means by linking fetishism and necromancy. We can be sure, however, that the necromancy of fetishism is related to the "divinatory" practice of hermeneutics. More specifically, our understanding of the term "necromancy" will depend on an illustration of the fetish that is not often invoked in discussions of Marx's theory of fetishism: "The physical form of the linen counts as the visible incarnation, the social chrysalis state, of all human labor" (*Capital* 159). Here Marx compares the commodity fetish to a "chrysalis," a site of transformation which is also somehow a "visible incarnation" of something that remains invisible, hidden. Moreover, the fetish is at once a *topos* and the image deposited in that place, a conception that immediately calls to mind the Hermetic art of memory—a concern of Renaissance philosophy that Pound invokes as informing the poetics of Imagism.

We can clarify the ambiguity between the chrysalis as the site and as the *image* of metamorphosis by considering more carefully the allusion (implied in the trope of the chrysalis) to an object, a living object, that changes from one state of existence to another: from worm to butterfly, from mundane to "sublime." The metamorphic properties of the fetish are evident from the start in Marx's famous introduction to this "enigmatic" object, with its "theological niceties." More fundamentally, as a symbol of metamorphosis or change, the chrysalis reflects Marx's view that the artifact becomes a fetish only in the act of exchange: "It is only by being exchanged that the products of labor acquire a socially uniform objectivity as values, which is distinct from their sensuously various objectivity as articles of utility" (*Capital* 166). Thus, the Marxian fetish is distinguished not only by its artifactuality, but by the transformation it undergoes in the act of exchange. The trope of the chrysalis therefore represents the dynamic process of exchange when the material "body" of the artifact is transformed into the "sublime" spirit of value. The chrysalis is a place—a *topos*—disguising its character as an image, from which another image, a phantasmic value, arises.

The trope of metamorphosis has a direct bearing on the *Doppelcharakter* of the fetish. As I indicated in Chapter 1, Marx repeatedly evokes the puzzling coexistence of physical and metaphysical qualities in the fetish. He vividly describes the exclusivity of the half-lives of the fetish: "So far no chemist has ever discovered exchange value either in a pearl or a diamond" (*Capital* 177). And, conversely, "Not an atom of matter enters into the objectivity of commodities as values; in this it is the direct opposite of the coarsely sensuous objectivity of commodities as physical objects" (*Capital* 138). More broadly speaking, the problem of an object that is at once material and phantasmic, perceptible and imperceptible, characterizes fetish discourse in general. Much of Freud's famous essay on fetishism, for example, dwells on the problematic act which brings the fetish substitute into existence, producing a phantasmic object (the material phallus) that is both perceptible and imperceptible, present and absent. Freud finally settles on the idea of "disavowal" as the proper term for this sleight of hand, after rejecting notions of repression or "scotomization." The fetish object, he concludes, is a remarkable hybrid born of illogic: "It is not true that, after the child has made his observation of the woman, he has preserved unaltered his belief that women have a phallus. He has retained that belief, but he has also given it up. In the conflict between the weight of the unwelcome perception [it is absent] and the force of his counter-wish [it is present], a compromise has been reached."[22] This compromise is the hybrid form—part fantasy, part object—of the fetish substitute. The double consciousness of the

22. Sigmund Freud, *Standard Edition of the Complete Psychological Works*, ed. James Strachey (London: Hogarth Press, 1960), vol. 21, pp. 153–154. More recently, Giorgio Agamben understands fetishism as a "model of knowledge" characterized by "operations in which desire simultaneously denies and affirms its object." Agamben, moreover, associates the fetish, which he describes as "the sign of an absence," with melancholia

object posited by Freud (at once present to the senses and imperceptible) reiterates the basic features of the Marxian fetish as a perceptible yet suprasensible object.

The modernist Image, as well, is "profoundly cracked" (to use a phrase of Georges Bataille's) in its antipoetic character and its resistance to visuality. Even Pound's most familiar and accessible definitions of the Image allude to a profound schism that produces the crypt effects of the Image. This is evident, to begin with, in the formal properties of the Image, as Pound describes it: "The 'one-image poem' is a form of super-position, that is to say it is one idea set on top of another" (*GB* 89). Furthermore, Pound relates the schismatic nature of the Image to a metamorphosis (something like the Marxian chrysalis), since the Image is said to appear at "the precise instant when a thing outward and objective transforms itself, or darts into a thing inward and subjective" (*GB* 89). The tension between inner and outer, subjective and objective, is so strong, in fact, that the Image divides in two:

> The Image can be of two sorts. It can arise within the mind. It is then "subjective." External causes play upon the mind, perhaps; if so, they are drawn into the mind, fused, transmitted, and emerge in the Image unlike themselves. Secondly, the Image can be objective. Emotion seizing up some external scene or action carries it intact to the mind; and that vortex purges it of all save the essential or dominant or dramatic qualities, and it emerges like the external original. (*SP* 374–375)

This surprising statement from Pound on the dual nature of the Image (which alternately disguises and resembles its object) cannot be isolated from his more prominent descriptions of an Image that is fractured internally. This progressive dislocation of subjective and objective, inner and outer, within the artifact, suggests that the modernist Image displays the essential duplicity of the fetish, masquerading alternately as spirit and thing, phantom and fact. The poet of radical positivism gazes at the spot where the spectral Image is said to appear and sees nothing, whereas the hermeneutical seer turns away from the letter, from fact, to summon the phantom of meaning.

---

and the cryptic space of memory. See Agamben, *Stanzas: Word and Phantasm in Western Culture*, trans. Ronald L. Martinez (Minneapolis: University of Minnesota Press, 1993), pp. xvii, 31–33.

Though the two kinds of Images described by Pound diverge in their relations to an external "original," both are products of a transformative process. The terms "subjective" and "objective," as Pound uses them, appear to have undergone a semantic inversion. The "objective" Image in particular raises interesting questions, since it emerges from a state of *possession,* an emotional seizure that Pound terms a "vortex." It is important to emphasize that the "objectivity" of the Image occurs not by purging emotion, but through the *agency* of emotion. In this description, one can begin to grasp the correlation between Pound's conceptions of the Image as a vortex and as a Freudian "complex" (*LE* 4). Clearly, the metamorphic character of the vortex resembles the Marxian chrysalis.

Returning, finally, to the Marxian trope of "necromancy," we can see that the dynamic of metamorphosis pertains to the art of conjuring the dead, as an emblem of fetishism. The chrysalis is the somatic crypt from which emerges the phantom of value, a memory cell holding a magically potent image. This can be understood in two ways. First, it reiterates the moment of exchange when the simple artifact is transformed into a fetish. In this sense, the art of necromancy is an image of the internal logic of the fetish itself. Yet we have seen that the trope can also be understood as representing the relation between the materialist critic or historian and the fetish object—that is to say, as the emblem of a particular interpretive economy. In this regard, discourse itself occupies the place of the fetish object. Marx says that the "metaphysical and theological niceties" of the commodity fetish emerge only through "analysis" of it, a process I have characterized as "sightless vision." Just as a phantom, or invisible object, emerges from the artifact in the moment of exchange—a process Marx compares to necromancy—so the critic conjures meaning from an object that appears to be meaningless. As an image of meaning retrieved from a dead object, an image of the critic's relation to the cryptic fetish, the trope of necromancy evokes the "divinatory" practice of hermeneutics. What's more, it equates the phantasms of exchange value and meaning, an equation that reveals the death discourse shared by fetishism and the Image to be the medium of a general crisis of representation.

Memory Cells

> Elegy presents everything as lost and gone, or absent and future.
> —Samuel Coleridge, *Biographia Literaria*

> I once said, perhaps rightly: The earlier culture will become a heap of rubble and finally a heap of ashes, but spirits will hover over the ashes.
> —Ludwig Wittgenstein, *Culture and Value*

What difference would it make to the history of Anglo-American poetic modernism if we were to read Pound as a poet whose progress begins and ends in the realm of the dead, the author (and protagonist) of a literary odyssey culminating in a political *inferno* haunted by his earliest poetic principles? What if we were to read Pound essentially as a poet of mourning—not elegiac precisely, but fetishistic and transgressive in his failed resuscitation of the inanimate and, with regard to politics, the nonexistent; a poet whose ideas about poetry, culture, and politics are consistently informed by tropes of decomposing objects and signs, reanimation, and violent states of "possession"? Would it be necessary to revise altogether the genre of poetic elegy, in order to accommodate a reverence for the dead that is distinguished by infidelity, license, and abuse? Perhaps not. More broadly speaking, does Pound's poetic Decadence, which is epitomized by his fascination with death, have any bearing on the conflation of art and life, aesthetics and politics, represented by the figure of the dandy—a persona adopted by Pound, at the very least, in his manner of dress?[23] Furthermore, how does one begin to disentangle certain Decadent paradigms subverting the categories of "art" and "life" from similar positions adopted by the avant-garde and fascist modernism? Finally,

---

23. Here is a description by Ford Madox Ford of Pound's appearance during the early years of their friendship (1909–1914): "Ezra had a forked red beard, luxuriant chestnut hair, an aggressive lank figure; one long blue single stone earring dangled on his jawbone. He wore a purple hat, a green shirt, a black velvet coat, vermillion socks, openwork brilliant tanned sandals . . . and trousers of green billiard cloth, in addition to an immense flowing tie that had been hand-painted by a Japanese Futurist artist." *Pound/Ford: The Story of a Literary Friendship,* ed. Brita Lindberg-Seyersted (New York: New Directions, 1982), p. 84.

is it possible that Decadent theorizing about "death-in-life" eventually finds political expression in the dialectical equation of construction and destruction that is characteristic of fascist ideologies?

I'd like to begin to consider the scope and significance of Pound's necrophilia by reviewing briefly one of the prevailing constructions of elegiac modernism. In his celebrated 1936 essay " 'In Memoriam,' " T. S. Eliot writes, "Tennyson is not only a minor Virgil, he is also Virgil as Dante saw him, a Virgil among the Shades, the saddest of all English poets, among the Great in Limbo, the most instinctive rebel against the society in which he was the most perfect conformist."[24] Among historians and critics of literary modernism, it is customary to view this passage (and the entire essay in which it appears) as cryptically self-referential, as a description not so much of Tennyson but of Eliot himself. Walton Litz, for example, claims that "in writing and rewriting the 1936 'In Memoriam' essay Eliot the poet-critic was confessing himself."[25] And Carol Christ notes, "Eliot could well be describing his own poetry when he remarks of Tennyson that he uses narrative situation only as an occasion for 'stating an elegiac mood.' "[26] As Christ's orientation suggests, this comparison can be made from the standpoint of a reader of Victorian as well as modern literature. Indeed, it was a scholar of Victorian literature, Arthur J. Carr, who first exploited Eliot's essay on Tennyson to make a case for the peculiar modernity of Tennyson's melancholy and his fascination with death. Citing Eliot's "Preludes" and "Prufrock" as evidence of Tennyson's influence, and echoing a famous theme of "The Waste Land," Carr situates Tennyson's modernity in "the interchanging play of memory and desire."[27] If, as Carr suggests, the character of Eliot's

---

24. T. S. Eliot, " 'In Memoriam' " (1936), reprinted in Frank Kermode, ed., *Selected Prose of T. S. Eliot* (New York: Harcourt Brace, 1975), p. 246.

25. A. Walton Litz, "T. S. Eliot's Victorian Inheritance," in U. C. Knoepflmacher and G. B. Tennyson, eds., *Nature and the Victorian Imagination* (Berkeley: University of California Press, 1977), p. 483.

26. Carol T. Christ, *Victorian and Modern Poetics* (Chicago: University of Chicago Press, 1984), p. 47.

27. Arthur J. Carr, "Tennyson as Modern Poet" (1950), reprinted in John Killham, ed., *Critical Essays on the Poetry of Tennyson* (London: Routledge and Kegan Paul, 1960), p. 48. For reference to Carr's essay, I am indebted to James R. Kincaid, "Forgetting to Remember: Tennyson's Happy Losses," *Victorian Poetry* 30, nos. 3–4 (Autumn–Winter 1992): 197–209. The Eliot-Tennyson team, I should add, has

modernity is indebted in some respects to the elegiac Tennyson, then one must, Carr claims, recognize Tennyson as "our true precursor" (42)—that is, as a protomodernist. In both poets, then, "the recurrent pattern is a transition through death, loss, or dream" (63), and their essential modernity is signaled by a preoccupation with death and loss.

While Carr's influential essay succeeded in revising (and to some extent reviving) interest in Tennyson's poetry, it also produced a residual (and revisionary) concept of elegiac *modernism* that would prove useful to historians and critics of twentieth-century poetry. Modernists such as Litz, for example, view Eliot's ostensive identification with Tennyson as an indication of the traditionalism of modern poetry, but also as evidence of its elegiac propensity. Eliot's cryptic confession of Tennysonian values becomes the basis not only for a pattern of influence but for a powerful, if submerged, expression of modernity. Thus, commenting on the "Little Gidding" sequence of "Four Quartets," Litz writes, "In this last and most moving dramatization of Eliot's primal theme, the meeting with a ghostly other self, all the divisions of his early criticism and poetry are put aside, and Tennyson joins Baudelaire as one of the dead masters of Eliot's art" (488).

Although the critical history of Eliot's submerged relation to Tennyson is not a topic that will generate much excitement these days, the conception of elegiac modernism is an idea eminently worth recovering. Yet the historical limitations of this conception, and its failure to be more persuasive generally, are due in part to the exclusive focus on Eliot and, to a lesser degree, Tennyson. In addition, the conception of elegiac modernism adumbrated by Litz, Christ, and others is hampered by its debts to Victorian scholarship; it fails to respond to experiences that are essential to specifically modernist representations of death, loss, absence, or mourning. A revised conception of elegiac modernism would therefore have to take into account more fully the catastrophic effects of World War I, the experience of exile, and the emergence of new technical media as modes of distanciation as well as preservation. These formative conditions resonate fully within the

---

remarkable staying power; it even makes a brief appearance in Kincaid's witty, deconstructive reading of Tennysonian remembrance (p. 200).

rhetoric of death, decomposition, and reanimation in Pound's writings. Perhaps it is not Eliot's but Pound's work that best illuminates the full scope of elegiac modernism—its preoccupation with loss but also with materiality, animism, imagery, and political violence.

Though the connection to Tennyson need not be scrapped entirely, the specific character of Pound's necrophilia (as well as his aversion to the dead) requires a shift of focus from the experience of melancholy to an aberration of mourning that verges upon mania and recalls the Image to its occluded origins as a cadaver and a ghost.[28] We find an important parallel to Pound's aberrant mourning in the work of Wyndham Lewis, whose fascination with death provides the key not only to his early (and unpublished) Decadent sonnets, but to his conception of Vorticist art. For Lewis, as for Pound, the difficult transition from aestheticism to the avant-garde occurs as a kind of mutation or sublimation of death.[29] I want to stress, however, that the recession

---

28. Marshall McLuhan makes a case for Tennyson as a precursor to Pound and Eliot, based on a fetishized conception of the image and on "the simultaneous order of a cabinet picture" (which would become the paratactic structure of "The Waste Land" and the *Cantos*): "It is precisely his fidelity to the vivisection of isolated moments that links Tennyson to the greatest works of his time and ours . . . It is to be related to the tendency to abandon succession for simultaneity when our instruments of observation acquired speed and precision." As this last sentence indicates, McLuhan's thesis about a Tennysonian and modernist poetics of the Image serves as the basis for his later speculations about the technical media. H. M. McLuhan, "Tennyson and the Romantic Epic," in Killham, ed., *Critical Essays on the Poetry of Tennyson*, pp. 93–94. On the relation between Imagism and Victorian conceptions of the picturesque, see McLuhan, "Tennyson and Picturesque Poetry," ibid., p. 70.

29. The necrophilic dimension of Lewis' early sonnets (written about 1910) is evident in the concluding sestet of "To the Spirit of Poetry":

> Our minds are all some buried savior's tomb,
> But rarely woken from pollution's gloom;
> And nought but a low mourning sound more
> Assails its depths,—no clamours of yore:
> One night shall not the watchers of the door
> Find a white angel in corruption's room?

Cited by Daniel Schenker, *Wyndham Lewis: Religion and Modernism* (Tuscaloosa: University of Alabama Press, 1992), p. 21. Given that death appears in this poem in a characteristically Decadent scene of "corruption," it is surprising to find that the idea of death remains central to Lewis' conception of Vorticism, of which he claims, "*Deadness* is the first condition of art." Wyndham Lewis, *Tarr* (Santa Barbara: Black Sparrow Press, 1983; orig. pub. 1918), p. 299.

of melancholy as the dominant feature of elegiac modernism does not imply the overcoming of loss or fascination in Pound's scopic regime of the dead. On the contrary, the effects of loss only become more recessive, more highly mediated (or mediumistic), and hence more pervasive.

Lewis, not surprisingly, was the most perceptive and persistent witness to Pound's phantasmagorical sense of modernity. From the beginning of their association, Lewis' assessment of Pound was rooted in the notion that "he [Pound] has never loved anything living as he has loved the dead."[30] Near the end of his life, Lewis returned once more to the issue of Pound's possession by "spirits" and his susceptibility to things that disappear and return again, to things mediated by "death." In 1954, eight years after Pound's incarceration for the Rome Radio broadcasts, Lewis published a short story called "Doppelgänger." The main protagonist of the story, "Thaddeus Trunk" (a pseudonym for Pound, whose paternal grandfather was named Thaddeus), is said to be "in love with the past."[31] He is also plagued by a "Stranger" who resembles him and who claims to have a "telepathic endowment" (216). In the end, the doppelgänger turns out to be "the real Thaddeus," whereas the original "Uncle Thad" is revealed to be "a bulky phantom of publicity" (222). In this story, Lewis reflects upon the ineluctable character of Pound's poetic investment in the economy of death, which is seen as migrating from his work to his life. Succumbing to the mimetic enchantment of the double and its telepathic powers, "Uncle Thad" becomes an index of the instability of the real and the chimerical, an effect of "publicity." More specifically, the doppelgänger is an emblem of the real "ghosts," the living dead, that haunted Pound's work and his cryptic enunciation of elegiac modernism.

I would like to begin my search for Pound's missing grave (and the tomb of the Image) by interviewing a few ghosts and by reviewing the books of the dead that Pound produced as monuments to their disappearance. In April 1916, almost four years after he coined the term

30. Wyndham Lewis, *Time and Western Man* (London: Chatto and Windus, 1927), p. 71.
31. Wyndham Lewis, "Doppelgänger," in *Unlucky for Pringle,* ed. Robert T. Chapman and C. J. Fox (London: Vision, 1973), p. 208.

"Imagism" and two years after he broke with Amy Lowell and the Imagist movement, Pound published his most important collection of writings on the subject of the Image. *Gaudier-Brzeska: A Memoir* appeared at a moment when Imagism as a movement had already faded from the memory of the London avant-garde, and when interest and activity in the Vorticist movement was also beginning to wane. (The last issue of *Blast* was published in July 1915.) The belated appearance of the book is not the only aspect of its anachronism; many of the essays in it are reprints of magazine articles that Pound published in 1913 and 1914, during the height of his involvement with the Imagist and Vorticist movements. Although Pound insists that he does not wish to revive the "journalistic squabbles" that accompanied the emergence of Imagism and Vorticism several years earlier, the sections of *Gaudier-Brzeska* written near the time of its publication are as contentious as the manifestos reprinted from *Blast*. Why does Pound, a brilliant strategist of the avant-garde, a man who is acutely aware of the importance of timing in the promotion of new art, publish a polemical work that is so obviously out of date? Is the memoir simply a pretext for a historical account of these movements, from the standpoint of an insider? Or is the motivation more strategic than its date would suggest? That is, is his memorial to Gaudier-Brzeska an attempt to revive the figure of the Image and to regain control of it from Amy Lowell, to whom he had relinquished it two years earlier?[32]

Uncertainty about the book's purpose, which is manifest in its belated appearance, is also evident in Pound's own statements about the book. On one hand, he says that the purpose of the book is to make Gaudier's work accessible to other artists, and, as the book's title suggests, "to leave as clear a record as possible of Gaudier's work and thought" (*GB* 19). Yet Pound later contradicts the need for such documentation when he says, "Mr. Brzeska's sculpture is so generally recognized in all camps that one does not need to bring in a brief

32. The first Imagist anthology, *Des Imagistes*, was organized by Pound and published in March 1914. Several months later Amy Lowell, a poet from Boston, arrived in London and proposed to Pound a second anthology, which would be published with her support and would also include some of her poetry. They quarreled over the content of the anthology, but Lowell persisted, and Pound was powerless or unwilling to stop her from pursuing the project. Lowell—without Pound's involvement—published three subsequent Imagist anthologies, in 1915, 1916, and 1917.

concerning it" (*GB* 93). Pound employs a legal analogy here to suggest that a defense of Gaudier's work would be superfluous. The end result of these inconsistencies is, as Donald Davie observes, a work that is "unfortunately the most incoherent though also one of the most important of his prose works."[33] Although I would dispute the implication that the work is important *in spite of* its incoherence, we may still ask what it is that prompted Pound to write the book, and how its curiously belated appearance and anachronistic materials are linked to its twin subjects, the death of a young sculptor and the "Image."

One of the most powerful and revealing tensions in *Gaudier-Brzeska* arises, as I have already suggested, from its disquieting mixture of elegy and polemic.[34] One moment Pound is reminiscing about an afternoon spent in Gaudier's studio, and the next he is revising the concept of the Image, or redressing the public's misunderstanding of Vorticism. The book is, after all, intended to be a work of memory, a public observance of the death of a young sculptor killed in World War I. Indeed, despite the author's forays into Vorticist polemics, we could justifiably call the book a work of mourning. Pound makes it clear that he does not *intend* to allow the memoir to become a manifesto: "I am not particularly anxious to make this book 'my book' about Gaudier-Brzeska . . . In so far as a knowledge of our [the Vorticists'] agreement is likely to lead to a clearer understanding or a swifter comprehension of Brzeska's work, in just so far will the general topic of vorticism be dragged into the present work" (*GB* 19). The proximity of death, however, in the loss of his friend and in the war at large, encourages Pound not only to review the controversies surrounding the Vorticist movement, but, more importantly, to revive an archaic figure of the Image that had been lost to him since his "conversion" to modernity in 1911 or 1912. Through his remembrance of the dead (and this is not the first time Pound dedicated a work to the memory of a dead painter or sculptor), he recovers the figure of the Image as

33. Donald Davie, *Ezra Pound: Poet as Sculptor* (New York: Oxford University Press, 1964), p. 54.
34. This conflict was noted by the book's earliest reviewers, including this critic from the *New York Times:* "Mr. Pound diminishes the value of his memoir by including a number of his own pronouncements on the subject of sculpture and of art in general." *New York Times Review of Books* (August 13, 1916): 314.

phantom or *ghost*. The convergence of elegy and Image (as well as Imagist polemic) indicates, I believe, that we must view *Gaudier-Brzeska*, which is essentially an encounter with the dead, as a vivid and perilous restaging of the poetics of Imagism. Indeed, Pound's puzzling disengagement from the Imagist movement in July 1914 may well have been precipitated by Gaudier's military enlistment in the previous month (June 1914).[35] Thus, Pound may be said to have revived the principles of Imagism by remembering the friend who, more than any other, embodied for him the spirit of that movement. Indeed, Pound is never closer to an illicit sense of the pleasure poetry affords than when he is exhuming or receiving the dead, thereby revealing a correlation between poetry, death, and pleasure that is encrypted in the figure of the Image. The specific correspondence between a recessive figure of the Image and Gaudier's phantom implies, therefore, certain important ramifications for an understanding of Pound's poetics. It suggests, first of all, that the rhetoric of death we encounter so frequently in Pound's work always refers obliquely to the problem of the Image. Thus, for example, the permutations and fate of Gaudier's phantom are those of the Image itself, both historically and ideologically. This suggests, furthermore, that Imagist poetics may be particularly susceptible to "psychological" (in the archaic sense of the term), psychoanalytic, or post-psychoanalytic readings.

Though it is not customary to think of Pound's Image in terms of dreams, ghosts, phantoms, and the underworld, it is precisely these associations that Pound would have encountered in reading Swinburne, Dowson, and other Victorian poets who influenced his earliest poetry. In addition, Pound's formalist agenda (the Image as a formal structure, ideogram, constellation, and so on) shows the influence of early psychological theory, a field that established itself on the basis of

---

35. It is possible that Pound's dissociation from the Imagist movement may have been influenced by Amy Lowell's antipathy for Gaudier. In her biography of Lowell, Jean Gould writes, "Amy could not abide Gaudier-Brzeska . . . He probably nurtured an equal dislike for the regal, immaculate appearance and the 'vivacious intelligence' of Amy Lowell. With his lank hair almost to his shoulders, his sparsely bearded cheeks, pointed chin, oddly slanted eyes topping off his slovenly clothes (almost identical to fellow artists of sixty years later), he was revolting to her." Jean Gould, *Amy: The World of Amy Lowell and the Imagist Movement* (New York: Dodd Mead, 1975), p. 127.

a work (Freud's *Interpretation of Dreams*) purporting to deal scientifically with phantoms of the mind. One of Pound's most influential definitions of the poetic Image is, in fact, specifically indebted to Freudian terminology. In the March 1913 issue of *Poetry,* Pound writes, "An 'image' is that which presents an intellectual and emotional complex in an instant of time. I use the term 'complex' rather in the technical sense employed by the newer psychologists such as Hart" (*LE* 4; Bernard Hart was one of the earliest and most sophisticated English proponents of psychoanalysis). Only rarely have critics taken into account the significance of this and other related statements Pound made—especially the challenge these statements pose to received notions of modern formalism.[36] Wallace Martin's perspicuous observation about the Image in this regard has gone largely unnoticed: "For Pound, the image is a psychological concept. It involves not sensation and ideation, but emotion and other unspecified psychic 'energies' . . . Hulme attempts to define the image philosophically; Pound discusses its psychological causes and effects, and emphasizes the fact that, like the 'complex,' it is endowed with energy. Hulme's concept of the image is derived from Bergson; Pound's was derived from Freud."[37] It is a measure of the power of Pound's formalist rhetoric that critics have almost entirely overlooked the psychological character of the Image and the corresponding associations with ghosts and phantoms. Yet it is crucial for a full understanding of Pound's poetics that these associations not be severed from the more prominent, formalist aspect of the Image.

Pound's memoir of Gaudier-Brzeska is, in effect, a literary crypt, a place that is haunted by the return of the young sculptor (in the form of images from the past), but also by the return of the spectral Image to Pound's thinking about poetry. A crypt is a place that preserves and conceals, a place that preserves the unspeakable pleasure Pound takes in the figure of death and the idea of being visited or haunted by images. The crypt also conceals, and what it hides is not only the

36. Martin A. Kayman provides an excellent account of the historical and intellectual context of Pound's definition of the Image as a "complex." See Kayman, "A Context for Hart's 'Complex,' " *Paideuma* 12, nos. 2 and 3 (Fall–Winter 1983–1984): 223–235.

37. Wallace Martin, *"The New Age" under A. R. Orage* (Manchester: Manchester University Press, 1967), p. 181.

absence of the dead but the disfiguring absence of the Image as phantom in Pound's enunciation of modern formalism. For although in *Gaudier-Brzeska* Pound offers a variety of figures for the Image (complex, ideogram, vortex, mask, and so on), he never describes it explicitly as a ghost or phantom. Yet it is precisely this figure of the Image that accounts for the book's anachronism and that impedes Pound's efforts to "modernize" his poetry. The book, like a crypt, is constructed around the absence of the dead, but also around the absence of a certain figure of the Image that is both ungraspable and unavoidable. The Image is allowed to return as a phantom only as an effect of mourning. Even then, it is forced to remain an inscrutable presence, an unspeakable pleasure corresponding to an unpronounceable word. These archaic associations continue to haunt Pound's formalist conception of the Image until he "buries" them—unsuccessfully—in 1920 in "Hugh Selwyn Mauberley."

By "exhuming" these archaic associations in Pound's work, we can uncover a narrative concerning the Image as phantom. This narrative is encrypted in a group of works that span Pound's early career, from 1908 to 1920. As I mentioned earlier, *Gaudier-Brzeska* is not the first work that Pound dedicates to the memory of a young painter or sculptor. Pound's first book of poems, *A Lume Spento* (1908), is dedicated in memoriam to "William Brooke Smith, dreamer of dreams," a young artist whom Pound had known in Philadelphia. Other works that develop explicitly the association of memory, Image, and phantom include Pound's translation of Book 11 of the *Odyssey* (the journey to the underworld), his translation of Cavalcanti's "Donna mi prega" (which resurfaces in Cantos 36 and 74), and "Hugh Selwyn Mauberley." All of these works—and numerous others—document various aspects of a struggle in Pound's work between divergent conceptions of the Image as artifact and phantom, and between a formalist agenda and what might be called the "desire" of the phantom that Pound encounters, repeatedly, in his own "books of the dead." One either fashions images in a material sense, or one is visited, haunted, by images. It is clear that the latter conception dominates Pound's earliest poetry. Nearly a third of the poems in *A Lume Spento* are addressed to the dead, or are crowded with apparitions, ghosts, and shades. The formalist rhetoric of the Image, which Pound hammered out between 1912 and 1914 and which is the basis of what most people understand to be Imagism, thus displaces an earlier, spectral figure of the Image.

Corresponding to the line of fracture in the Image is a rift that separates the two types of Image makers that appear in Pound's books of the dead. The first type is a "dreamer," a "hedonist," a "somnambulistic medium" (*GB* 106); he is sensitive and passive. The second type is active, energetic, irascible, phallic. The first type is haunted by images; the second masters the medium through "technique." The painters, sculptors, and "outlaws" who appear in Pound's books of the dead often show traces of both types. These types correspond to two kinds of memory. One is active, selective, transformational; it shares certain features with Freud's description of the "work" of mourning. The other is passive, receptive; memories come upon the mind as in a dream.

It is important to bear in mind that *Gaudier-Brzeska* is ostensibly a book of reminiscence, and that memory, for Pound, is fundamentally a question of remembering the dead, or at least dealing with images in the mind—"resurgent EIKONES"—that function like ghosts (*C* 74: 460). This visualization almost always implies recollection: to see is to remember, an equation that helps explain the ambiguous visuality of the Image. Pound's fascination with the powers of memory spans his entire career, from his early interest in Cavalcanti's neoplatonic theory of memory, to the Pisan cantos, where Pound actually repeats the adage, "The Muses are the daughters of memory" (*C* 74: 459). The art of memory, understood as a revival of the dead, lies at the very heart of Pound's poetic agenda. A good example of the way in which Pound's conception of memory informs his poetics occurs in the celebrated series of essays titled "I Gather the Limbs of Osiris," published in 1911–1912 (the same period during which he was translating Cavalcanti's "Donna mi prega"). Pound uses the myth of Osiris (which he borrows from the Egyptian Book of the Dead) as a metaphor to illustrate the vocation of the poet. The poet's essential task, as Pound sees it, is to gather the scattered limbs of the slain god, to reunite the disparate members of the dormant tradition: *to re-member the dead*. In order to assume the role of the one who re-members (who becomes the memory of the race), Pound must take the position of

Isis, the sister-lover of Osiris. (The female gendering of the one who re-members the dead—of the Imagist poet—is rendered most conspicuously in Pound's nomination of H.D. as the prototypical "Imagiste." Indeed, the fictitious "H.D." is equivalent to the Image itself, even as she is encrypted historically as an Imagist poet.)[38] In the Osiris articles, Pound announces a program for modern poetry based on the idea of remembrance, and also articulates for the first time what he calls "the method of the luminous detail" (*SP* 21–23), a concept that prefigures the "radiant node or cluster" of the Image. The "radiant" detail or Image is, in fact, an instrument of remembrance. By isolating such details, which stand in a synecdochical relation to the lost tradition they evoke, one can recover what has been lost or forgotten: the past. In a quite literal sense, and in a manner that corresponds to a long tradition of memory theory, the luminous detail—the forerunner of the Image—is a mnemonic device.

A major influence on Pound's understanding of memory came from his reading and translations of Guido Cavalcanti, a medieval Italian poet whose most famous poem is the canzone "Donna mi prega." Pound's interest in Cavalcanti makes its first appearance in Pound's book of critical essays *The Spirit of Romance* (based on a series of lectures he delivered in the summer of 1909). Later, between April and November 1910, Pound translated nearly all of Cavalcanti's poetry; he published these translations in December 1912, along with an introduction, under the title *Sonnets and Ballate of Guido Cavalcanti*. Between 1910 and 1931, Pound expanded this introduction to an essay of nearly sixty pages, which he published under the title "Cavalcanti" in 1934.[39]

---

38. In her memoir of Pound, H.D. offers a double portrait of her former lover: "The two men, diametrically opposed, set off each other, the London 'opposite number' of my life-long Isis search, and Odysseus-Pound descended into the land of shades in the Pisan Cantos." H.D., *End to Torment: A Memoir of Ezra Pound*, ed. Norman Holmes Pearson and Michael King (New York: New Directions, 1979), p. 32. In this passage, H.D. describes Pound as the dismembered Osiris (to her Isis). Osiris and Odysseus (the two personae H.D. ascribes to Pound) are "diametrically opposed" because Osiris is one of the lost dead, whereas Odysseus, alive, journeys to Hades to recover the dead. In this respect, the position of Odysseus is identical to that of Isis. Hence, by assuming the Isis role in his "Osiris" articles, Pound anticipates his later persona as Odysseus.

39. For an exhaustive account of Pound's many projects relating to Cavalcanti, see David Anderson, *Pound's Cavalcanti* (Princeton: Princeton University Press, 1983).

Pound published a revised translation of "Donna mi prega" in *The Dial* in 1928. He continued to rework this translation, and it appeared in another revision as Canto 36 in 1934. Fragments of the poem are also strewn throughout the Pisan cantos (a section of the *Cantos* that is haunted by personal memories). Pound's lifelong preoccupation with "Donna mi prega" and his repeated renderings of it testify to his belief that the poem contained an enigmatic key to a conception of memory combining erotic love, death, and visual form. The poem became, for Pound, a virtual fetish, its arcane terms recurring like emblems in his work.

"Donna mi prega" is a philosophical poem steeped in neoplatonic thought and the Provençal tradition—a poem that seeks to describe the correlation of visuality and memory in erotic love. Pound's first translation of the poem begins with the following dedication: "To Thomas Campion his ghost, and to the ghost of Henry Lawes, as prayer for the revival of music." These words suggest immediately the relation of the poem's subject (memory) to ghosts and the art of setting words to music (poetry). In his "Cavalcanti" essay, Pound produces a critical anatomy of these features of the poem's exposition. According to his reading of the poem, the inscribing force of affection carves a "forméd trace" *(un formato locho)* in memory, which is the "latent intellect" *(possibile intelletto)*. Affection comes from visible form *(Vien da veduta forma)*, and takes its place in memory *(In quella parte dove sta memoria prende suo state)*.

All of these ideas derive from classical and medieval conceptions of memory. According to tradition, the "art of memory" was invented by the Greek poet Simonides, who is also said to have initiated the tradition of *ut pictura poesis* (the correspondence, or comparison, of verbal and visual arts). As the story goes, the principles of the art of memory occurred to Simonides after attending a banquet at which all of the guests were killed when the roof over their heads collapsed. Moments before the disaster occurred, Simonides was called outside by two strangers—the twins Castor and Pollux in disguise—to whom Simonides had just dedicated a song of praise. The bodies of the dead, buried under the rubble, were mutilated beyond recognition, making it impossible for friends and family to identify their remains. Simonides, however, was able to identify the bodies by recalling *the places of the dead.* From this constellation of dead bodies emerged the art of memory as a system of ordered places, equating remembrance and a deferral of visuality. It is important to emphasize from the outset that the *art* of memory is not a theory of "natural" memory but a mnemonic calculus, a system of artificial memory that is designed to supplement and extend the powers of natural memory. The art of memory is an invisible tool, a technique that is said to endow its practitioners with "divine" powers (hence Simonides' debt to Castor and Pollux), allowing them to retrieve words and things—in the form of images— from a "secret place." Furthermore, heavily influenced by medieval theories of atomism, the art of memory is implicated historically in the development of cryptography, mathematical calculus, and artificial— especially graphic—languages (such as ideogrammic notation). As such, the historical discourse on the art of memory anticipates in remarkable ways the modern discourse on technology and the technical media. The same kinds of magical—and destructive—powers are ascribed to both phenomena. The art of memory, which discloses and exploits the transitivity of a certain kind of "dwelling" place (the *locus*), acts as a *medium* between word and image, oblivion and disfigurement, between the realms of the living and the dead. Questions of topography, and a confusion between place and image, trace the art of memory forward to psychoanalytic theories of language and technology conjured from the translational space of the crypt.[40]

According to ancient sources, which include Cicero, Quintillian, and others, the "art of memory," following Simonides' method, is based on a mnemonic system of places and images (*loci* and *imagines*): "A *locus* is a place easily grasped by memory, such as a house, an intercolumnar space, a corner, an arch, or the like. Images are forms, marks, or simulacra of what we wish to remember."[41] In order to expand the powers of natural memory, we must first visualize in our

---

40. The psychoanalytic concepts of the crypt and cryptonymy, to which my speculations on memory are indebted, originate in Nicolas Abraham and Maria Torok, *The Wolf Man's Magic Word: A Cryptonymy,* trans. Nicholas Rand, foreword by Jacques Derrida (Minneapolis: University of Minnesota Press, 1986). A philosophical and historical account of the cryptic space of memory can be found in Giorgio Agamben, *Stanzas: Word and Phantasm in Western Culture.*

41. My account of the historical and practical features of the art of memory is entirely dependent on Frances A. Yates, *The Art of Memory* (Chicago: University of Chicago Press, 1966), p. 6.

mind a house or dwelling of many rooms *(loci)*, each with a distinctive character. This arrangement of places becomes a permanent setting in which we can deposit, or from which we can withdraw, images that stand for various "things." To recall a word or thing from memory, we enter the dwelling of memory and seek out the *locus* where the image for that word or thing has been deposited for safekeeping. Frances Yates comments, "We have to try to imagine the memory of a trained orator of that period as architecturally built up with orders of memorized places stocked with images in a manner inconceivable to us" (43).

The "theory of images," like the theory of places, alludes to the necrophilic origins of the art of memory. A text by Thomas Aquinas, for example, refers to *imagines* as *phantasmata*, or ghosts (*Art of Memory* 69–71). One should not, moreover, think of the images deposited in the *loci* of memory as mere objects or still figures. Indeed, the "fields and spacious palaces" (as Augustine refers to the *loci* of memory) are thronged with *imagines agentes* (active images), which bring to mind dreadful scenes from the underworld.[42] Augustine's description of the *imagines* recalls Odysseus' encounter with the shades of the dead in Book 11 of the *Odyssey:* "Others rush out in troops, and while one thing is desired and required, they all start forth, as who should say, 'Is it perchance I?' These I drive away with the hand of my heart from the face of remembrance" (*Art of Memory* 46). One is to imagine a palace of the dead, with innumerable rooms, populated by "the *imagines agentes,* fantastically gesticulating from their places and arousing memory by their emotional appeal" (26). As in the *Odyssey*, the *phantasmata* of memory clamor for attention, to be remembered, to speak to (and for) the living.

The *imagines* of memory display "a love of the grotesque, the idiosyncratic." An anonymous source of the first century B.C. advises that memory images will be more effective "if we assign to them exceptional beauty or singular ugliness; if we ornament some of them, as with crowns or purple cloaks; or if we somehow disfigure them by

---

42. It is interesting to note that the art of memory, as it is conceived by Latin sources, often reflects the tastes of imperial Rome: "I came to the fields and spacious palaces of memory, where are the treasures of innumerable images, brought into it from things of all sorts perceived by the senses" (Yates, *The Art of Memory*, p. 46). Augustine's description suggests an analogy whereby the palace of memory is filled with exotic images gathered from the distant provinces of the senses.

introducing one stained with blood or soiled with mud or smeared with red paint" (*Art of Memory* 10). To produce memorable figures, therefore, we must disfigure them; the familiar—that which is to be remembered—must become unfamiliar, grotesque, strange, in order to escape oblivion. The allure of disfigurement recalls the mutilated corpses buried under the rubble of Simonides' banquet. In this respect, the innumerable *loci* of memory, each containing a disfigured image, should be understood as a network of catacombs, or, in the view of medieval theorists of memory, as the "places of Hell."

Once it is marked or disfigured, the image itself becomes a field of inscription, a characterization that is usually reserved for the *locus* or setting of the memory image. Cicero compares the art of memory to an inner writing: "We shall employ the places and images respectively as a wax writing-tablet and the letters written on it" (*Art of Memory* 2). Indeed, hieroglyphs and other ciphers were used as memory images, suggesting that the progression from spectral image to ideogram in Pound's formulation of the Image may subscribe to a logic similar to that of the art of memory. The crypt (or *locus*) holds an image that is both phantom and cipher. According to the conception of memory as a system of writing, it is the *locus* that receives the mark of inscription. Yet the image, as we have seen, can also be marked or disfigured in some fashion, suggesting that a firm distinction between *locus* and *imagines* may not be tenable. A similar uncertainty undermines even more basic distinctions between place and image: "The same set of loci can be used again and again for remembering different material. The images which we have placed on them for remembering one set of things fade and are effaced when we make no further use of them. But the loci remain in memory and can be used again by placing another set of images for another set of material" (*Art of Memory* 7). The art of memory therefore depends on the assumption that the *locus* is permanent, whereas the image is fleeting, or transient. Yet the imaginary *locus*, we must remember, is nothing more than an image. Indeed, it is an image of considerably greater power than the memory image itself, precisely because it disguises its identity as an image—that is to say, it conceals its ephemerality, its susceptibility to oblivion. (The obsessive power of the image—Marx's conception of the commodity fetish, for example—is always due to this sort of concealment.) Freed, however, from the illusion of permanence, the architectural *locus*—the crypt—assumes the phantasmic properties of the image. The art of memory is revealed to be a system of figures disfigured by other figures, images encrypted in images. The translatability of image and place (of the image and its *crypt*) is evident in our current usage of the term "topos" (or "topic"), which Aristotle and other Greek sources used to denote the memory *locus*. As we use it, the word "topic" refers to a general image or subject. Hence, the role of the memory image has been transferred to its site: we use the word meaning "place" when we wish to refer to the image it holds.[43]

The "theory of places," as it was known for nearly two thousand years, refers frequently and unmistakably, in its accumulation of practical detail, to the necrophilic origins of Simonides' invention. The eccentric and even "grotesque" character of the memory places (which are said to deform classical architecture) alludes to an expressive and thematic context that is often articulated in the form of advice on the selection of *loci*. According to one classical rhetorician, "It is better to form one's memory loci in a deserted and solitary place, for crowds of passing people tend to weaken the impressions. Therefore the student intent on acquiring a sharp and well-defined set of *loci* will choose an unfrequented building in which to memorize places" (*Art of Memory* 7). Other authors reflect a similar bias: "Those wishing to reminisce withdraw from the public light into private obscurity" (68). A medieval commentator advises, "When memorizing, the matter should not be read out in a loud voice, but meditated upon in a murmur. And it is obviously better to exercise the memory by night, rather than by day, when silence spreading far and wide aids us" (51).

Such evocations of dark and deserted places are concerned with more than the pragmatics of memorization. Indeed, these silent, nocturnal places are meant to evoke the cryptic space of memory itself, and to refer, obliquely, to the places of the dead at Simonides' banquet. These lonely places are not only empty but pervaded by a sense of melancholy—an inducement, perhaps, to morbid recollection. We might speculate that these associations of memory and wild, deserted

43. Yates observes, "Topics are the 'things' or subject matter of dialectic which came to be known as topoi through the places in which they were stored" (*The Art of Memory*, p. 31).

places contributed, distantly, to neoclassical and Romantic tastes for ruins and graveyards. Indeed, if we were to put into practice the advice of these commentators, we could find no better place to memorize a set of *loci* than a cemetery. One medieval commentator, in fact, goes a step further and compares the *loci* of memory to a map of the underworld: "The places of Hell, varied in accordance with the nature of the sins punished in them, could be regarded as variegated memory *loci*" (94). Lodged in these infernal cells would be images of the damned.

There is another feature of the art of memory that confirms but also complicates its association with the realm of the dead. Tending the cryptic space of memory, as Quintillian describes it, is a guardian: "The images by which the speech is to be remembered are then placed in imagination on the places which have been memorized in the building ... All these places are visited in turn and the various deposits demanded of the custodians" (3). Another commentator writes, "When it is required to revive the memory, one begins from the first place to run through all, demanding what has been entrusted to them, of which one will be reminded by the image" (22). Little else is said about the shadowy figure of the guardian, but we may compare him to Charon, the ferryman who controls access to the underworld. We may also compare the custodian of memory to the guardian that Freud posts at the antechamber of the unconscious. In the art of memory, the figure of the guardian introduces the problem of repression and, by implication, desire. The image encrypted in the *locus* of memory evokes desire, yet also, and more important, it is subject to certain restrictions or resistance. Hence, there is a principle of negativity built into the memory *locus* and its cryptic space—a complication that recalls the problematic visuality of the modernist Image.

The translatability of place and image comes to light only with the disclosure that the art of memory is founded on an omission: the architectural *locus,* or crypt, like the fetish it preserves and conceals, is subject to the laws of ephemerality and transference that govern the phantasmic image. Something is missing; something has been lost; or, rather, the place itself has been misplaced. We are inclined to take seriously Cicero's jest that the art of memory is a "science of forgetting" (*Art of Memory* 17). Indeed, some critics of the art of memory express concern that "all those places and images would only bury under a heap of rubble whatever little one does remember naturally" (19). "Memory," another skeptic warns, "is crushed beneath a weight of images" (19). These passages, which allude to the ruins of Simonides' banquet, remind us that the art of memory originates in a scene of devastation. The faculty of "natural" memory is analogous to a mutilated corpse buried under the weight of images. We may also view the palace of artificial memory, built on the ruins of natural memory, as a monument to the renunciation of memory.[44] Thus, as a system of visualization and remembrance that is founded on blindness and the obliteration of memory, the art of memory prefigures in remarkable ways not only the essential negativity of the modernist Image—its resistance to visuality—but its cryptic relation to the dead. In this regard, as in the discourse of scientific objectivity, to see is not to remember but to forget.

To return to Pound's efforts at translating Cavalcanti's poetic treatise on memory, it is precisely the problematic distinction between place and image that engages Pound in his diverse renderings of the phrase *formato locho* (a variation on the Latin term *locus*). Initially, in the 1912 edition, Pound chooses a textual variant, *non formato locho*, which he renders as "unforméd space." Needless to say, this is exactly contrary to his ultimate choice, in 1928, of "forméd trace" (which adheres closely to the traditional understanding of mnemonics as a form of inscription). This dichotomy—the place (which is also an image) as formed or unformed—is less puzzling if we acknowledge that it replicates, in some fashion, the (non)distinction between *locus* and image in the art of memory. Pound recognizes that the problems of translating the phrase *formato locho* turn on this distinction. In the textual notes to his translation, he writes, "The 'formato locho' is the tract or locus marked out in the 'possible intelletto' . . . I do not think Egidio is sound in thinking the 'formato *locho*' is a single image. Determined locus or habitat would be nearer the mark" (*LE* 188). In

44. To the extent that artificial memory anticipates the cryptic effects of the technical media, my view of the relation between "natural" memory and artificial memory echoes the following statement by Laurence Rickels on the media in general: "Every point of contact between a body and its media extensions marks the site of a secret burial." Rickels, *Aberrations of Mourning: Writing on German Crypts* (Detroit: Wayne State University Press, 1988), p. 360.

making this decision, Pound authorizes, in the context of his own poetics, the image that hides its identity as an image (the *locus,* the crypt). The choice to translate *formato locho* (and hence to designate the image) as place or "habitat" (as a crypt) must be understood as a gesture in the struggle between the Image as artifact and the Image as phantom.

Yet this gesture, which betrays Pound's formalist agenda, is no more stable than the distinction between place and image in the art of memory. For when the phrase *formato locho* surfaces again, in the Pisan Cantos, it is no longer identified as a "determined locus or habitat" but has become an image and phantom. In a revealing passage from Canto 74, the tropes of memory, imagery, and death converge:

> and that certain images be formed in the mind
> to remain there
> *formato locho*
> Arachne mi porta fortuna
> to remain there, resurgent EIKONES
> and still in Trastevere
> for the deification of emperors. (*C* 74: 460)

The *formato locho* (forméd trace) is associated here with images that are described as "resurgent EIKONES."[45] The word *eikōn* in Greek means ghost or phantom, as well as image or likeness. A synonymous term, *eidōlon* (idol), is used by Homer to designate the "cadaverous dead" in Book 11 of the *Odyssey*. Through his translation of this episode in Canto 1, Pound was certainly aware of the double meaning of both terms; what motivated him to choose one over the other is explained by reference to "Trastevere." The Santa Maria Basilica in the Trastevere quarter of Rome contains Byzantine *icons* in the form of mosaics.[46] Hence, Pound's choice of *eikōn* rather than *eidōlon* to designate the ghostly images of memory suggests that these images are comparable to mosaics. By associating the mosaic aspect of the

---

45. To give a complete account of Pound's *formato locho,* it is important to note that the following line occurs in Canto 70: "And in the mirror of memory, formato loco" (*C* 70: 410). With the association of the mirror, Pound's understanding of *formato loco* treads specifically on the historical rhetoric of the Image.

46. Carroll F. Terrell, *A Companion to the Cantos of Ezra Pound,* 2 vols. (Berkeley: University of California Press, 1980), vol. 2, p. 385.

Image, which emphasizes the tessellated or fragmentary nature of memory, with the spectral "EIKONES," Pound produces a dialectical figure (the *formato locho*) that stages the differences between the Image as artifact and phantom.

A similar dialectic emerges in Pound's most famous Imagist poem, "In a Station of the Metro," and in his account of the poem's composition. Pound worked on the poem sporadically from 1911 to 1913, a period of tremendous ferment and change in his poetry (and, incidentally, the period in which he produced his translations of Cavalcanti). Pound reprints the poem in his memoir of Gaudier:

> The apparition of these faces in the crowd:
> Petals, on a wet, black bough. (*GB* 89)

Bearing in mind Pound's affection for medieval concepts of memory, the "station" of the metro can be compared to the *locus* of memory in which the "apparitions" *(imagines)* appear. What's more, Hugh Kenner argues that the poem records a descent "underground," and recalls Odysseus' encounter with the souls of the dead in Hades.[47] The "faces in the crowd," like the "EIKONES" of memory, are "apparitions": they emerge into visibility (as images), yet they are also phantoms. Obviously, this poem, which is cited by Pound (and everyone else) as a paradigm of the modern, formalist Image in poetry, is haunted by other conceptions of the Image. Indeed, Pound portrayed the "Metro" poem as a crucial turning point in his career, a work that forced him into an "impasse" (*GB* 89). He struggled during a period of a year and a half to complete the poem, and cut it down from thirty lines to a single sentence. Pound leaves no doubt that the "Image" of the poem is ultimately a product of shaping and carving resistant materials. The Image is made, not received. Yet the content of the poem alludes to the Image as phantom, even as its mode of creation identifies it as an artifact. Hence, we can understand the "Metro" poem as the moment in Pound's career when the Image as phantom begins to assume the artifactual properties of the formalist Image.

Yet the metamorphosis of the Image never succeeds entirely; Pound's attempts during the teens to "modernize" his poetry and his

---

47. Hugh Kenner, *The Pound Era* (Berkeley: University of California Press, 1971), pp. 184–185.

conceptions of the Image are continually interrupted and garbled by the return of archaic associations in the form of ghosts, burials, and books or poems for the dead. This explains, in part, the curiously belated appearance and anachronistic features of the memoir of Gaudier-Brzeska. Even as Pound seeks to establish a formalist agenda, these archaic associations assert themselves in ever more powerful ways. In a letter of July 1916 (the year in which he published *Gaudier-Brzeska*), Pound writes that he is working on an "adaptation" of Book 11 of the *Odyssey* (*L* 87). In the *Nekuia* (the journey to the underworld to question the dead), Pound discovers the "primal scene" of his encounter with the phantoms of memory, and all the poetic values associated with such an encounter.

In order to appreciate fully the crypt effects of *Gaudier-Brzeska* and the poet's recurrent desire to mourn but also to revive the figure of the youthful sculptor or painter, we must take a closer look at the character of Elpenor in the *Odyssey,* and his curious relationship to Odysseus. Elpenor is a minor figure who makes a brief appearance at the end of Book 10 and the beginning of Book 11. He is the youngest of Odysseus' crew, a position that recalls that of Gaudier in the Vorticist group. Homer describes him as "neither very strong in combat nor very well constructed in his thoughts" (*Odyssey* 10: 553); the term he uses, *arērōs* (ill-fitted, poorly constructed), is a metaphor drawn from carpentry. Elpenor, then, is both less virile and less pragmatic than his fellow warriors. His manner of thinking is unsound with regard to its craft or *technē;* he is a dreamer, and his character has a distinctly feminine quality.

Near the end of Book 10, on the eve of Odysseus' departure from Circe's island, Elpenor climbs up on Circe's roof for a breath of fresh air. There he falls asleep until dawn, when he is awakened by the sound of the crew making preparations to leave. Startled, and anxious to join his companions, he misses the ladder and tumbles off the roof, breaking his neck (*Odyssey* 10: 552–560). He dies, and his soul descends to Hades. Although Odysseus and his crew are aware of Elpenor's accidental death, they depart, for reasons that are never explained, without burying him or observing his death properly. In Pound's translation (which is the opening segment of the *Cantos*), Odysseus sails to a place where he finds "the ocean flowing backward" (*C* 1: 3). The backwardness of Pound's own journey to the underworld (through translation and memory) is clearly essential to his conception of poetry. To embark on the writing of the *Cantos,* Pound must make a journey in reverse: he must return to a place he has never been. This is why Tiresias greets Odysseus/Pound on the latter's arrival in Hades with the question, "A second time?" (This phrase does not occur in the original Greek.)

The law of repetition that drives Odysseus/Pound to "return" to the place of death becomes dramatically evident as he prepares to interview the dead. The first shade he encounters, among the hundreds clamoring for his attention, is that of Elpenor. And Pound makes it clear that this meeting is of no little importance, for in Canto 1 he devotes twice as many lines to Odysseus' meeting with Elpenor as he does to the conversation with Tiresias. (This is not the case in the original: Homer devotes considerably more attention to Tiresias.) On seeing the shade of Elpenor, Odysseus breaks into tears and asks how Elpenor could have arrived in Hades so quickly (*Odyssey* 11: 55–58). Elpenor warns Odysseus that his journey home to Ithaca will be jeopardized if he does not make proper arrangements for Elpenor's burial. Odysseus agrees to all of Elpenor's requests, including the one that prefigures Odysseus' own fate: Elpenor asks Odysseus to plant his (Elpenor's) oar on top of his burial mound. Only fifty lines later, Tiresias instructs Odysseus to take a journey inland until he is stopped by a stranger who mistakes his oar (that of Odysseus) for a winnowing fan (*Odyssey* 11: 119–130). Though the oar serves here to mark the difference between the living and the dead (Odysseus and Elpenor), it is also an inscrutable implement that unites the two men. The dreamy Elpenor is clearly an alter ego for Odysseus *polymetis.*

Carroll Terrell argues that Elpenor "stands for the luckless incidental companion of the hero (or poet) whose only fame after death rests in the fact that the hero has placed his name on record."[48] Though it may be true that the Elpenor type survives for us only as result of the poet's words, it certainly is not the case that he is an

---

48. Terrell, *A Companion to the Cantos of Ezra Pound,* vol. 1, p. 2. A peculiar notoriety continues, however, to shadow the figure of Elpenor: his name survives in what neuropathologists call the "Elpenor Syndrome" or "incomplete awakening." Paul Virilio discusses the correlation between the Elpenor Syndrome and technologies of "topographical amnesia" such as wireless telegraphy. See Virilio, *The Vision Machine,* trans. Julie Rose (Bloomington: Indiana University Press, 1994), pp. 10, 11.

"incidental" figure for Pound (as the emphasis of his translation indicates). On the contrary, Pound is haunted by the Elpenor type as late as the composition of "Hugh Selwyn Mauberley" (1919–1920). Just as Odysseus was haunted by Elpenor, so Pound is haunted by the phantoms of Will Smith, Gaudier-Brzeska, and Mauberley. Indeed Pound draws an explicit connection between Elpenor and Mauberley when he describes Mauberley's grave on "the unforecasted beach":

> Then on an oar
> Read this:
> "I was
> And I no more exist;
> Here drifted
> An Hedonist." (P 203)

In this context, Elpenor's oar not only marks the place of death, but signifies the kind of Image that Mauberley creates ("an art in profile")—a signifier on which Mauberley's epitaph is inscribed.

Pound's imaging of the Elpenor type in his work is complicated and often contradictory. Obviously, not all of the figures, real or fictional, who become Elpenor to Pound's Odysseus resemble one another closely, nor is their correspondence to Elpenor's character ever precise. Indeed, the Homeric Elpenor does not possess the most prominent characteristic of the Elpenor types in Pound's work: Will Smith, Gaudier-Brzeska, and Mauberley are all creators of images. What's more, Gaudier's forceful personality contrasts sharply with the feminine qualities of the dreamer, the hedonist, the aesthete. Yet he fulfills the Elpenor type for Pound in certain essential ways; most important, Gaudier's sudden, premature death at the age of twenty-three—his transformation into a restless phantom—nominates him as a double of the Elpenor figure.

To understand fully Gaudier's significance, we must return to the first Elpenor figure in Pound's life and work: the painter William Brooke Smith, whom Pound described as a "Dreamer of dreams" and who died, like Gaudier, a premature death. Pound first met Smith, who was an art student in Philadelphia, at the age of fifteen or sixteen. Smith died of tuberculosis in 1908, when he was twenty-five. In a letter of 1921 to William Carlos Williams, Pound writes, "Any studio

I was ever in was probably that of some friend or relative of Will Smith, who avoided a very unpleasant era of American life by dying of consumption to the intimate grief of his friends. How in Christ's name he came to be in Phila.—and to know what he did know at the age of 17–25—I don't know. At any rate, thirteen years are gone; I haven't replaced him and shan't and no longer hope to" (*L* 165). The closeness of their friendship—and perhaps something more than friendship—can be inferred from several recently discovered letters that Smith wrote to Pound in 1907.[49] Much later, in one of the Pisan Cantos, Pound remembers Smith as "the wraith of my first friend" (*C* 77: 479), echoing Dante's description of Cavalcanti. Pound published his first book of poetry, *A Lume Spento,* the year Smith died (1908), and dedicated the book to him. The book was originally to be titled *La Fraisne* (after the poem that opens the book), but Pound changed it to its present title in observance of Smith's death.

The phrase *a lume spento,* which Pound translates as "with tapers quenched," comes from Dante (*Purgatorio* 3: 132). Although the funereal connotations of the phrase are immediately evident, its deeper revelations of Smith's character and Pound's intentions are available only through Dante's text and the scholarly apparatus attending it.

---

49. One of Smith's letters addresses Pound as "My ever dear Boy" and closes with the following:

> "These days of awakening life and throbbing pulses 'like veins swollen with delight,' have perhaps made me wish to see everything through a golden veil, rather than through a violet mist. The whole world of jade and sapphire is calling to me, and with God in his heaven surely there is a song of joy and gladness. I can't sing the song, so you must, because you are part of me. 'The wine must taste of its own grapes.'
> Goodbye. You are very dear to me.
> W."

A second letter from Smith ends even more frankly:

> "Don't forget to write to me whenever you can. Dear boy, take the best care of yourself, especially the part that isn't seen, and believe that I am with you always.
> With love,
> Will"

These letters were discovered in the Beinecke Collection by James J. Wilhelm, and are reproduced in his article "The Letters of William Brooke Smith to Ezra Pound," *Paideuma* 19, nos. 1 and 2 (Spring–Fall 1990): 163–168.

The phrase *a lume spento* occurs in a passage in which the heretic Manfredi speaks sadly of his unburied remains, which are exposed to wind and rain (*"Or le bagna la pioggia e move il vento"; Purgatorio* 3: 130). This scene clearly recalls the circumstance of Elpenor's death. Concerning the phrase *a lume spento,* Charles Singleton writes: "It was the custom to bury the bodies of the excommunicated and of heretics with candles extinguished."⁵⁰ Furthermore, he writes, "it was the custom to *exhume* [emphasis added] the bodies of those who had been excommunicated and cast them outside the city" (63). Hence, the title, *A Lume Spento,* referring to Smith, tells us that the young painter was a heretic of sorts, a renegade, and that Pound's elegiac gesture corresponds to the exhumation and reburial of his corpse. By dedicating the book to Smith as he does (with the phrase *a lume spento*), Pound enacts a burial befitting a heretic (who, in this case, is also the beloved) and identifies his own first book of poems as a literary crypt. Out of this crypt, another phantom, named Gaudier-Brzeska, will later arise.

In Pound's writings, the figure of the painter or sculptor who dies in his youth is both somehow oddly inaccessible (for it returns to him from afar, with unavowable sentiments) and unavoidable. Maurice Blanchot writes, "The act of haunting is not the unreal visitation of the ideal: what haunts is the inaccessible which one cannot rid oneself of, what one does not find and what, because of that, does not allow one to avoid it. The ungraspable is what one does not escape."⁵¹ Indeed, Pound's encounters with the phantom in *Gaudier-Brzeska* (whoever that phantom may be) have all the markings of the uncanny—insofar as his recollections involve a *familiar* stranger. This coincides with Nicolas Abraham's observation that the phantom "gives rise to endless repetition."⁵² To begin with, the phantom named Gaudier-Brzeska inherits from Will Smith a certain iconoclastic nature; he is described as an "outlaw," a renegade (*GB* 53, 141). Pound goes so far as to suggest that Gaudier fled to London from

50. Charles S. Singleton, *Purgatorio, Vol. 2: Commentary* (Princeton: Princeton University Press, 1982), p. 64.
51. Maurice Blanchot, *The Gaze of Orpheus,* trans. Lydia Davis (Barrytown, N.Y.: Station Hill Press, 1981), p. 84.
52. Nicolas Abraham, "Notes on the Phantom: A Complement to Freud's Metapsychology," trans. Nicholas Rand, *Critical Inquiry* 13, no. 2 (Winter 1987): 289.

Paris after being involved in some kind of failed rebellion (*GB* 47). Pound's sense that Gaudier embodies a restless, atavistic force gives rise to "an unverifiable fancy" that "an almost exact portrait of Gaudier" is to be found "carved on some French cathedral façade" (*GB* 76). The idea that Gaudier is a double of some lost figure, "a return of what does not come back" (as Blanchot describes the image), is felt even more keenly in the following statement by Pound: "He [Gaudier] was, of course, indescribably like some one whom one had met in the pages of Castiglione or Valla, or perhaps in a painting forgotten" (*GB* 48). The forgotten painting in this case would be a self-portrait of Pound at age twenty-three. For when Pound first met Gaudier, it provoked in him an image of his own youth and thoughts of mortality (at age twenty-nine):

> I was interested and I was determined that he should be. I knew that many things would bore or disgust him, particularly my rather middle-aged point of view, my intellectual tiredness and exhaustion, my general scepticism and quietness, and I therefore opened fire with "Altaforte" and "Piere Vidal," and such poems as I had written when about his own age . . . He even tried to persuade me that I was not becoming middle-aged, but any man whose youth has been worth anything, any man who has lived his life at all in the sun, knows that he has seen the best of it when he finds thirty approaching; knows that he is entering a quieter realm. (*GB* 45–46)

The tone of these reflections is uncharacteristic for Pound; his normal vigor and confidence are undercut by a powerful sense of exhaustion, resignation, and withdrawal. Though his words reveal an unmistakable note of affection for Gaudier, the most important experience seems to be a loss of some part of himself. Thus, even before his death, Gaudier communicates to Pound a powerful sense of things forgotten and buried. As his reading of "Altaforte" suggests, however, Pound is not timid in his efforts to retrieve what is lost, or to revive the dead.

The combination of melancholy and bravado that we find in Pound's reminiscence is, I think, symptomatic of a more profound sense of disorientation that Pound experiences in the cryptic space of memory. At the close of Chapter 3 of the memoir, for example, Pound comments on the haphazard nature of his recollections: "That is the way memory serves us, details return ill assorted, pell mell, in confusion" (*GB* 40). Four pages later, however, at the beginning of Chapter 5, Pound is ready to apply a "method," or discover some kind of "order" in his memories: "To give the man as I knew him, there is perhaps no better method, or no method wherein I can be more faithful than to give the facts of acquaintance, in their order, as nearly as I can remember them" (44). Yet this attempt to arrange things gives way, once again, several pages later, to confusion. At the beginning of Chapter 6 he writes, "My memory of the order of events from then on is rather confused" (51).

We find in these comments a record of a struggle to give order to memory, to render it coherent, to prevent a deluge of images from overwhelming both the one who remembers and the reader. The experience of remembering and mourning is, from this perspective, an active, transformative labor of separation. Yet this is not the limit of Pound's experience of remembrance, nor is it perhaps even the primary one. For the process begins with the "return" of details, "ill assorted, pell mell, in confusion." From this perspective, the one who remembers is profoundly passive; what he remembers is what is visited upon him, what haunts him, and what he cannot avoid. At one point, Pound acknowledges that even the memories he constructs with words, in contrast to photographs, are destined to be no more than phantoms: "The rest is perforce impressions and opinion, mine and those of Mr. Bennington's camera. And Mr. Bennington's camera has the better of me, for it gives the subject as if ready to move and to speak, whereas I can give but diminished memories of past speech and action" (*GB* 38). Pound's impressions of Gaudier suggest a restless, unpredictable spirit that is ruled by instinct. Pound tells us that Gaudier liked "to feel as independent as the savage" (40), and describes him as "a well-made young wolf or some soft-moving, bright-eyed wild thing" (44). Apparently, Gaudier appeals to Pound as a kind of primitive spirit—volatile, stealthy, and potentially dangerous. This impression is reinforced by Pound's description of Gaudier's sudden departure at their first meeting: "And he disappeared like a Greek god in a vision" (44).

Pound first met Gaudier by chance at a gallery in London, at the opening of an exhibition of the sculptor's work. Their meeting was precipitated by a peculiar incident involving Gaudier-Brzeska's name.

Pound writes, "I turned to the catalogue and began to take liberties with the appalling assemblage of consonants: 'Brzxjk'—I began. I tried again, 'Burrzisskzk'—I drew back, breathed deeply and took another run at the hurdle, sneezed, coughed, rumbled, got as far as 'Burdidis'—when there was a dart from behind the pedestal and I heard a voice speaking with the gentlest fury in the world: 'Cela s'appelle tout simplement Jaersh-ka. C'est moi qui les ai sculptés'" (*GB* 44). Initially the phantom, who is heard but not seen, instructs Pound with a kind of "fury" in the pronunciation of an unpronounceable name. He then disappears "like a Greek god in a vision." Pound is duly intrigued by this apparition: "I wrote at once inviting him to dinner, having found his address in the catalogue. He did not arrive ... The morning after my date I received *a letter addressed to me as 'Madame'* [emphasis added], inviting me to the studio. Then a meeting was arranged through a mutual acquaintance" (44–45). These words suggest, among other things, that Pound's first encounter with Gaudier-Brzeska was charged with sexual tension and ambiguity.

Gaudier took the name Brzeska because he was living with Sophie Brzeska, "a Polish woman much older than himself whom he referred to as his sister."[53] The enigmatic character of their relationship and Gaudier's decision to take her name are reflected in the shadowy nature of her presence in *Gaudier-Brzeska*. She is virtually absent from the book; Pound refers to her only once or twice as "Miss Brzeska," and indicates that she provided him with some biographical information on Gaudier. This omission is surely not accidental. In addition, Pound almost never refers to Gaudier-Brzeska by his full name, in spite of the fact that Gaudier-Brzeska identified himself as such at least as early as 1911. For Pound it is always simply "Gaudier."

It is no coincidence that the unutterable (and not merely unpronounceable) half of Gaudier-Brzeska's name is female. Gaudier-Brzeska, as Pound remembers him, is a cryptic figure in a struggle between divergent concepts of imagery and memory, and between the artist as pragmatist and the artist as dreamer. These antithetical conceptions display, as we have discovered, distinct gender associations.

---

53. Noel Stock, *The Life of Ezra Pound* (San Francisco: North Point, 1982), p. 146.

The Image as artifact (as well as the artist who produces such Images) is associated, implicitly, with the masculine; whereas the Image as phantom (and the artist who receives such Images) is associated with the feminine. By repressing the feminine name, as well as the woman behind the name (Sophie Brzeska), Pound "motivates" the fracture in Gaudier-Brzeska's name, and forces it to become symptomatic of the central struggle in the poetics of Imagism.

The phantom that is preserved and concealed in Pound's literary crypt is therefore also a "silent word" that gives rise to an "undecipherable fetish" (*Wolf Man* 81–83). According to Abraham and Torok, the crypt is the place of the excluded word-thing, the unspeakable name. Of the "silent word," Derrida writes, "It is the very tombstone of the illicit, and marks the spot of an extreme pleasure, a pleasure entirely real though walled up, buried alive in its own prohibitions."[54] Hence, the word hidden and preserved in the crypt is the cipher of an unspeakable pleasure. Pound's crypt holds such a word, an unnameable feminine word, and this "pleasure word" leads us back to the moment Pound receives a letter from the dead addressed to him as "Madame." In this moment, Pound becomes a woman and takes the place of the unnameable word-thing: "Jaersh-ka."

The name Gaudier-Brzeska is a broken symbol, half of which is sealed within the crypt. The "silent word" in the crypt (which is also a phantom) can become conscious only if it takes the form of an "undecipherable fetish" (which Abraham and Torok call the "Thing"; *Wolf Man* 81). The "Thing" is the visual image of a cryptonym, a tableau of a variant meaning of the pleasure word. In essence, it is a rebus or hieroglyph of the pleasure word. In Pound's text, the tableau-fetish of the silent word, *Brzeska*, is the moment Pound is addressed as a woman by a dead man. This tableau corresponds to the unspeakable pleasure that Pound takes (but cannot acknowledge) in assuming a feminine role—the role of someone who is visited or haunted by memories and images (rather than someone who makes them). The fact that the pleasure of cross-dressing lies in the "inner safe" of Pound's crypt, sealed by a woman's proper name, only confirms the logic of cryptonymy. For, as Abraham and Torok observe,

---

54. Jacques Derrida, "*Fors*: The Anglish Words of Nicolas Abraham and Maria Torok," foreword to Abraham and Torok, *The Wolf Man's Magic Word*, p. xxxiv.

"the silent word" is "love disguised and dressed up in a 'painting'" (83). The Image is a transvestite of the word.

The exhumation and reburial of a single figure, which constitutes the central focus of *A Lume Spento* and *Gaudier-Brzeska*, becomes, in "Hugh Selwyn Mauberley," a double burial of separate characters. In 1919 and 1920, three years after the publication of *Gaudier-Brzeska*, Pound wrote "Hugh Selwyn Mauberley," a poem that dramatizes the central conflict in Pound's aesthetic between the artist as pragmatist and the artist as dreamer. The two main protagonists of the poem, E.P. and Mauberley, personify the antithetical values that inhere symbolically in Gaudier-Brzeska's fractured name. Traditionally, critics have viewed the poem as Pound's sardonic farewell to the London scene and to the Decadent qualities of his own poetry. K. K. Ruthven writes, "Ideally, Pound hoped to exorcise Mauberley and cultivate E.P."[55] The evidence of the poem, however, is far more ambiguous. Ruthven's choice of the term *exorcise* is certainly apt, because Mauberley is a return of the Elpenor type—the dreamer, the "hedonist." On the other side of the coin is E.P., the pragmatist, who "strove to resuscitate the dead art of poetry" (*P* 187) and whom Pound compares to one of his favorite poet-outlaws, Villon.

The poem is constructed around a double burial and a dialogue between the two protagonists that is carried on after death. E.P. and Mauberley bury each other in the course of the poem, and each one has a section in the poem that is spoken from the grave. Donald Davie quotes Pound as saying, "Mauberley buries E.P. in the opening poem; gets rid of all his troublesome energies."[56] Indeed, the opening poem is an epitaph for E.P. titled, "Ode Pour L'Election de Son Sepulchre" (after Ronsard's poem), spoken, presumably, by Mauberley. What we have is an exact reversal of the situation in Pound's earlier "books of the dead": here, Mauberley the wraith buries E.P. the man. Yet E.P. later delivers Mauberley's epitaph from the grave (*P* 203), and even offers a beautiful pastiche of a Renaissance seduction poem, exploiting the tropes of sexual love and death ("When our two dusts with Wal-

---

55. K. K. Ruthven, *A Guide to Ezra Pound's "Personae"* (Berkeley: University of California Press, 1969), p. 126.
56. Donald Davie, "Ezra Pound's 'Hugh Selwyn Mauberley,'" in B. Ford, ed., *The Modern Age* (Harmondsworth: Penguin, 1961), p. 320.

ler's shall be laid / Siftings on siftings in oblivion"). Pound also makes an extremely important admission in the poem that serves to elide certain differences between dreamer and pragmatist. He makes it clear that the ultimate goals of E.P. and Mauberley are the same: "His true Penelope was Flaubert." This phrase first appears in relation to E.P., but it is also applied later to Mauberley (*P* 187, 198). Hence, the question of the Image as phantom or artifact is displaced, finally, by a teleological sleight of hand.

Whether or not the poet of the *Cantos* arose from the sublation of these two figures, he certainly was never able to lay to rest the ghosts of Elpenor, Will Smith, Gaudier-Brzeska, and Mauberley. (This phantasmic and erotic lineage survives, for Pound, in the figure of another young artist-heretic: George Antheil.) Quoting Apollinaire in *Gaudier-Brzeska,* Pound writes, "On ne peut pas porter *partout* avec soi le cadavre de son père" (82). Yet that is precisely what occurs in the book: Pound is unable to part with the "cadaverous dead," to complete the task of mourning. The poet's lost male companions become remote and inexorable *fathers* to his writing. In a very real sense, death both quickens and captures Pound's writing. "The work of the phantom," Nicolas Abraham writes, "coincides in every respect with Freud's description of the death-instinct" ("Phantom" 291). Haunted by a series of ghosts, Pound continually seeks to return to a place he has never been, to converse with the dead. His experience of the dead (which is the experience of the unknown or the impossible) and his conception of memory converge with the poetics of the Image. If, indeed, Images and the phantoms of memory are analogous in Pound's mind (as in the phrase "resurgent EIKONES"), then we should view the poetic Image as the return of a lost or dead object, a moment in which the subject is *haunted* by reality. The Image is life imaged as death, a *living death,* as the Egyptian Book of the Dead taught Pound and others (including Yeats and Wyndham Lewis) around the turn of the century.

Images pieced together like mosaics, "in little splotches of color" (as Pound described the genesis of the "Metro" poem), arise from a place that hides its identity as an Image, a place that is no place: the crypt. The *formato locho* is Pound's first important figuring of the crypt, a place that is the site of the death of pleasure (the loss of the beloved) but also a place that knows the word that says pleasure. Contradictory forces erect and sustain the crypt: to allow the dead, or the beloved, or anything real, to return in the form of an Image, Pound must lie in his own grave (the grave containing the pragmatist and the formalist agenda of the Image). He must assume the place of the one who bears the unutterable feminine name, the transvestite word. Only then will she receive a letter from a dead man, and only then will she remember the slain god who is her brother and her lover. For if Pound assumes the name-place of Sophie Brzeska, who is the "sister" and lover of Henri Gaudier, then he fulfills the role of Isis, who remembers the god Osiris.

Corpse Language

To the readers of a journal called *Aryan Path* in 1939, Ezra Pound offered his thoughts on the subject of sacrifice: "Animals are now killed in abattoirs; the sight of killing can remind us, in the midst of our normal semi-consciousness of all that goes on in our vile and degraded mercantilist ambience, that life exists by destruction of other life. The sight of one day's hecatomb might even cause thought in the midst of our democracy and usuriocracy" (*SP* 68). The main point here, stated with characteristic circuity, is that in a so-called democracy one segment of society inevitably lives at the expense of another; and more specifically, that usurers feed off the vitality of society at large. But there is a more insidious implication: the sight of ritual killing might incite the masses to overcome their victimization—that is, to destroy the usurers in order to preserve the life of the community. One might therefore infer, especially in the context of Pound's vehement anti-Semitism, that the reference to the abattoir is merely a pretext for the subject of *human* sacrifice. Given Pound's obliquity with regard to such matters, it is not implausible to identify this view of sacrifice as a veiled fantasy of mass death.[57]

57. In his book on Pound's anti-Semitism, Robert Casillo argues, "To ignore the darker and concealed significance of Pound's ritualism is to embrace the *méconnaissance* which enables victimization to continue." Casillo, *The Genealogy of Demons* (Evanston, Ill.: Northwestern University Press, 1988), p. 276. Casillo also addresses the problem of interpreting Pound's many allusions to the desirability of political violence against

Death's ritual and figurative power, which Pound invokes quite explicitly in his statement, first emerges in his poetry and criticism long before his engagement with fascism and, indeed, before his remembrance of Gaudier-Brzeska. Necrophilia emerges as an important feature of Pound's work with the publication of his earliest poetry. The rhetoric of death attains its historical—and more sinister—form, however, only when he begins to resist its power. Pound's resistance to his own fascination with death, and to the materiality of the dead in particular, fuels the gradual emergence of the figure of the Image in his poetics. Indeed, Pound fashions the Image as a kind of talisman or charm that would lead him out of the realm of the dead, out of the delirium and passivity of Decadence. Yet he fails, as often as he tries, to lay the dead to rest, to resist their erotic and imaginative appeal. Hence, the Image remains saturated with the very ideas about death that it pretends to exclude. The Image emerges as both an embodiment of the dead and a weapon in Pound's assault on the materiality of the dead.

In an early poem, Pound proposes an inversion of the fundamental values of life and death: "What . . . if? 'Tis out of death we come, / And not thereto . . ." (*CEP* 254). If this inversion establishes the inaugural terms of Pound's poetic, then he can succeed in his "search for the real"—which discloses the Image—only by singing of the dead and what Mary Douglas calls the "sad wit of pollution." Furthermore, the Image that lies in the crypt, once it is summoned, inevitably engenders confusion over what is living and what is dead. In Pound's mind, the dead always display an alarming vitality, and the living, or the works they produce, often resemble the dead. Indeed, we should view the whole project of Imagism as a deconstruction of "death" in poetic language. As Pound seeks more and more violently to isolate his early poetry and its influences from his sense of modernity (a turning point in his career that critics identify with Imagism), the distinction

---

the Jews and others: "Is Pound suggesting expulsion or extermination? Although tantalized by political violence, Pound is often vague, tentative, equivocal in discussing the subject, for the anti-Semitic propagandist usually knows that the open endorsement of violence will in most cases get him nowhere. Like Pound, who offers his audience images of Jewish sacrifice, he plants the seeds of vengeance in the listener's mind, without making clear what specific expression the vengeance is to take" (p. 265).

between the living and the dead becomes increasingly incoherent, and ripe for exploitation in the realm of politics. Indeed, I think it is essential to regard Decadent theorizing about "death-in-life" (or a form of death that is somehow magically alive) as the precursor of the fascist equation of survival and sacrifice, construction and destruction.[58]

In a covert fashion, the rhetoric of the Image is embroiled in a struggle for power over "dead language" and various other forms of cultural filth and decay. Before we examine this struggle more closely, however, we should establish conclusively the extent of Pound's infatuation with death prior to the Imagist movement. We must also demonstrate that this fascination continued long after his break with the movement per se—indeed, for as long as the figure of the Image commanded his attention. To begin with, the sheer quantity of his early writing concerned with death is remarkable—even for a young poet steeped in the necrophilic poetry of Ernest Dowson, Arthur Symons, and Lionel Johnson. More than a third of the poems in his first six books of poetry (including the 1912 edition of *Ripostes*) treat the subject of death in some fashion (76 of 214 poems in the *Collected Early Poems*). In addition, the poems printed in *Lustra* (which includes work written or published from 1913 to 1915) displays a similar, though diminished, affinity for the dead. References to ghosts, phantoms, tombs, corpses, and the underworld are numerous; frequently, the poet addresses the dead, or undergoes the experience of death himself. As a graduate student at the University of Pennsylvania, Pound's tastes reflected a similar inclination. Initially, he hoped to do his thesis on the Latin poets of the Renaissance, whom he praised as "the men who were most persistent in their effort to bring the dead to life" (*SR* 223). When the young Pound arrived in London and registered at the British Library in 1908, he listed the Latin poets of the Renaissance as his research topic (*SC* 99).

In one of his first letters home in 1908, Pound describes his morbid tastes to William Carlos Williams in the following manner: "Perhaps you like pictures painted in green and white and gold, and I paint in

58. Citing Walter Benjamin's linkage of Decadence and fascism, Alice Yaeger Kaplan discusses what she calls the "polarity machine" of fascist ideology, in which terms such as "construction" and "destruction" become dialectically equivalent. Kaplan, *Reproductions of Banality*, pp. 28–30.

black and crimson and purple" (*L* 6). Already the "colors" of death and the making of images are paired in his mind. In 1912 Pound writes, "It is a manner of speech among poets to chant of dead, half-forgotten things, there seems no special harm in it; it has always been done" (*LE* 8). This statement should be viewed as an apology for his own inclinations as a young poet. In 1909 he wrote enthusiastically to his father about Frederic Manning's poem "Persephone," and composed a poem in response to it entitled "Canzon: The Yearly Slain" (*CEP* 133). In addition, one of Pound's early collections of poetry *(Canzoni)* bears an epigraph from Propertius which dedicates the work to Persephone, queen of the underworld (*CEP* 130). Pound translates the quote (which also appears in section 6 of "Homage to Sextus Propertius") as "My not unworthy gift to Persephone" (*P* 219). Furthermore, in *Personae* (1926), Pound appends the phrase to his selection of poems from *Ripostes,* suggesting—through a kind of back-formation—that the first examples of Imagism (the poems in *Ripostes*) appeared under the sway of Persephone (*P* 57). In the poem "Religio," Pound notes the goddess of the underworld as one of his tutelary figures (*SP* 48), and indeed she continues to fill that role throughout the *Cantos*.

Pound's necrophilia is also evident in his fondness for writing epitaphs, three of which he selected for inclusion in *Personae* (1926). His feelings are even more apparent, however, in the subject matter of many of his early poems. The poem "Threnos," for example, is addressed "to the fair dead," and celebrates, according to Hugh Witemeyer, "the Swinburnian ecstasy of death" (*CEP* 30).[59] Pound's tastes are even more explicit in "Redondillas":

> They tell me to "Mirror my age"
> God pity the age if I do it,
> Perhaps I myself would prefer
> To sing of the dead and the buried . . .
> I sing of risorgimenti
> Of old things found that were hidden. (*CEP* 218)

Out of this desire "to sing of the dead and the buried" evolves a conception of poetry which is articulated through a metaphorics of

---

59. Hugh Witemeyer, *The Poetry of Ezra Pound: Forms and Renewal, 1908–1920* (Berkeley: University of California Press, 1969), p. 71.

death: writing and poetic composition are understood in terms of decomposition, burial, exhumation, and demonic possession. In the poem "Epilogue," for example, Pound writes, "I who have labored long in the tombs, / Am come back therefrom with riches" (*CEP* 209). The idea that the poet is a kind of grave-robber can also be inferred from the epigraph to the poem, "Sestina: Altaforte," where Pound poses a question to the reader that states the basic evaluative criterion for his cryptaesthetic: "Have I dug him up again?" (He is referring to the main protagonist of the poem, Bertrand de Born.) A successful poem is one in which the poet digs up a corpse and sets it out for the reader's curiosity or pleasure. Ten years later, in a letter to James Joyce, Pound reiterates his belief—this time with a note of desperation—that his talents pertain to the dead: "Signore Sterlina [the nickname that Joyce's children had bestowed on Pound] is perhaps better at digging up corpses of let us say Li Po, or more lately, Sextus Propertius, than in preserving this bitched mess of modernity" (*P/J* 148).

Other early poems depict the poet as a figure who is inspired or even possessed by the dead. "To E.B.B.," for example, offers the following portrait of the poet:

> Poor wearied singer at the gates of death
> Taking thy slender sweetness from the breath
> Of the singers of old time. (*CEP* 262)

The poem "Histrion" provides a minor *ars poetica* on this inspirational mode, which involves a form of possession and, ultimately, self-extinction:

> . . . the souls of all men great
> At times pass through us,
> And we are melted into them, and are not
> Save reflexions of their souls . . .
> So cease we from all being for the time,
> And these, the Masters of the Soul, live on. (*CEP* 71)

The self-effacement implied in assuming a mask dignifies the poet, for it rehearses the *mysterium* of death and incorporation.

As the following lines from "Und Drang" confirm, the writing of poetry is associated, in Pound's mind, with deliberate, repeated death: "I have lived long, and died, / Yes I have been dead, right often"

(*CEP* 169). The idea that death is emblematic of the creative experience gives rise to other poems in which the poet imagines his own death in greater detail. A number of Pound's early poems fall into this category, including "The Tomb at Akr Çaar," "Redivivus," "And Thus in Nineveh," and "Anima Sola." Often these poems are set in the narrator's tomb, the site of a dialogue with his ghost or corpse. Pound's exploration of this topos culminates in sections 3 and 6 of "Homage to Sextus Propertius," when the poet imagines his own funeral.

With regard to style as well as subject matter, we cannot easily distinguish Pound's transition from his so-called early poetry to his Imagist phase. It is important to emphasize that the earliest and least understood aspect of Imagism (the cryptic "Doctrine of the Image") does not require Pound to abandon his literary necrophilia; rather, it suggests an obscure development of this unavowable and aggressively "poetic" economy. The best evidence for Imagism's necrophilic dimension is the anthology *Des Imagistes,* which Pound compiled in 1913 but did not publish until 1914. The opening poem of the anthology, "Choricos," by Richard Aldington, had already appeared (on Pound's recommendation) in *Poetry* in November 1912, as one of the earliest examples of Imagist poetry. The morbid qualities of Aldington's poem, and its verbal archaisms, are representative of a number of the poems that Pound selected for the anthology:

> The ancient songs
> Pass deathward mournfully. . . .
> O Death,
> Thou art an healing wind . . .
> Thou art the dusk and the fragrance;
> Thou art the lips of love mournfully smiling;
> Thou art pale peace of one
> Satiate with old desires;
> Thou art the silence of beauty. . . .
> Thou sealest our eyes
> And the illimitable quietude
> Comes gently upon us.[60]

---

60. Ezra Pound, ed., *Des Imagistes: An Anthology* (New York: Boni, 1914), pp. 7–9. The anthology was reprinted in 1917.

Other poems in the anthology by Aldington, Skipwith Cannell, H.D., and Pound himself confirm the Decadent wellsprings of Imagism. Quite obviously, at this stage, the concept of the Image has not yet emerged from the crypt.

Furthermore, one of Pound's crypt poems, titled "Middle-Aged," is the occasion for the earliest recorded usage of the term "Imagiste." In a letter to Harriet Monroe in August 1912, Pound describes the poem as "an over-elaborate post-Browning 'Imagiste' affair" (*L* 10). In his crypt poetry, Pound finds pleasure in gazing at the dead, or conversing with them, or even allowing the dead to penetrate and finally displace his own being. "Middle-Aged" teaches us that all of these cryptic pleasures are bodily pleasures, for the poet's infatuation with death in this case is genuinely erotic. The pleasure of being dead is not unequivocal, however, because the poem is prompted, as its title indicates, by the poet's awareness of his aging body, by the reign of death in life. Nevertheless, by imagining himself as a "buried king" in the tomb of a pyramid, the poet transforms his aging body into a homoerotic spectacle:

> As the fine dust, in the hid cell
> Beneath their transitory step and merriment,
> Drifts through the air, and the sarcophagus
> Gains yet another crust
> Of useless riches for the occupant,
> So I, the fires that lit once dreams
> Now over and spent,
> Lie dead within four walls
> And so now love
> Rains down and so enriches some stiff case,
> And strews a mind with precious metaphors,
> And so the space
> Of my still consciousness
> Is full of gilded snow. (*P* 236)

Pound wrote this poem on "middle age" when he was only twenty-six years old. A year or so later the question of middle age arose again with great poignancy when Pound first met the sculptor Gaudier-Brzeska. It is quite possible, therefore, that the experience of aging is merely a conceit, a pretext for the pleasure he derives from placing himself in a crypt that is also an Image. The pleasures afforded by death and imagery are always intertwined in Pound's mind, often through the medium of the body.

The poem imagines a group of tourists "frolicking" on the roof of a hidden burial cell. Their movement dislodges the "fine dust" that drifts down onto the dead ruler. The poem is ambiguous, however, as to the effect of the "gilded snow" on the inhabitant of the crypt. On the one hand, the dead man is unaware of these "useless riches"; yet the dust is also compared to love and to metaphors strewn upon the mind. Indeed, the dirt that rains down on the corpse of the pharaoh, which becomes the corpse of the poet, is also gold and semen and figurative language. The dead man is "touched" by this protean substance.

Pound's infatuation with the dead was not lost on his contemporaries, or on his later critics. Wyndham Lewis, for example, wrote of Pound, "Life is not his true concern . . . His field is purely that of the dead . . . whose life is preserved for us in books and pictures" (Lewis, *Time* 87). Elsewhere, Lewis described Pound as "a bombastic galleon" with "a skull and crossbones" flying from its mast.[61] Richard Aldington's parody of the famous "Metro" poem also registers Pound's necrophilic bias:

> The apparitions of these poems in a crowd:
> White faces in a dead black faint. (*SC* 191)

As for Pound's critics, Hugh Witemeyer has described "Hugh Selwyn Mauberley" as an "elaborate autopsy" (*Poetry of Ezra Pound* 162), and Humphrey Carpenter describes Pound's fifth volume of poetry, *Canzoni,* as "the last twitch of a poetic corpse, the body being recognizably that of the Pre-Raphaelites" (*SC* 157).

The foregoing summary has, I hope, demonstrated not only the prominence of death in Pound's early poetry and his thinking about poetry, but the potency and desirability, in Pound's view, of anything associated with death. His frank and sometimes morbid relations with "the dead and the buried" embody his sense of tradition, but they also harbor an illicit pleasure. These attitudes reflect some of the most

---

61. Wyndham Lewis, *Blasting and Bombardiering* (London: Calder and Boyars, 1967; orig. pub. 1937), p. 272.

powerful influences on his early poetry, including Swinburne's enormously complex and eroticized conception of death. Pound also admired poets of the 1890s such as Ernest Dowson and Lionel Johnson, whose work included some striking examples of necrophilia in verse. In a preface to Johnson's poetry, for example, Pound notes sympathetically Johnson's "fear of life," and singled out for praise the following line from the poem "Nihilism": "I shall be calm soon, with the calm death brings" (*LE* 368). The languid eroticism of poems such as "Morbidezza" by Arthur Symons—another poet whom Pound admired—also made its mark on his early work, and survived the upheaval in his poetics that occurred in the name of the Image.

Although death is often the bearer of whatever is most profound or pleasurable to Pound in his early poetry, there are also signs that he was becoming increasingly uneasy with his absorption in death and its Decadent overtones. In 1911, in a poem titled "Canzon: The Vision," Pound asks, "Were jewelled tales / An opiate meet to quell the malady / Of life unlived?" (*CEP* 145). The idea of the living dead, which had formerly been the locus of various literary and erotic transferences, was now a "malady." A "life unlived" was now less likely to be the source of poetic treasure.

As the rhetoric of the Image moved into the foreground of Pound's poetic discourse during the years 1912 to 1914, he began to associate death more and more frequently with anything that he considered to be evil or despicable. (And he did this despite the fact that death continued to be the bearer of many positive values with regard to the Image.) Indeed, the idea of death underwent a remarkable transvaluation in Pound's writing during this period. With the emergence of Imagism, Pound repudiated his first six books of poetry (he later referred to them as "a collection of stale cream puffs"; *CEP* 314) and many of the literary influences that had shaped his early poetry. He attacked what he called "rhetoric" in poetry, equating it with "dead language." The aim of Imagism was to lay the dead to rest, to extinguish dead language, dead poetry, and the influence of dead minds. Pound described *Lustra* (1916), his first book of poems after launching the Imagist movement, as "absolutely the *last* obsequies of the Victorian period" (*L* 23). The underscoring of the word *last* suggests that Pound had already tried, unsuccessfully, to bury his illicit past; and indeed, he would go on making such attempts at least as late as "Hugh Selwyn Mauberley." This desire to shed his infatuation with the dead helped unite his disparate interests; his review of Allen Upward's *Divine Mystery* in 1913, for example, yields the sublimating logic of Imagism: "Primitive man turns from his worship of the dead . . . to a worship of the life-giving Helios" (*SP* 404). There can be little doubt that this "primitive" scenario depicts Pound's own wishes.

Using the principles of Imagism as a kind of litmus test, Pound hoped to distinguish between the living and the dead in art. He wrote, "We apply a loose-leaf system to book-keeping so as to have the live items separated from the dead ones" (*LE* 18). Furthermore, Pound was inclined to encourage "good criticism, chiefly in form of attacks on dead language" (*L* 178). Elsewhere, he identified the object of his criticism—and the antithesis of the Image—as "corpse language" (*L* 296). Obviously, anything worthy of an attack is hardly dead or inert; indeed, the necessity for such an attack confirms its potency—hence the instability of the distinction, in Pound's mind, between the living and the dead.

In his attacks on literary or cultural stagnation, Pound frequently deploys analogies emphasizing the materiality of death: "In England the mental corpses lay about in the streets, no one desired to touch them but the general feeling was they must be kept" (*SP* 54). As an Imagist poet, Pound assumes the figurative role of a caste that not only touches but eliminates the corpses infecting the streets. In the context of Vorticism, the outcast begins to resemble an anarchist seeking to rid literary culture of the highly charged matter of death. Pound's description of Wyndham Lewis, for example, offers a glimpse of his own posturing at the time: "A volcanic and disordered mind like Wyndham Lewis's is of great value, especially in a dead, and for the most part rotted, milieu" (*SC* 245). Later in his career, Pound continues to view himself as "the last living Rhadamanthus" (*L* 274; an allusion to the king who judged the dead in the underworld), yet he grew weary of his role, and encouraged younger writers to carry on his ambiguous campaign against dead things: "I don't propose to deal with dead matter and negations. In fact, the younger generation ought to do the killing and carrying away of corpses" (*L* 328).

These comments leave little doubt that the rhetoric of Imagism registers a virtual transformation in Pound's attitudes toward death and the world of the dead. Death becomes, in part, a figure for anything despicable or malevolent. Yet it is never merely antithetical to the brilliant figure of the Image, for Pound's infatuation with death persisted in spite of his newly discovered revulsion to it; indeed, revulsion may have enhanced his infatuation. His old longing for the "life unlived" continued to inform his work and tastes. His scholarly interests, for example, still gravitated toward the macabre. In 1916 he translated twelve dialogues from Fontenelle's *Dialogues des morts,* and published them in *Pavannes and Divagations.* He also became interested about this time in Walter Savage Landor's "interviews" with the dead, *Imaginary Conversations.* Pound himself wrote a series of "Imaginary Letters." In 1917 his taste for the arcane surfaced in an article praising a work by Thomas Lovell Beddoes titled *Death's Jest Book* (*SP* 378–383). We should also recall, of course, that during this period Pound was translating material from the *Odyssey* that would become the opening segment of the *Cantos:* the descent by Odysseus to the underworld. Indeed, it could be argued that the idea of death continued to dominate his later conceptions of the *Cantos* as a whole. In 1927, for example, he identifies in the *Cantos* three primary structural "moments":

A. Live man goes down into the world of Dead

B. The "repeat in history"

C. The "magic moment" or moment of metamorphosis (*L* 210)

The three-part scheme of the poem that he provides here suggests that the *Cantos* remains entirely captivated by the figure of death, though it now embraces historical and mythological modalities that make it compatible with the ideology of fascism.

The Vorticists, Pound writes, are "arrogant enough to dare to intend to 'wake the dead'" (*GB* 117). Indeed, Pound, despite his inclination to label as deathlike anything he opposes, remains in thrall to death. The Image, according to Pound, is "impersonal," rigorous, and hard as stone. It stands in opposition to the "caressable in art" (*GB* 97). These qualities adumbrate a poetic language made in the image of death. When Pound describes the qualities he admires most in poetry or prose, he often turns to adjectives such as "hard" and "clear cut." In his criticism, the reader repeatedly encounters expressions such as, "We can be thankful for clear, hard surfaces, for an escape from softness and mushiness" (*P/J* 33). When Pound praises Joyce's early work, he writes, "It is a joy to find in Mr. Joyce a hardness and gauntness" (*P/J* 32). Surely the hard and gaunt qualities of Joyce's prose are not far removed from the rigor of death, which is precisely why they are a source of "joy" to Pound. These are also the essential qualities of Imagist poetry. Imagism emphasizes "technique," and is therefore "impersonal," according to Pound (*GB* 85).

In certain respects, the poetic discourse of "objectivity," with its disdain for subjective and socially constructed meaning, may be regarded as a more advanced symptom of cultural Decadence, insofar as it resembles the hermeticism of its aesthetic counterpart, the *l'art pour l'art* movement. Hence, by espousing objectivity in the name of the Image, Pound secretly retains the Decadent principles of his earliest poetry. Furthermore, the implications of "impersonality" have not, perhaps, been thoroughly articulated: not only does it require, as I discussed in Chapter 1, a mortification of the subject, but a more puzzling and phantasmatic severance from the empirical object. The peculiar and somehow potent deadness of the modernist Image is captured most fully by Wyndham Lewis in his explication of the Vorticist aesthetic:

> *Deadness* is the first condition of art. The second is the absence of the *soul*, in the sentimental human sense. The lines and masses of the statue are its soul. No restless, flame-like ego is imagined *inside* of it. It has no inside. This is another condition of art; *to have no inside*, nothing you cannot *see*. Instead then of being something impelled like an independent machine by a little egoistic fire inside, it lives soullessly and deadly by its frontal lines and masses.[62]

Pound thought this passage important enough to cite it, with explicit approval, in his review of *Tarr* in 1920 (*LE* 430)—even going so far as to suggest that the concept of deadness helps explain the epiphanic moments in Joyce's fiction.

It is hardly necessary to emphasize that Lewis' notorious celebration of "deadness" in art all but describes the sculpted image as a cadaver,

---

62. Wyndham Lewis, *Tarr*, pp. 299–300. Though published in 1918, Lewis' novel was written before 1914.

and that its resistance to hermeneutic profundity is a cardinal feature of modern positivism and its privileging of the image as the sign of radical exteriority (that is, objectivity). Nevertheless, Lewis inadvertently discloses a cryptological dimension of the Image that is keyed to its implacable yet reductive visuality. For the proscription against seeing into the interior of the artifact suggests a desire on the part of the spectator to do just that. The "deadness" of the Vorticist Image is intended, however, to obstruct, to resist the desire to glimpse something inside the Image. Though Lewis claims there is "no inside" to the Image, it's clear that the potent negativity of the Image depends on a resistance to visuality, on the assumption that there may, at least in the spectator's mind, be something to see inside the Image. Like the cells of artificial memory that oscillate between *locus* and image, the Vorticist Image is at once a cadaver and the crypt that conceals the absent dead.

As an emblem of "impersonality," the Image assumes the strange autonomy of a corpse, estranged at once from any kind of subjective experience (except the task of mourning) and from its vanished referent (the living "thing"). So extreme, however, is the autonomy—the negativity—of the Image, that its deadness becomes the precondition for a kind of sinister animation, but also for "life" itself. Indeed, we have seen that for Pound the material waste of the cadaver is deceptively and dangerously *alive*. Indeed, Lewis concedes that the Vorticist Image "*lives* soullessly and deadly by its frontal lines and masses," that it must, therefore, be viewed as an emblem of the *living* dead. Yet the strange "life" of the Image can be construed only in terms of excess, since that vitality is borrowed not only from its human maker (who must remain impassive, thinglike), but also somehow from its estranged referent, the living "thing" that it disavows. It is precisely in regard to the excessive and indeed "perverse" vitality of the Image that the Vorticist aesthetic engages most directly the problem of the fetish. For the discourse of fetishism has, from its historical origins in the colonial period, been consistently associated with the "perversion" of animism, with the "savage" attribution of vitality to inanimate things, and with the erosion of the distinction between the living and the dead that accompanies the regime of fetishism.

If we therefore take into consideration the entire spectrum of

Pound's attitudes about death, it is obvious that the rhetoric of Imagism is fueled by tremendous ambivalence. On the one hand, anything opposed to the Image is attacked as being corpselike, filthy, inert, or bereft of vitality. Yet the most prominent features of the Image itself are deathlike: its impersonality, its rigor, its severance from the empirical object, and its assertion of a polarity between art and life. This ambivalence is clearest in the borderline poems that announce the Imagist project, yet fail to rid themselves of "rhetoric," sentimentality, archaicism, "softness," and other qualities the Imagist poet deplores. "Revolt against the Crepuscular Spirit in Modern Poetry," for example, illustrates perfectly this formal contradiction of poetic principles. The first line of the poem, as well as its title, announces the poet's desire to put off his infatuation with death, both in spirit and letter: "I would shake off the lethargy of this our time," he writes (*CEP* 96). The archaic diction of the line indicates, however, that the poem is still under the spell of the "crepuscular spirit." By the end of the poem, all trace of revolt has departed, leaving a perfect specimen of "corpse language":

> Great God, if these thy sons are grown such thin ephemera,
> I bid thee grapple chaos and beget
> Some new titanic spawn to pile the hills and
> This earth again. (*CEP* 97)

What is it then that enables Pound to distinguish between the "corpse language" of his early poetry and the supposedly vital language of Imagism? Is the distinction that Pound draws between two kinds of language—living and dead—purely figurative, as it must be in a poetic doctrine concerned with the Image? Would that explain why the prehistory and the afterlife of the Image always inhabit, or dictate, its immediate significance?

Pound sacrifices to "modernity" the language of his youth, which is not only the language of the dead but a material embodiment of the dead. Youthful language and dead language, once combined and suppressed, become a "corpse language" so powerful that it must be slain time and time again. Pound sacrifices a forbidden tongue, his own "first" language and that of the dead, in order to preserve it. In this discursive and poetic act of incorporation, all of the sinister and erotic powers associated with death come to reside in the Image. Yet at the heart of Pound's "Doctrine of the Image" lies a confusion over what is living and what is dead. This confusion is evident in the instability of the term "dead," as Pound employs it. He describes, for example, his "research into something so dead as a complicated aesthetic of sound . . . which ain't dead in the least, though I dare to say the canzone is too mummified to walk on its own pins again" (*L* 157–158). Is the aural aesthetic of the canzone dead, or not? Exploiting a similar kind of ambiguity, he writes of the Dadaists, "They have expressed a desire to live and to die, preferring death to a sort of moribund permanence" (*P/J* 186). Is the death chosen by the Dadaists real, or not? This ambiguity suggests that Pound is well on his way to losing track of this distinction (a path that leads to his veiled threats of violence against the Jews during World War II).

The rhetorical play on the word "dead" points to uncertainties of a more fundamental nature. One of Pound's "Imaginary Letters" contains a rather free translation of part of a sonnet by Baudelaire ("Le Vampire"). The translation is the focus of an elaborate deconstruction of death and vitality in language, executed by the persona who writes the letter, Walter Villerant. Villerant is not entirely candid, however, as to the origins of the sonnet, describing it merely as "Baudelarian." Hence, the discussion begins on a note of ambiguity. The poem resembles, in many respects, Pound's early crypt poetry. It concerns an erotic encounter with a corpse—which turns out to be alive:

> One night stretched out along a hebrew bitch—
> Like two corpses at the undertakers—
> This carcass, sold alike to jews and quakers,
> Reminded me of beauty noble and rich.
> Although she stank like bacon in the flitch,
> I thought of her as though the ancient makers
> Had shown her mistress of a thousand acres,
> Casqued and Perfumed, so that my nerves 'gan
>   twitch . . . (*PD* 74)

Immediately shocking is the lurid necrophilia of the poem: the speaker describes himself and the prostitute as "corpses," and compares the site of their coupling to a morgue. Her "carcass" reminds him of "beauty noble and rich," and he is aroused sexually by imagining her stinking flesh as an embodiment of ancient splendor. Even more disturbing, considering Pound's anti-Semitism, is the fact that the central figure in this erotic tableau of the living dead is a Jewess.

The morbid sexuality of the poem is emblematic of the wider concern of the "imaginary letter," which is the illusory nature of "vigor" in language. Villerant introduces the poem by noting that in Baudelaire's time "the poetic language had grown stiff" (*PD* 75). This observation, of course, sounds suspiciously like Pound's assessment of his own era. Faced with the impediment of dead language, Baudelaire forged a new poetry that is praised generally for its vigor. A closer look, however, convinces Villerant that "the Baudelaire 'vigour' seems to me now too facile a mechanism. Any decayed cabbage, cast upon any pale satin sofa will give one a sense of contrast" (*PD* 75). Hence the vigor of Baudelaire's language is illusory; it is facile, mechanistic; it is, in fact, a *dead* language. The poem's shock effect is derived not from the vitality of its language but from its morbid subject matter, which imagines a living body as dead. The language of the poem, on the other hand, is an emblem of the living dead: it appears to be alive but is actually dead.[63] Villerant ends his commentary on the poem with a crucial observation; he compares the illusory vigor of language to the illusionistic properties of a graphic image: "The stuff looks more vigorous than it is ... As indeed bad graphic art often looks more skillful than it is" (*PD* 76). Thus, the realism of "bad graphic art," like Baudelaire's appalling words, projects the uncanny effect of the living dead.

The inscrutability of death in language, which Pound discovers in the Baudelaire poem, signals a fundamental ambiguity in his own sense of language. As Pound describes it, "corpse language" is often alive

63. It is interesting to note that a "corpse" turns up in the English version of the poem. Something is rotten in this translation: the line "she stank like bacon in the flitch" is an interpolation on Pound's part. Nothing even resembling this line appears in the original. What's more, the entire line has a colloquial ring that is misplaced in the poem. I would tend to view these curiosities as elements of a linguistic disturbance or rupture, which takes place in a poem that is concerned with the "revival" of language.

in an uncanny fashion; it seethes with hidden powers and invisible vermin; it is truly menacing. The supposedly vital language of the Image, on the other hand, is said to be purged of rhetoric and sentiment, of any trace of desire; it is hard and stiff as a corpse. Hence, the dead, for Pound, possess an alarming vitality, whereas the living are often deathlike. When he condemns a poem as "dead" or corpselike, the statement is therefore bound to be ambiguous, since he is also infatuated with the dead and the past. The attack on "corpse language" is always underwritten by desire, and his infatuation with the dead is always tinged with hostility.

Hyperaesthetics and the Cult of Mourning

The rhetoric of death articulated by modern Imagists such as Pound, Lewis, Aldington, and H.D. often harbors an elegiac dimension, a poetics of mourning, that translates the image-cadaver into a ghost, into a phantasmic and mediumistic figure of transmission. In Pound's case, the "translation" of an Image into the economy of mourning almost always entails a "conversion" of the male poet's gender. Earlier in this chapter, I emphasized the role of Pound's grief in his reappropriation and revision of the Image, and indicated that he was capable of mourning the dead only by assuming the place of the "unutterable feminine name," the position of the feminine. In doing so, Pound may be said to share, or adopt, the fictive identity of the prototypical Imagiste: "H.D." The disincarnation of the Image (as a ghost) is mirrored by the transformation of the poet's gender. This moment of "conversion" evokes the images of metamorphosis that Pound (and H.D.) used to characterize their youthful love affair between 1905 and 1907. Further, H.D.'s choice to sign her letters to Pound *throughout her life* as "Dryad" (the name given to her by Pound)—a spirit of the woods—evokes what she later calls the "incalculable element" in their relationship. Describing in 1958 the impetus for her memoir of Pound, *End to Torment,* she writes, "Dr. Erich Heydt [H.D.'s analyst] injected me with Ezra, jabbing a needle into my arm. 'You know Ezra Pound, don't you?' This was almost five years ago. It took a long time for the virus or the anti-virus to take effect. But the hypodermic needle did its work, or didn't it? There was an incalculable element."[64]

The element untouched by virulent memory almost certainly concerns the metamorphic character of "H.D.," but also the reciprocity of the identities of lover and beloved. In "Hilda's Book," the collection of love poems that Pound presented to H.D., the beloved (that is, H.D.) is repeatedly associated with the myth of metamorphosis and described as a "tree-born spirit of the wood" (*End to Torment* 84). The "madness" of the girl's becoming a tree recurs throughout Pound's early poetry (*P* 3, 4, 62, 91), as an image not only of the beloved but of the poet himself. Indeed, Pound chose "The Tree"— a poem that originally appeared in "Hilda's Book"—to open his volume of selected poems, *Personae* (1926): "I stood still and was a tree amid the wood, / Knowing the truth of things unseen before" (*P* 3).

Pound's preoccupation with metamorphosis, and with what he calls the "transsentient" character of his relation to H.D. (*CEP* 8–9), informs, implicitly, the important series of articles titled "I Gather the Limbs of Osiris" (published in 1911 and 1912). In what is essentially a manifesto of modern poetics and critical method, Pound places himself in the position of Isis (sister and lover of Osiris), who *re-members* the scattered limbs of the slain god. He adopts a similar strategy, as I indicated earlier, in mourning the dead sculptor Gaudier-Brzeska. Hence, in Pound's view, the one who mourns, the one who gives voice to the pain of loss and is therefore able to love the dead as part of herself, is always feminine (or at least a mimicry of femininity) and usually adolescent. Indeed, most of the female figures in Pound's death cult are teenagers. The *locus classicus* for Pound's adolescent figures (and their susceptibility to states of "possession") can be found in a line of Propertius, which Pound translates as "My genius is no more than a girl" (*P* 217). Indeed, in the postscript to his translation of Rémy de Gourmont, Pound cites this line in relation to Fenollosa on "image making" and the physiology of style (*NPL* 158). In the twilight zone of Pound's early poetry, young girls, by virtue of their passivity and their absorption in the materiality of the body

64. H.D., *End to Torment*, pp. 20–21.

(according to Pound), enjoy a privileged relation to the dead. In his view, these girls are "linking objects" to a realm of poetry that is at once intensely pleasurable, menacing, and forbidden (that is, the realm of the dead, which is populated by shades or Images).[65] The most intensely erotic encounters with the dead, which occur in his crypt poetry, are therefore nearly always enacted from the standpoint of a young girl. Contrary to what one might expect, Pound's views on these subjects are not merely, or even primarily, psychological. They reflect, as we shall discover, the influence of Victorian social codes governing the role of gender in mourning.

Changing gender, as a poetic device, also exposes Pound to the illicit pleasure of being visited or haunted by *images* (an experience that always enacts the return of a dead or lost object). Hence, one is "haunted" by reality when one *receives* images, instead of making them. The pleasure of receiving images is illicit, in part, because Pound associates feminine passivity with Decadent poetry. As he sees it, the masculine values of "technique" and pragmatic action are constantly threatened by the death-obsessed and hedonistic instincts of the feminine. Whenever the male poet assumes the voice and body of a young girl, he succumbs not only to the passivity of death but to the passivity of the Image (which institutes the servitude of idolatry). He denies, on one hand, what Pound views as the active character of the male body, and therefore allows himself to be inhabited by ghosts (a pleasure that derives, essentially, from a denial of corporeality). Yet he also extinguishes his intellectual powers, as Pound sees it, by mimicking the girl's absorption in materiality (a sacrificial pleasure that transforms not only the Image, but the poet himself, into an eroticized corpse). Thus, by assuming the place of the unutterable feminine name, the poet runs the risk of becoming either a live dwelling for the spirits of the dead, or a corpse. He succumbs to a force that is essentially passive and a pleasure that is not only irresistible but fatal to the explicit aims of his poetry.

In an essay on Rémy de Gourmont, a subject that inevitably elicits

---

65. On the concept of "linking objects" between the living and the dead, see Vamik Volkan, *Linking Objects and Linking Phenomena: A Study of the Forms, Symptoms, Metapsychology, and Therapy of Complicated Mourning* (New York: International Universities Press, 1981).

from Pound his most uninhibited thoughts on the relation of poetry to the body, Pound remarks, "Sex, in so far as it is not a purely physiological reproductive mechanism, lies in the domain of aesthetics" (*LE* 341). We would rightfully assume, in an essay that refers to Gourmont's "sexual intelligence," that this statement associates aesthetic pleasure with bodily pleasure. After all, in his reflections on Gourmont's *Natural Philosophy of Love,* Pound compares the production of Images to an outburst of sexual energy (*NPL* 153). This poetic absorption in the sensuality of the body is closely linked to Gourmont's "sense of beauty," an aesthetic orientation that plays a decisive role in Pound's early poetry and persists in the rhetoric of the Image. Pound describes Gourmont's keen sensitivity to beauty as "hyperaesthesia," comparing it to a kind of "genius" (*NPL* 155). Pound writes in 1919, "I do not think it possible to overemphasize Gourmont's sense of beauty. The mist clings to the lacquer. His spirit was the spirit of Omakitsu; his *pays natal* was near to the peach-blossom fountain of the untranslatable poem" (*LE* 343). It is quite evident from this passage that the pleasure derived from beauty and corporeality remains a powerful temptation for Pound.

In spite of his inclination to identify Imagism as an art that springs from the body, Pound is just as likely to separate poetry and pleasure. The Image is not a formation of pleasure but an object that fills the empty space of pleasure. In the first issue of *Blast,* Pound writes, "Hedonism is the vacant place of the vortex, without force, deprived of past and future" (*EPVA* 151). This statement, echoing the antihedonistic views of Sorel and Hulme, veers away from the Decadent and corporeal origins of the Image, toward the values of rigor and asceticism, which represent a mortification of the body. Pleasure is conceived here as functioning in a temporal framework that responds only to the immediate sensual requirements of the body. More important, pleasure is understood as a "vacant place" with no "force" of its own. The site of pleasure is essentially passive; its true function is to receive and hold the forceful impression made by the vortex. Indeed, Pound's rejection of "hedonism" is predicated on a distinction between passive and active, or "receiving" and "conceiving": "You may think of man as that toward which perception moves. You may think of him as the TOY of circumstance, as the plastic substance

RECEIVING impressions. OR you may think of him as DIRECTING a certain fluid force against circumstance, as CONCEIVING instead of merely observing and reflecting" (*EPVA* 151). Pound views the "phallic" poet as superior because such a poet shapes or sculpts the raw matter of the body, of circumstance, of imagery. In contrast, the poet who assumes the place of the young girl surrenders himself to pleasure. He becomes a mere plaything, "the TOY of circumstance," a "plastic substance RECEIVING impressions." Feminine passivity is therefore associated in Pound's mind with idleness, servitude, and inert materiality. The danger that he associates with these qualities is characteristic of what Blanchot calls "the immense passivity of death, which escapes the logic of decisions, which can perfectly well speak but remains secret, mysterious, and undecipherable because it bears no relation to light."[66] The image, too, according to Blanchot, has "a characteristic passivity: a passivity that makes us submit to it, even as we are summoning it."[67] Hence, when Pound rejects the passivity of the feminine, along with the passivity of death, yet places himself in the position of an idolater before the figure of the Image, he exposes himself to the dangers of materiality that haunt the "vacant" site of pleasure.

We can further illuminate Pound's reaction against pleasure and the temptations of "beauty" by examining the character of Mauberley in "Hugh Selwyn Mauberley." Six years after condemning "hedonism" in *Blast*, Pound is still trying to bury the figure of the hyperaesthetic, pleasure-loving poet. Mauberley, who stands in contrast to the more virile and pragmatic character of E.P., is an Imagist writer who practices "an art in profile," though he is "lacking the skill to forge Achaia"—that is, to maintain the standards of classical engraving (*P* 198). His "fundamental passion" is the "urge to convey the relation / of eye-lid to cheekbone / By verbal manifestation; / To present the series / Of curious heads in Medallion—" (*P* 200). The fact that his fundamental passion is aesthetic and not sexual is confirmed by his deferred and thoroughly attenuated response to the

---

66. Maurice Blanchot, *The Space of Literature*, trans. Ann Smock (Lincoln: University of Nebraska Press, 1982), p. 102.
67. Maurice Blanchot, *The Gaze of Orpheus*, trans. Lydia Davis (Barrytown, N.Y.: Station Hill Press, 1981), p. 80.

sexual overtures of a young woman (*P* 200). Mauberley's aesthetic vision is thus a form of blindness to "natural" pleasure; his pleasure is self-absorbed and passive, "his desire for survival, / Faint in the most strenuous moods" (*P* 202). Ironically, Mauberley's deferral or mediation of carnal pleasure ensures its fatal influence. The desire for pleasure, sufficiently abstracted, thus usurps the desire to live. Death captures the poet who is captive to pleasure. Mauberley's epitaph, we should recall, reads: "I was / And I no more exist; / Here drifted / An hedonist" (*P* 203).

The year that Pound composed "Hugh Selwyn Mauberley" (1919), ridiculing the hyperaesthetic tastes of its central character, was also the year that he praised Gourmont's incomparable "sense of beauty." The date of this statement suggests that Pound's own hyperaesthetic tastes persisted in spite of his repeated attacks on hedonism. Rather than abandon his pleasure-loving ways, which always lead back to the figure of the Image, Pound routes his desires through a complex circuit of idolatry and transsexuality. Access to the pleasures of the grave (passivity, materiality, sentimentality) is secured initially through a fascination with dead girls, or girls inhabited by death. (I must reiterate: I say "girls" because most of the female figures in Pound's death cult are teenagers.) Pound situates his morbid idolatry in the context of what he calls "the cult of the dead Beatrice," modeled after Dante's reverence for his absent beloved. An early poem of Pound's, "La Nuvoletta," begins with an explanatory note indicating that the speaker of the poem is "Dante to an unknown lady, beseeching her not to interrupt his cult of the dead Beatrice" (*CEP* 151).

Pound substitutes a number of candidates for the "dead Beatrice," including Ignez de Castro, a character from Camoens' epic poem "Os Lusiades." In an essay on the Portuguese author, Pound contends, "Modern interest in the poem centers in the stanzas of the third canto which treat of Ignez de Castro" (*SR* 218). The "modern interest" that Pound refers to is, of course, his own necrophilia. In the second of the so-called Ur-cantos, he devotes twenty-five lines to the story of "her dug-up corpse."[68] She also appears twice in the *Cantos* (*C* 3: 12 and 30: 148). As Pound tells her story, Ignez is a peasant girl loved

---

68. Pound, "Three Cantos II," *Poetry* 10, no. 4 (July 1917): 180–188.

by Pedro, the prince of Portugal. Conspirators at court have her murdered before she and the prince are able to marry. Years later, when he becomes king, he digs up her corpse, crowns her, and forces the courtiers to pay homage to the dead queen. As is the case with most of the girls who figure in Pound's cult of the dead, Ignez de Castro functions quite literally as an idol. We should also note that the dead idol serves as a weapon. The story involves a beloved figure that turns to filth (a corpse) and is subsequently used as a weapon against the king's enemies. This scenario approximates the rise to power of the Image in Pound's career. The fetishized language of Swinburne, which Pound adores, turns to "corpse language," and he subsequently uses it to attack his literary foes. Yet the despised "corpse language" is transformed into a luminous Image, just as the corpse of Ignez becomes a queen.

Sigismundo Malatesta, one of Pound's most prominent alter egos in the *Cantos,* likewise indulges in morbid idolatry (and is described by Pound as a "necrophiliast"; *C* 10: 44). Malatesta built a mausoleum, the Tempio, to house the remains of his third wife, Isotta. Pound celebrates this fact by composing an epitaph for her crypt (*C* 9: 40–41), and refers to her as "Divae Ixottae" (the Divine Isotta; *C* 76: 473). His interest in epigraphy and images of the dead is also evident from a poem by Giacomo Leopardi, which Pound translated as "Her Monument, the Image Cut Thereon" (*CEP* 154–155). Other graphic images mixing the themes of death and erotic love also hold a prominent place in his "cult of the dead Beatrice." The Pre-Raphaelite portraits of women painted by Edward Burne-Jones, for example, were a favorite of Pound's. The ekphrastic poem "Yeux Glauques," which is based on a Burne-Jones sketch, reveals Pound's belief that the erotic appeal of these women survives in their eyes, which "Became the pastime for / Painters and adulterers" (*P* 192). Indeed, the entire epoch of Swinburne, Rossetti, and Ruskin, which Pound recalls with such ambivalence, is preserved in the "vacant gaze" that stares out from "the half-ruined face" (*P* 192).

The "vacant gaze" of a female icon, which arouses hostility as well as desire, appears in two other brief ekphrastic poems by Pound, each based on the painting "Venus Reclining," by Jacopo del Sellaio (1442–1493). The first one is titled "The Picture," which I quote in full:

> The eyes of this dead lady speak to me,
> For here was love, not to be drowned out,
> And here desire, not to be kissed away.
> The eyes of this dead lady speak to me. (*CEP* 197)

The second poem, titled "Of Jacopo dell Sellaio," is scarcely longer than the first and also ends with the line, "The eyes of this dead lady speak to me" (*CEP* 197). As in the case of "Yeux Glauques," the eyes of the dead are eroticized because they turn the idolatrous gaze of the viewer back upon himself. Not only the dead girl in "The Picture" but the image itself returns the poet's gaze, causing his voice to fall silent (hence the brevity of the poem and the hint of incredulity in the repeated line). Yet the poet knows that the gaze of the image is terrifying only so long as it remains mute or "vacant." Hence, he attempts to mitigate its power by lending his voice to the dead girl's eyes. In this respect, the poet's fetishized relation to the image resembles a ventriloquist's act. The secret desires of the poet issue from the "vacant" eyes of a dead girl, as though they were her own. Yet her gaze reveals nothing of herself—only Pound's inexhaustible longing for the dead. The image, like a cadaver, remains strangely mute and impassive, even as the viewer succumbs to "the opaque meaning of a thing that is being eaten and that also is eating, being swallowed up and recreating itself in a vain effort to turn itself into nothing" (Blanchot, *Orpheus* 54).

The two poems on the Sellaio painting may also help us understand what role the "cult of the dead Beatrice" played in Pound's personal life. We know from Dorothy Shakespear's letters that Pound recommended the painting to her and that she did go to the National Gallery "to interview the Sellaio" (*P/S* 120). It is not unlikely, therefore, that Pound associated his "beautiful young wife" (as Yeats described Dorothy) with the Sellaio painting. Ultimately, however, his marriage revealed the consequences of extending his fascination with imagery and death to real circumstances, for Pound once said of his wife: "I fell in love with a beautiful picture that never came to life" (*SC* 241).

Pound's correlation of certain archaic and eroticized images with a kind of adolescent death cult lends itself, of course, to a complex but rather predictable reading from the standpoint of psychosexual politics. I wish to point out only one aspect of such a critique: Pound's willingness to adopt the ostensive passivity of his archaic and girlish icons intersects quite obviously with the discourse of fetishism. For a kind of "perverse" exchange takes place between the fetishist and his inert object of desire: conventionally, the fetish object assumes a magical potency as the fetishist surrenders reason, volition, and "vitality" to the image, becoming more and more subservient and "slavish." (Hence, the practice of fetishism by Africans became, in the hands of European intellectuals, a means of legitimating the slave trade.) The loss of "vitality" suffered by the fetishist is often regarded, according to W. J. T. Mitchell, as a "projection which results in the symbolic castration or feminization of the fetishist."[69] In Pound's case, the gaze emanating from the fetishized portrait, a gaze that conveys the poet's voice even as it robs him of it, is also the gaze of Medusa, threatening to rob him of his virility. I would also argue that Pound's idolatrous relation to the dead Beatrice is *intended*, surreptitiously, to transgress the bounds of gender and to disrupt the poet's sexual identity. By surrendering his virility, his authority, to the fetish, Pound adopts the young girl's passivity, which grants him access to the illicit pleasures of the grave. In a sense, he exchanges places with the idol: he becomes the dead girl he adores.

Pound's early poetry and certain aspects of his personal life offer considerable evidence that he took interest in figures who disturbed the ideological boundaries of gender, and also that he himself was inclined to experiment with the sexual identity of his persona. In his writing, Pound is never closer to the material and sentimental pleasures of poetry (which constitute the prehistory and the afterlife of the Image) than when he assumes the voice of a girl who is wounded by loss, a girl inhabited by death. The pleasure of mourning allows him not only to acknowledge, at a distance, the shameful but intensely pleasurable origins of his own poetry, but to revive these pleasures in the clandestine form of the Image as a corpse or phantom. In order to gain access to the dead, however, Pound finds it necessary to devise a "subversive mourning art," a strategy that allows him to cross the "liminality of grief" by dismantling certain gender formations.[70]

69. Mitchell offers a lengthy discussion of the problem of fetishism in *Iconology*, p. 194.

70. I have borrowed these phrases from Neal Tolchin's study of Victorian social codes

Pound's private life yields details which can be read as clues or symptoms of a gender disorder that becomes fully "legible" only in his crypt poetry. In his early correspondence to Dorothy, for example, Pound frequently closes letters with the phrase, "I kiss your eyes" (*P/S* 94, 114, 136, 145, 175). On Pound's lips, this quaint expression inevitably recalls the "yeux glauques" of the beggar maid in Burne-Jones's painting. It also suggests that Pound's obsession with a dead lover's eyes (who in this case happens to be alive) may have more in common with Mauberley's attenuated "passion" than with a frank expression of sexuality. The words seem to convey a diffident, almost chaste affection. Indeed, after expressing her own desires for sexual satisfaction, Dorothy discreetly acknowledges Pound's reluctance to consummate their "friendship" (*P/S* 9). Their sexual roles are further complicated by Pound's habit of referring to Dorothy, his fiancée, as "Little Brother" and "Coz," terms of affection usually reserved for a male companion (*P/S* 6, 37, 114).

These "symptoms" would remain largely unintelligible were it not for other, more explicit evidence that Pound took pleasure in exploiting ambiguities of gender or sexuality in his personal life. Most readers and critics of Pound know that in 1908 he was removed from his position as an instructor at Wabash College in Indiana. The dismissal occurred when it was discovered that he had shared his rooms for a night with a young woman from out of town. Pound defended himself against insinuations of sexual misconduct, but was swiftly relieved of his position on the faculty. It is not widely known, however, that the woman in his room that night was a transvestite—"a lady-gent impersonator," in Pound's own words (*SC* 76). In addition, Pound shared his rooms with the impersonator not once but *twice,* and it was only after the second incident that the college felt compelled to dismiss him (80). Whether or not any sexual impropriety occurred, Pound was delighted by the notoriety gained from the incident. In a letter to H.D., he wrote, "They say in Wyncote [Pound's hometown in Pennsylvania] that I am bi-sexual and given to unnatural lust" (81).

---

in the articulation of mourning. See Tolchin, *Mourning, Gender, and Creativity in the Art of Herman Melville* (New Haven: Yale University Press, 1988).

My point in drawing attention to this episode and other ambiguities in Pound's sexual character is not to establish a new biographical topos but to furnish a textual *locus* with fresh *images*.[71] I want simply to emphasize that Pound's *imagination* is drawn to the predicament, or desire, of the transvestite, an affinity that has an oblique yet powerful bearing on the elegiac dimension of the Image. The translation of "corpse language" into the radiant figure of the Image may be understood as a form of "cross-dressing." According to Abraham and Torok, the "silent word" that inhabits a crypt is "love disguised and dressed up in a painting" (*Wolf Man* 83). The cryptic place of the Image preserves and conceals a transvestite word: not merely a corpse made up to look as though it were alive, but a female word disguised as a male Image.[72] The "gender bending" required of the male poet to grieve or to find pleasure in the body (acts that lead him to the hidden ground of the Image) is an effect of gendering word and Image. The male poet becomes a woman to counteract the "perversity" of Imagism, to restore the Image to its "original" gender.

We can track the anomalies of Pound's sexual identity from his private life to his poetry and literary activities, a sphere that yields a more substantial portrait of the transvestite or transsexual poet. At the height of his involvement in the Imagist movement, for example, Pound organized half of a new magazine titled *The Cerebralist,* of which only a single issue appeared, in December 1913. The magazine was a forum for the Cerebralist movement, founded by E. C. Grey, whose book *The Mysticism of Sex and Happiness* (1914) provided the "philosophical" basis for the movement. The magazine contained an article by Grey describing the "uni-sex" philosophy of Cerebralism and its central figure, the "modern Womb-Man." The issue also contained an article on the "Imagistes" by "R.S." (perhaps Richard Aldington) and a piece called "Ikon" by Pound.

---

71. This is not to say that the biographical possibilities are entirely without substance. In *End to Torment,* H.D. mentions rumors surrounding the Wabash incident, and marvels at Pound's allusion to bisexuality as early as 1908 (pp. 14–15).

72. On the relation of fetishism and transvestitism, see Victor N. Smirnoff, "The Fetishistic Transaction," in Serge Lebovici and Daniel Widlöcher, eds., *Psychoanalysis in France* (New York: International Universities Press, 1980), pp. 309–310.

IKON

It is in art the highest business to create the beautiful image; to create order and profusion of images that we may furnish the life of our minds with a noble surrounding.

And if—as some say, the soul survives the body; if our consciousness is not an intermittent melody of strings that relapse between whiles into silence, then more than ever should we put forth images of beauty, that going out into tenantless spaces we have with us all that is needful—an abundance of sounds and patterns to entertain us in that long dreaming; to strew our path to Valhalla; to give rich gifts by the way.

To find Pound making such a statement in December 1913 is truly astonishing. At a time when he is vigorously promoting the formalist conception of the Image (and condemning the notion of the Image as ornamentation), he is here situating the "beautiful image" in the realm of the dead, and describing it in terms of "entertainment" and "gifts" strewn along the path to the underworld (for whom? the monsters along the way?). More significant for our purposes, the notion of the Image as an accoutrement of the dead arises in the context of a magazine devoted to subverting traditional assumptions about gender and sexuality. Hence, the "hyper-aesthetic" of the beautiful Image is linked not only to the realm of the dead but to a disordering of gender.

It is clear from Pound's early poetry that female figures play a crucial if mysterious role in the process of sublimation that I have linked to the formation of the Image. In the poem "The Alchemist," for example, Pound induces the magical transubstantiation of base metal into gold by chanting a long list of women's names (*CEP* 225–229). In the introduction to his translations of Cavalcanti, he explains, "The equations of alchemy were apt to be written as women's names and the women so named endowed with the magical powers of the compounds" (*T* 18). This link suggests that the sublimation of corpse language into imagery is precipitated by a transformation of gender in the male poet, who must invoke the unutterable feminine name (as in the case of Gaudier-Brzeska) in order to practice the alchemy of Imagism. The male poet is thus possessed by the magical powers of the feminine name, as if by a spirit or demon.

We know from Pound's poetry and from his library that he was interested in the subject of demonology, and especially in the sexual figures of the incubus and succubus (evil spirits believed to descend upon and have sexual intercourse with sleeping bodies). In a footnote to the "Note Precedent to 'La Fraisne'" (1908), he refers to a work titled *De Daemonialitate, et Incubus et Succubus* (translated in 1879 as *Demonality; or Incubi and Succubi*), by the seventeenth-century theologian Lodovico Sinistrari. (This same footnote also contains a reference to the Egyptian Book of the Dead.) Later, in 1913, when Pound is living with Yeats at Stone Cottage, he writes home to his father in Philadelphia, asking for his copy of the book. A letter of January 22, 1914, from Dorothy to Ezra indicates that she, too, is reading the book—on his recommendation, one would assume (*P/S* 305).

This resurgence of Pound's interest in demonology during the period of the Imagist movement has its origins in the preoccupation with death that haunts his early poetry. Entering the realm of the dead (the realm of Images) often coincides with a change of gender. In the poem "Shalott," for example, the ghost of Tennyson's melancholy Lady of Shalott becomes the "Lord of Shalott," a spectral figure of the poet who roams with the wind over the earth (*CEP* 252). Other poems, some of which actually take place in a crypt, present a more complex disordering of gender and sexuality. In these crypt poems, the phantom is often engaged in some kind of sexual liaison, though its gender is usually not revealed, making it impossible to determine whether the relation is heterosexual or homosexual. In the poem "I Wait," for example, the speaker declares,

> As some pale-lidded ghost that calls
> I wait secure until that other goes . . .
> I wait secure and waiting know I not
> A bite of anger at thy littleness, nor even envy
> Of that other one that bindeth thee
> Within the close-hewn shroud of womanhood. (*CEP* 251)

Not until the "other" departs, freeing the beloved from the "shroud" of the body, can the "soul" find the satisfaction it desires. Who or what is the "other"? The phantom's pleasure awaits the departure either of its own material body or of a rival lover who is still alive.

Hence, the speaker, who is already dead, awaits the death of the beloved, an event that would allow their souls to mingle and "beget mighty fantasies"; or, alternately, the departure of the rival lover, which would permit the *incubus* to "descend" upon her sleeping lover.

The most accomplished of Pound's crypt poems is "The Tomb at Akr Çaar," which recalls the poem "Middle-Aged" (as well as "Dance Figure") in its Egyptian setting, frank eroticism, and nostalgic tone.[73] The speaker of the poem is the soul of Nikoptis, whose mummified body has occupied the tomb for some five thousand years:

> I am thy soul, Nikoptis, I have watched
> These five millennia, and thy dead eyes
> Moved not, nor ever answer my desire . . .
> See, the light grass sprang up to pillow thee,
> And kissed thee with a myriad grassy tongues;
> But not thou me. (*CEP* 183)

The soul addresses its reminiscences, its longings, its complaints, to the dead body. It claims never to have received an "answer" to its desire, yet it also declares, "I have been intimate with thee, known thy ways." The soul takes its pleasure on the insensate body:

> And three souls came upon Thee—
> And I came.
> And I flowed in upon thee, beat them off;
> I have been intimate with thee, known thy ways.
> Have I not touched thy palms and finger-tips,
> Flowed in, and through thee and about thy heels? (*CEP* 183–184)

Although there is no clear indication as to the gender of the soul, the tone of the poem and its treatment of sexual passion have a distinctly Sapphic quality. The trope of "light grass" may be an allusion to fragment 2 of Sappho:

> trembling shakes my body
> and I turn paler than

---

73. One is surprised to discover a lengthy passage from "Akr Çaar" cited by a Washington reporter in 1945 as a description (or prefiguration) of Pound's imprisonment on charges of treason. This reference to the most prominent example of Pound's crypt poetry occurs in Austine Cassini's column, "These Charming People," in the *Times-Herald* (Washington, D.C.), 11 December 1945.

> dry grass. At such time
> death isn't far from me.[74]

As in the case of "I Wait," the soul is preoccupied with the experience of waiting, the muted pain of loss or separation, and deferred longing. Indeed, the tomb, a place of utter darkness, is radiant with desire:

> And no sun comes to rest me in this place,
> And I am torn against the jagged dark,
> And no new light beats upon me, and you say
> No word, day after day. (*CEP* 184)

The voice is plaintive, inconsolable, yet lucid in its powers of observation. By assuming the place of the feminine, the poet discovers the emotional resonance of human loss: something was there and is now no longer there. Something has disappeared.

Yet the one who mourns also knows the pleasures of the body at the limits of materiality. The soul deprived of its body becomes a sexual outlaw, a succubus preying on a corpse. The soul discovers the power residing in the margins of the body: a living body becomes a corpse, and the entire body crowds into the margins of the body. As a corpse, the body exists only marginally, thus attaining its most powerful and affective condition. Grieving at the death of pleasure and consumed by the unspeakable pleasures of the body, the poet also discovers the place of the Image. For the Image, too, signifies loss and death: something was there and is no longer there. Something has disappeared. Yet the Image, by virtue of its materiality, is what "remains"; it is the refuge of pleasure, of the body: "What hope do I have of attaining the thing I push away? My hope lies in the materiality of language, in the fact that words are things, too" (Blanchot, *Orpheus* 46).

Deprivation and a keen sense of the impassioned materiality of existence are united in the Sapphic voice that echoes in "The Tomb at Akr Çaar." This voice is the matrix of what many readers and critics regard as Pound's most affecting poetry. The plaintive voice of "The River Merchant's Wife," for example, has its origins in the neutered voice of the crypt. The humility and tenderness that many critics

---

74. Mary Barnard, *Sappho* (Berkeley: University of California Press, 1958), p. 29.

admire in the Pisan Cantos derive, I would argue, from a poetry absorbed in loss and redeemed by materiality. Yet the mutation of gender that often occurs in crypt poetry is shadowed by a more sinister erotic transformation: a human takes the form of an animal. Indeed, the metamorphosis of human into beast may be the ultimate reference of any form of sexual mutation, as well as a terrifying metaphor for representation itself. The Image, as such, would therefore be the alluring monster produced by tampering with gender. In the poem "Yeux Glauques," for example, the "vacant gaze" of the beggar maid stares from a "half-ruined face" that becomes "that faun's head of hers" (*P* 192). The title of the poem suggests that the eyes of the dead girl are those of an owl (from the Greek word *glaux*, meaning owl).

The themes of necrophilia and bestial transformation also converge in striking fashion in the poem "Piere Vidal Old," which reworks the legend of a troubadour who turns into a wolf. The poet's lust for blood in battle is compared to the wolf's savage instincts, which are linked in turn to sexual passion. The crucial turn in the poem occurs when the poet is conquered by love and returns to human form:

> Hot is such love and silent,
> Silent as fate is, and as strong until
> It faints in taking and in giving all.
> Stark, keen, triumphant, till it plays at death.
> God! she was white then, splendid as some tomb
> High wrought of marble, and the panting breath
> Ceased utterly. Well, then I waited, drew,
> Half-sheathed, then naked from its saffron sheath
> Drew full this dagger that doth tremble here.
> Just then she woke and mocked the less keen blade.
> Ah God, the Loba! and my only mate!
> Was there such flesh made ever and unmade. (*CEP* 110–111)

In this extraordinary passage, the poet's reversion from wolf to human form, a reversion precipitated by love, coincides with his lover's apparent passage from life into death. Hence, bestial transformation is linked to the inscrutable difference between life and death. The curious thing is that the depravity of the poet's necrophilia surfaces only after he has reverted to human form, as if the human mind were the soil of bestial desires. Yet the blood lust of the wolf in battle is viewed as being entirely "natural." The decisive moment comes as the poet prepares to lower himself into the "white tomb" of his lover's dead body: she suddenly returns to life and mocks his state of arousal. Just as the difference between life and death is always unstable for Pound, so the erogenous fantasy of moving between human and bestial forms is fraught with danger.

There is yet another "wolf man" in Pound's life, one who occupies the cryptic place of the Image: Gaudier-Brzeska is "like a well-made young wolf or some soft-moving, bright-eyed wild thing" (*GB* 44). Indeed, in a "Praefatio" that appeared only in the first edition of the memoir, Pound suggests that the incidents and individuals described in his memoir somehow fulfill the mythical topos of "lycanthropy." In a brief discussion of the consequences for Germany of its belligerent actions in the Great War, Pound observes, "Lycanthropy in the individual is, in the nation, a clinging to atavistic ideals. The nation which breaks the peace of the unity of nations is on a par with the individual who breaks peace within the nation. There is no reason why the offending nation should not be treated as *caput lupinum*" (as a wolf-like individual).[75] The young wolf of Pound's fantasies can often be found at the threshold of the Image-crypt: Pound cherished, for example, the drawing (of a wolf) Gaudier made for "The Tomb at Akr Çaar" (*GB* 45). In "Villanelle: The Psychological Hour," Pound assumes the female voice of the crypt to mourn Gaudier's absence and to announce, even as he disguises, his illicit desire (*P* 158–159; *SC* 216). Yet werewolves eat children and are said to indulge in cannibalism.[76] Cryptonymy is a "fantasy of incorporation." Freud's Wolf Man is altered by devouring others. Lycanthropy is thus the silent name of an encrypted desire that produces the monstrosity of the Image. Consumed by the work of mourning, Pound devours the corpse of Gaudier and is transformed into a wolf; yet he, in turn, is

---

75. Pound, *Gaudier-Brzeska* (London: John Lane, 1916), p. 1. For later editions of the memoir, Pound made a number of changes in the text, as well as deleting the "Praefatio."

76. Caroline Oates, "Metamorphosis and Lycanthropy in Franche-Comté, 1521–1643," *Zone: Fragments for a History of the Human Body,* Part 1 (1989): 307, 322.

devoured by the wolf man at the threshold of the crypt (a disappearance that summons the Image and Pound's most affecting poetry). Should we then ask, with H.D., "Was it love of the incomparable 'Lady Loba' that lured him to Radio Rome and that, in the end, was his undoing?" (*End to Torment* 27). To what degree does the lycanthropy of the avant-garde become, for Pound, the "lycanthropy" of fascist Italy, as well as a figure for his postwar "madness"?[77]

77. In the late 1950s, following more than a decade of incarceration at St. Elizabeths, Pound published a translation of a poem that finds the Wolf Man in asylum:

> Werewolf in selvage I saw
> In day's dawn changing his shape,
> Amid leaves he lay,
> and in his face, sleeping, such pain
> I fled agape.

The poem, by Jaime de Angulo, appears in Ezra Pound, *Pavannes and Divagations* (London: Peter Owen, 1960), pp. 242–243.

CHAPTER 4

Anathemata

The Sad Wit of Pollution

> The world decomposes into facts.
> —Ludwig Wittgenstein, *Tractatus Logico-Philosophicus*

Imagism, we are often told, marks the origin of Anglo-American poetic modernism. Yet the so-called modernist Image functions more precisely as a *medium* between symbolic economies (Victorian and modern) that were identified by the modernists, for strategic purposes, as incommensurable. Through the figure of the Image, a substantial body of Decadent theory and practice is *translated* into an incipient formation of the avant-garde. As such, Imagism represents a moment of conversion (in effect, a conversion experience) that is peculiar to the origins of modernism in a variety of media. From the standpoint of a *critique* of modernism, however, this conversion portends the recovery of Decadence as an essential aspect of modernity.

In Pound's case, as we have seen, this translation via the Image (from Decadence to avant-garde, and vice versa) is permeated by the rhetoric and economy of death. One of the most prominent features of Pound's necrophilia, and of his repudiation of death, is a concern with materiality, both in terms of contamination and physical evidence. The corpse becomes an object of revulsion, even as it embodies the poet's most exalted desires. As an emblem of material objectivity, the cadaverous Image is always in danger of reverting to a state of ethical and aesthetic pollution. The danger of contamination therefore haunts the exalted principles of literary positivism (with its emphasis on empirical evidence). In this regard, the ambiguous character of materiality reflects "death's double position as anomalous, marginal, repressed, and at the same time masterful, central, everywhere manifest."[1] In its most extreme aspect (which I will discuss in Chapter 6), the Image deriving from material contamination becomes associated with radioactivity, a form of waste that constitutes an invisible order of fatality, as well as a medium of invisible images and images of the unseen. With its telegraphic properties and a half-life that exceeds historical time, the radioactive Image is at once immortal and lethal in its effects, an emblem of death and unending life.

We can make Pound's conception of the Image reveal its backwardness, its inscrutable desire, its apology for filth, if we examine more closely what it endeavors to exclude. Between 1911 and 1912, Pound's taste in poetry underwent a dramatic reversal. He disavowed most of his own early poetry, as well as poets such as Swinburne, Ernest Dowson, and Lionel Johnson, whose work had partly inspired it. According to these revisions, Pound claimed that Victorian poetry was plagued by imitative, or mimetic, values and by what he called "rhetoric." In an effort to correct these distortions associated with the materiality of language, Pound proposed the Image as an emblem of representational authority and exactitude, endowing it with certain redemptive powers. In more ominous terms—which Pound was not afraid to use—the Image appears as a "totalitarian" structure, capable of restoring to language and poetry a lost order of signification. Richard Sieburth explains that the Image in this regard represents "a fundamental attempt to get his poetry off the gold standard, to defetishize the signifier."[2] The problem of this strategy, of course, is that the verbal Image has been viewed historically, and is also viewed by Pound, as a refuge of sensuality and materiality (in part because of its

1. Elisabeth Bronfen and Sarah Webster Goodwin, "Introduction," in Bronfen and Goodwin, eds., *Death and Representation* (Baltimore: Johns Hopkins University Press, 1993), p. 19.
2. Richard Sieburth, "In Pound We Trust: The Economy of Poetry / The Poetry of Economics," *Critical Inquiry* 14, no. 1 (Autumn 1987): 146.

association with the graphic arts) but also, more prominently, as the privileged medium of modern literary empiricism.[3] The materiality of the Image guarantees its "objectivity." Thus, Pound turns to a "modern" version of the fetish—the Image—in order to counteract the fetishized language of Decadence. The perversity of this strategy is fundamental to those hidden dimensions of the Image that are the object of this study. We encounter the "crypt effect" of the Image whenever this kind of "homeopathic" logic dominates Pound's literary or cultural conceptions.

The link between the materiality of late Victorian poetry (its "Decadent" properties) and the empiricism of the modernist Image suggests a hidden continuity between the archaic values of Pound's earliest poetry and the "modernity" of the Image. Of course, he is obliged to suppress any evidence that such a continuum exists, and it is precisely this continuum that is submerged in the lost "Doctrine of the Image." When the turn in Pound's career occurs around 1912, he begins to attack poets in whose work language or poetry "goes rotten, i.e., becomes slushy and inexact, or excessive and bloated" (*LE* 21). Armed with this scatological rhetoric, Pound launches his vision of modern poetry. Imagism emerges out of this contempt for certain dimensions of language, yet the Image, a verbal artifact, necessarily emerges from the abomination of language—an icon recovered from the putrid, excessive body of Victorian poetry.

The materialist poetics of the Image should therefore be understood as an allegory of sublimation: the magical conversion of base matter into gold, excrement into imagery. By elevating the Image, Pound fashions an idol out of the contemptible material of language. Freud's

---

3. The long tradition of viewing the image as a material simulacrum can be traced back as far as the Judeo-Hellenic roots of Western culture. The material image usually functions in a hierarchy that elevates the abstract over the sensory, or vice versa. The god of the Old Testament, for example, inaugurates the long tradition of Western iconoclasm by forbidding the production of graven images. Likewise, Plato divides objects of perception into images that are intelligible only to the mind's eye and images that can be perceived by the external eye. On the history of the distinction between images of the mind and material images, see W. J. T. Mitchell, *Iconology: Image, Text, Ideology* (Chicago: University of Chicago Press, 1986), pp. 5–52. Also, for an account of the difference between Hebraic and Hellenic attitudes toward imagery, see Françoise Meltzer, *Salomé and the Dance of Writing* (Chicago: University of Chicago Press, 1987), pp. 73–111.

theories of sublimation and anality teach us that through a process of negation and idealization what is lowest becomes highest. Yet the ideal retains, in an altered state, all of the despicable qualities of its origins. Pound's Image is essentially *anathematic:* its exalted character, which looks forward to the ethical dimension of the "ideogrammic method," derives from its capacity to shock and repel. The forbidden tongue of Swinburne is permitted to speak only through the perversely ideal form of the Image.

The regime of negativity that I have associated with the Image (which is the foundation of its "objectivity") appears most forcefully in Pound's efforts to circumscribe a realm of material contamination that is usually associated with the body. Thus, the material objectivity of the Image is founded on a mortification of the body. This negation, however, is dialectical; it always produces, as I have argued, a material and political afterlife. Julia Kristeva writes, "The abject is edged with the sublime," a comment indicating the relevance of Freud's theory of sublimation to the necrophilic dimension of the Image and to its particular rendering of the negative.[4] Freud's theory of sublimation subscribes to a logic of dialectical negation: "The subject matter of a repressed image or thought can make its way into consciousness on the condition that it is *denied*. Negation is a way of taking account of what is repressed; indeed, it is actually a removal of repression, though not, of course, an acceptance of what is repressed."[5] Hence, sublimation, which views continuity as an effect of exclusion, helps account for the persistence of necrophilia in the poetics of the Image.

"Sublimations," according to Norman O. Brown, "are negations of the body which simultaneously affirm it."[6] Moreover, Pound's dialectical negations of materiality, which inaugurate the poetics of Imagism, evince the representational economy of death: "Every representation of death necessarily represses what it purports to reveal. It

---

4. Julia Kristeva, *The Powers of Horror: An Essay on Abjection,* trans. Leon S. Roudiez (New York: Columbia University Press, 1982), p. 11.

5. Sigmund Freud, "Negation," *Collected Papers,* ed. James Strachey (New York: Basic Books, 1959), vol. 5, p. 182.

6. Norman O. Brown, *Life against Death* (New York: Random House, 1969), p. 297.

also necessarily serves other purposes that may or may not be overtly acknowledged . . . Representations of death, with their structural dialectic of revealing and concealing and their inevitable configurations of power and powerlessness, are rich texts for studying the ways art answers threats to its own powers of representation."[7] We could therefore argue that the concept of sublimation shares with the rhetoric of Imagism an emphasis on the body as a site of ideological struggle. The repression of materiality in the name of the Image is always haunted by the army of cadavers produced by World War I (and, more intimately, by the dead bodies in Pound's early poetry).

In print, Pound's formulations of Imagism, or of the approach to Imagism, usually depend on a vigorous repudiation of Decadent corporeality: "For Milton and Victorianism and for the softness of the 'nineties' I have different degrees of antipathy or even contempt" (*LE* 362). In 1912 he explains:

> As to twentieth-century poetry, and the poetry which I expect to see written during the next decade or so, it will, I think, move against poppy-cock, it will be harder and saner . . . It will be as much like granite as it can be, its force will lie in its truth . . . I mean it will not try to seem forcible by rhetorical din, and luxurious riot. We will have fewer painted adjectives impeding the shock and stroke of it. At least for myself, I want it so, austere, direct, free from emotional slither. (*LE* 12)

Statements such as these do not, however, usually appear without a gesture of self-incrimination. In the same article, for example, Pound observes, "As for the nineteenth century, with all respect to its achievements, I think we shall look back upon it as a rather blurry, messy sort of period, a rather sentimentalistic, mannerish sort of period. I say this without any self-righteousness, with no sense of self-satisfaction" (*LE* 11). The equivocation and blurriness of this statement about a supposedly blurry period of literature is frankly ironic, and it ends on a note of humility for good reason: the first six volumes of Pound's own poetry provide many examples of the "blurry" poems that he must condemn as an Imagist.

---

7. Bronfen and Goodwin, *Death and Representation*, p. 19.

Pound's battle against a "riot" of luxury and decay in poetry often focuses on the term "rhetoric." He announces, for example, that "the 'image' is the furthest possible remove from rhetoric" (*GB* 83). Ironically, he borrowed the term "rhetoric," and much of the polemic in which it is embedded, from those writers he attacked in the name of the Image. Arthur Symons, for example, describes the spirit of Decadence as "a revolt against exteriority, against rhetoric, against a materialistic tradition."[8] Pound, having embodied in his own early poetry what he now calls the "rhetoric" of late Victorian poetry, identifies with the writers of Decadence even as he attacks them. His revolt against materialism eventually comes to focus on what he calls "the power of putrefaction," which poses a threat to the Image and is therefore to be associated with those whom he calls "The Iconoclasts": "The power of putrefaction aims at the obfuscation of history . . . The power of putrefaction would destroy all intrinsic beauty. Whether this power is borne by certain carriers, or by certain others, remains to be determined. It is spread like the bacilli of typhus or bubonic plague, carried by rats wholly unconscious of their role. Suspect anyone who destroys an image, or wants to suppress a page of history" (*SP* 317). Though Pound seeks to prevent the decomposition of images, he seems to be entirely unaware of the possibility that his own conception of the Image may be one of the unknown "carriers" of the "power of putrefaction"—that the Image is itself an eroticized corpse, an emblem of radical materiality.

The "power of putrefaction" is not restricted to the uncanny effects of "corpse language" or the power of the dead. Indeed, it refers to the dangers inherent in many forms of pollution and filth. In the name of the Image, Pound attacks "the dung-minded, dung-beared, penny a line, please the mediocre-at-all-cost doctrine" (*P/J* 66). He deplores "the washy rhetoricians, this back flush of dead symbolism, dead celticism, etc." (*PD* 63), and condemns "the futurist diarrhea, rhetorical slush" (*L* 78). He declares that "vomit, carefully labelled 'Beauty,' is still in the literary market" (*PD* 74), and rages against "the *London Mercury* or the *Athenaeum* or a dozen and one of these other mortuaries for the entombment of dead fecal mentality" (*L* 154). The

---

8. Arthur Symons, *The Symbolist Movement in Literature* (New York: Haskell, 1971; orig. pub. 1899), pp. 8–9.

Anathemata

Imagist poet condemns Victorianism as "a bog, a marasmus, a great putridity in place of a sane and active ebullience" (*LE* 21).

Pound's obsession with various kinds of filth (including the corpse) is a response to what Mary Douglas calls "pollution dangers."[9] Building upon "the old definition of dirt as matter out of place" (*Purity and Danger* 35), Douglas argues that "reflection on dirt involves reflection on the relation of order to disorder, being to non-being, life to death" (5). "Dirt," she concludes, "is essentially disorder" (2). Dirt offends against order, and makes correct definition or discrimination impossible. "Pollution behavior," Douglas explains, "is the reaction that condemns any object or idea likely to confuse or contradict cherished classifications" (36). Dirt, one might say, is the residue of ambiguity. Given Pound's abhorrence of ambiguity and his equation of "intrinsic beauty" with order (embodied in the figure of the Image), we should not be surprised that the rhetoric of the Image resembles, at times, a pollution ritual. Pound's efforts to rid poetry of various kinds of filth are deeply concerned with questions of form and the restoration or discovery of new forms in art. Douglas confirms this link between pollution and form: "Pollution arises from the interplay of form and surrounding formlessness. Pollution dangers strike when form has been attacked" (104).

"The quest for purity," Douglas writes, "is pursued by rejection" (161). The idea of a subject that constitutes itself through exclusion and repression is also, as I indicated in Chapter 1, the basis of Julia Kristeva's theory of "abjection." Acknowledging her debt to Douglas and to Bataille's concept of heterogeneity, Kristeva contends that the abject is founded on "the logic of prohibition".[10] The abject is what every system excludes, a residue of otherness that remains, nonethe-

---

9. Mary Douglas, *Purity and Danger: An Analysis of Concepts of Pollution and Taboo* (London: Ark, 1966), p. 104.

10. Kristeva, *The Powers of Horror*, p. 64. Georges Bataille's work on the cultural dimensions of ritual pollution is an important precursor to that of Douglas and Kristeva. I have chosen, however, not to pursue Bataille's theories in detail, because of their emphasis on sacrifice, laughter, sexuality, and other forms of ecstatic release. These topics, it seems to me, are not directly relevant to Pound's own excremental economy. Bataille's concept of heterogeneity, however, remains central to my understanding of the image in Pound's poetics. Georges Bataille, *Visions of Excess: Selected Writings, 1927–1939*, trans. Allan Stoekl (Minneapolis: University of Minnesota Press, 1985).

less, intrinsic to the system. In this regard, Pound's conception of the Image may be described as a formation of the abject. The Image is constituted by what it excludes—by "corpse language" and by other forms of pollution that are intrinsic to its nature. Pound fashions the Image as he spews out abominations over the corpse of his own language. The expulsion of impurities is lined with the "glamor" of the Image, as Kristeva explains: "The purification rite appears then as that essential ridge, which, prohibiting the filthy object, extracts it from the secular order and lines it at once with a sacred facet" (*Powers of Horror* 65).

Considering Pound's violent repudiation of cultural and poetic decay, one would not expect him to insist on an intimate relation between beauty and filth. Yet this is precisely what he does. "Kulchur," he contends, "occurs in or above the stinking manure heap, and cannot be honestly defined without recognition of the dungheap" (*L* 294). Furthermore, "Disgust with the sordid is but another expression of a sensitiveness to the finer thing. There is no perception of beauty without a corresponding disgust" (*LE* 415). These passages articulate a thesis similar to Douglas' understanding of pollution and Kristeva's theory of abjection: beauty and order depend on filth, on the scorned presence of the other. A dialectical relation exists between what Pound calls the "cult of beauty" (embodied by the Image) and the "cult of ugliness" (enthralled by death and excess).[11] "The cult of beauty and the delineation of ugliness are not in mutual opposition" (*LE* 45). The "power of putrefaction" engenders the fetishistic appeal of the Image; the abject is lined with sublimity.

On several occasions, Pound takes the relation between beauty and filth a step further: he implies that the seed of beauty or creativity is embedded in the rotting corpse of materiality. The last of the Hell Cantos, for example, depicts a scene in the Palux Laerna, the swamp where Hercules confronted the Hydra:

11. Mary Douglas draws upon the topos of the image to illustrate the relation between sacred beauty and filth: "In painting such dark themes, pollution symbols are as necessary as the use of black in any depiction whatsoever. Therefore we find corruption enshrined in sacred places and times" (*Purity and Danger*, p. 179). In this passage, pollution is compared to the black color of delineation, without which (she argues) no image is possible. All representation, or any system, thus depends upon some form of contamination for its legibility or meaningfulness.

> Palux Laerna,
> the lake of bodies, aqua morta,
> of limbs fluid, and mingled, like fish heaped in a bin
> and here an arm upward, clutching a fragment of marble.
> And the embryos, in flux,
> new inflow, submerging,
> Here an arm upward, trout, submerged by eels;
> and from the bank, the stiff herbage
> and the dry nobbled path, many known, and unknown,
> for an instant;
> submerging,
> The face gone, generation. (C 16: 69)

The scene depicts a watery death, a place where life is submerged, disappearing. The swamp is a "lake of bodies," either dead or dying, their limbs mingled with one another and with the dead water ("aqua morta"). In short, the scene is one of horrifying decay, viewed from the safety of a "dry path" (which recalls the scene at the end of the same canto, where the poet escapes from the bog with the help of Medusa). There are certain details, however, that do not agree with the prevailing atmosphere of death and decay—the arms thrust out of the mire, for example, one of which is "clutching a fragment of marble." This defiant gesture, which suggests a remnant of classical tradition, is surely nostalgic, if not hopeful. And there are also "the embryos, in flux," floating in the awful lake. The final two lines suggest that these embryos will survive: "submerging, / The face gone, generation." The disappearance of life is therefore the occasion for "generation," for new life. The "lake of bodies," which resembles a giant corpse teeming with vermin, is also the source of new bodies, new forms.

Mary Douglas, in her study of pollution symbols, discovers a similar logic: "Granted that disorder spoils pattern, it also provides the materials of pattern" (94). This insight leads her to question the "problem" of sublimation: "We must therefore ask how dirt, which is normally destructive, sometimes becomes creative" (*Purity and Danger* 159). This question also confronts the most perverse features of Pound's conception of the Image. The erotic infatuation with the dead in Pound's early poetry is replaced by his fetishistic regard for the Image. The swamp of "rhetoric" becomes the Image suffused with light and the sun's genius. The revolting materiality of "corpse language" survives in the elegant and articulate brush strokes of the ideogram. "Dead fecal mentality" informs the arcane Image associated with science and mathematics.

One discovers in Pound's "Metro" poem (the most famous of all Imagist poems) a striking illustration of the principle of sublimation informing the Image. In his "Vorticism" essay, published in the *Fortnightly Review* in September 1914, Pound offers his readers a detailed account of the origins and compositional history of the "Metro" poem, as an exposition of Imagism in practice. He dates the genesis of the poem to a moment three years prior to the writing of the "Vorticism" essay, which would be 1911—the same year he wrote "Silet," the opening poem of *Ripostes*. Following what Pound calls "the impasse in which I had been left by my metro emotion" (*GB* 89), he writes a series of drafts of the poem, each more condensed than the previous one. By eliminating what he calls material of "second intensity," Pound shrinks the poem from thirty lines to a single sentence. Clearly this process, whose principles Pound formulates during the "impasse" between 1911 and 1913, represents the essential negativity of the Image—that is, the regime of elimination and prohibition that I have described as fundamental to the "objectivity" of Imagist poetics.

The sublime aspect of the Image derives from its irrepressible "substance"; indeed, the negative practice of Imagism serves not to eliminate but to *preserve* the "life" of the crypt: its elegiac feeling, its eroticism, its fatality. The remains of language—the Image—render the volatile materiality of the crypt; the ascetic mode of the Image draws attention to the body by making it disappear. Though Pound presents the "Metro" poem as a paradigm of modernist practice, its reference to an apparitional event in an underground "station" quite obviously links it, as I indicated in the previous chapter, to the Decadent properties of Pound's crypt poetry. Indeed, the archaic dimension of the "Metro" poem is more pronounced than Pound suggests. He dates the origin of the poem to 1911, without indicating any possible precedent in his earlier published poetry. K. K. Ruthven has demonstrated, however, that the specific "image" of the "Metro" poem derives from a very early poem of Pound's, "Laudantes Decem

Pulchritudinis Johannae Templi," published in *Exultations* (1909).[12] One section of the poem, addressed to "my beloved of the peach trees," describes "the vision of the blossom":

> the perfect faces which I see at times
> When my eyes are closed—
> Faces fragile, pale, yet flushed a little,
> > like petals of roses:
> these things have confused my memories of her. (*CEP* 119)

The essential features of this "vision" survive intact in the "Metro" poem:

> The apparition of these faces in the crowd:
> > Petals, on a wet, black bough. (*GB* 89)

It is essential to emphasize that the original "vision" occurs with *eyes closed,* and that the visuality of the Imagist poem must therefore be described as highly ambiguous, if not dependent on a kind of blindness.

By 1913 (if not from the outset) the "vision of the blossom" becomes associated in Pound's mind with Japanese poetry (haiku). Indeed, the "vision of the blossom" continues to circulate in his work in a manner that eventually discloses its specifically archaic, or nostalgic, dimension. An early manuscript of Canto 4, composed in 1918, contains the following lines: "the thousand-year peach trees shed their flakes / into the stream, out of a former time."[13] These lines suggest that the apparitional petals of the "Metro" poem should be viewed as drifting "out of a former time," as ghosts. The "peach trees in magical blossom" appear in yet another context, in Pound's essay on Rémy de Gourmont, published in March 1919: "I do not think it possible to overemphasize Gourmont's sense of beauty ... His *pays natal* was near to the peach-blossom fountain of the untranslatable poem" (*L* 343). The "vision of the blossom," which we now understand to be an apparition of the dead, is described here by Pound as "an untranslatable poem." Indeed, we could argue that the "*pays natal*"

---

12. K. K. Ruthven, *A Guide to Pound's "Personae" (1926)* (Berkeley: University of California Press, 1969), p. 153.
13. Cited in Christine Froula, *To Write Paradise: Style and Error in Pound's Cantos* (New Haven: Yale University Press, 1984), p. 40.

of the modernist Image is an "untranslatable poem"—a poem encrypted in the Image, a vision preserved and concealed by the negative praxis of Imagism. Yet the phantasmic "substance" of the "Metro" poem differs not at all from its antecedent, its forgotten ancestry, in *Exultations*. Thus, the "Metro" poem emerges as the nucleus of a constellation of apparitional poems spanning the entire Imagist period, from 1909 to 1919.

If we search for other traces of the "untranslatable poem," or at least intimations of the sublime logic of the Image, we discover in several of Pound's early poems an interest in alchemy and the idea of the transmutation of metals, an archaic figure for the process of sublimation. "The Alchemist," for example, is a chant sung to Persephone, linking the themes of sublimation and death (*CEP* 227). More revealing is the poem "Capilupus Sends Greeting to Grotus," in which the poet uses the figure of alchemy to illustrate his own conception of poetry:

> The test tubes of your alchemy give me the figure
> For some fluid that you call a certain long equation,
> Plus some new substance,
> Is no longer the same fluid but a new,
> Though all the elements thereof
> Be known unto thy father's father in thine art.
> Yet as ever by some new combination of old elements
> Ye do seek the gold, so seek I perfection. (*CEP* 268)

Understood as a form of alchemy, poetry is essentially a process of experimenting with various "fluids" in order to produce a precious commodity. The gold of alchemy or poetry is produced not by introducing a new element but "by some new combination of old elements." The basic materials of the alchemical "equation" are "known unto thy father's father"—that is, they are familiar to the dead and, as possessions of the dead, can be understood as embodiments of the dead. The crucial feature of this equation is that no new material is required to produce the precious substance. The essence of gold is latent in the base materials from which it is composed—as in the case of the "Metro" poem. Something new is derived from something old, and fluids harden into gold, yet there is no *substantive* difference between the dead base and the living essence. The sublime logic of alchemy also governs, as we have seen, the transformation of "corpse language" into the luminous Image. Pound's naïve appropriation of the figure of alchemy masks the dialectical forces that would found his poetry on the violence of abjection.

The essential alchemy of Pound's poetry takes place in a crypt, a vessel in which dead words are "translated" into vital Images. The "rhetoric" and materiality of language (including its mimetic powers) are sealed in a tomb, only to return under the guise of the Image. The unspeakable pleasures of "corpse language" are accessible to Pound only through the materiality of a modern fetish, the Image. By murdering the language of his youth (which is also the language of the dead, his literary forebears), he unwittingly devours it in a manner that fails to preserve the dead as living. This crisis signals a refusal to mourn, or an aberration of mourning, that eventually produces the bulky citations of the *Cantos*. The dead are indeed lodged within his work, but *as dead,* as other. Consequently, "the place that shuns symbolization and is the site of the death of pleasure, knows the word that says pleasure."[14] This cryptic place harbors a word that has become a thing, an "exquisite corpse" that is ravaged and yet somehow untouched by the ancient rivalry of word and image.

Plastic Surgery

I have argued that the figure of the Image displaces the corpse in Pound's poetics and becomes, through a process of sublimation, a legitimate object for his illicit infatuation with the dead body. The rhetoric of the Image is thus best understood as a rite of purification intended to rid poetry, and ultimately society, of various kinds of pollution. The inscrutable relation between the Image and the body is not limited, however, to necrophilia and the repudiation of bodily filth. The negative character of these obsessions is dialectical and therefore affirmative of a larger concern with the status of the *living* body. The erotic appeal of a corpse and the sensual pleasure historically associated with imagery of all kinds mask a deeper concern with hedonism

14. Nicolas Abraham and Maria Torok, *The Wolf Man's Magic Word: A Cryptonymy,* trans. Nicholas Rand (Minneapolis: University of Minnesota Press, 1986), p. 81.

and sexual pleasure in Pound's work. Similarly, his preoccupation with decay and contamination in poetry and politics (or economics) shows a concern with the body proper (a clean body, a body I call my own), as distinguished from what is foreign or extrinsic to it.

In her analysis of the concept of pollution, Mary Douglas observes, "The focus of all pollution symbolism is the body; the final problem to which the perspective leads is bodily disintegration" (*Purity and Danger* 173). The pollution dangers that threaten any structure, be it social, religious, or aesthetic, are conceived therefore in corporeal terms: "The body is a model which can stand for any bounded system. Its boundaries can represent any boundaries which are threatened or precarious" (115). The danger of pollution arises when the conventional boundaries of a system or concept come under attack and become confused or ambiguous. Douglas writes, "Any structure of ideas is vulnerable at its margins. We should expect the orifices of the body to symbolize its specially vulnerable points . . . Spittle, blood, milk, urine, feces, or tears by simply issuing forth have traversed the boundary of the body . . . The mistake is to treat bodily margins in isolation from all other margins" (121). Hence, "all margins are dangerous" (121). Pollution control therefore depends on establishing a rigorous distinction between what is proper or intrinsic to the body and what is extrinsic to it. Anything dirty or menacing belongs outside. The difference between the inside and the outside is the basis of somatic identity, or the identity of any stable element. Hence, those activities that disturb the inside/outside distinction, such as eating, excretion, or sex, or any invasive act such as surgery, are potentially menacing and enormously powerful.

It is not a coincidence that the inside/outside distinction is called into question by the major theoretical discourses I have brought to bear on the rhetoric of the Image and Pound's necrophilia. Kristeva, for example, in her analysis of melancholy, combines a deconstructive emphasis on marginality with Mary Douglas's thesis that dirt is "matter out of place," to situate the violent uncertainty of abjection: "It is thus not lack of cleanliness or health that causes abjection but what disturbs identity, system, order. What does not respect borders, positions, rules. The in-between, the ambiguous, the composite" (*Powers of Horror* 4). Significantly, for our purposes, the abject shares its borderline existence with the "sublimating discourse" of aesthetics (7). In other words, poetry is borderline speech, tainted by having traversed the boundary of inside/outside.

Given the emphasis on marginality in the philosophy of deconstruction, we should not be surprised to find that Derrida's interest in Abraham and Torok's theory of cryptonymy focuses primarily on the *topography* of the crypt. Through an act of incorporation, a lost object (which may be a word) is encrypted within the subject. A secret vault is constructed within the subject to preserve and conceal the ineffable word that says "pleasure." A thing that belongs on the outside is brought within. Hence, according to Derrida, the crypt establishes "an inside heterogenous to the inside of the self."[15] And further, "One might go on indefinitely switching the place names around in this dizzying topology (the inside as the outside of the outside, or of the inside; the outside as the inside of the inside, or of the outside, etc.)" (xix). What fascinates Derrida about the crypt is that it violates, inexorably, the distinction between inside and outside. It is no longer possible to designate what is proper or intrinsic to the body.

Pollution behavior, abjection, cryptonymy—each of these conceptions is linked (by its reliance on the power of negation) to aesthetics and to ideas about poetry such as Imagism. The "accursed share" (as Bataille calls it) produces pleasure, though it is founded on a logic of prohibition, by swallowing the other, by contaminating itself and traversing its own boundaries. A similar contradiction arises when we compare the rhetoric of the Image to Pound's appropriation of the body and medical terminology. The rhetoric of the Image, as we have seen, stems from a logic of prohibition: it resembles a kind of pollution behavior; it is an expression of the abject; the language of Pound's youth is sealed in a crypt. Each of these formations, it must be stressed, is articulated through a metaphorics of the body, a body that exists only insofar as it observes the distinction between inside and outside. Yet when Pound "handles" the living body, it is always with the intention of transgressing this boundary, dissolving the difference between inside and outside, altering the body, or inventing it anew. Why must the body of the Image, which is a corpse in disguise, be protected

15. Jacques Derrida, "*Fors:* The Anglish Words of Nicolas Abraham and Maria Torok," trans. Barbara Johnson, *The Wolf Man's Magic Word*, p. xvi.

from every kind of filth, including dead flesh, which is the most sickening of all wastes? And why must the poetic Image, which is necessarily composed of words, never be "degraded to the status of a word"? Is it possible that Pound's attempt to distinguish rigorously between the inside and the outside of the Image is subverted by attempts to *violate* this distinction in his work?

That the rhetoric of the Image sublimates various parts and functions of the human body is discernible from its emphasis on materiality. Yet Pound makes the link between Image and body in far more explicit ways. For example, in the November 1918 issue of *Little Review,* Pound published a rough translation of Voltaire's anti-Semitic essay "Genesis." He does not identify Voltaire as the author, however, and thus encourages the reader to view the anonymous author as a medium for Pound's own opinions. In one section, the Pound-Voltaire figure states, "One cannot make images save of bodies. No nation imagined a bodiless god, and it is impossible to picture him as such" (*PD* 170). In all probability, Pound enjoyed this statement as an affront to Hebraic sanctions against imagery and, hence, as an expression of paganism and idolatry. Yet the indeterminacy of the phrase "make images of bodies" suggests that the link between image and body is something more than thematic. Indeed, the phrase admits the possibility of images *composed* of bodies, and words made of flesh.

Pound identifies the latter figure (the word made flesh) as expressing the qualities he admired most in the work of Rémy de Gourmont, who exerted a powerful influence on Pound's ideas about sexuality and the body. In an attempt to characterize the "sensual wisdom" of Gourmont's writing, Pound cites the following sentence from *Physique de l'Amour:* "My words are the unspoken words of my body" (*LE* 341). As if to underscore the importance of these words to his own understanding of poetry and materiality, Pound repeats a variation of this statement in the same essay (written shortly after Gourmont's death): "My true life is in the unspoken words of my body" (*LE* 342). Words encrypted in the body; the mute force of words that continue to speak after death; words that return again and again precisely because they are unspoken; haunting words. The unspoken word of the body is nothing other than the Image.

The idea of mute words spoken from the body defines the act of ventriloquism, which has a special relevance to Pound's poetics and, more specifically, to his work as a translator. James Joyce, for example, once described him as a "ventriloquist Agitator" (*P/J* 266). And Pound himself linked his use of the *persona,* or mask, to Imagist poetics (*GB* 85). Ventriloquism, from the Latin "to speak from the belly," involves a displacement *within* the body that appears to be a displacement *of* the body. The speech of ventriloquism comes from the "gut," from the region of the intestines, with the implication that such words are necessarily crude and materialistic. ("To speak from the gut" also means to speak from one's instincts, and perhaps from the unconscious.) Words that are engendered in the belly of one body issue from the mouth of another, from an *image,* a "dummy," a mute. Ventriloquism is therefore a means of invigorating the inanimate, or making the dead speak. Words engendered in the labyrinth of the body (the intestines) fill the empty mouth of an Image.

Invigorating a moribund body is a central aim not only of Imagist poetics but of Pound's interest in medical procedures. As a "physician" he can draw upon a repertory of techniques to save the patient (literature), but one of his favorites is the idea of "exotic injections." Pound characterizes a number of historical "revivals" in this fashion, including the salutary effect on Victorian literature of Swinburne's and Rossetti's translations. British literature, according to Pound, "was kept alive during the last century by a series of exotic injections" (*LE* 33–34). His own work fulfills a similar role in twentieth-century letters. From Paris, he writes that he is seeking "a triple extract for export purposes . . . a poetic serum to save English letters from post-mature and American letters from pre-mature suicide and decomposition."[16] Just as the ventriloquist plants his words in the lifeless dummy, so the literary physician injects the moribund body with a "poetic serum." Yet the words that make up this serum are foreign or "exotic," suggesting that such an injection might not only "quicken" the patient but expose him to the dangers of a foreign substance. The propriety of the body would therefore be violated: what belongs outside is disseminated within.

By examining more closely certain aspects of Pound's desire to

16. Ezra Pound, "The Island of Paris: A Letter," *The Dial* 69, no. 4 (October 1920): 406.

"doctor" the features of poetry, we can gain a more articulate sense of his understanding of the body. Frequently, the specific nature of Pound's medical interests coincides with his poetic agenda. As a graduate student at the University of Pennsylvania, for example, his eyesight was impaired by astigmatism, and he consulted the Philadelphia ophthalmologist George Milbry Gould (1848–1922). Later, during the heyday of the Imagist movement, Pound became interested in Gould's theory about the effect of eyestrain on creativity (*P/S* 180–181). In a six-volume work titled *Biographic Clinics,* Gould analyzed the personalities of various English authors in light of his optical theories. An awareness of Pound's interest in Gould helps explain some of his more eccentric practices and judgments. For example, Pound's use of abbreviation in his texts is notorious. When he makes a remark such as "Abbreviations save *eye* effort" (*L* 322), we are in a better position, knowing Gould's influence, to interpret his motivations. Pound's extraordinarily harsh judgment of Milton, who went blind, may also have been confirmed and thereby sharpened by Gould's influence.

The real significance of Pound's interest in Gould's eccentric science is simply that it coincides with the problematic visuality of the Image. A pathology of the eye is linked to a visual aesthetic. Anxiety over the effect of eyestrain on creativity suggests that Pound is already committed poetically to the sublimating power of visuality. Yet his aesthetic and ideological investment stands on perilous ground, as several of his letters to James Joyce reveal. Having become adept at diagnosing his own visual ailments, Pound recommends Gould's work to Joyce when Joyce's eyesight begins to deteriorate. What is remarkable about Pound's attempt to save Joyce's eyes are the attempts to *limit* the realm of the visible that accompany his medical advice. A discussion of the "realism" of *Ulysses* draws the following censure from Pound: "Abnormal keenness of insight O.K. But obsessions arseoreial, cloacal, deist, aesthetic as opposed to arsetheti, any obsession or tic shd. be very carefully considered before being turned loose" (*P/J* 158). Pound attempts to circumscribe the authority of Joyce's visual exactitude by limiting the realm of visibility. Celebration of the visible is immediately confronted by a concern with the invisible, by a prohibition against looking and an account of what should remain *unseen*.

According to the logic of sublimation, what must remain invisible in a formation such as the Image is the "obsession" with bodily wastes (and cadavers) lurking at its borders. The dialectical negativity of modernist vision helps, in this regard, to explain the perversity of one of Pound's most famous anecdotes. Louis Agassiz, the story goes, ordered a graduate student to stare at a dead fish for three weeks, as a lesson in empirical observation: "At the end of three weeks the fish was in an advanced state of decomposition, but the student knew something about it" (*ABC* 17–18). In Pound's narrative, the strange correspondence between visuality and decomposition, though it is presented as the very foundation of realism, somehow eludes the disembodied eye of positivism. The "power of putrefaction" remains incidental even as the eye is engrossed (and instructed) by it.

Whatever the true sources of his interest in medicine, Pound believed that he possessed an intuitive gift for medical diagnosis from an early age. Indeed, he claimed in "Indiscretions," a family history and memoir of his childhood, that he was able to make a correct diagnosis of his own ailments by the time he was two years of age! (*PD* 42). As a figure of speech, diagnosis is present in his earliest thinking about poetry. In a letter of 1908 to his friend William Carlos Williams, he writes, "As for preaching poetic anarchy or anything else: heaven forbid. I record symptoms as I see 'em. I advise no remedy. I don't even draw the disease usually. Temperature 102 3/8, pulse 78, tongue coated, etc., eyes yellow, etc." (*L* 4). Throughout his career, Pound repeatedly describes the most effective sort of critical intelligence in terms of medical diagnosis. To assess the condition of poetry accurately requires the intuition and skill of a physician interpreting the symptoms of a sick patient. In his essay "The Serious Artist" Pound remarks, "It takes a skillful physician to make certain diagnoses or to discern the lurking disease beneath the appearance of vigor" (*LE* 48). The possibility of misreading bodily symptoms, and mistaking sickness for health, recalls Pound's effort to discern the dead language lurking in Baudelaire's sonnet "Le Vampire." The inscrutable difference between the living and the dead in poetic language is ultimately grounded in the body.

Pound compares the art of evaluating poetry to a hermeneutic of the body. The aim of the physician is to penetrate to the secretive interior of the body and determine its actual condition. This figurative penetration is achieved through a process of diagnosis, which involves reading bodily symptoms. But symptoms are ambiguous, and a doctor may judge a body to be healthy when it is in fact close to death. Just as the latent meaning of a symptom "lurks" beneath the surface (and may therefore remain inaccessible), so the fate of the body depends on its internal organs, which are hidden from the outside. Pound's desire to penetrate the body and discover its innermost secrets went well beyond a figurative notion of literary criticism (although its significance should never be isolated from his literary agenda). For a time, he was interested in the work of a Dr. Louis Berman in London, who developed a theory of the glands as the seat of most illnesses, including psychological disorders (*SC* 414). Pound discussed Berman's theories in an article in *New Age* of March 1922, and later recommended him to T. S. Eliot, whose wife Vivien was suffering from severe depression at the time.

It is no coincidence that two areas of medical science claimed Pound's attention during the course of his career: endocrinology and ophthalmology. These two fields, which treat the glands and the eyes, replicate the arc of sublimation, which links the functions of the so-called lower organs and the eyes. Moreover, Pound's symptomology and his curiosity about the internal organs are primarily concerned with *illegibility* and with things that resist understanding. A symptom that remains unintelligible draws the "physician" into the secret interior of the body, and blurs the essential distinction between inside and outside. Unless the doctor physically opens the body, however, the art of diagnosis can be nothing more than surmise, a fabrication of what remains hidden. Julia Kristeva links the formation of the abject to the "symptom," which she defines as "a language that gives up, a structure within the body, a non-assimilable alien, a monster, a tumor, a cancer that the listening devices of the unconscious do not hear, for its strayed subject is huddled outside the paths of desire" (*Powers of Horror* 11). "In the symptom," she concludes, "the abject permeates me. I become abject" (11). The symptom may therefore be described as a cyst of meaning that makes interpretation difficult (but not impossible), a crypt lodged within the body. In order to identify the occupant of a crypt as living or dead, to make a good diagnosis, one must traverse the border between inside and outside. As readers, we must disturb the sleep of the dead and unravel the body in order to mark its fragile boundaries.

Through an anecdote that Pound once told to Charles Olson, we discover that his interest in endocrinology was linked in his mind to a literal penetration or incision of the body. Olson quotes Pound as saying, "There was a Jew, in London, Obermeyer, a doctor of the endocrines, and I used to ask him what is the effect of circumcision. That's the question that gets them sore . . . that sends them right up the pole. Try it, don't take my word for it, try it" (*SC* 362). The association between "reading" glands and circumcision suggests a leap from figurative to literal penetration of the body, from diagnosis to surgery (which, in this case, is performed in order to mark the male body—a mark of faith). With regard to the body's integrity, the difference between diagnosis and cure (or inscription) is essentially a matter of degree: the cure is more invasive, more violent. Both procedures, however, take place in an atmosphere of wondrous uncertainty and peril—precisely because the limits of the body are in flux.

Surgery is a favorite trope of Pound's for the art of writing poetry. Yet critics are more apt to note his fondness for speaking of poetry in terms of sculpture—an art that Pound associates with the "daemonic" energy of Gaudier-Brzeska (*GB* 39–40). Sculpture, according to Pound, requires not only the capacity to conceive forms but the physical strength to execute them in recalcitrant materials such as stone and wood. More important, sculpture represents for Pound a process of separation and excision that is fundamental, generally, to his sense of artistic practice. In an interview in 1914, for example, he observes: "There are two ways of presenting beauty—by satire, which clears away the rubbish and allows the central loveliness to reveal itself; and by direct presentation of beauty itself" (*P/S* 324–325). Although Pound is often inclined to think of the Image in terms of "direct presentation," it should also be evident that this "presentation" often depends on a logic of exclusion. A poet makes an Image by carving away various kinds of filth and "rubbish," thereby allowing the essential form to stand out clearly. By Pound's definition, therefore, the Image is a form of satire. Yet the sculptural techniques of satire, and the satiric emphasis on materiality, derive not from chiseling stone but from an encounter with the human body: "Satire is surgery, insertions and amputations," Pound writes (*LE* 45). The master trope is not sculpture but surgery.

Pound liked to believe that his poetry continued the tradition of writers who possessed a "surgical" intelligence. Thus, "Ovid, before Browning, raises the dead and dissects their mental processes" (*SR* 16). Not only do we discover that Pound views his forbears as surgeons, but surgery figures prominently in his relation to the dead, and to cadavers in particular. The reference to "dissection" suggests that the virtues of realism and exactitude are represented here as a kind of anatomy lesson (a familiar event to medical students). Furthermore, the rhetoric of medicine and surgery later came to occupy a prominent place in Pound's anti-Semitic attacks. He was intrigued, for example, that Céline (a notorious anti-Semite) was trained as a physician. His solutions for the problem of usury were often couched in medical terms that recall his literary criticism: "USURY is the cancer of the world, which only the surgeon's knife of fascism can cut out of the life of nations" (*SP* 300).

Kristeva compares the individual permeated by abjection to a surgeon, and refers to "the scalpel that carries out his separations" (8). Pound, too, employs the tools of the surgeon to carry out the separations upon which the rhetoric of the Image is founded. Carving an Image in words is analogous to cutting away the diseased or rotting portion of an ailing body. Walter Villerant, the persona of the "Imaginary Letters," contends that "Pound's sterilized surgery" removes the "decayed-lily verbiage" of the "Wilde school" (*PD* 73–74). Elsewhere, speaking in his own voice, Pound contrasts "the very cleanliness of the tools, the health of the very matter of thought itself" to language that "goes rotten, i.e., becomes slushy and inexact, or excessive and bloated" (*LE* 21). These statements reiterate in medical terms the basic logic of Imagism: Pound takes up the scalpel to rid language of impurities, thereby separating proper from improper and maintaining the "natural" boundaries of the body.

The work of the scalpel is undertaken in the name of "realism." Toward this end, Pound urges, "let an unknown man write clear and clean realism; let a poet use the speech of his predecessors, either being as antiseptic as the instruments of a surgeon" (*PD* 91). Yet surgery, as a metaphor for realism, is more than just pruning; it may, as Pound indicated, require "incisions" and "amputations," activities that expose the inner organs and alter the body's shape. Michael Fried has argued that surgery, when it functions as an emblem of realism in painting, is "an art of necessary violence."[17] Fried pursues his thesis by examining *The Gross Clinic*, a painting by Thomas Eakins that depicts the dissection of a cadaver (a subject we have already noted in Pound's reference to the "surgical" intelligence of Ovid and Browning). Fried contends that Eakins' "realism" produces an image of the cadaver that is "disfigured" by foreshortening and other techniques. This aesthetic "disfiguration" corresponds to the mutilation that is actually being performed on the cadaver in the painting. Ultimately, Fried wishes to identify Eakins' disfiguration of the body as one of those moments in the history of realism "when tactics of shock, violence, perceptual distortion, and physical outrage were mobilized against prevailing conventions of the representation of the human body specifically in order to produce a new and stupefyingly powerful experience of the 'real' " (64).

Pound's conception of the Image represents a similar moment in the history of "absorptive realism." Like Eakins, Pound employs the figure of surgery to express the violent and invasive character of "realism." Surgery, in Pound's hands, safeguards the body by ridding it of contamination, but it also mutilates the flesh. Pound invades the body of language by making "sterile" incisions, in order to probe beneath the surface. By gaining access to the mysterious inner organs, he breaks down the distinction between inside and outside. Not only do the inner organs become visible or externalized, they become vulnerable to contamination. As an Imagist poet, Pound also performs "amputations": piercing, cutting, shrinking, molding, or scraping the body as realism requires. A new realism demands an alteration or "disfiguration" of the body. For Pound, surgery means remaking the body, reshaping it, inside and out, fashioning it to resemble his own vision of what poetry should be.

Fried claims that the main concern of his essays on realism is "the *materiality* of writing" (xi). The violence associated with writing,

17. Michael Fried, *Realism, Writing, Disfiguration* (Chicago: University of Chicago Press, 1987), p. 62.

when it is conceived as a form of surgery, becomes the object of a powerful ambivalence. Hence, in the representations that Fried examines, "the materiality of writing turns out to be simultaneously elicited and repressed" (xiv). The result is that "the definitive realist painting would be one that the viewer could not bear to look at . . . At this extreme the enterprise of realism required an effacing of seeing in the act of looking" (65). Pound's conception of the Image displays, I have argued, a similar resistance to visuality. On one hand, Imagism calls for a surgical procedure that strips the body (language) of "glamor," filth, and contamination. This ensures not only the accuracy of the Image but its visibility or legibility. Realism thus depends on establishing a stable border between what belongs to the body and what is foreign to it. Surgery, on the other hand, is necessarily a violent act; it mutilates and alters the body. The fragile boundary between inside and outside is destroyed. Once this occurs, the body can be "sculpted" or revised to assume abstract or inhuman form. Thus, the very act that secures the visibility and precision of the Image makes it unutterably foreign and resistant to visuality. The realistic Image, in its most extreme form, is always *apotropaic,* or simply unrecognizable. Surgery, for Pound, is always plastic surgery, just as the "monstrous plasticity of the dead" escapes recognition when it assumes the form of the Image.

Pound's most extreme revisions of the poetic body occur in a postscript to his translation of Rémy de Gourmont's *Physique de l'Amour,* a translation published in 1922. (The first signs of Pound's interest in Gourmont appear considerably earlier, during the Imagist period.) Pound begins with the thesis that "the brain itself, is, in origin and development, only a sort of great clot of genital fluid held in suspense or reserve" (*NPL* 199). This thought sets the stage for an imaginary account of what takes place inside the body, and, more important, a bizarre speculation on "new organs" and the future of the body. Elaborating on the idea of a "spermatozoic" brain, Pound contends that "creative thought," which includes the production of *Images,* is "a sudden out-spurt of the mind" (*NPL* 153). This "power of exteriorizing a form" (*NPL* 149) extends, in a mysterious fashion, to physiological changes in the body. "I believe," writes Pound, "that the species changes as suddenly as a man makes a song or a poem, or as

Anathemata

suddenly as he *starts* making them, more suddenly than he can cut a statue in stone, at most as slowly as a locust or long-tailed Sirmione false mosquito emerges from its outgrown skin. It is not even proved that man is at the end of his physical changes" (*NPL* 153). This leads Pound to speculate on what new organs may be in store: "Let us suppose man capable of exteriorizing a new organ, horn, halo, Eye of Horus. Given a brain of power, comes the question, what organ, and to what purpose? . . . The 'next step,' as in the case of the male organ of the nautilus, is to grow a tool and detach it" (*NPL* 154). Analogous to the exteriorization of Images from the body, the eruption of organs that are at once archaic and unprecedented progresses from the eye of Horus to what may be construed (in the nautilus image) as the missing phallus of Osiris (the only member of the god that his sister Isis does not recover). The eye is displaced by a "tool," a fetish that apparently continues to elude the poet who had once outlined his poetic program in a series of articles titled "I Gather the Limbs of Osiris."

Pound's speculations about the future of the body echo in remarkable ways his thinking about imagery. The hypothesis of externalized organs and faculties, for example, corresponds to his conception of the "phantastikon" (the image-making faculty), which exists *outside* the body—like a "soap-bubble" (*SR* 92). As extensions of the human sensorium, the new organs resemble the technical media. Not only is the body transformed into a medium, but its new organs are analogous, Pound claims, to *Images*. At this point, Pound's speculations on the body converge with his theorization of the Image, revealing not only the corporeal dimension of the Image but the mediumistic character of the body.

Pound's thinking about the body also reveals the degree to which Image making imperils the corporeal distinction between interior and exterior. Each time the body produces an Image, it turns itself inside out, externalizing a fragment of its mysterious inner life. The Image emerges from the body like a horn or a halo (or the lost phallus of a god)—a feature of the body that is inhuman or even monstrous. One thinks of Bataille's figure of the "pineal eye," a monstrous protuberance emerging from the top of the head.[18] The pineal eye is a vestigial

---

18. Bataille, "The Pineal Eye," *Visions of Excess*, pp. 79–80.

organ that Descartes associates with the soul, and Bataille with the potency of the abject. As an "organ" of heterogeneity and visuality, the pineal eye corresponds to the Images and new organs bursting from a body that has been the subject of a sudden evolutionary change, or of medical experimentation. Indeed, by practicing the arts of diagnosis and "surgery," the Imagist poet subjects the body of language to unforeseen alterations.

Is there a link then in modernist poetics between Image making, medical experimentation, and teratogenesis? The idea that the "surgical" techniques of Imagism could release from the (female) body an exquisite monster does, in fact, find expression in an unpublished poem that Pound sent T. S. Eliot after reworking "The Waste Land." The poem is entitled "Sage Homme" (a pun on the French word for midwife, *sage-femme*):

> These are the poems of Eliot
> By the Uranian Muse begot;
> A Man their Mother was,
> A Muse their Sire.
> How did the printed Infancies result
> From Nuptials thus doubly difficult?
> If you must need enquire
> Know diligent Reader
> That on each Occasion
> Ezra performed the Caesarian Operation.
> Cauls and grave clothes he brings,
> Fortune's outrageous stings,
> About which odour clings,
>   Of putrefaction,
> Bleichstein's dank rotting clothes
> Affect the dainty nose,
> He speaks of common woes
>   Deploring action.
> He writes of A.B.C.s
> And flaxseed poultices,
> Observing fate's hard decrees
>   Sans satisfaction;
> Breeding of animals,
> Humans and cannibals,
> But above all else of smells

> Without attraction.
> Vates cum fistula. (*L* 170)

The poem treats the commonplace idea of giving birth to a work of art from the standpoint of what Pound calls his "obstetric effort" (*L* 171). The offspring ("The Waste Land") is the result of a collaboration between a Muse, its mother, and a midwife, who delivers Eliot (its mother) of the anomalous creature that was incubated during Eliot's mental breakdown in London. (I believe I am fair in describing "The Waste Land," with its heteroclite structure and assortment of voices, as an anomaly—especially when we consider the role of madness in its conception.) The most problematic aspect of the poem is its portrait of the *sage-homme*, or male midwife, whose first name is "Ezra" and last name is "Bleichstein." It is extremely odd that Pound, who performs the "Caesarian Operation" that delivers the poem, would cast himself in the role of Bleichstein (who revives the character "Bleistein" from Eliot's anti-Semitic poem "Burbank with Baedeker: Bleistein with a Cigar"). Given Pound's identification with the figure of a decrepit Jewish physician (who is also the object of his anti-Semitic fears), we may safely assume that Bleichstein is one of the "demonic doubles" that haunt Pound's anti-Semitic rhetoric.[19]

The figure of Bleichstein (whose real-life counterparts may be the endocrinologists Berman and Overmeyer) seems to have risen from the grave: he wears "dank rotting clothes" and gives off an odor of "putrefaction." He brings with him, as though he were also an undertaker, the accoutrements of death: "grave clothes" and "cauls." The word "caul," which can mean either a "skull-cup" or the "membrane surrounding a fetus," unites the doctor's two functions as obstetrician and emissary of death. Like Pound, Bleichstein is therefore both a medium for the dead and a midwife for the unborn.[20] Clearly, then, Pound views the figure of the Jewish doctor as an emissary from the realm of the dead. Moreover, Bleichstein's interest in the "breeding

---

19. Robert Casillo's account of "mimetic violence" in Pound's work appears in *The Genealogy of Demons: Anti-Semitism, Fascism, and the Myths of Ezra Pound* (Evanston, Ill: Northwestern University Press, 1988), pp. 250–252, 298–310.

20. The uncanny resemblance between Pound and Bleichstein is augmented by the fact that Bleichstein "writes of A.B.C.s." A decade or so after writing this poem, Pound began to publish a series of articles and books with titles such as "ABC of Economics" and *ABC of Reading*.

of animals, humans and cannibals" does indeed suggest a link between poetry, surgery, and teratogenesis. The experimental procedures of the *sage-homme* conform, in this respect, to the logic of the abject, which, according to Kristeva, "kills in the name of life . . . It lives at the behest of death—an operator in genetic experimentations" (*Powers of Horror* 15). The Jewish physician, with whom Pound identifies, is thus an extremely powerful figure that combines the "power of putrefaction" with the arts of diagnosis and surgery. The corporeal rhetoric of the Image and the rhetoric of Pound's anti-Semitism converge in this uncanny figure.

CHAPTER 5

Impossible Effigies

> One can gauge the degree of the historical sensibility an age possesses by the manner in which it translates texts and by the manner in which it seeks to incorporate past epochs and books into its own being.
> —Friedrich Nietzsche, "On the Problem of Translation"

> It were as wise to cast a violet in a crucible that you might discover the formal principle of its color and odor, as seek to transfuse from one language into another the creations of a poet. The plant must spring again from its seed, or it will bear no flower.
> —Percy Bysshe Shelley, "Defence of Poetry"

> To declare its impossibility is not an argument against the possible splendor of the translator's task. On the contrary, this characterization admits it to the highest rank and lets us infer that it is meaningful.
> —José Ortega y Gasset, "The Misery and the Splendor of Translation"

Lingering over the sublime body of the Image, we are reminded of the *Doppelcharakter* of the fetish: its entrancing, or merely inscrutable, alternation between materiality and abstraction, body and spirit. In its historical and technical aspects, the modernist Image is essentially a *medium,* a form of exchange or translation in the service of memory, negotiating the perilous relations between the living and the dead. Indeed, the cryptological dimension of the Image receives its most explicit formulation in Pound's theory of translation; for Pound views his translations not only as Images, but as images of the dead. In this regard, Pound's translation discourse is his most formidable contribution to the art of memory. Pound's many translations, as well as his thoughts on translation, are routinely cited by scholars from diverse fields as being among the most original and influential in Western literary history.[1] Taking this broader spectrum of opinion into account, we could argue that Pound occupies a more secure position in literary history as a translator than as a poet, and—what is more significant—that translation emerges in early modernist poetics as a critical and creative mode equal to, and at times surpassing, poetry. Yet gauging the significance of evaluations of this kind is fraught with difficulties, for the internal contradictions of translation discourse are so extreme as to border on a kind of madness. Since the late eighteenth century, writing about translation repeatedly and inexplicably enters into reflection, and departs from it, with the assumption that translation—especially of poetry—is *impossible*. Given the absurdity (and potency) of a discourse that starts from the premise of its own nonexistence (what Paul Mann calls a "theory-death"), I hesitate even to ask what bearing impossibility may have on Pound's achievements as a translator, or on the relation of translation to Imagism. Yet it may be wise, before I consider the place of the Image in Pound's discourse of translation, to say a few words about impossibility, about what John Dryden calls "the disease of translation." (Can this be the same poet-critic who neatly divides translation into the archetypal categories of metaphrase, paraphrase, and imitation?)[2] For the impossibility of translation always evokes a possible, if inconceivable, exchange.

1. George Steiner, for example, writes, "List Saint Jerome, Luther, Dryden, Hölderlin, Novalis, Schleiermacher, Nietzsche, Ezra Pound, Valéry, MacKenna, Franz Rosenzweig, Walter Benjamin, Quine—and you have very nearly the sum total of those who have said anything fundamental or new about translation." Steiner, *After Babel: Aspects of Language and Translation* (London: Oxford University Press, 1975), pp. 269. In addition, any monograph, or major anthology of essays, on the subject of translation is likely to contain references to Pound, by scholars who cite his views on translation in relation to topics ranging from anthropology to German Romanticism. See the sources cited in this chapter; also William Arrowsmith and Roger Shattuck, eds., *The Craft and Context of Translation* (Austin: University of Texas Press, 1961).

2. Indeed, it is; Dryden's crack about the "disease of translation" appears in his preface to *Sylvae: Or, the Second Part of Poetical Miscellanies* (1685), five years after his categorical description in the "Preface to the Translation of Ovid's *Epistles*" (1680). One assumes that the evolution from schematics to pathology is due to the burden of his greater experience as a translator. See *Essays of John Dryden*, ed. W. P. Ker (New York: Russell and Russell, 1961), vol. 1, pp. 237, 251.

This possible exchange is to be recovered, however, not from the ineluctable activity of translation in a pragmatic sense (translation occurs and will continue to do so), but from the veritable doctrine of untranslatability that translation discourse has produced from the late eighteenth century to the present. Indeed, given the eerie uniformity of historical opinion regarding the impossibility of translation, it is hard not to detect a trace of fanaticism, an overture to what exceeds language and reasoning—a demonology, as though in defending the idea of untranslatability one sought to maintain an *impossible* position. In a recent historical anthology of writings on translation, the paradigm first appears historically in Schopenhauer's comment that "poems cannot be translated; they can only be transposed."[3] One can then trace a direct line from Romantic Germany to Ortega y Gasset's superb essay on "the misery and the splendor of translation," which presents itself as a meditation on "the demon of the impossible."[4] Roman Jakobson, though ostensibly less "Romantic," is likewise given to absolutes on the subject of translation: "The pun, or to use a more erudite, and perhaps more precise term—paronomasia, reigns over poetic art, and whether its rule is absolute or limited, poetry by definition is untranslatable. Only creative transposition is possible."[5] Octavio Paz summarizes these views admirably, "The greatest pessimism about the feasibility of translation has been concentrated in poetry . . . The consensus is almost unanimous that the translation of connotative meanings is impossible . . . Poetry is a fabric of connotative meanings and, consequently, untranslatable."[6] In this particular anthology, the "unanimity" of opinion culminates with Yves Bonnefoy's peremptory dismissal of the question: "The answer to the question, 'Can one translate a poem?' is of course no."[7]

In a more philosophical context, we could argue that impossibility

---

3. Arthur Schopenhauer, "On Language and Words," trans. Peter Mollenhauer, in Rainer Schulte and John Biguenet, eds., *Theories of Translation* (Chicago: University of Chicago Press, 1992), p. 33.

4. José Ortega y Gasset, "The Misery and the Splendor of Translation," trans. Elizabeth Gamble Miller, ibid., p. 99.

5. Roman Jakobson, "On Linguistic Aspects of Translation," ibid., p. 151.

6. Octavio Paz, "Translation: Literature and Letters," trans. Irene del Corral, ibid., p. 155.

7. Yves Bonnefoy, "Translating Poetry," ibid., p. 191.

also exercises a sovereign influence over recent poststructuralist revisions of translation theory. Derrida, for example, refers to "the necessary and impossible task of translation, its necessity *as* impossibility"; thus, "for a poetic text or a sacred text, communication is not the essential."[8] Emphasizing at once the material and telegraphic nature of the contact between original and translation, Derrida formulates his position in response to an implicit question concerning the translatability of a proper name, a signature, or, I would add, an image: "Since no meaning bears detaching, transferring, transporting, or translating into another tongue (as meaning), it commands right away the translation that it seems to refuse. It is transferable and untranslatable. There is only the letter" ("Babel" 204). Friedrich Kittler, echoing Schopenhauer's terms, makes a similar claim: "The transposition of media is thus an exact correlate of untranslatability."[9] For Kittler, modernism, with its emphasis on materials and particularity, emerges from the deterioration of translatability implied in the positivity of the new technical media. The triumph of difference and untranslatability thus spells the decline of hermeneutics and a certain conception of "poetry" that is modeled after translation.

Though untranslatability played a role in thinking about translation prior to the nineteenth century, it was only with the emergence of hermeneutics and the poetics of Romanticism (primarily in Germany) that the impossibility of translation became a generative concept, a positive value upon which a modern theory of translation (and poetics) could be constructed. Antoine Berman associates the evolving relation of translation and culture with what he calls "the experience of the foreign," a concept in which the strangeness of the original text—if it is not entirely inaccessible—must be recovered and preserved at any cost (including the destruction of the native tongue).[10] Berman concludes, "The untranslatable, in reality, is not anything in particular, but the totality of the foreign language in its strangeness and its dif-

8. Jacques Derrida, "Des Tours de Babel," trans. Joseph F. Graham, in Joseph F. Graham, ed., *Difference in Translation* (Ithaca: Cornell University Press, 1985), pp. 171, 180.

9. Friedrich Kittler, *Discourse Networks 1800/1900,* trans. Michael Metteer, with Chris Cullens (Stanford: Stanford University Press, 1990), p. 274.

10. Antoine Berman, *The Experience of the Foreign: Translation and Culture in Romantic Germany,* trans. S. Heyvaert (Albany: SUNY Press, 1992), p. 60.

ference" (*Experience of the Foreign* 60). Assuming the properties of the ineffable and the unspeakable, untranslatability in the Romantic period becomes the index of a certain conception of poetry, and poetry becomes the measure, the limit, of translation.

The impossibility of translation suggests that translation subscribes to the logic of the crypt: something is hidden, ineffable, remote, unspeakable. Or is it that in light of the impossibility of translation, the *original* becomes a crypt, a fact that would explain the untranslatability of poetry? In any case, as Ortega y Gasset observes, the "misery and the splendor of translation" refer, however obliquely, to a reserve of secrecy and silence: "The stupendous reality, which is language, will not be understood at its root if one doesn't begin by noticing that speech is composed above all of silences . . . From this we deduce the enormous difficulty of translation: in it one tries to say in a language precisely what that language tends to silence. But, at the same time, one glimpses a possible marvelous aspect of the enterprise of translating: the revelation of the mutual secrets that peoples and epochs keep to themselves" ("Misery and Splendor" 110). In its untranslatability, then, the original arrives from a distant realm of secrecy and silence. Indeed, distance enchants and speaks through the possible exchange that transpires in the impossibility of translation. All translation, in this respect, is *telegraphic;* whatever reaches us does so from afar. Translation, as Derrida observes, discloses what "distance means in writing and the voice."[11] Yet the impossibility of translation suggests more than distance; it implies forms of exchange that are inexplicable, governed by unreason, illogic, or chance. Thus, Derrida speaks of writing "in the trance of the *trans—*" ("Living On" 172), and asks, "On what condition is this transferential magneticization possible between what are called textual bodies?" (178) The impossibility of translation must therefore be understood as a refuge not only for telegraphic but *telepathic* relations (if there is any distinction between the two). We cannot dismiss the possibility (since the possible is determined, in this case, by the impossible) that one text might "read" or even "love" another, or that a text might "converse" with the dead. Indeed, the law of the impossibility of translation dictates

11. Jacques Derrida, "Living on / Border Lines," trans. James Hulbert, in H. Bloom et al., *Deconstruction and Criticism* (New York: Continuum, 1979), p. 77.

that translation can occur only outside the bounds of reason and natural language. According to a logic that tolerates the possibility of impossible exchange—a "mad hypothesis"—anything is possible. Yves Bonnefoy intimates as much when he asks, "Under what circumstances is this type of translation, the translation of poetry, not completely mad?" ("Translating Poetry" 191).[12]

Untranslatability, then, becomes the distinguishing feature of poetic texts, whether sacred, archaic, or Romantic; hence the abiding notion that poetry is what is lost in translation. At the same time, however, poetry (as Novalis observes) becomes equivalent to translation, or at least to the form of exchange that survives the impossibility of translation: "To translate is to write poetry as much as creating one's own works" (Novalis, cited in Berman, *Experience of the Foreign* 105). All meanings, all things, all discourses, are susceptible, convertible, to the "pure speech" of poetry, so that it is not poetry but words and things that are lost in translation. Poetry, as translation, shares the "phantasmagorical modality of hermeneutics," which "excludes all particularities in favor of a general equivalent" (Kittler, *Discourse Networks* 115, 265). Exploiting the phantasmic effects of the impossibility of translation, poetry exercises a principle of unrestricted exchange, in which all things are translated into an afterlife (into meaning) and, inadvertently, into history. Poetry, then, becomes the pivotal term in a dialectic of untranslatability and absolute transferability, a dialectic that is articulated most fully by the historical discourse on hieroglyphics (which coincides with the Romantic interest in translation).

As Kittler's use of the term "general equivalent" suggests, a powerful valence exists between translation discourse and the Marxian vocabulary of political economy. Any reflection on the nature of translation immediately gains historical and ethical dimensions by invoking certain analogous principles of Marxian economics. Yet it would be a mistake to assume that this affinity is merely figurative or that it reveals a deficiency in translation discourse, thereby confirming its inherently subordinate character. On the contrary, just as Marx's analogy of the commodity as a hieroglyph can be understood as echoing and elaborating the great translational event of Champollion's decipherment of

---

12. On the relation between translation and psychosis, see Louis Wolfson, *Le schizo et les langues* (Paris: Gallimard, 1970).

hieroglyphic characters in 1819, so his theory of exchange value—and its discursive object, the commodity fetish—resonate with the great debate on translation that emerged from German Romanticism and the philosophy of hermeneutics. Recall, for example, Goethe's inclination to speak of his concept of *Weltliteratur* in terms of a *Weltmarkt,* a world market for material goods (Berman, *Experience of the Foreign* 55–57); or Friedrich Schlegel's comment that translation constitutes a "market to which the most distant merchants come with their wares" (cited in Kittler, *Discourse Networks* 71). According to Marx, the simple artifact, which is characterized by its use value, assumes the properties of a fetish only when it is exchanged.[13] Yet the exchange of objects that are fundamentally dissimilar in their use, origin, and material character can occur only through the mediation of a "general equivalent." Thus, the central "enigma" of the commodity fetish concerns the creation of exchange value as a medium that permits disparate objects to be substituted for one another, and to enter into "phantasmagorical" relations with one another. Indeed, as Thomas Keenan observes of Marx's analysis of commodity fetishism, "we can say that Marx poses the 'transformation problem,' or that Marxism is a theory of change"—that is, a theory of translation.[14]

It is essential, before I proceed any further with Marx, to note that the correspondence between fetishism and translation does not originate in the specific features of the Marxian analysis of capital; rather, Marx inherits this correspondence from the colonial origins of fetish discourse. Fetishism may thus be understood as an effect of translation, not merely in the context of Marx's theory of exchange value, but according to the specific historical circumstances from which the concept of the fetish emerges. In his work on the history of fetish discourse, William Pietz argues that the fetish concept "originated in the

---

13. Marx explains, "It is only by being exchanged that the products of labor acquire a socially uniform objectivity as values." See Marx, *Capital: A Critique of Political Economy,* vol. 1, introd. Ernest Mandel, trans. Ben Fowkes (Harmondsworth: Penguin, 1976), p. 166. In addition, he writes, "A commodity's simple form of value is contained in its value-relation with another commodity of a different kind, i.e., in its exchange relation with the latter" (152).

14. Thomas Keenan, "The Point Is to (Ex)Change It: Reading *Capital* Rhetorically," in William Pietz and Emily Apter, eds., *Fetishism as Cultural Discourse* (Ithaca: Cornell University Press, 1993), p. 159.

cross-cultural spaces of the coast of West Africa during the sixteenth and seventeenth centuries," and, more broadly speaking, that the fetish, as a discursive object, represents "a cross-cultural relation formed by the on-going encounter of the value codes of radically different social orders."[15] Pietz is quite explicit about the relevance of translation to this milieu: "The pidgin word *Fetisso* . . . may be viewed either as a failed translation of various African terms or as something itself, a novel word responsive to an unprecedented type of situation" ("Problem of the Fetish" 6). Whether the term *fetish* emerges historically as a "failed translation" or as an instance of creative translation, it is symptomatic of "cross-cultural spaces" whose function is to "translate and transvalue objects between radically different social systems" (6). The idea of the fetish can therefore be said to have arisen from the essential condition of translation, from "the clash of incommensurable difference" (13).

One could argue quite plausibly that the Marxian theory of exchange value resurrects (and is haunted by) the essential features of colonial fetish discourse: the problem of "incommensurable difference," the effects of "mistranslation," and the "transvaluation" of disparate objects. Indeed, Thomas Keenan argues that Marx's analysis of the commodity fetish is dominated by questions that motivate the history of translation discourse: "How is exchange possible? What common terms could there be between different objects?" ("The Point" 170). As to the possibility of exchange in the realm of objects, Marx responds, according to Keenan, in a manner that echoes the doctrine of untranslatability: "It remains impossible and it happens all the time" (171). Thus, Marx's theory of fetishism, like the history of translation theory, remains transfixed by "the question of the possible impossibility of exchange" (169).

For Marx, as for those who espouse a doctrine of untranslatability, the act of exchange and the creation of exchange value is nothing short of miraculous, since no common term can be found for things that are intrinsically different: "This making alike can only be something foreign to the true nature of things" (*Capital* 151). The foreignness of exchange (which makes disparate things alike) is a countersign of

---

15. William Pietz, "The Problem of the Fetish, Part 1," *Res* 9 (Spring 1985): 5, 11.

its impossibility; indeed, the fetish is a "mystical" and "enigmatic" object precisely because it is the residue of an impossible exchange. Though there is no logical or material basis for it, the exchange of objects, like the translation of texts, does in fact take place. This can occur, however, only if a medium between things is created through a process of "total abstraction." Thus, Keenan explains, "In the face of difference, abstraction is required, even if it is not necessarily possible" ("The Point" 165). The strain of this incongruity is indicated by the rhetorical extravagance that Marx displays in his attempt to characterize the possibility and the effects of impossible exchange. For Marx, the abstraction of translation that occurs in the moment of exchange is nothing less than a loss of life. The Marxian view of exchange is articulated fully by Adorno and Horkheimer: "Abstraction, the tool of the Enlightenment, treats objects as did fate, the notion of which it rejects: it liquidates them."[16] Abstracted from the intrinsic properties of its use value in the moment of exchange, the object undergoes a kind of death, a decomposition, that results in the creation of the "phantom objectivity" of exchange. Thus, in the eyes of Marx, translation is equivalent to decomposition, to the dematerialization of the object (a death that mysteriously reanimates the object with a peculiar vitality). In this regard, Marx struggles in his analysis of fetishism to defend the *poetry* of the object from the mortification of exchange. Keenan, whose essay is superbly attentive to the necrophilic dimension of Marx's theory of fetishism, remarks of exchange value, "This phantom makes possible the relation between (or within) things or uses, grants the common axis of similarity hitherto unavailable, precisely because it is a ghost and no longer a thing or labor" ("The Point" 168). Thus, he concludes, "Without ghosts, no exchange" (168).

The rhetorical elaboration of death in the Marxian analysis of the fetish is an immediate effect of the theoretical impossibility of exchange, but it is also a residue of the tension between impossibility and memory. For exchange value, according to Marx, depends on the "disappearance," or forgetting, of the material object—the basis of its existence as a form of embodied labor (*Capital* 128). Further-

16. Theodor W. Adorno and Max Horkheimer, *Dialectic of Enlightenment*, trans. John Cumming (New York: Continuum, 1970), p. 13.

more, according to W. J. T. Mitchell, modern fetishism envelops the disembodied (and forgotten) artifact in the oblivion of rationalized commerce:

> The magic of the fetish depends on the projection of consciousness into the object, and then a forgetting of that act of projection . . . Commodity fetishism can be understood, then, as a kind of double forgetting: first the capitalist forgets that it is he and his tribe who have projected life and value into commodities in the ritual of exchange . . . But then, a second phase of amnesia sets in that is quite unknown to primitive fetishism. The commodity veils itself in familiarity and triviality, in the rationality of purely quantitative relations.[17]

In what is ostensibly an entirely different context, Freud draws a similar conclusion regarding the origins of fetishism: "When the fetish is instituted some process occurs which reminds one of the stopping of memory in traumatic amnesia."[18] Hence, the most influential modern theorizations of fetishism situate their elusive object in a dialectic of forgetting and remembering that possesses all of the phantasmic properties of the art of memory. The aim of Marxist cultural criticism is to retrieve the material artifact from the crypt of exchange value, to recover the lost object from death and oblivion. Given the correlation in Marx between death, memory, and the possibility of impossible exchange, it should come as no surprise that translation discourse labors under a similar fascination with death. Indeed, the rhetoric of death in Marx only confirms the degree to which the problem of translation dominates his theory of fetishism. For the history of translation discourse is extraordinarily morbid in its rhetorical coloring. As in the case of Marx, this coloring must be viewed as an effect of the impossible. To cite Dryden, who has descended to us, erroneously, as a paradigm of reasonableness and reticence: "A good poet is no more like himself in a dull translation, than his carcass would be to a living body."[19] Schopenhauer employs a similar figure to illustrate his in-

17. W. J. T. Mitchell, *Iconology: Image, Text, Ideology* (Chicago: University of Chicago Press, 1986), p. 193.
18. Sigmund Freud, *Standard Edition of the Complete Psychological Works*, ed. James Strachey (London: Hogarth Press, 1960), vol. 21, p. 155.
19. John Dryden, from his preface to *Sylvae: Or the Second Part of Poetical Miscella-*

terdiction of poetic translation: "Every translation either remains dead and its style appears forced, wooden, and unnatural, or it frees itself of the constraints of adherence to language and therefore is satisfied with the notion of an *à peu près*, which rings false. A library of translations resembles a gallery with reproductions of paintings" ("Language and Words" 33). (Schopenhauer's correlation of dead translations and images is not, as I will explain in a moment, without significance.) Death also looms over Friedrich Schleiermacher's reflections on translation: "Paraphrase seeks to overcome the irrationality of languages, but only in a mechanical way . . . Thus paraphrase labors its way through an accumulation of loosely defined details . . . The living speech has been irretrievably killed."[20] In the twentieth century, we find Paul Valéry troubled by the mortal danger of translation: "Where poetry is concerned, fidelity to meaning alone is a kind of betrayal. How many poetic works, reduced to prose, that is, to their simple meaning, become literally nonexistent? They are anatomical expressions, dead birds! Sometimes, indeed, untrammeled absurdity swarms over these deplorable corpses . . . Verse is put into prose as though into its coffin."[21] Finally, Vladimir Nabokov acknowledges the risk of mortality in translation, but claims that it is inherent in the original text: "I take literalism to mean 'absolute accuracy.' If such accuracy sometimes results in the strange allegoric scene suggested by the phrase 'the letter has killed the spirit,' only one reason can be imagined: there must have been something wrong either with the original letter or with the original spirit, and this is not really a translator's concern."[22]

All of these accounts of death in translation evoke, as Antoine Berman explains, a danger that is associated with translation conceived in terms of mortality:

---

nies, p. 253. He also cites approvingly a comment by John Denham: "Poetry is of so subtle a spirit, that, in pouring out of one language into another, it will evaporate; and if a new spirit be not added in the transfusion, there will remain nothing but a *caput mortuum*." Dryden remarks, "I confess this argument holds good against a literal translation." From his "Preface to the Translation of Ovid's *Epistles*," p. 241.

20. Friedrich Schleiermacher, "On the Different Methods of Translating," trans. Waltraud Bartscht, in Schulte and Biguenet, eds., *Theories of Translation*, p. 40.
21. Paul Valéry, "Variations on the *Eclogues*," trans. Denise Folliot, ibid., p. 116.
22. Vladimir Nabokov, "Problems of Translation: *Onegin* in English," ibid., p. 141.

> Translation is situated precisely in that obscure and dangerous region where the disproportionate strangeness of the foreign work and its language runs the risk of striking down with all its force on the translator's text and his language, thus ruining his undertaking and leaving the reader only with an inauthentic *Fremdheit* [strangeness]. But if the translator refuses this danger, there is the risk of falling immediately into another one: the danger of killing the dimension of the foreign. (*Experience of the Foreign* 155)

Death, it would seem, is all but inescapable in translation; in its wake, we are apt to be set upon by a ghost, or to discover a corpse (of the original, of the translator's text and her language, of meaning, and so on). Nor should we assume that the historical obsession with death in translation discourse merely illustrates certain pragmatic constraints; rather, the mortality of translation, like that of the artifact in the Marxian theory of exchange, stems directly from the theoretical impossibility of translation. The whole spectacle of the living dead, of cadavers and ghosts and "necromancy," results directly from the injunction against translation, from the transgression of this law, and from the extravagant economy of the impossible.[23] All translation, according to Walter Benjamin, bears within it the force of transgression: "Hölderlin's translations in particular are subject to the enormous danger inherent in all translations: the gates of a language thus expanded and modified may slam shut and enclose the translator with silence. Hölderlin's translations from Sophocles were his last work: in them meaning plunges from abyss to abyss until it threatens to become lost in the bottomless depths of language."[24] Benjamin suggests that the nihilism of translation, entertaining the impossible, delivers the translator into an abyss of silence and meaninglessness. Yet one could also argue that by enacting the impossible (translation), the transla-

23. In a fine essay titled "Gender and the Metaphorics of Translation," Lori Chamberlain suggests that the rhetoric of death in translation discourse can be attributed to the danger of ideological transgression: "The reason translation is so overcoded, so overregulated, is that it threatens to erase the difference between production and reproduction which is essential to the establishment of power . . . That the *difference* is essential is argued in terms of life and death." In Lawrence Venuti, ed., *Rethinking Translation: Discourse, Subjectivity, Ideology* (London: Routledge, 1992), pp. 66–67.

24. Walter Benjamin, "The Task of the Translator" (1923), in *Illuminations,* ed. Hannah Arendt, trans. Harry Zohn (New York: Schocken, 1969), pp. 81–82.

tor enters the realms of magic, death, and madness. Thus, by evoking death, translation discourse (including the Marxian theory of exchange) evokes the impossible, the unknowable, the ineffable.[25] Yet the impossible, as Georges Bataille observes, overwhelms utility, truth, and meaning, and thus engenders through translation unspeakable (and inconceivable) forms of exchange.[26] Indeed, the impossibility lodged within translation is itself death, madness—and originality.

The epigraph to Pound's first major translation project, *Sonnets and Ballate of Guido Cavalcanti* (published in 1912), announces an obligation, a compulsion, under which Pound will labor throughout his long career as a translator: "I have owned service to the deathless dead / Grudge not the gold I bear in livery." Though it is tempting, and perhaps entirely valid, to view Pound's conception of translation as symptomatic of the necrophilic orientation of his early poetry (and therefore related to the Image), it may be more accurate, though also more demanding, to view his entanglement with death as an effect of the trance of translation, a trance that yields a mnemonic conception of modern poetics. Such an interpretation would certainly find encouragement in the formula I have just outlined, which derives the death-discourse of translation from the extravagant economy of the impossible.

It is no secret that Pound conceived of translation as the scene of memory, evoked most prominently in his translation of a translation of Book 11 of the *Odyssey*, a palimpsest that serves as the opening sequence of the *Cantos*. Kenner, for example, views Pound's transla-

---

25. The most important contemporary account of the doctrine of impossibility in translation is Abraham and Torok's theory of cryptonymy, which derives from an effort to translate the multilingual puns of the Wolf Man. Although the logic of the crypt, as it is constituted by the Wolf Man's psychosis, admits, initially, only the possibility of transposition (a "word translated into an image"), the success of Abraham and Torok's hermeneutic project—their ability to decipher the encrypted words—testifies eloquently to the possibility of translation: that is, to the survival of meaning.

26. Georges Bataille, *The Impossible,* trans. Robert Hurley (San Francisco: City Lights, 1991), pp. 9–10, 157–164.

tions as "interchanges of voice and personality with the dead, the handful of enduring dead, across centuries and millennia of snow-drifting events."²⁷ Moreover, he claims, "The Poundian homage consists in taking an earlier poet as guide to secret places of the imagination" ("Introduction" 12). A more recent commentator characterizes Pound's work as a translator in a similar manner: "Finding something of value in a former age or different language, something relegated as it were to the realms of Lethe, the translator ferries it into modern English."²⁸ These descriptions, of course, are only echoes of Pound, who repeatedly emphasizes the mediumistic and telegraphic properties of translation. Explaining, for example, his aim in translating Lope de Vega, he writes, "One seeks to resurrect the damaged shade of the author" (*SR* 182). Variations and refinements of this statement appear throughout Pound's writings on translation.

The tenor of Pound's comments (which I will explore more thoroughly in a moment) suggests that it would be fruitful to think of translation in terms of elegy and mnemonic ritual, an idea that Rosanna Warren has recently explored. Regarding elegy as "a communion perpetually renewed in light of death," she attempts "to define a private ritual figure for translation, the perhaps fictive origin of elegy as the art associated with funerals, and thus with death."²⁹ Translation, she argues, enacts the rites of elegy:

> Just as the work of mourning proceeds by rehearsal of the trauma and ritual self-mutilation to detachment from the deceased and acceptance of a symbolic substitute, so the work of translation repeats the destruction of the original, dismembers and digests it as in the Thracian sacrifice of Orpheus or the rites of Dionysus, and finally offers a transubstantiated version as consolation for, and recognition of, loss. ("Sappho" 206)

27. Hugh Kenner, "Introduction," in *The Translations of Ezra Pound* (New York: New Directions, 1963), p. 14.
28. David Anderson, *Pound's Cavalcanti* (Princeton: Princeton University Press, 1983), p. ix.
29. Rosanna Warren, "Sappho: Translation as Elegy," in Rosanna Warren, ed., *The Art of Translation: Voices from the Field* (Boston: Northeastern University Press, 1989), p. 202. Warren's essay is also appealing in that it offers a "sketch of translation as an elegiac genealogy," a genealogy that leads from Sappho to Catullus to Baudelaire to Swinburne. Pound, who translated Sappho under the influence of Swinburne, would occupy the final position in this "elegiac genealogy."

Though we should retain the idea that translation is an elegiac mode, and especially the possibility that as a ritual it may represent the *origin* of elegy, we must also alter Warren's paradigm to reflect more accurately the idiosyncrasies of Pound's elegiac translations. We should insist, for example, that his translations be understood as "aberrations of mourning," since they are always about a *disavowal* of loss.[30] That is, they enact what Derrida calls *le deuil du deuil,* the obstruction of mourning that Freud first recognized in the "libidinal explosion of the maniac."[31] In Pound's elegiac translations, the manic inversion is signaled above all by the virtual absence of melancholy in his obsession with the dead (a distinctive feature, generally, of elegiac modernism). His translations therefore witness the jubilant return of the original, even as it remains sequestered, concealed from the one who gives voice to it. Enacting a frenzied incorporation of the dead, the mania of translation represents the primary economic effect of the doctrine of untranslatability (the failure to remember, to recuperate what is lost).

Pound often declines to use the verb "to translate," preferring instead a calque from the Latin such as "to bring over" or "bring across." Such a concern for definition is symptomatic of the chronic instability of translation, yet it also indicates Pound's desire to convey something of the "desolate undertaking" of translation, as well as its transitivity. In a famous comment about "Homage to Sextus Propertius," he writes, "There was never any question of translation . . . My job was to bring a dead man to life" (*L* 149). Pound's comment almost certainly alludes to the character of the original poems (which bear the title *Elegies* in Latin), but it also suggests that there is something repellent or dreadful about the task of translation. Although Pound took pleasure in the idea of circulating among the dead and bringing them back to life, he is often reticent in his approach. For

---

30. For an ingenious discussion of this problem, see Laurence Rickels, *Aberrations of Mourning: Writings on German Crypts* (Detroit: Wayne State University Press, 1989).

31. Derrida, "Living On," pp. 115, 111. On the enigmatic relation between melancholia and mania, Freud writes, "The most remarkable characteristic of melancholia, and the one in most need of explanation, is its tendency to change round into mania— a state which is the opposite of its symptoms." *Standard Edition of the Complete Psychological Works,* ed. James Strachey (London: Hogarth Press, 1960), vol. 14, p. 253. Further, he claims, "the content of mania is no different from that of melancholia . . . Both disorders are wrestling with the same 'complex' " (p. 254).

the dead are often perceived as sublime figures of authority, who inspire fear and hostility as well as veneration. Indeed, Pound often experienced moments of reluctance and trepidation at the shrine of the dead. Concerning his translations of Cavalcanti, he wrote, "That there might be less interposed between the reader and Guido, it was my first intention to print only his poems and an unrhymed gloze" (*T* 24). Here Pound discloses a fetishistic regard for the original that would have precluded translation altogether. Yet the implications of the term "gloze" suggest that even the most literal translation threatens to obscure the original. For "gloze" can mean simply "commentary," but also "flattery" or "specious talk." Indeed, the paradox of extreme literalism (that the most faithful translation is also unintelligible) haunts not only Pound's view of translation but the positivism of the Image. Pound's trepidation at exhuming the dead is nowhere more evident than in the following quote from his essay on the early translators of Homer: "But then all translation is a thankless, or is at least most apt to be a thankless and desolate undertaking" (*LE* 268). The pun on the final word, whether intentional or not, is particularly revealing. As we shall see, the sense of "desolation" that Pound experiences cannot be isolated from the "atrocities" committed in the act of translation.

Pound approaches the task of memory implied by translation with extraordinary ambivalence; he wishes "to touch the untouchable"—as Derrida describes the translator's impulse ("Babel" 191). It is a question of establishing *contact* with the dead through words, names, or signatures that we can regard, following the precepts of the art of memory, as disfigured *images* of what has been lost or forgotten. As relics of the dead, the fetishized words enable the sensation of *contact*.[32] Pound conceives his relation to literary tradition in a similar fashion: "Besides knowing living artists I have come *in touch* with the tradition of the dead . . . There is more in this sort of Apostolic Succession than a ludicrous anecdote, for people whose minds have been enriched by *contact* [emphasis added] with men of genius retain the

---

32. In *Totem and Taboo,* Freud describes such beliefs as the basis of what he calls the "omnipotence of thoughts." *Totem and Taboo* (1913), trans. James Strachey (New York: Norton, 1950), p. 81.

effects of it."³³ Elsewhere Pound writes of "the feeling of being in contact with the force of a great original" (*LE* 271). The sensation of contact, which is also the site of an exchange, can have various consequences. As this passage suggests, contact with a remote literature from the past (which Pound calls the "tradition of the dead") can, paradoxically, result in a transfusion of vital energy from the original to a moribund literature in the present. Pound asserts, for example, that British literature in the nineteenth century was "kept alive" by "exotic injections" of foreign literature through the translations of Swinburne, Rossetti, and Fitzgerald (*LE* 33–34). Much more frequently, however, Pound alludes to a process whereby the original author or text is brought to life, resurrected, through a depletion of the translator's vitality, or, more seriously, through a reification, a deadening, of his native language.

There is a terrible risk, of course, in feeding the dead from the store of one's own vitality. As many writers on translation have warned, the translator's linguistic identity, and perhaps even certain features of his native tongue, may be impaired or extinguished in the moment of exchange, when his words become the property of the dead. Pound not only acknowledges the "mortal" danger of translation, he embraces it as the essential experience of the translator. In an early poem called "Histrion," he explains his theory of the persona, which forms the basis of his early translational poetics:

> Translucent, molten gold, that is the "I"
> And into this some form projects itself:
> Christus, John, or eke the Florentine;
> And as the clear space is not if a form's
> Imposed thereon,
> So cease we from all being for a time,
> And these, the masters of the soul, live on. (*CEP* 71)

In this stanza, Pound describes the poet or translator as a "clear space" that ceases to exist as it takes on the "form" of Dante or of some other "master" in the moment of exchange. Translation, therefore, requires sacrifice. In Pound's translations, according to Daniel Hooley, this

33. Ezra Pound, "How I Began," *T.P.'s Weekly* (June 6, 1913): 707.

negative capability produces a "remarkable innovation."[34] "Homage to Sextus Propertius," in particular, shows the effects of a sacrificial exchange between the translator and the imagined persona of the original author: "The tone of ennui and stupefying inertia is present not only in the language and phrasing Pound uses, but even in the very *process* of his translation—as if the jaded persona Pound infers from the text were itself translating the poem" ("Pound's Propertius" 1035). As Pound the translator merges with the personality of the author, "the interpreted Propertius is, as it were, given the opportunity to re-compose his poem" (1041).

The voice of the translator, then, expires, while "the masters of the soul live on." The idea that the original survives through the afterlife of translation is fundamental to some of the most influential thinking about translation in the twentieth century. Walter Benjamin, for example, explains,

> Just as the manifestations of life are intimately connected with the phenomenon of life without being of importance to it, a translation issues from the original—not so much from its life as from its afterlife. For a translation comes later than the original, and since the important works of world literature never find their chosen translators at the time of their origin, their translation marks their stage of continued life. The idea of life and afterlife in works of art should be regarded with an entirely unmetaphorical objectivity . . . The concept of life is given its due only if everything that has a history of its own, and is not merely the setting for history, is credited with life. In the final analysis, the range of life must be determined by history rather than by nature. ("Task of the Translator" 71)

If the concept of "life" is determined not by natural but by historical longevity, then "death" merely initiates an afterlife that must be considered part of the life of the object. Later, Benjamin will claim that life is a natural fact whereas death is a social one, implying that the death of an object or a text is equivalent to its afterlife, its true historical existence. Thus, for Benjamin as for Pound, translation falls properly within death's dominion, which is the domain of history and its phantasmagorical modality.

---

34. Daniel Hooley, "Pound's Propertius Again," *MLN* 100, no. 5 (December 1985): 1035.

Like Pound's theory of *personae* (which is a theory of ghosts), one of Derrida's most substantial treatments of translation is built around the concept of "living on." (Derrida's essay "Living On" responds directly to Benjamin's historiological conception of death.) Derrida writes, "Translation is neither the life nor death of the text, only or already its living *on,* its life after life, its life after death" (103). From the phrase "living on" he extracts a sense of translation as afterlife, a living death (life after life), but also as a text "living on" another text: a parasite, a succubus, a ravenous ghost. Thus, the translation "lives off and dies of the other, preserves the other and loses the other" (167). Furthermore, Derrida observes, "the translation effect" incorporates the "effects of transference, of superimposing, of textual superimprinting" (91)—a conception that pertains directly to Pound's notion of translations as Images.

The figurative death of the translator described by so many theorists (and by Pound) is, of course, a linguistic event. "Death" occurs via the medium of language, and can therefore be conceived as a literary historical phenomenon, as a kind of legacy. In this regard, Pound was never coy about the influence of the great Victorian translators on his own theory and practice of translation. Concerning his translations of Cavalcanti, for example, he writes, "In the matter of these translations . . . Rossetti is my father and my mother" (*T* 20). Much Victorian translation, according to Susan Bassnet-McGuire, is based on "an immense respect, verging on adulation, for the original . . . Moreover, the original text is perceived as *property,* as an item of beauty to be added to a collection . . . The translator appears as a skillful merchant offering exotic wares to the discerning few."[35] The essential point, of course, is that Victorian translation tends to produce a kind of commodity steeped in nostalgia. One of the most obvious features of these "exotic wares" is the use of archaisms. And archaism happens to be, along with scholasticism, the feature of Victorian translation that most influenced Pound's work as a translator. Usually the "archaic" tone of a translation by Swinburne or Morris, for example, derives not from linguistic usage of an actual historical period but from the luster of neologisms and historical oddities drawn from various periods. The

---

35. Susan Bassnet-McGuire, *Translation Studies* (London: Methuen, 1980), pp. 69, 71.

result, which springs from a desire to preserve the historical otherness of the original, is entirely ahistorical. In this sense, Pound conceived of archaism simply as another material resource of the language. Archaism is called for, according to Pound, when "there is not ready-made verbal pigment" to render the "fervour" of the original (*LE* 200). Archaism is therefore not a style or decorative reminder of the past, but a verbal substance that magically embodies the original—like the untranscended materiality of the fetish—because it is "possessed" by the dead language of the original. The fetishistic appeal of archaism may help explain Pound's continued use of it, both in his poetry and in his translations, long after archaism had fallen out of literary fashion.

Archaism therefore has two functions: to recall magically a distant time or place, and to catch the eye of the elite "consumer." Both aims are related to fetishism, although the effects of the former are less obvious and more destructive. The use of archaism springs from a fetishistic desire to serve the original, to preserve its historical difference. Yet as George Steiner points out, archaism produces only "the illusion of remembrance" ("After Babel" 347). Furthermore, Steiner argues, "Archaism internalizes"; it incorporates the original in such a manner that the original is effectively forgotten. What is ostensibly an act of remembrance and fidelity therefore depends on a moment of amnesia or betrayal. Just as the magical luster of the commodity depends on the oblivion surrounding its material origins, so, too, the effect of archaism in translation may make the original less rather than more accessible to the reader (though this inaccessibility is also held to be the sign of an authentic translation).

The larger question of the translator's distance from an alien text, and whether this distance may be conceived as productive, is especially germane to Pound's first volume of translations from the Chinese, *Cathay* (published in 1915). For he completed these "translations" without any knowledge of the Chinese language. What conception of exchange between languages would allow us to call these poems "translations"? In his essay on the Anaximander fragment, Heidegger justifies an obscure rendering of a particular term with the following explanation: "The translation of τό κρεών as 'usage' has not resulted from a preoccupation with etymologies and dictionary meanings . . .

Impossible Effigies

The word 'usage' is dictated to thinking in the experience of Being's oblivion."[36] Although this passage can be fully elucidated only in the context of Heidegger's philosophical disclosure of "Being," the association of dictation and oblivion speaks generally to a fundamental condition of translation, and, more specifically, to Pound's oblivious translations from the Chinese. According to Heidegger, genuine translation is received only in "the experience of oblivion"; it is dictated out of forgetfulness—a forgetting of "dictionary meanings." In Pound's translation, according to Massimo Bacigalupo, there is a similar dialectic of nearness and distance: "Pound's translation is *apocalyptic*, as L. S. Dembo first suggested: it *reveals* an identity where one saw only distances, and does so, I will add—by making that distance absolute."[37] The notion of apocalyptic translation, which must be viewed as yet another excessive formation stemming from the doctrine of impossibility, necessarily evokes the phantasmagorical dimension of translation. Derrida, for example, refers to "an apocalyptic superimprinting of texts: there is no paradigmatic text. Only relationships of cryptic haunting from mark to mark" ("Living On" 137). Pound's oblivious relation to Chinese rules out the possibility of a "paradigmatic text" (which would depend on a matrix of "dictionary meanings"), so that apocalyptic translation, if it is to have any "contact" with the original, must receive its instructions from the dead under the veil and compulsion of mediation.

What would it mean for Pound's translations to be "dictated" from "oblivion"? We must emphasize, first of all, the essential passivity of the translator, the one receiving "dictation." But this passivity or subservience is also, I will argue, a license, a precondition for hermeneutical violence and abuse. The source of what is dictated, for Pound, can be nothing other than "the tradition of the dead." When Pound writes of his attraction to Chinese literature, "I desire to hear the music of a lost dynasty" (*L* 128), he intends to revive through his translations not only the dead poets but the milieu of Chinese antiquity. Pound's translations are therefore a kind of "haunted

---

36. Martin Heidegger, "The Anaximander Fragment," trans. David Knell and Frank A. Capuzzi, *Early Greek Thinking* (New York: Harper and Row, 1975), p. 54.

37. Massimo Bacigalupo, *The Formed Trace: The Later Poetry of Ezra Pound* (New York: Columbia University Press, 1980), p. 183.

writing," in which a dead author dictates to the translator, out of the oblivion of language or history—out of the impossibility of recovering certain specific meanings. (This problem is most acute, and therefore most revealing, in Pound's translations of Cavalcanti.) Avital Ronell has developed the concept of the "writing couple" to account for the space in which a dead author subjects a living author or translator to the "we position."[38] The essential feature of this telegraphic relation, as I have indicated, is that it derives from "the experience of oblivion." Equating modern poetics with the art of memory, Pound's translations are efforts to "resurrect a forgotten mode" and "a forgotten speech" (*LE* 11; *SR* 58). They are relics, fragments of a lost tradition, and the words themselves are magical because they are thought to be part or possession of the dead. The translator, by taking these words into his "empty mouth," acquires the qualities possessed by the dead and the lost tradition they represent.

Although the necrophilic dimension of Pound's translation theory quite obviously sustains the traditional imagery of mortality in translation, thereby engaging the problem of untranslatability, it is not clear in Pound's case what bearing the rhetorical cipher of death may have on the traditional categories of translation, such as metaphrase, paraphrase, or imitation. Does this elaborate metaphoric of death help us understand whether his translations correspond essentially to the *verbum de verbo* (word for word) tradition or to the *sensum de sensu* (sense for sense) tradition in translation? Is there a way of linking the critical and speculative dimensions of translation discourse? We can begin to formulate a response to these questions by observing that Pound conceived of his translations not only as reanimating the dead but as images—indeed, as *images of the dead*. Only by establishing a correlation between Pound's translation theory and his ideas about poetry can we view the cryptic features of his translations as symptoms of a larger crisis of representation in language and culture.

Though critics have noted an affinity between Imagism and the development of Pound's ideas about translation, neither the details nor the larger significance of this correlation has been examined care-

---

38. Avital Ronell, *Dictations: On Haunted Writings* (Bloomington: Indiana University Press, 1987). The phrase "we position" is from N. Christoph de Nagy, *The Poetry of Ezra Pound: The Pre-Imagist Stage* (Bern: Francke, 1960), p. 145.

fully. Hugh Kenner, for example, suggests that Pound's principles as a translator and the practice of Imagism display similar strategies in meeting the "test" of representation: "Pound has always written as if to meet a test of this kind, in a spirit of utter fidelity to his material, whether a document or an intuition. He has told of working six months to fix a complex instantaneous emotion in fourteen words" ("Introduction" 10). In a recent article on *Cathay*, Ming Xie is somewhat more specific when he suggests that there is a corresponding development between Pound's elegiac translations and his theory of the Image:

> Pound's own gradual evolution from his experiments with "hokku-like" sentences, the epigrams and epitaphs in the earlier poems, to the longer *Cathay* poems in which the elegiac mood prevails, indicates his gradual generic modulation of the epigrammic into the elegiac, paralleled by his developing theory of the Image. As a result, Pound extended the repertoire of elegy by modulating it into a mixture of styles and moods . . . all to be unified in a cluster of simple, natural, and distinct images.[39]

What remains implicit in Ming Xie's thesis—namely, the correlation of images, translations, and ghosts—finds expression in Jackson Mathews' explanation of Pound's "apocalyptic" rendering of Chinese ideograms: "Pound has explored these written traces of the pictures that went into their formation—an old *Imagiste* engaged in a kind of etymological archaeology. What he has hunted for are the shadowy images, the shades that may or may not haunt the penumbra of the Chinese mind . . . He is doing what he has always believed to be the business of poetry, taking care of language. Revivifying the faded image, reviving the meaning lost in banality and dead usage."[40] Although Mathews' comments are suggestive, they provide even less specific evidence for the comparison of images and translation than do the observations of Kenner and Xie.

To make a thorough comparison, we must return to the writings of Pound which form the basis of these critics' observations. In the

39. Ming Xie, "Elegy and Personae in Ezra Pound's *Cathay*," *ELH* 60, no. 1 (Spring 1993): 267–268.

40. Jackson Mathews, "Third Thoughts on Translating Poetry," in Reuben Brower, ed., *On Translation* (New York: Oxford University Press, 1959), p. 69.

late 1920s Pound undertook an ambitious scholarly and creative project to publish in translation the complete works of Guido Cavalcanti. This edition, which would have included photoreproductions of various manuscripts (an unorthodox method at that time) was to have been the culmination of Pound's long interest in Cavalcanti's poetry. The project was never published in its entirety. Among the unpublished papers of the edition is an introductory note that includes the following statement by Pound: "The translation of a poem having any depth ends by being one of two things: Either it is the expression of the translator, virtually a new poem, or it is as it were a photograph, as exact as possible, of one side of the statue" (cited in Anderson, *Pound's Cavalcanti* 5). Although this passage is unusual for its reference to photography, it is nevertheless representative of Pound's inclination to speak of translation in terms of analogies drawn from the graphic arts.

Indeed, this was not the first time Pound spoke of his translations of Cavalcanti in relation to the graphic arts. The introduction to *Sonnets and Ballate of Guido Cavalcanti,* published in 1912, begins with an epigraph from Dante that compares the relative values of Giotto and Cimabue. Why Pound would begin an introduction to a set of translations with a reference to painting becomes evident only when he makes a more explicit appeal to the art of William Blake: "I would liken Guido's cadence to nothing less than line in Blake's drawing . . . The line is unbounded, it marks the passage of a force, it continues beyond the frame" (*T* 23). The fact that Guido's "line" violates the boundaries of the frame makes possible not only Pound's interlingual translations but the intermedial figures that he uses to describe translation. When Pound revises the introduction for the "Complete Works" project in 1927, he updates the analogy: Miró replaces Blake. "And the mastery, a minor mastery, will lie in keeping this line unbroken, as unbroken in sound as a line in one of Miro's latest drawings on paper" (*LE* 197). Indeed, analogies drawn from the graphic arts inform Pound's most basic categories of translation. On the final page of *Umbra,* a collection of poems and translations published in 1920, Pound offers a typology of his translations. His more literal renderings fall under the heading of "études" or "portraits"—terms drawn from the vocabulary of painting. In a review of Laurence

Binyon's translation of Dante, Pound writes, "If Binyon has given us an engraving, he has put the original color on the opposite page" (*LE* 207). Elsewhere in the same review, Pound speculates on what might be lost if a Giotto fresco were "translated into oils" by Joshua Reynolds, and he cites the sculptor Brancusi to suggest the comparable demands made by sculpture and translation (*LE* 194, 206).

I cite these analogies to demonstrate that the poetics of Imagism, which Pound formulated during the period of his most intense involvement with translation (1910–1918), plays an important role in Pound's ideas about translation. This should not be at all surprising, since a theory of translation necessarily implies not only a theory of literature but a theory of language. Indeed, Pound emphasizes the "unity of intention" between his poetry and his translations (*SP* 41). Discussing the origin of the concept of the Image, he writes, "I began this search for the real in a book called *Personae*, casting off, as it were, complete masks of the self in each poem. I continued in a long series of translations, which were but more elaborate masks" (*GB* 85). In this passage Pound indicates that the Image, which emerged as a primary figure in his "search for the real," originated with the use of "masks" and that these two figures are contiguous. The aesthetic and epistemological aims of the Image in poetry are therefore closely related to Pound's agenda as a translator.

Pound's comparison of translation and the graphic arts is based in part on certain powerful ideological assumptions regarding the nature of graphic and verbal imagery. Traditionally, a realistic painting is understood to share certain material properties with what it represents. The relation of a pictorial sign to its referent is said to be "motivated" or iconic. When language is employed as a verbal "image," it takes on, by implication, the qualities of painting or sculpture. Translation, too, has traditionally been regarded as iconic: a word imitates a word; the relation of the medium to its referent is somehow less arbitrary than the relation between word and thing. As a result of these assumptions about the iconicity of graphic imagery and translation, both are conditioned by notions of debt, obligation, and fidelity to an original. It is precisely these assumptions regarding the ostensibly natural advantages of the image as a sign that predisposed the discourse of positivism toward the image as the privileged sign of objectivity. Thus, as images, Pound's translations labor under the same doctrine of extreme literalism (and its phantasmagorical effects) as the literary positivism of the poetic Image. What distinguishes translation discourse historically—and what makes deconstructive theorists so enamored of it—is its nihilism: its repeated admission that extreme literalism—the very principles that condition translation itself—is *impossible*. In other words, translation discourse proclaims with self-destructive candor what is often forgotten or submerged in the history of aesthetic philosophy and literary criticism: a realistic image is no more possible than an exact translation. The fact that the discourse of poetic objectivity blinds itself to the possibility of the impossible does not, I have argued, spare its images from the phantasmic effects of exchange. Indeed, the sorting of images (and translations) into categories of literal and free, proper and improper, should be read as a symptom, a residue of the impossible—a degraded symbol of the phantasmatic powers of negation. Such divisions, of course, invite impropriety, in that they refer obliquely to the impossible. Thus, as Images, Pound's translations aspire to a kind of "transparency" (a term in translation discourse that is equivalent to "fidelity"), though they are more likely to obscure the original, to become suddenly opaque, in their violent procedures and their efforts to dislocate the "receiving medium" (the target language) into the space of revelation. The opacity of Pound's translations exhibits the resistance to visuality (to transparency) that is characteristic of the modernist Image.

The modernist Image also reflects the unpredictable graft of translation—one text "living on" another—in its duplicity, its *Doppelcharakter:* "The one-image poem is a form of super-position, that is to say it is one idea set on top of another" (*GB* 89). The very wording of Pound's definition recalls, once again, Derrida's cryptological reading of translation: "An effect of 'superimposing' images inscribes itself *en abyme*" ("Living On" 129). It is precisely the haunting of one text by another, the obscene notion of live words "covering" a dead text, that accounts for the apocalyptic character of Pound's translations. Furthermore, a translation is an Image by virtue of its composite nature. For an Image, according to Pound, is also a "radiant node or cluster," a dynamic structure composed of heterogeneous elements (*GB* 92). Regarding his method of composing "Homage to Sextus Propertius," Pound writes, "I certainly omitted no means of definition that I saw open to me, including shortenings, cross cuts, and implications derived from other writings of Propertius" (*L* 231). These violent procedures would later serve as the basis for the "ideogrammic" model of discourse; they also subscribe to the formal logic of the fetish, which, according to William Pietz, always produces a "composite fabrication" made up of "heterogenous elements" ("Fetish: 1" 7).

The heterogeneity of Pound's translations is also evident in the fact that many of them are not freestanding, so to speak, but are embedded in larger texts. From Pound's first book of criticism, *The Spirit of Romance*, published in 1910, to the drafts and fragments of the final Cantos, the role and circumstance of translation in Pound's work is remarkably constant. Indeed, *The Spirit of Romance*, although it is a work of prose criticism, offers a surprising precedent for the method of the *Cantos:* translations interspersed with commentary. Pound calls the translations in *The Spirit of Romance* "illustrations" (*SR* 154). Yet the discursive structure that supports these illustrations groans under the weight of evidentiary material. Indeed, the proportion of translated material to commentary in *The Spirit of Romance* is over fifty percent, suggesting that these "illustrations" have clearly exceeded their ostensibly subordinate role in Pound's argument. A similar displacement occurs in the *Cantos* where the poet's own voice is frequently eclipsed entirely by translated material. Pound's translations begin as illustrations and end as hieroglyphs stripped of all explanatory or discursive context. They are mounted and displayed like emblems or precious amulets. Indeed, Pound makes it clear in *The Spirit of Romance* that one of his primary impulses is to preserve certain texts from extinction. These translations function therefore as *memento mori*, cherished possessions of the dead that are displayed like charms to guard against loss.

By viewing Pound's translations as Images, as he intended we should do, we see clearly that both these concepts in his work are conditioned by notions of accuracy and fidelity, which figure prominently in the discourse of objectivity. Moreover, the fact that these strictures produce in translation discourse a doctrine of impossibility suggests that the modernist Image is functioning under a similar regime of impossibility. The phantasmic or necrophilic dimension of the Image would therefore signal, as it does in the case of Pound's translation theory, a kind of madness that follows from invoking, and indeed practicing, the impossible. Exactitude in translation, however, is not precisely the same thing as objectivity in the doctrine of Image—or let us say, it is figured with considerably greater complexity. This is certainly the case with Pound. Indeed, we can learn a great deal about the problem of extreme literalism in the poetic Image (its positivity) by considering more carefully how Pound conceived of literalism in translation.

Pound generally divides his translations into two groups that seem to correspond, at first glance, to the conventional categories of paraphrase and imitation (that is, literal translations and free translations). In a brief appendix to *Umbra* (1920), he offers a typology of his translations to date. Under the heading "Major Personae" he lists "Homage to Sextus Propertius" and the poems of *Cathay*, whereas he describes his translations of Cavalcanti and Arnaut Daniel as "Etudes." Pound maintains this division throughout his writings and uses a number of different terms to characterize the differences within the ensemble of his own translations, or between his translations and those of other writers. Most of these terms arise from the recurring problem of how to characterize his translations of Cavalcanti. In a letter of 1912, responding to a review of *Sonnets and Ballate of Guido Cavalcanti* that appeared in the *Times Literary Supplement*, Pound writes, "Surely Rossetti's preface and mine show the reader that there could be no possible clash or contention between the aesthetic method and my scholastic one; he was avowedly intent on making beautiful verses as I am on presenting an individual" (Anderson, *Pound's Cavalcanti* xviii). In another letter, Pound describes the contrast somewhat differently: "I do not think, however, that homage has scholastic value" (*L* 178). The use of the term "homage" is almost certainly meant to refer to the specific qualities of "Homage to Sextus Propertius," thereby confirming the typology sketched out in *Umbra*.

Varying his terms slightly in an essay from *The Spirit of Romance*, Pound contrasts Rossetti's translations in verse ("verse in one language for verse in another") with his own "exegetical" translations (*SR* 106). Later, in his unpublished notes for the *Rime* edition of

Cavalcanti translations (published in Genoa in 1932), the contrast becomes one between Rossetti's "poetic" translations and his own "gloze" (cited in *Pound's Cavalcanti* 5). In a related comment, Pound describes his renderings of Cavalcanti and Arnaut as "diagrammatic translations" (*L* 179). Finally, in the long essay on Cavalcanti that he prepared for the "Complete Works" edition, Pound speaks of the difference between what he calls "interpretive translation" and translation that falls "in the domain of original writing" (*LE* 200). Taking all of these comments into account (including the contrast I cited earlier between translation as a "photograph" and translation as "original expression"), we can produce a fairly consistent and descriptive typology of Pound's translations. Gathered together, these terms display more readily their affinity for the historical categories of paraphrase and imitation.

Paraphrase (strict)	*Imitation (free)*
scholastic	aesthetic
exegetical	verse
gloze	poetic
interpretive	original
photograph	expression
étude	persona
diagrammatic	homage

Although this tabulation of Pound's views is certainly helpful in placing his translations in a traditional context, it tends to mask the originality of Pound's conceptions, as well as a certain tension between his notion of literalism (indicated by terms such as "exegetical" and "scholastic") and more conventional notions of fidelity in translation.

We should note that it is the Cavalcanti translations in particular which Pound consistently associates with the problem of exactitude, and that it is therefore these translations (along with "The Seafarer") which reflect most effectively the principles and permutations of the Image. In this regard David Anderson observes, "Writing for the 'Complete Works' in the late 1920s, Pound was to recall his early labors in the Cavalcanti atelier, and strongly to suggest that his Florentine Master had been the immediate source of those aesthetic principles that revolutionized his poetry after 1912" (*Pound's Cavalcanti* xiv). It is not only the problem of exactitude, however, or its "impossible" effects, that links the doctrine of the Image to Pound's translations of Cavalcanti. Indeed, Anderson argues that in the introduction to *Sonnets and Ballate of Guido Cavalcanti* (1912), "we find pronouncements couched in as yet uncertain critical vocabulary that look directly forward to Pound's imagist period" (xiv). Anderson is referring in part to the impact on Pound of Cavalcanti's conceptual *precision* (and his obscurity), but also to the obsessive *visuality* of Cavalcanti's love poems.[41] Furthermore, visuality and the experience of seeing in these poems (exemplified by the lover's glance) inevitably entail not only blindness but a kind of death. The correlation of vision and death quite obviously dominates Cavalcanti's imagination: of the thirty-five sonnets and fourteen ballads translated by Pound, all but a handful elaborate a persistent motif of death as a moment of vision eclipsed (and fulfilled) by the fatality of love, an "impossible" fusion of visibility and blindness. In Sonnet 22, for example, Pound translates, "Love bore away thy heart, because in his sight / Was Death grown clamorous for one thou lovest,"[42] Sonnet 26 bears the title "Of Love in a Dead Vision" (*Sonnets and Ballate* 53), and the lover in Ballata 1 is made to observe, "Were not death turned pleasure in my sight / Then Love would weep to see me so offended" (75). Among many other examples, we might also note these lines from Sonnet 4: "Then seems that on my mind there rains a clear / Image of a lady, thoughtful, bound / Hither to keep death-watch upon that heart" (9).

I think it is fair to say that this early volume of translations represents

---

41. The visuality of Cavalcanti's poems has not been lost on Lowry Nelson, for example, who writes, "Intrinsically connected with the intensity of Cavalcantian love and lyric drama is his vivid visuality. . . He seems more than other poets before him to register the sharpness and immediacy of visual images: first comes the direct striking of the image on the eye, then the psycho-physiological process of receiving it and contemplating it; there is also the character and significance of his glance and her glance, in the sense that a glance or a look is both receptive and also expressive." *The Poetry of Guido Cavalcanti* (New York: Garland, 1986), p. xl. According to Giorgio Agamben, who traces a cryptology of the lyric to its origins in troubadour and *duecento* poetry, Cavalcanti "conceived of love as an essentially phantasmatic process, involving both imagination and memory in an assiduous, tormented circling around an image painted or reflected in the deepest self." See Agamben, *Stanzas: Word and Phantasm in Western Culture,* trans. Ronald L. Martinez (Minneapolis: University of Minnesota Press, 1993), p. 81.

42. Pound, *Sonnets and Ballate of Guido Cavalcanti* (Westport, Conn.: Hyperion, 1983; orig. pub. 1912), p. 45.

a decisive, though largely underestimated, development in Pound's poetics. At a moment when he is formulating an aggressively modern poetics of the Image that would require him to put aside or at least disguise the necrophilia of his early poetry, Pound discovers in Cavalcanti's poems a conception of the Image that *preserves* the enigmatic power of death. Indeed, we could argue that the disparate features of the Image (intense feeling, problematic visuality, definitional rigor, and a fascination with death) coalesce in Cavalcanti's poetry—in the translation of a remote and archaic vision. A passage from Pound's original introduction to the translations indicates that he views Cavalcanti as the prototypical Imagist:

> Than Guido Cavalcanti no psychologist of the emotions is more keen in his understanding, more precise in his expression; we have in him no rhetoric, but always true description, whether it be of pain itself, or of the apathy that comes when the emotion and possibilities of emotion are exhausted, or that stranger state when the feeling by its intensity surpasses our powers of bearing and we seem to stand aside and watch it surging across some thing or being with whom we are no longer identified.[43]

It is important to note that Cavalcanti's precision (the prototype of the Imagist sensibility) tends toward melancholy, and toward a "stranger state" that resembles a kind of aberrant mourning. The title of Pound's 1932 Italian edition of Cavalcanti indicates that this melancholy association persisted in Pound's mind throughout his many revisions of the translations: the volume, *Le Rime,* is subtitled *Edizione rappezzata fra le rovine* ("Edition patched together amid the ruins").

In Pound's earliest translations of Cavalcanti, then, we discover an indispensable key to the necrophilic dimension of the Image, but also to its problematic visuality. It is not simply that Pound conceives of his Cavalcanti translations as images and as a means of resurrecting the dead, but that he actually discovers in Cavalcanti's poems (via the impossibility of translation) a correlation between vision and death that serves as the basis both for his conception of translation and for his doctrine of the Image. Thus, it is through his translations of

---

43. Pound, "Introduction," in *Sonnets and Ballate of Guido Cavalcanti,* p. xii. Pound dates the introduction November 15, 1910—another indication that Imagist poetics originated considerably earlier than the Imagist movement in 1913.

Cavalcanti that Pound first conceives of the Image that blinds and annihilates, the Image that resists visuality and thereby invokes the extravagant economy of the impossible.

Given the density and originality of this great translational event in Pound's career, it is not surprising if we find, on returning to Pound's reflections on translation, that most of his attempts at defining his own practice were focused on his translations of Cavalcanti. Indeed, the formal and imaginative resistance offered by Cavalcanti's poems provoked what are generally regarded as his most original contributions to the discourse of translation. (The "translations" of *Cathay* are justly admired for their elegiac beauty, but they did not yield the kind of formal and speculative innovations—in terms of translation—which arose over the long course of Pound's engagement with Cavalcanti.) For Pound, such innovations arise only in response to the demands of extreme literalism, to the textual resistance associated with an obligation to be faithful to the letter of an original (the same resistance that conditions the doctrine of the Image). Though the nature of his terminology sometimes suggests otherwise, these innovations are almost always motivated by an impulse to greater fidelity—indeed, this incongruity is the first clue to the originality of these conceptions. Thus, Pound considers the "exegetical" translations of Cavalcanti (his term for the kind of translation that is bound by certain obligations to the letter of the original) to be examples of what he called "criticism by translation" (*LE* 74).[44] (One might also subject a text to "criticism via music, meaning definitely the setting of a poet's words"; *LE* 74.) Elsewhere, Pound describes translation as a "contrast or cross-light" that helps illuminate features of the original that might otherwise remain submerged (*LE* 256). Thus, his translation of "Donna mi prega" is not "an equivalent" but an "instrument" to probe the original (*LE* 172).[45]

---

44. The concept of "criticism by translation" has generated considerable interest among theorists of translation. Antoine Berman, for example, writes, "Ezra Pound's translations and his reflection on poetry, criticism, and translation are of fundamental importance here, and it would be interesting to confront the theory of *criticism by translation* with the Romantic theories of translation by criticism." Berman, *The Experience of the Foreign*, p. 179.

45. Though Pound's Cavalcanti translations have become the most prominent example of "criticism by translation," the concept pertains as well to other translations

It must be remembered that these conceptions (which fall in the categories of "exegetical," "scholastic," or "interpretive" translation) are motivated by fidelity, by a kind of realism. The peculiarity of Pound's approach indicates, however, that poems as enigmatic, both historically and semantically, as Cavalcanti's require extreme and unorthodox measures to produce an *Image* of the text. Realism can be achieved only by employing certain violent or controversial procedures. Thus, in the introduction to *Sonnets and Ballate,* Pound explains, "It is conceivable the poetry of a far-off time or place requires a translation not only of word and spirit, but of 'accompaniment,' that is, that the modern audience must in some measure be made aware of the mental content of the older audience, and of what these others drew from certain fashions of thought and speech" (*Sonnets and Ballate* xii). In order to resurrect not only the dead poet but the milieu of a "far-off time or place," Pound must employ a variety of practices. The actual translation may therefore be "accompanied" by photoreproductions of various historical manuscripts, by a list of textual variants, by historical and interpretive annotations, and perhaps even by a musical performance of the original. (Only Pound's "scholastic" translations appeared with the original *en face,* unlike *Cathay* or "Homage to Sextus Propertius.") Thus, the translation itself is only a single component in the larger work of "diagrammatic" translation. This constellation of elements is the matrix of "criticism by translation" and can be described as an Image because it resembles, and almost certainly anticipates, the nondiscursive model of the ideogram. All the same, the motivation behind the elaborate strategies of accompaniment (and the complexity of the ideogram) is a simple one: greater fidelity and accuracy. Indeed, concerning his Cavalcanti translations Pound once claimed, "What we need now is not so much a commen-

---

by Pound. Indeed, the earliest correlation of translation and criticism occurs with Pound's publication of "The Seafarer," which appeared in November 1911 as the first installment of the series of articles titled "I Gather the Limbs of Osiris." Pound describes the translation of "The Seafarer" as an "illustration of 'The New Method' in scholarship"; *New Age* 10, no. 5 (November 30, 1911): 107. The fact that Pound initiates his twelve-part discursus on "the new method in scholarship" with a translation suggests that translation is not merely an aspect of the "new method" but its foundation. The new method in scholarship is, of course, a blueprint for the "new method" in poetry—that is, Imagism.

tator as a lexicon. It is the precise sense of certain terms *as understood at that particular epoch* that one would like to have set before one" (*LE* 162). Thus, Pound's elaborate translations of accompaniment (like the ideogram) aspire to the accuracy and transparency of a *lexicon;* each translation, like a kind of Rosetta stone, aims to *decipher* the original (a conception that evokes the problem of hieroglyphics).

Just as the ideogrammic Image is prone to obscurity and hermeticism, so it is often difficult to reconcile the procedures used in Pound's translations of accompaniment with a doctrine of literalism in translation. Concerning his translations of Cavalcanti, Pound writes, "I have found out what I have found out by concentration on the text" (*LE* 162); and even more emphatically, "the essential fact is THERE ON THE PAGE" (*LE* 208). Although this position represents an extreme, quasi-mystical preoccupation with the letter of a text, it is by no means restrictive, as Pound's translations demonstrate. For he advocates what he calls a "violence of language," albeit controlled (*L* 182). Describing the language of his early Cavalcanti translations as "katachrestical" (cited in Anderson, *Pound's Cavalcanti* 4), Pound insists that translation requires a "sacrifice of values" (*LE* 168). A radically material translation, like the Image-vortex, is a violent "channel" that transmits ideas and phantoms from a lost tradition, or from an inscrutable present, into the present. In Pound's view, the materiality of a foreign text, once it is cleared of static cultural "readings" and other forms of mediation, transmits an array of signals, formerly unintelligible, from its original milieu. The improvisatory character of his translations derives, paradoxically, from an ethic of extreme literalism.

Probably the most extreme example of Pound's "katachrestical" translations is his rendering of "The Seafarer," a work closely associated with the procedures of Imagism as a result of its publication in late 1911 as an installment of "I Gather the Limbs of Osiris" and because it appeared in *Ripostes* (1912). As we have seen, Pound presents the "Seafarer" translation as an illustration of "the New Method in Scholarship," which he describes otherwise as "the method of the Luminous Detail" (*SP* 21). We should also note the poem's elegiac tone and its emphasis on the experience of exile, features that it shares with the later translations of *Cathay* (1915). Yet "The Seafarer" corresponds most closely, in its methodological concerns, to the Cavalcanti translations, since Pound characterizes only these two projects as instances of "criticism by translation." Pound undertook both projects during the same period in his career (1910–1911), and both evolved as the result of his overriding concern with literalism—the key term in the translational doctrine of impossibility. In the February 15, 1912, issue of *New Age,* for example, Pound says that his rendering of "The Seafarer" is "as nearly literal, I think, as any translation can be." Like the Cavalcanti poems, "The Seafarer" evinces a preoccupation with death and materiality that bears significantly, from the translator's point of view, on the enchanted materiality of the text:

> Waneth the watch, but the world holdeth.
> Tomb hideth trouble. The blade is layed low.
> Earthly glory ageth and seareth.
> No man at all going the earth's gait,
> But age fares against him, his face paleth,
> Grey-haired, he groaneth, knows gone companions,
> Lordly men are to earth o'ergiven, . . .
> And though he strew the grave with gold,
> His born brothers, their buried bodies
> Be an unlikely treasure hoard. (*P* 66)

In all likelihood, the poem's preoccupation with exile and death helped persuade Pound to adopt a variation of the poem's Anglo-Saxon rhythms in Canto 1, itself a translation of Book 11 of the *Odyssey,* in which Odysseus descends to Hades.

The poet of "The Seafarer" describes the experience of exile as a kind of living death: "My lord deems me to this dead life" (*P* 65). Moreover, Pound equates exile and death in a more explicit fashion in an early poem, "Epilogue," composed in 1912, the year following his work on "The Seafarer":

> I, who went out in exile,
>   Am returned to thee with gifts.
> I, who have labored long in the tombs,
>   Am come back therefrom with riches. (*CEP* 209)

These lines describe the poet's "medieval studies, experiments, and translations" in terms of an encounter with the dead, yet they also introduce the experience of *exile* as a figure for translation. Exile, according to "The Seafarer," brings with it affliction, sorrow, and bitterness, yet "the heart's thought" in exile also seeks out "a foreign fastness" (*P* 65)—a cryptic space that exceeds the dull life of "the Burgher." Moreover, although the poet of "The Seafarer" belies the poem's preoccupation with death by asserting that "buried bodies / Be an unlikely treasure hoard," the poem's *translator* (Pound) insists that the tomb—the "foreign fastness" sought in exile—yields abundant riches.

Exile, as a figure for translation, becomes equivalent in this context to a kind of grave-robbing. More specifically, in the case of "The Seafarer" (as well as Pound's Cavalcanti translations), it is the effects of extreme literalism in translation that bear comparison with grave-robbing, so that the ransacking of graves, even if it verges on the romance of archaeology, demands to be read as an image of katachresis in translation. Some of Pound's techniques in translating "The Seafarer" can indeed be described as katachrestical, even as they represent a clandestine laboring "in the tombs," a desecration of the crypt by looting it of material "devices" associated with the dead. The most striking examples of katachresis in "The Seafarer" occur when Pound "translates" certain Anglo-Saxon terms or phrases by substituting English homonyms. K. K. Ruthven has described this practice in detail:

> As a result he has given us "reckon" (1) for *wrecan* ("to make, compose"); "stern" (23) for *stearn* ("a tern"), "moaneth" (37) for *monað* ("makes mindful of, urges"; in l. 51 *gemoniað* is translated literally as "admonisheth"); "berries" (49) for *byrig* (dative of *burh,* "a town"); "twain" (70) for *tweon* ("to doubt"); "mirth" for *mærþo* ("glory"); and "blade" (90) for *blæd* ("glory," translated literally as "blast" in l. 80). This technique can cope not only with single words but also with phrases: *on eorþan* becomes "on earth then" (33; "then" is superfluous); *sumeres weard* ("guardian of summer") becomes "summerward" (55); and *eorþan rices* ("kingdom of the earth") becomes "earthen riches" (83).[46]

---

46. K. K. Ruthven, *A Guide to Ezra Pound's "Personae" (1926)* (Berkeley: University of California Press, 1969), p. 213.

With such practices the poet reaches the enchanted boundaries of literalism in translation. In this case, the materiality of the archaic and anonymous text is charged with a kind of magical authenticity and expressiveness that permits translation only as *transposition*—a gesture that often implies a violation of the original's *meaning*. Though Pound paints this process in terms of recovering the "possessions" of the dead—their "fashion," their "craft," their habits—the logic of "possession" encourages us to view the translator of "The Seafarer" as someone enthralled by the enigmatic but often mutilated *corpus* of the text, conjuring a spirit from its enchanted substance in a manner that violates its meaning.

The combination of reverence and abuse directed toward the "dead" original evokes in the strongest possible manner not only the latent animism of the artifact but the ephemeral character of the object's "vitality." In her theory of artifactual reciprocity, Elaine Scarry emphasizes that our magical attachment to made objects always carries a threat of violence: "A useless artifact, whether a failed god, or a failed table, will be discarded."[47] Furthermore, she explains, "Civilization restructures the naturally existing external environment to be laden with human awareness, and when a given object is empty of such awareness, we routinely ask the garbage collector (himself a direct emissary of the platonic realm of ideal civilization) to carry it away to the frontier, beyond the gates of the beloved city" (*Body in Pain* 305). A failure of reciprocity on the part of the artifact usually ensures its disappearance (because it is no longer sentient), and indeed the violence directed against the artifact simply reverses the power of life and death exercised by the fetish over its maker.[48] Accounts of fetishism are ways of talking about images, and a theory of imagery is, inevitably, also a theory about the fear and hostility aroused by images.[49] Thus,

---

47. Elaine Scarry, *The Body in Pain: The Making and Unmaking of the World* (New York: Oxford University Press, 1985), p. 182.
48. According to William Pietz, Enlightenment theorists associated the essential "delusion" of fetishism (and its social efficacy) with a fear of death: "The fetish would supernaturally cause the physical death of those who broke faith. Fetishism thus represented a principle of social order based on an irrational fear of supernaturally caused death rather than a rational understanding of the impersonally just rule of law." Pietz, "The Problem of the Fetish: Part 3a," p. 106.
49. W. J. T. Mitchell makes this argument in *Iconology*, pp. 3, 159.

most accounts of fetishism, whether colonial, medical, or economic, tend to emphasize the subservient and passive orientation of the fetishist. William Pietz, for example, summarizes the view of Enlightenment theorists, inherited from colonial travel narratives: "The slavishness of the situation of the fetish worshipper lay in the infantile submission of his inner autonomous will to the random determinations of the mechanism of natural events" ("Fetish: 3a" 12). Similarly, in his book on fetishism in nineteenth-century literature, David Simpson summarizes the view of fetishism that Marx inherited from ethnography and Romantic aesthetics: "Roughly speaking, fetishism occurs when the mind ceases to realize that it has itself created the outward images or things to which it subsequently posits itself as in some sort of subservient relation."[50]

These views, as I have suggested, fail to take into account the violence and abuse characteristic of fetishism, which is evident in colonial travel narratives. Writing in 1737, John Atkins, for example, observes that a fetish may be kept "until the Proprietor could not observe any of the usual effects, or was improsperous; and thus whether he imputes it to the Age and Decay of the Fetish, I cannot tell; but takes a newer and consequently a better."[51] Similarly, writing in 1699, the Dutchman Willem Bosman quotes an African, who explains, "If our Design prove successful, we have discovered a new and assisting God, which is daily presented with fresh Offerings. But if the contrary happen, the new God is rejected as a useless Tool, and consequently returns to his Primitive Estate . . . We make and break our Gods daily, and consequently are the Masters and Inventors of what we Sacrifice to."[52] From its earliest appearances in colonial discourse, then, the idea of the fetish is associated with what Pietz calls a "primary and carnal rhetoric of identification and disavowal" ("Fetish: 1" 14). The animism of the artifact is signaled not only by the submissiveness of the fetishist, but by the violence that may be directed toward the object if it loses its powers of enchantment. Bosman's "informant"

50. David Simpson, *Fetishism and Imagination* (Baltimore: Johns Hopkins University Press, 1982), p. xiii.
51. John Atkins, *A Voyage to Guinea, Brasil, and the West-Indies* (London, 1737), pp. 83–84.
52. Willem Bosman, *A Description of the Gold Coast of Guinea* (London: Cass, 1967; orig. pub. 1705), p. 368.

also reveals the remarkable continuity between colonial fetish discourse and the modernity of commodity fetishism: "We make and break our Gods daily, and consequently are the Masters and Inventors of what we sacrifice to." Marx, of course, argues that modern fetishists are less enlightened than their "primitive" counterparts, because they remain ignorant of their creative role. Indeed, Marx's analysis of the commodity can be viewed as an exhortation to master the object, to realize the destructive powers of the fetishist by disenchanting our "possessions." The Freudian analysis of fetishism, on the other hand, echoes the colonial paradigm more clearly, since Freud argues that the fetishist is never merely passive or subservient before the object of his passion: "To point out that he reveres his fetish is not the whole story; in many cases he treats it in a way which is obviously equivalent to a representation of castration . . . Affection and hostility in the treatment of the fetish—which run parallel with the disavowal and the acknowledgement of castration—are mixed in unequal proportions in different cases" (*Standard Edition* 21: 157). Thus, the veneration conventionally associated with sexual fetishism often entails a symbolic deletion or mutilation of the fetish object. The Freudian correlation of fetishism and abuse also surfaces in the context of modern art in the "sadistic literary and visual content" of the Surrealist "object."[53]

The idea that affection and hostility, reverence and abuse, subservience and domination can be contained in a single perspective is essential in explaining the contradictions in Pound's achievement as a translator. His entire poetic agenda is based on a profound reverence for literary tradition, yet his translations are notoriously violent; originals are frequently dismantled and willfully rearranged. "Take these scraps, and the almost impossible conclusion, a tag of Provençal rhythm, and make them a plenum" (*LE* 196). His tactics can produce monstrosities of sense or diction. Yet he undertakes all of this in the spirit of what Stephen MacKenna calls "a chaste freedom, a freedom based rigidly on a preservitude" (cited in Steiner, *After Babel* 268). If, indeed, we regard Pound's translation practice as a highly influential form of literary and cultural memory, then we must recall that the art

---

53. On fetishism and Surrealism, see Jack J. Spector, "The Avant-Garde Object: Form and Fetish between World War I and World War II," *Res* 12 (Autumn 1986): 130, 131, 136.

of memory prized, as stimulants to "natural" memory, images that had been *disfigured* in some manner. Thus, the monstrosities of Pound's translations signal not only the artificiality of translation as a form of memory, but its technological aspect.

In those translations that are governed by the contradictory logic of the Image, Pound offers the reader examples of what Phillip Lewis calls "abusive translation," a practice that belongs to "an experimental order, an order of discovery."[54] Lewis contrasts the Marxist concept of use value with abuse, arguing that great translation goes against the grain of conventional "usage" ("Translation Effects" 58). Abusive translation would therefore be associated with the figural properties of exchange value. Following Lewis' conception, Cynthia Chase calls for "a strategy of rigorously abusive translation, which would counter what is lost in the translation with an addition, a supplement. The translator commits an excess, performs an abuse—but not just anywhere."[55] For Pound, the seeds of abuse are embedded in the original; certain "enigmas" or "obscurities" in the original text invite experimentation (*LE* 259, 268–269). Thus, as I have already indicated, he acknowledges the need for a "violence of language," and describes his early Cavalcanti translations (and, by implication, his rendering of "The Seafarer") as "katachrestical."

In response to charges that the "mistakes" in his translations are inadvertent or unintentional, Pound writes, "As to the atrocities of my translation, all that can be said in excuse is that they are, I hope, for the most part intentional, and committed with the aim of driving the reader's perceptions further into the original than it would without them have penetrated" (cited in Anderson, *Pound's Cavalcanti* xxi–xxii). Furthermore, he explains, "In some places I hope mistranslation may serve to concentrate attention on a passage" (5). Here again we find the characteristic ambivalence of fetishism: the translator's fidelity is demonstrated by various "atrocities" committed against the original. If we recall the necrophilic dimension of Pound's translations, we might say (with Derrida) that translation "calls forth what it forbids:

54. Phillip Lewis, "The Measure of Translation Effects," in Graham, ed., *Difference in Translation*, p. 45.
55. Cynthia Chase, "Paragon, Perergon: Baudelaire Translates Rousseau," ibid., p. 65.

the death of the other whom it is supposed to preserve" ("Living On" 166). Intentional mistranslation (an effect of the impossibility of translation) becomes a procedure that is at once solicitous of the original and an instrument of originality. Conditioned by the metaphorics of gender in translation, originality and the recovery of an original always come at the expense of violence. (And this expenditure subscribes to the logic of the crypt, as Antoine Berman notes: "Where there is revelation of something hidden there is violence"; *Experience of the Foreign* 171.)

The politics of originality also dictate Pound's intolerance of violence committed against the "organism" of the *langue maternelle*.[56] He is quick to attack anyone who violates the "natural wording" of English (*LE* 270). He condemns, for example, the "stilted unsayable jargon" of Browning's *Agamemnon* (*LE* 268). In the extreme case, Pound's loyalties are clearly defined: his fidelity to the syntax of English is absolute. In contrast to this conservatism about English sentence structure, however, are the wild fluctuations of diction in Pound's translations. The "pigment" of archaism, for example, is a resource that Pound employs with surprising regularity in his translations. In addition, the reader is occasionally startled to find Confucius speaking African-American English or Cockney dialect. Along with these "monstrosities" of diction, Pound is not afraid to produce lapses of meaning in a text (a "sacrifice of values"). Unlike the *syntactic* monstrosities generated in the target language by extreme literalism (which Benjamin prized in Hölderlin's translations), Pound's atrocities are usually committed against what he perceives to be inherited or historical "sediment" that obscures the original meaning, a strategy that produces a corresponding "enigma" in the sense or diction of the translation.[57] Thus, Pound explains, "What obfuscated me was not the Italian but the crust of dead English, the sediment present in my available vocabulary" (*LE* 193). In his Cavalcanti translations, then, Pound anticipates the principles of Imagism, by pursuing a dream of

56. I would refer the reader once again to Lori Chamberlain's superb essay "Gender and the Metaphorics of Translation," where she notes "the persistence of what I have called the politics of originality and its logic of violence in contemporary translation theory" (p. 64).

57. On Benjamin's taste for such "monstrosities," see Carol Jacobs, "The Monstrosity of Translation," *MLN* 90, no. 6 (1975): 762.

translation *without remainder*. Yet the dream, as we have seen in the case of the Image, only produces another corpse.

The Freudian analysis of fetishism can be particularly helpful in identifying the greater interests of a veneration that presupposes or requires the mutilation of its object. To what end is fetishistic ambivalence directed? Its function is essentially conservative: the fetishist aims to preserve his fantasy of the maternal phallus (which would allay his fears of castration). Alan Bass calls the fetish "a fantastic mistranslation of sexual difference," a thesis which derives from Freud's reference to the "indelible trace" left in the unconscious by the fantasy of the maternal phallus.[58] The fetishist "mistranslates" the "indelible trace" of the maternal phallus in order to preserve it.[59] A similar logic is at work in Pound's translations: not only do they betray contrary impulses to preserve and to transform the "trace" of the original, but Pound commits his "mistranslations" with the aim of preserving a fantastic figure encrypted in the words of the original.

Bass extends the analogy of translation and fetishism further when he describes the fetish as a "rewriting of history that reinterprets indestructible pictures of early fantasies in terms of current needs" ("History of Mistranslation" 128). As fetishes, Pound's translations fulfilled a similar revisionary function: to "rewrite" literary history in accordance with the contemporary requirements of Pound's larger poetic project. Often, his work as a translator provided a laboratory for his poetic experiments. Thus, Pound's translations of a canzone by Cavalcanti or a lyric by Li Po tend to resemble atavistic shades of his own mercurial diction, or the "costly" signatures of his ear. As

---

58. Alan Bass, "On the History of Mistranslation and the Psychoanalytic Movement," in Graham, ed., *Difference in Translation*, p. 137.

59. In a humorous parable about mistranslating proper names, Pound inadvertently reveals the phallic dimension of translation. He writes, "The phonetic translation of my name into the Japanese tongue is so indecorous that I am seriously advised not to use it, lest it do me harm in Nippon. (Rendered back *ad verbum* into our maternal speech it gives for its meaning, 'This picture of a phallus costs ten yen.' There is no surety in shifting personal names from one idiom to another" (*LE* 259). While this anecdote is obviously light-hearted, it is nevertheless brimming with significance. For it describes a moment in which Pound's own signature, his proper name, is disseminated into another tongue, letter by letter, and returns to him in all of its foreignness, as an image. The consequence, therefore, of utter fidelity to the materiality of a word is a monstrosity; depravity is the outcome of chastity.

Victor Smirnoff remarks, "the fetish-object represents *restoration* of a lost continuity."[60] And this is precisely the aim of Pound's fetishized translations: to resurrect a lost tradition, to rewrite literary history through the reverential "abuse" of foreign texts. Translation in Pound's poetics is therefore not only a medium to resurrect the dead, but a *mediator* of literary history.

A translation in which abuse becomes a technique of fidelity summons a question that hovers persistently about Pound's doctrine of literalism in poetry and translation (a question, surely, that has already troubled the reader): Is it reasonable to describe as accurate or faithful a translation that depends on katachresis and mistranslation? Clearly, Pound's sense of exactitude in translation diverges sharply from conventional notions of metaphrase or paraphrase (hence the originality of his conceptions). Yet surely it would be a mistake to suggest that Pound is not motivated by a sense of obligation to an "original," given the extraordinary procedures he devised to ensure the greatest possible accuracy. Perhaps we can trace the problem to assumptions regarding the nature of the object of translation; perhaps we should ask a question that I have already posed in relation to the poetic Image, a question that is decisive in determining the nature of realism or objectivity in Pound's poetics: What, then, is the object of Pound's translation of a poem by Cavalcanti? I mean, what does it pretend to be faithful to? Of what is it an Image? Is it a rendering of the letter of the poem (as we might expect of a translator who is concerned with accuracy), or the "spirit" of the poem (its "meaning"), or some other dimension of the thing?

We know that the poetic Image (as I discussed in Chapter 1) dissociates itself almost entirely from the empirical object. The Image presents not the physical object but something that resists appearing altogether. The same is true of Pound's "exegetical" translations: it is quite clear that he is not concerned with rendering Cavalcanti's poem word by word, or even with reproducing its "music." In the unpublished notes to his "Complete Works" project, for example, Pound observes, "The ideal translation of G.C. [Guido Cavalcanti] will use

---

60. Victor Smirnoff, "The Fetishistic Transaction," in Serge Lebovici and Daniel Widlöcher, eds., *Psychoanalysis in France* (New York: International Universities Press, 1980), p. 322.

a simpler language than either Rossetti or I have attained, and will concentrate on the meaning and cut loose, a great deal looser from the actual phrase" (cited in Anderson, *Pound's Cavalcanti* 255). This comment recalls the idea that his "scholastic" translations aspire to the condition of a lexicon. From a historical standpoint, therefore, he claims (in regard to translations of Homer), "The quality of translations declined in measure as the translations ceased to be absorbed in the subject matter of the original" (*LE* 247). Given these comments by Pound, it might seem plausible to argue that his "exegetical" translations, strange as they may be, are examples of the "sense for sense" tradition of translation: his translations are Images not of the letter of the original but of its meaning. This characterization, however, is untenable for a number of reasons (particularly in light of the techniques Pound used in "The Seafarer"). Borges once remarked of Pound's work as a translator, "Scholars accuse Pound of making gross errors, demonstrating his ignorance of Anglo-Saxon, Latin, or Provençal; they are unwilling to grasp that his translations reflect elusive forms and not the substance of a work."[61]

To understand Borges' comment, we must recall Pound's view that his task as a translator is to "resurrect the damaged shade of the author." Discussing in 1926 the danger of revising his early Cavalcanti translations, Pound offers a glimpse of the telepathic properties of translation: "Even if I now managed to get back into Guido's skin, or into some skin that I for a moment hallucinate myself into thinking of as the skin of Guido, it is a different me, and I enter the pelt from a different angle" (cited in Anderson, *Pound's Cavalcanti* 5). More prosaically, he claims that he attempts in his translations "to embody in the whole of my English some trace of that power which implies the man" (*T* 24). In another context, Pound once made a peculiar comment about what is *missing* in Rossetti's translations of Cavalcanti. What Rossetti fails to do, according to Pound, is to give the reader a sense of "Euclid inside his cube" (*LE* 193). By this, Pound means the

---

61. Jorge Luis Borges, "Note sur Ezra Pound, traducteur," *L'Herne* 6 (1965): 233 (my translation). The original reads, "Les érudits accusent Pound de tomber dans les erreurs crasses, démontrant son ignorance du saxon, du latin ou du provençal; ils ne veulent pas comprendre que ses traductions réfléchissent les formes insaisissables et non le fond."

force and mystery of "personality" that dwells within the form of a great work—whether that form is in stone, in words, or in the laws of geometry. What Pound seeks to do in his translations is to bring back to life the force of a unique "personality," and to feed it, if necessary, with the vitality of his own tongue.[62] He often speaks of an author's personality informing a work, of "Marlowe's unbridled personality moving behind the words" (*SR* 194), or Cavalcanti's "lofty, austere spirit moving behind the verse" (*SR* 113). Often, Pound loses sight of the distinction between the force of personality and the actual words of a text. Not only might an author's words be understood as a possession, an extension, of his personality, but Pound actually conceives of this personality as a kind of text. About Villon, he says, "He is a lurid canto of the *Inferno,* written too late to be included in the original text" (*SR* 177). When Pound writes, "My endeavor was not to display skill in versification but to present the vivid personality of Guido Cavalcanti" (Anderson, *Pound's Cavalcanti* 5), we understand that this translation must be something like a verbal effigy, rudely fashioned and charged with the "omnipotence of thoughts." This statement is similar to his disclaimer about translating Propertius: his job is "to bring a dead man to life." Pound seems to want to emphasize the crudity and supernaturalism of his enterprise. His translations are not quite texts, or objects, or phantoms, but are amalgams of all three: verbal effigies of powerful literary figures from the past whom he alternately reveres and abuses according to the present needs of his own poetic project. We are reminded of Yeats's description of

---

62. The idea of "translating" the personality of a dead author (who bears traces of a lost "dynasty" of meaning) suggests that Pound, through his translations, wishes to make "contact" with an entity (a lost time or place) that exists prior to the actual words of the original text. A comment by Freud suggests that an image (or translation) of a lost place comprises the oblivion of fetishism. Freud writes, "When the fetish is instituted some process occurs which reminds one of the stopping of memory in traumatic amnesia . . . It is as though the last impression before the uncanny and traumatic one is retained as a fetish" (*Standard Edition,* 21:155). Although recognition of the missing object "institutes" the fetish, the object or material translated into a fetish actually derives from a moment in time that *precedes* the traumatic scene of recognition. Thus, in the realm of fetishism, effect precedes cause. If applied to translation, this temporal inversion of cause and effect would suggest that a translation may antedate the original that precipitates it. This would help explain Pound's insistence that a translation must resurrect the author behind the original text. The translation therefore embodies a force that precedes the original text, though it also necessarily derives from the original.

Pound as a "brilliant improvisator translating at sight from an unknown Greek masterpiece"—a comment that deftly conveys the sense of a reckless and even perilous rendering of an original that is not only "dead" but lost.

In the process of translating, as in the poetics of Imagism, Pound seeks not so much to render the empirical object (the literal features of the original) as something behind or within the object—a phantom that appears reluctantly if at all. This does not imply, however, that Pound is primarily concerned with meaning or content in a traditional sense; rather, translation permits an exchange between languages that is at once mnemonic, impossible, and nonrepresentational. It permits one language to be possessed by the habits of another, in material and stylistic terms, via the "person" of the dead author. If we take Pound's obsessive revisions of Cavalcanti's "Donna mi prega" as emblematic of his translations of accompaniment, then there can be little doubt that the phantasmatic event of translation stems from its own impossibility. For the ingenious (and desolate) strategies of Pound's translations reveal nothing so much as the fact that the meaning of Cavalcanti's poem is truly forgotten, lost, unrecoverable. Since the impossibility of translation can arise only as the consequence of an excessive obligation to the original, we must conclude that Pound conducts the séance of his imagistic translations according to the demands of extreme literalism—though the object the séance summons has disappeared. In their uncompromising fidelity to the dead, Pound's translations are faithful to nothing that exists. Conceived as an art of memory, translation—which is then distinguished by its technical aspect—threatens to submerge, even as it enhances, the powers of "natural" memory.

CHAPTER 6

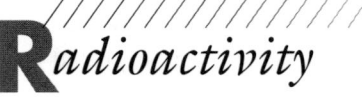
Radioactivity

> *La Radia* shall be
>
> The reception amplification and transfiguration of vibrations emitted by living beings living or dead spirits dramas of wordless noise-states.
>
> The reception amplification and transfiguration of vibrations emitted by matter.
>
> —F. T. Marinetti and Pino Masnata, "La Radia" (1933), trans. Stephen Sartarelli

> I go my way with the assurance of a somnambulist.
>
> —Adolf Hitler, radio speech, March 14, 1936

Radium

Pound's fascist radio broadcasts, delivered twice weekly over Rome Radio from January 1940 to July 1943, provided the legal basis for his indictment on charges of treason in 1945, as well as the motive, ultimately, for his twelve-year confinement in a mental asylum.[1] These broadcasts are also rightly viewed as evidence of his mental instability during the war and as the most virulent expression of his fascist and anti-Semitic beliefs. In spite of the historical and symbolic significance of these broadcasts in Pound's career (and in the evolution of postwar American poetry), critics have made little effort to correlate the materials of these broadcasts, or the significance of Pound's choice to use

---

1. For a brief historical sketch indicating how Pound's radio speeches were written, recorded, and broadcast, see Leonard Doob's introduction to his compilation of the radio scripts, *"Ezra Pound Speaking": Radio Speeches of World War II*, ed. Leonard W. Doob (Westport, Conn.: Greenwood, 1978), pp. xi–xv.

RADIO CORPSE

a technical medium, with his literary and cultural values. To be sure, thinking about the medium of radio and its special relation to fascism hardly seems an appropriate conclusion to a book about Pound's conception of the Image. What possible bearing could radio, a medium that is understood to be intrinsically nonvisual and phonocentric, have on a theory of images? At best, on the surface of things, we might expect a discussion of radio in the larger context of modern "images" to articulate in unexpected ways the dialectic of verbal and visual values that finds expression in the history of the modernist Image. Yet the terms of Pound's earliest speculations on the nature of poetic imagery require a much stronger claim concerning the relevance of radio (and fascist radio in particular) to the principles of Imagism. Indeed, I believe that we must regard Pound's fascist radio broadcasts, if we take into account his theories of material and translational images, as marking the practical and theoretical horizons of Imagism. Furthermore, if we view the medium of radio as a specific political formation of the imaginary, then the imaginary (and ideological) correspondences between telegraphy and radiation, between broadcasting and radiography, must be considered germane to the poetics of the modernist Image.

These correspondences may be said to arise, in part, from Pound's dialectical concern with various kinds of waste and contamination, as well as from the mediumistic conception of the body that issues from his speculations on the relation between imagery and corporeality. The waste material of the cadaver, which survives in the phantasmatic *substance* of the Image, finds its most extreme expression in radioactive materials such as radium. The corpse, as an Image, becomes radioactive, thereby representing a principle of nonorganic life and, at the same time, assuming the properties of a medium. The radio corpse, as such, transmits a cryptonymous account of the Image and its political afterlife. A kind of "meaning" somehow emanates from the inert materiality of the corpse, though the cadaverous Image may also be regarded as an emblem of "objectivity" and of the eclipse of meaning in modernist poetics.

We should therefore generally understand the radiological character of the Image as an effect of "meaning"—that is, as signaling the magical and perilous recuperation of subjective and socially constructed meaning in the context of literary and philosophical positivism. Within the discourse of objectivity, then—whether it pertains to "science" or to fascist historiography—meaning becomes equivalent to radiation, to a form of "energy" that is magically potent (in its capacity to carry electrified speech or to "see through" objects) but also deadly. This improbable discourse of radio images pertains to the superstitious properties attributed to meaning by theorists ranging from Walter Benjamin and Ernst Jünger to Wittgenstein (who, for example, draws a comparison between meaning and cursing).[2] The telephonic order of radio becomes equivalent, in this regard, to telepathy, but also to the lethal effects of radioactivity.

By "radio images" I mean images whose invisibility corresponds directly to the magical effects of transmission, translation, and exchange (which stem from the "decay" of the body). In Pound's case, the discourse of radio images, which emerges fully only in the context of fascism, can be traced directly to his earliest speculations concerning the nature of poetic imagery. These early discussions of a "mythological" conception of the Image draw heavily, as many critics have noted, on the emerging science of electromagnetism.[3] Pound

2. Several eminent theorists of modern imagery display a surprising configuration of interests. Pound's is not the only career that veers between a preoccupation with images and a significant engagement with radio. Walter Benjamin's programming for children in the early years of German broadcasting is beginning to find a place in the critical history of his work. See Jeffrey Mehlman, *Walter Benjamin for Children: An Essay on His Radio Years* (Chicago: University of Chicago Press, 1993). We should also consider carefully the place of radio in the influential theories of E. H. Gombrich, who from 1939 to 1945 monitored German broadcasts for the B.B.C. Listening Post. Gombrich's own reflections on broadcasting can be found in his *Myth and Reality in German War-Time Broadcasts* (London: Athlone, 1970). Finally, we should recall that Rudolf Arnheim, another prominent theorist of modern visual culture, produced a book-length study of the new medium titled *Radio: An Art of Sound* (London: Faber and Faber, 1936).

3. The influence of popular science on Pound's poetics is the subject of two fine books: Ian F. A. Bell, *Critic as Scientist: The Modernist Poetics of Ezra Pound* (London: Methuen, 1981); and Martin Kayman, *The Modernism of Ezra Pound: The Science of Poetry* (London: Macmillan, 1986). More specifically, Kayman's essay "Ezra Pound: A Model for His Use of Science," *Biblos* (Coimbra), vol. 57 (1981), provides a very helpful sketch—to which I am indebted—of the scientific milieu around the turn of the century and a chronology of the major discoveries and theoretical advances in the emerging science of electromagnetism. He also describes the activities of the Society for Psychical Research (founded in 1882), an influential group of scientists whose interests provide the immediate context—via Yeats—for Pound's alignment of science and mysticism.

views Cavalcanti's visionary poetry, for example, as disclosing "the radiant world . . . a world of moving energies," and more specifically, as depicting "magnetisms that take form, that are seen, or that border the visible" (*LE* 154). Furthermore, as he explains in his introduction to his translations of Cavalcanti, "Modern science shows us radium with a noble virtue of energy. Each thing or person was held to send forth magnetisms of certain effect; in Sonnet xxxv, the image of his lady has these powers. It is a spiritual chemistry, and modern science and modern mysticism are both set to confirm it" (*T* 18). Later, in relation to the mediumistic properties of the Noh drama, Pound continues to emphasize the "magnetic" properties of the Image: "The image has a sort of centripetal force, drawing in the mind upon beauty, and in each case upon some particular beauty."[4]

Pound's early theorizing about radiant images (which "border the visible") also yields, not surprisingly, some of his earliest speculations about atomic structures (which contribute to his conception of the ideogram): "The Art of Poetry consists in combining these 'essentials to thought,' these dynamic particles, *si licet* this radium" (*SP* 330). This view of poetry as something like a radioactive substance informs Pound's most celebrated conceptions of the Image, as when he calls the vortex a "radiant node or cluster" (*GB* 92) and writes in 1913 (the year in which he launched the Imagist movement), "The thing that matters in art is a sort of energy, something more or less like electricity or radioactivity, a force transfusing, welding, and unifying" (*LE* 49). In the "unifying" power of "radioactive" images we discover the origins of paideuma—the fascist "world-picture"—in which the disparate features of history are fused into mythological coherence.

According to Kayman, members of the society included: William James (president of the society in 1896), Sir Oliver Lodge (professor of physics and one of the inventors of the wireless), Henri Bergson, Sir William Cookes (discoverer of Thallium and inventor of the radiometer), Lord Rayleigh (Nobel physicist in 1904), and Sir J. J. Thompson (discoverer of gamma rays). Corresponding members included Heinrich Hertz, Sigmund Freud, Carl Jung, and Marie Curie. Among the phenomena investigated by the society were "telepathy, automatic writing, clairvoyance, and the 'survival of bodily death.' " More generally, according to Kayman, it sought to foster "the production of a scientific discourse of the mystical" (p. 518).

4. This comment occurs in a recently discovered and unpublished essay that Pound wrote in 1915: "Affirmations VI: The 'Image' and the Japanese Classical Stage," *Princeton University Library Chronicle* 53, no. 1 (Autumn 1991): 18.

More remotely, we also discover in Pound's theory of radioactive art the origins of a conception of radio as a medium that is capable of unifying the "subconscious energies" of an entire population. Indeed, at least provisionally, I will make a case for what Alice Yaeger Kaplan calls "the insistence of the radio in the fascist unconscious."[5] That is to say, fascism discovers in radio not only a technical medium that is essential to its practical dissemination, but its proper ideological medium as well. In Pound's case, the ideological medium of radio has its origins in his speculations about the Image—a trajectory that recapitulates the historical spectrum of radio waves: "Begin in a radio dreamland, end in a radio war."[6]

Pound found corroboration for his early theory of "radioactive" images in Fenollosa's conception of the ideogram. Fenollosa describes the Chinese written character as enveloped by "a nimbus of meanings."[7] Furthermore, he explains, "a word is like a sun, with its corona and chromosphere; words crowd upon words, and enwrap each other in luminous envelopes" (*Chinese Written Character* 32). In the manuscript from which Pound constructed his revised version of Fenollosa's essay, Fenollosa refers to the "radiation" and "coronal" harmonies produced by the ideogram.[8] This conception of "radiant" meaning appears as well in an earlier essay of Fenollosa's titled "The Nature of Fine Art." There he writes that poetry "demands full words, charged with intense meaning at the center, like a nucleus and radiating out toward infinity, like a great nebula."[9] Quite clearly, the radioactive properties of the ideogram must have appealed to Pound not merely

---

5. Alice Yaeger Kaplan, *Reproductions of Banality: Fascism, Literature, and French Intellectual Life* (Minneapolis: University of Minnesota Press, 1986), p. 138.

6. This characterization of radio history is Gregory Whitehead's, from his essay "Out of the Dark: Notes on the Nobodies of Radio Art," in Douglas Kahn and Gregory Whitehead, eds., *Wireless Imagination: Sound, Radio, and the Avant-Garde* (Cambridge, Mass.: MIT Press, 1992), p. 256. Concerning the dialectic of the "radio dreamland," he writes, "Just beneath the promise of a lightning connection to a world of dreamy, invisible things, lurks a darker potential for spotlessly violent electrocution, for going up in smoke, or going down with the ship" (p. 256).

7. Ernest Fenollosa, *The Chinese Written Character as a Medium for Poetry*, ed. Ezra Pound (San Francisco: City Lights, 1936), p. 25.

8. From Fenollosa's original manuscript, cited in Laszlo Géfin, *Ideogram: History of a Poetic Method* (Austin: University of Texas Press, 1982), p. 23.

9. Fenollosa, cited in Lawrence W. Chisolm, *Fenollosa: The Far East and American Culture* (New Haven: Yale University Press, 1963), p. 216.

as a counterpart to the "magnetic" images of Cavalcanti but as a means of "radicalizing," so to speak, the electromagnetic spectrum.

At the figurative core of Pound's (and Fenollosa's) theory of "radiant" images is the substance of radium, whose radioactive properties were discovered in 1898, and which Poincaré, the French mathematician, called in 1905 "that grand revolutionist of the present time." In 1895, only three years prior to the discovery of radium's "mystical" energy, the German physicist Roentgen disclosed the revolutionary imaging effects of X-rays. Among the early names for the negative images produced by these rays were "radiograms" and "skiagrams" (shadow writing). Just as Pound had conceived of radium as producing images "bordering the visible," so the physical properties of X-rays introduced dramatic new possibilities for penetrating and imaging the unseen. With regard to the development of the modernist Image, it is significant that the phenomena of radium and X-rays are both identified in the public mind—not surprisingly, given the historical proximity of their discoveries—with the existence of a world of hidden energies or forms, and with visual registrations of invisibility. On one hand we have a substance whose radiant energy is invisible, whereas on the other we have a form of radiant energy that produces images of the unseen. In Pound's theory of translational or visionary images these categories collapse into each other: the Image is not *produced* by radiation but rather is itself a radiant substance, transmitting yet also somehow depicting the hidden "world of energies." The translational Image is radioactive: it is at once a form and a transmission of the invisible, an ambiguity that recalls Pound's antithetical translations of the memory *locus* as the "forméd trace" and "unformed space." This tension between inscription and transmission also informs the development of sound reproduction from phonography to radio broadcasting.

We can therefore view Pound's fascination with radium and radioactivity as one of the essential sources of what I have called the negativity of the modernist Image—a negativity that is signaled by the Image's resistance to visuality. Furthermore, as Lorraine Daston and Peter Galison have observed, the assimilation of X-ray technology to emerging ideologies of vision and objectivity was immediate and profound: "In part the ability of X-rays to penetrate where ordinary vision could not bestowed on the medium an aura of superhuman power. But in addition, by its very nature, X-ray technology was parasitic on the widespread assumption that the photograph does not lie . . . The image of the X-ray appeared (in court, at least) to preempt and displace all other forms of knowledge."[10] Thus, the image produced by radiation—or, in Pound's case, the radioactive Image—derives from its objectivity powers that are "superhuman" (that is to say, "magical"). As a powerful new index of objectivity, radiation—the medium of *invisible* images—simply reinforces the negativity of the modernist Image. More obscurely, the autonomy of the Image—an effect of its essential negativity—is signaled by the interminable half-life of radium, by its immortality. As a dialectical emblem of that which kills and cannot be killed, of mortality and immortality, radium must therefore be regarded as one of the most fertile and puzzling figures in Pound's cryptology of the Image.

Conceived as a radioactive substance, the modernist Image appears in a certain physical and ideological "frequency," yet is continually verging, from its inception, upon radiography (the art of radio images) and the "tribal medium" of radio. What is more important, the physical spectrum of the modernist Image is an ideological spectrum, across which are distributed the historical distinctions between words and pictures, or voices and images. The fact that this spectrum is, both physically and ideologically, a continuum implies that light verges on sound: pictures, under certain historical circumstances, become words (and vice versa). In this regard, I am defining a nominalist position similar to that articulated by W. J. T. Mitchell, who argues that "there is no *essential* difference between poetry and painting," but that "there are always a number of differences in effect in a culture which allow it to sort out the distinctive qualities of its ensemble of signs and symbols."[11] From this perspective, it is possible for a medium (painting, for example) to migrate or travel along an ideological spectrum of historically determined values and to occupy the "frequency" of another medium (such as poetry). Insofar as these categories (words

10. Lorraine Daston and Peter Galison, "The Image of Objectivity," *Representations* 40 (Fall 1992): 111.

11. W. J. T. Mitchell, *Iconology: Image, Text, Ideology* (Chicago: University of Chicago Press, 1986), p. 49.

and pictures) are inflected and indeed determined historically by configurations of race, class, and gender, then we must view the radiological properties of the modernist Image as a cryptic revelation of its *political life*. Thus, in the course of its development, the Image is displaced along a spectrum that is at once material and ideological: the Image conceived as a "radiant" corpse becomes the voice of fascism, converted by the medium of radio into the ghost of a lost aesthetic.

To deconstruct the medium of the Image in this way implies, of course, that radio, its antithetical medium, is constructed according to a similar series of oppositions and that radio, as a medium, is therefore also susceptible to a kind of ideological migration. Gregory Whitehead, a theorist and practitioner of radio art, subjects the medium of radio to spectral analysis when he argues that

> the material of radio art is not just sound. Radio *happens* in sound, but sound is not really what matters about radio. What does matter is the bisected heart of the infinite dreamland/ghostland, a heart that beats through a series of highly pulsed and frictive oppositions: the radio signal as intimate but untouchable, sensually charged but technically remote, reaching deep inside but from way out there, seductive in its invitation but possibly lethal in its effects. Shaping the play of these frictions, the radio artist must then enact a kind of sacrificial autoelectrocution, performed in order to go straight out of one's mind and (who's there?) then diffuse, in search of a place to settle. Mostly, this involves staging an intricate game of position, a game that unfolds among far-flung bodies, for the most part unknown to each other. ("Out of the Dark" 254)

Whitehead's sense of radio as an "intricate game of position" may be extended to radio's ideological construction as a medium. Thus, although I have emphasized a dialectical relation *between* verbal and visual values—between the radio broadcasts and the modernist Image—it is essential to note that this dialectic operates *within* each of these media. Pound's conception of the graphic Image, as I have emphasized repeatedly, is haunted by its spectral and phantasmatic origins, and continually threatens to revert from a figure of inscription to a figure of transmission. A similar dialectic informs not only Pound's radio speeches (which were prerecorded in batches of ten or twenty at a time), but the discourse of sound reproduction, which, according to Douglas Kahn, is dominated by three figures: vibration, inscription, transmission.[12]

As the names "gramophone" and "phonograph" indicate, the "registration" and objectification of the voice (which converts sound into a commodity) is conceived in graphic terms—that is to say, as a mode of writing or inscription. In an essay on the history of phonographic media, Kahn describes "the protophonographic trends leading to the birth of the phonographic voice, the writing technologies embodied in the resurrection or animation of youth."[13] Among the "writing technologies" contributing to the realization of phonography, Kahn cites the development of "universal languages and alphabets," as well as "speech synthesis and automata in general" (85). The phonographic media therefore descend, in part, from experimentation with ideogrammic notation, suggesting that Pound's formulation of the ideogrammic method, as a "writing technology," anticipates in unexpected ways his political experiments with a disembodied voice conveyed through the medium of radio. Moreover, the entire spectrum of "writing technologies," from ideogrammic writing to phonography, subscribes, as Kahn indicates, to a teleology that focuses on "the resurrection or animation of youth." The phonographic dimension of radio therefore perfects the "divinatory" technique of the ideogram—without, however, sacrificing any of its graphic or "scientific" properties. Indeed, the gramophone was frequently invoked during the period of its initial penetration into public and private life as an emblem of positivism. (For example, in his *Tractatus*, Wittgenstein refers to the gramophone as being analogous to his picture-theory of language—an analogy that Moholy-Nagy, in 1922, calls the "groove-manuscript.")

Transmission, on the other hand, dematerializes the mark, the object of sound. Kahn explains, "Transmission was basically the return and invigoration of objects and bodies that had been fixed by inscription to the space implied by vibration" ("Histories of Sound" 20). Thus, transmission revives at a distance the object of inscription, the

12. Douglas Kahn, "Histories of Sound Once Removed," in Kahn and Whitehead, eds., *Wireless Imagination*, p. 14.
13. Douglas Kahn, "Death in Light of the Phonograph," ibid., p. 85.

image of the voice, recovering its lost or decayed origin, which *returns* as a ghost. Moreover, Kahn observes,

> Phonography established the objecthood of sound and the ability to replicate a myriad of objects, but it did not strongly imply sounds from a distance. Wirelessness immediately meant great distances . . . This structure was anthropomorphized in several accounts of radio and transmission in general to ideas of unmediated communication, thought transference, and signal as corporeal sensation. A technology that had already been heavily invested with human fears and desires was elevated to vitalistic, prosthetic, and necrotic tropes. (21)

Oscillating between inscription and transmission, phonography and telephony, the production of Pound's radio speeches replicates in a technical medium the oscillation of the modernist Image between positivism and hermeneutics, between direct "registration" and the magical space of words at a distance. In this regard, it is probably helpful to remember that the modern art of cryptology originates with the military use of the wireless during World War I—also the burial site of Pound's cryptology of the Image.[14] Moreover, when radio—the medium that spawns the modern discipline of "cryptanalysis"—emerges from its origins in counterespionage, it does so as the new medium for poetry.[15]

To get a preview of Pound's radiophonic enchantment (which amounts to a *performance* of fascist ideology) as well as a glimpse of the radio phantom rehearsing its lacerating effect, we must turn to Pound's music criticism, especially *Antheil and the Treatise on Harmony,* published in Paris in 1924. It was during this period (or shortly afterward) that Pound was reading Frobenius and Leibniz for the first time, and these readings in turn initiated his mythological reformulation of the ideogram. In addition, during the mid-1920s Pound took a strong interest in three artists who were associated with Dada and

---

14. Manuel DeLanda discusses the military origins of wireless cryptology in his book *War in the Age of Intelligent Machines* (Cambridge, Mass.: MIT Press, 1989), pp. 180–212.

15. In his essay "Soundplay: The Polyphonous Tradition of German Radio Art," Mark E. Cory explains, "In Germany the earliest programming marking the transition of radio from a military tool to a cultural medium included music and the recitation of poetry." In Kahn and Whitehead, eds., *Wireless Imagination,* p. 334.

Surrealism: Picabia, Cocteau, and the young American "composer" George Antheil.[16] Pound regarded Picabia as what we would now call a "conceptual artist" (*SP* 458), while he appreciated Cocteau primarily for his radiophonic techniques (*SP* 454). Pound's infatuation with the sonic art of Antheil was therefore in keeping with the provisional or experimental nature of his (Pound's) interest in Surrealism, which permitted him to explore the technologized spaces between traditional media. The peculiar instability of medial boundaries in Pound's Surrealism almost certainly contributed to his speculations in 1928 about "a new medium, a sort of expression half way between writing and action" (*SP* 217). Not only does Pound assimilate Surrealism primarily as a sonic or "conceptual" art, but his ideas about music and telephony are strongly colored by Surrealism. This orientation is quite obvious in several passages of the Antheil book: "After the 'fool in the outer ear' has been put to sleep by the rhythm; after the ear's rebellion against the first *shock to its habit* has worn off, the little whiskers of the ear's interior 'miniature piano' begin to wave quite nicely in the ebb and flow of this different sort of sound current; a nostalgia of the sun overtakes one; the music is, and is rightly, an enchantment."[17] Pound's views on music can be compared to those of the Belgian Surrealist Paul Nougé, whose 1928 essay "Music is Dangerous" describes the "haunting" character of sound: "It would reach us in its most pervasive forms; the song rising from the lips of those about us, of such and such a stranger, perhaps in the most haunting circumstances; that mechanical music which floats our way from the background of deserted places; and sly and most dangerous of all, the voice that suddenly materializes from some forgotten corner of our memory."[18]

Nougé's idea of sound evoking "deserted places," as well as his references to oblivion and memory, articulate the implied topos of Pound's subliminal and "nostalgic" dimension of sound. The art of

16. The best account of Pound's interest in Dada and Surrealism is Richard Sieburth, "Dada Pound," *South Atlantic Quarterly* 83, no. 1 (Winter 1984), pp. 44–68.

17. Pound, *Antheil and the Treatise on Harmony* (Chicago: Pascal Covici, 1927), pp. 124–125. This first American edition of Pound's text contains notes not included in the original edition, published in Paris in 1924 by Bill Bird's Three Mountains Press.

18. Paul Nougé, "Music is Dangerous" (1928), cited in Christopher Schiff, "Banging on the Windowpane: Sound in Early Surrealism," in Kahn and Whitehead, eds., *Wireless Imagination*, p. 179.

sound, especially as it becomes technologized, is clearly, in the views of these writers, an art of memory. As such, Pound's developing sense of sonic and telephonic practice, which will culminate in the Rome Radio broadcasts, represents the final stage in his ongoing reformulation of the concept of the medium—a process dominated by the figure of the Image. The ostensibly visual medium of the Image realizes fully its negativity by migrating into the "frequency" of radiographic images and, ultimately, into the spectral medium of radio. In Pound's case, the question of the medium, whether one is speaking of poetry or of the technical and occult media, is always a question of memory, of reconfiguring death and reviving the dead.

Pound's eccentric "treatise" on music anticipates, primarily by its receptivity to Surrealist ideas, the nostalgic character of his radiophonic practice. There is also, however, a personal and psychological "complex" embedded in the book that looks forward to the mediumistic character of the radio broadcasts. For Pound's music theory is inseparable from his idolatrous regard for Antheil, the self-described "Bad Boy of Music."[19] The scale of Pound's infatuation stands in marked contrast to the relative insignificance of Antheil's compositions in the history of twentieth-century music. Indeed, even Antheil admitted, "Nobody could have been a tenth as good as Ezra made me" (*Bad Boy* 120). What is it, then, that fuels Pound's enthusiasms for the scandalous "concerts" staged by Antheil? In my opinion, Pound's *Treatise* on Antheil is enflamed by nostalgia, not only for his own youthful participation in the Vorticist movement, to which he compares the Surrealist milieu, but for the "bad boy" whom Antheil resembles: Gaudier-Brzeska.[20] Indeed, Pound explicitly compares Antheil to

---

19. George Antheil's memoir *Bad Boy of Music* was published in 1945 (Garden City: Doubleday).

20. The resemblance between Gaudier and Antheil may have some physical basis, if we compare the photo of Gaudier reproduced by Pound in his memoir of the sculptor (an image showing Gaudier with longish hair) to Christopher Schiff's description of "a Man Ray photo of Antheil—taken after one of the pianist's Berlin concerts—sporting a Louise Brooks haircut. While this might not seem remarkable now, the image of a male wearing a hairstyle that had been developed for women who wished to appear androgynous was almost as shocking in its time as was either the star that Duchamp had shaved on his head or Dali's mohawk." Schiff, "Banging on the Windowpane," p. 188, n. 100. Antheil's androgyny is not without significance, if we recall Pound's feminization of Gaudier in the memoir. Furthermore, the cult surrounding Gaudier after his death

Radioactivity

Gaudier, referring to "Antheil's criticism of other composers, the turns of phrase, the abruptness recalling Gaudier's manifestos" (*Treatise* 56–57). Both men, he concludes, have about them an air of "savagery."[21] Clearly, Pound has reopened Gaudier's crypt (and the burial site of the Image) by publicizing and theorizing his infatuation with Antheil. His nostalgic revival of a dead Imagist (via the medium of Antheil's celebrity) is a harbinger of fascism's nostalgic appeal.

What must be emphasized about Pound's close encounter with Surrealism is that his speculations on the subliminal and nostalgic character of sound coincide with a celebrity figure (Antheil) whom he charges with subliminal and nostalgic "energies." Antheil is moreover prominently associated with the *mechanization* of sound, a profile that aligns him with phonographic and telephonic media. These media have historically been closely associated with a technology of memory, but also with telepathy and reanimation, thus providing Pound with a belated index of the mnemonic and cryptological features of the "radiant" Image. Charles Cros, the inventor (with Edison in 1877) of the gramophone, calls his machine a "paleograph," instructing it, "You will write what has (already) taken place . . . You will rewrite, you will remember me."[22] Edison himself wrote of the phonograph, "This tongueless, toothless instrument, without larynx or pharynx, dumb, voiceless matter, nevertheless utters your words, and centuries after you have crumbled to dust will repeat again and again to gen-

---

bears some resemblance to the largely male hysteria surrounding Antheil. Schiff writes, "the Surrealists—particularly expatriate Americans such as Man Ray—attended his concerts religiously, assaulting anyone who expressed displeasure with the performance" (p. 176).

21. The "scene" of Pound's first meeting with Gaudier in 1912 (*GB* 44–45) bears an uncanny similarity to Antheil's description of his first meeting with Pound in Margaret Anderson's apartment in 1923: "He [Pound] was unusually kind and gracious to me; and as I left he asked for my address and said that he would someday come around to see me. Ezra turned up early the next morning, in a green coat with blue square buttons; and his red pointed goatee and kinky red hair above flew off from his face in all directions" (*Bad Boy of Music*, p. 117). Pound's eccentric attire recalls Ford Madox Ford's description of his Vorticist costume prior to World War I (see Chapter 3, note 23, above), suggesting that Pound is literally replaying his role as a Vorticist impresario, courting Antheil as he once did Gaudier.

22. Charles Cros, "Note au sujet du phonographe de M. Edison," cited in Charles Grivel, "The Phonograph's Horned Mouth," trans. Stephen Sartarelli, in Kahn and Whitehead, eds., *Wireless Imagination*, p. 44.

erations that will never know you, every idle thought, every fond fancy, every vain word that you choose to whisper against this thin iron diaphragm."[23] Moreover, following the invention of the phonograph, Edison became embroiled in public disputes about the afterlife, and even worked for a time on a device intended to establish contact with the "memory swarms" of the soul.[24] A similar "outbreak of ancient speculations"—to use Pound's phrase—occurs with the invention of telegraphy. In the *Century* magazine in 1902, for example, a writer observes of the wireless, "It would be almost like dreamland and ghostland, not the ghostland created by a heated imagination, but a real communication from a distance based on true physical laws."[25]

Views such as these—a mere sampling of a pervasive orientation—suggest that Pound, by embracing radio in the context of fascism, transposes into a technological and highly politicized realm his most esoteric concerns with death, memory, and radioactive energies. The nostalgic and fetishized properties of the Image—its cryptic dimension—find direct material and technical expression in the medium of radio as it develops under fascism. Indeed, given the associations hovering about the phonographic and telephonic media, I am inclined to say that the ideological medium of radio is always present in the most archaic configurations of the modernist Image, whether we have in mind the magical and lethal effects of radiation, the ventriloquism of Pound's translations of the dead, the art of memory, or the genealogical tracing of the ideogram to primitive "drumming languages" (*GK* 98). This persistent emphasis on lost, dead, or forgotten phenomena culminates, I would argue, in the fascist discourse of mythological "possession," in which the disparate features of political and economic life are magically unified and frozen into an image of the past.

As an implement of what Michael Taussig calls "State fetishism," the radio is distinguished from the gramophone above all by its character as a *mass medium,* and is therefore implicated historically in the

---

23. Edison, cited in Kahn, "Death in Light of the Phonograph," p. 93. Kahn's essay probes the necrophilic dimension of the history of phonographic media.

24. Wyn Wachhorst discusses Edison's interest in parapsychology in *Thomas Alva Edison: An American Myth* (Cambridge, Mass.: MIT Press, 1981), pp. 137–141. See also Kahn, "Death in Light of the Phonograph," for a more speculative reading of the convergence of technology and spiritualism in Edison's work.

25. P. T. McGrath, cited in Whitehead, "Out of the Dark," p. 254.

Radioactivity

discourse of crowd psychology. In a paper on the relation between crowd psychology and the avant-garde, Robert Nye observes, "Crowd psychologists [such as Gustave LeBon] also paid homage in their writings to the power of modern communications networks to create vast crowds—'publics'—by the simultaneous generation of 'mental images' and currents of opinion."[26] Hitler, who was a disciple of LeBon's theory of crowds, appears to have assimilated directly into the radio practice of National Socialism these opinions regarding the susceptibility of crowds to "mythological" images.[27] Alice Yaeger Kaplan develops what she calls "the concept of the radio crowd" in relation to fascism, explaining, "The fascist position on radio was figuratively, not literally, collective: the ideal fascist broadcast, whether monitored individually or in a crowd, should extend the listener into an imaginary crowd spirit" (*Reproductions of Banality* 136). Pound's conception of radio is likewise permeated by the "crowd spirit": he repeatedly emphasizes its "democratic" properties, even as he condemns its pernicious effects on the "herd." From a broader perspective, his "surrender" to the medium of radio can be viewed as recuperating his interest in the "Unanimisme" of Jules Romains (a proto-avant-garde movement that constitutes a shadowy dimension of the earliest writings on Imagism).

In her essay on the fascist radio broadcasts of the French collaborator Lucien Rebatet, Kaplan writes, "The persuasive efficacy of radio was not merely a historic factor in the success of fascism. A discourse on radio, as well as a discourse *miming* radio, played an important role in the versions of successful social reality propagated by fascist intellectuals" (*Reproductions of Banality* 138). I want to make a similar claim about Pound: long before radio became a significant element of his cultural and political practice, Pound displayed in his theorization of the Image an affinity for figures that are essential to the history of phonographic and telephonic media (inscription, transmission, radiation, and reanimation). Having said this, I must emphasize, in

26. Robert A. Nye, "Savage Crowds, Modernism, and Modern Politics," paper delivered at a conference titled "Prehistories of the Future: Primitivism, Modernism, Politics," California Institute of Technology, 1992.
27. My source for the information concerning Hitler's knowledge of LeBon's crowd theory is Gombrich, *Myth and Reality in German War-Time Broadcasts*, p. 4.

Pound's case, that his views about radio, and the technical media in general, are not simply dialectical but antithetical. Thus, as I have indicated, Pound views radio as a natural extension of fascism's transformative, mythographic character, yet he also equates it with the "subhuman transmissions" of Jewish influence (*RB* 159). Radio is at once the essence of fascism and the mediumistic equivalent of the Jew. A similar schism develops in his conception of radio as a medium that both fosters and inhibits expression or thought. In 1940 Pound declares, "Free speech without freedom of radio is a mere goldfish in a bowl" (*SP* 303)—a view that he is fond of repeating in his broadcasts. Yet he also attacks radio as a "devil box" that pacifies the "herd" of "goyim," as a medium bearing "unconscious agents . . . poisonous as the germs of the bubonic plague" (*RB* 100, 238). Radio is at once the last refuge of "free speech" and a modern pestilence, a kind of shock therapy that either electrifies or electrocutes the mind.

In certain respects, the contradictory nature of Pound's position merely reflects the ambiguity characterizing society's response as a whole to new technical media. Concerning the public reception of the phonograph, for example, Charles Grivel writes, "Demand and suppression went together, the desire to preserve the voice and anxiety generated by the spectacle of one's own self (its excessive coherence, its 'eternity')" ("Horned Mouth" 41). There is a special significance, however, to the antithetical character of Pound's response to radio, since he recognizes, with some displeasure, a basic correspondence between radiophonic practice and the ideogrammic technique of the *Cantos:* "I anticipated the damn thing [radio] in first third of Cantos" (*L* 343). When Pound talks about radio, therefore, he is also reflecting upon the formal innovation that is most prominently associated with the *Cantos:* the ideogrammic technique. He is also, more obliquely, reflecting upon the political unconscious of the ideogrammic medium. Pound's antithetical discourse on radio offers a devastating anatomy— a deconstruction—of the imagistic basis of the *Cantos.*

Phantom Transmissions

Two years before he died, Pound added a brief foreword to the 1970 edition of his memoir of the sculptor Gaudier-Brzeska. His final assessment of the memoir, which was originally published in 1916, is almost apologetic in tone: "It falls into place as a footnote on what was visible to one spectator in 1913 and 14."[28] In retrospect, he claims, the memoir is merely a "footnote" to an era he once called (in one of his radio speeches) "the romantic period of my life" (*RB* 245). What's more, the memoir is said to be the work of a "spectator"—a modest claim, indeed, for a work whose polemical vigor often disturbs the task of mourning. The unassuming yet anomalous presence of this stranger, who appears for the first time in the appended foreword, alerts the reader to a silent breach, a schism, in the one who remembers the dead.

According to views that Pound held during the time he compiled the materials for the memoir, the passive figure of the spectator would be harshly judged as a relic of antiquated poetic values, a counterpart to the "sensitive" poet who is susceptible to ghosts. Clearly, the "spectator" Pound refers to is not himself as he was in 1913, a militant figure in the artistic developments of the period, but the Pound of 1970: an observer of the distant past, a man on the brink of his own grave, who installs the passive figure of the spectator in a final attempt to appease the vengeful ghosts of Gaudier's crypt. The memoir is thus a footnote to a "text" that can be deciphered—and suppressed—only from the vantage point of the "spectator." As "a footnote on what was visible," it also anchors and eventually betrays the *invisible* features of an era dominated in Pound's mind by the Image. That is to say, the memoir of Gaudier-Brzeska harbors a traumatic figure (the Image) that will appear only "in translation"—in the broadcast transmissions of Radio Rome. Further, the belated foreword to this book of mourning, so easily overlooked, is a *Vor*-text of passivity that threatens to engulf the defiant voices of its narrator and its subject. Thus, even as late as 1970, the memoir, and the doctrine of the Image that it enunciates, are haunted by a passive regime of spectatorship and spiritualism.

A footnote "falls into place" beneath a mound of words as a cadaver falls away from itself into resemblance (Latin *cadere,* "to fall"). Pound calls the memoir "a footnote on what was visible," a garbled missive

28. The foreword appears on the unnumbered frontispiece to *Gaudier-Brzeska: A Memoir* (New York: New Directions, 1970).

RADIO CORPSE

from the grave that falls outside the picture, so to speak—a blindspot in the purview of the "spectator." The memoir is, after all, a literary crypt, a dwelling place for Gaudier's restless phantom. Yet as a footnote to a missing text, the memoir is a crypt of another sort: a place that holds what must be sequestered from discourse, a place that is the underworld of a text, the origin of certain unwelcome transmissions. Amplified by textual and biographical coincidence, these transmissions eventually intercept the fascist radio broadcasts that Pound makes during World War II. Swayed by the "tribal magic" of radio, Pound automatically "translates" the signals emanating from Gaudier's crypt—a footnote broadcasting the garbled "text" to which it will one day be appended, but only in retrospect. These phantom transmissions must therefore be understood as effects of an unmournable death: not only the loss of Gaudier, but the final interment of the Image as corpse and phantom. In the radio broadcasts, the submerged pattern of mourning that disfigures the memoir is projected into the technical media (principally radio), which Pound views as extensions of the artist's hypersensitive faculties. Hence, the Image lying in Gaudier's crypt looms as a vengeful ghost in the radio broadcasts. Ultimately, Pound's use of the radio should be understood as a media séance with the dead—a final, devastating episode of Imagism.

Since the link between Gaudier's crypt and the radio broadcasts is not strictly one of influence, and since the remoteness of one voice from the other is essential to their proximity, it may be useful to say a few words about the unorthodox channels that sustain my reading of the radio speeches. The broadcasts are the catastrophic end to a period of aberrant mourning that coincides with the spell exerted by the Image over Pound's poetry and thought. Not surprisingly, the phantom that wreaks vengeance on Pound through the broadcasts is reluctant to identify itself. Although it is Gaudier's crypt that transmits the interference translated by Pound, the identity of the phantom exceeds that of Gaudier alone; for Gaudier already displaces an earlier figure, Will Smith (another dead Image-maker). The phantom Gaudier is, moreover, both magnetized and contaminated by the disquieting celebrity of Antheil, as well as by various phantasmic relations in Pound's family history. Though the phantom's identity remains ambiguous, we can detect its disruptive presence in the panoply of bizarre voices, the incoherence, and the vicious accusations repeated obsessively in the broadcasts. Nor is Pound's own account of his relation to the phantom any more revealing, since his words are constrained by his debt to a legendary—that is to say, phantasmic—figure whose premature death in World War I shocked and saddened the London avant-garde. As we shall see, Pound's debt arises from a death wish that inadvertently comes true. "Such a debt," according to Avital Ronell, "always falls due to a figure whose loss is as deeply desired as it is regretted."[29]

In certain limited respects, the phantom that disfigures Pound's voice in the radio broadcasts can be understood as a source of speech, a cache of real words, vengefully conceived and later summoned by the "medium" of radio to fulfill its disastrous end. The atrocious enthusiasm of Pound's views on race and economics, for example, might be heard as an imitation of youth, a replay that is also a disfiguring, an attempt to master Gaudier's "Paleolithic Vortex" ("written from the trenches"):

> This war is a great remedy.
> In the individual it kills arrogance, self-esteem, pride.
> It takes away from the masses numbers upon numbers of
>   unimportant units, whose economic activities become noxious,
>   as the recent trade crises have shown us. (*GB* 27)

Remembering his friend, Pound writes, "In undertaking this book I am doing what little I can to carry out his desire" (*GB* 19). This "undertaking" culminates in the radio broadcasts, where Pound mingles his own desire with that of Gaudier. Authorized by twenty years of silence, the words of the phantom surface unexpectedly, rising to a question that is nothing more than a lure for ghosts, a question so simple that Pound cannot answer it alone: "Well, why pick on the Jew? I have heard the term 'Jewish impertinence,' in fact Gaudier-Brzeska used to use it" (*RB* 53). This statement, which Pound made during one of the broadcasts, evokes a passage that he excised from later editions of his memoir of Gaudier. In the original edition of the memoir, Pound cites a notebook of Gaudier's, which includes, he

29. Avital Ronell, *Dictations: On Haunted Writings* (Bloomington: Indiana University Press, 1986), pp. 4–5.

claims, "a consideration of 'La Question Juive,' containing the statements that 'Un *Juif* a tort d'abord parce-que *Juif* est un être pratiquant une religion *absurde*,' and that Christ's reform was 'contre le nationalisme.' "[30] (" 'A *Jew* is wrong first of all because *Jew* is a being who practices an *absurd* religion'; Christ's reform was 'against *nationalism*.' ") This passage, absent from the current edition of the memoir, not only confirms the importance of Gaudier as a source for Pound's anti-Semitism, but helps establish the actual character of Gaudier's phantasmatic influence on the radio broadcasts. The mingling of anti-Semitism and nationalism in Gaudier's views must surely have seemed prescient to Pound in 1942. Aside from the question of whether Gaudier's influence is real or virtual, however, the phonographic aspect of the radio speeches (which were prerecorded) establishes the idea of a posthumous voice. Indeed, as Alice Kaplan notes, "It is the *reproduced* voice, rather than the voice itself, that conveys the archaic values demanded by so-called antimodernist fascist rhetoric" (*Reproductions of Banality* 134). Recording technology allowed Pound to lay his own voice—or that of a phantom—to rest, so that it might rise from the tomb of the Image.

In spite of the paucity of direct evidence, the pressure exerted by the phantom in the radio broadcasts is unmistakable. The source of this pressure, according to Nicolas Abraham, is not words actually spoken by the dead, but the *unspeakable*: "The words which the phantom uses to carry out its return . . . do not refer to a source of speech . . . Instead, they point to a gap, that is, the unspeakable."[31] What haunts Pound, therefore, is not, by and large, Gaudier's actual words, but "the gaps left within us by the secrets of others" ("Notes on the Phantom" 287). The radio speeches are haunted by the unspeakable: not only by views and opinions that are unforgivable among the living, but by words the dead never dared to utter. Pound is forced to speak *for* the dead. During the broadcasts, for example, he is continually alert to what he calls "the history of secret controls" (*RB* 326) exerted over himself and others. "Roosevelt," he declares, "is MOVED by others; and does not act *propio motu*" (*RB* 94).

---

30. Pound, *Gaudier-Brzeska* (London: John Lane, 1916), p. 42.
31. Nicolas Abraham, "Notes on the Phantom: A Complement to Freud's Metapsychology," trans. Nicholas Rand, *Critical Inquiry* 13, no. 2 (Winter 1987): 290.

Roosevelt is no more than a zombie, according to Pound—an automaton manipulated by forces beyond his control. Elsewhere, Pound warns his audience of dangers that have a special bearing on his own internal predicament: "Can you MEET one another? Your air isn't free. Open organizations have been 'put inside' . . . Nothing but SECRET organization" (*RB* 68). Although Pound would not admit to external controls operating within himself, he declared to the foreign minister of the Salò government that his broadcasts were "guided by an interior light" (*SC* 632).

At the other end of the line is Gaudier's crypt, haunted not only by the ravenous ghost of the young sculptor, but by the specter of mass death rising from the battlefields of World War I. The correspondence between Gaudier's crypt and the radio broadcasts may be said to originate in a common awareness of death, both public and private. Beyond this rudimentary observation, however, the trail disappears. The inscrutable link between one place of hiding and another, between transmitter and receiver, can be recovered from the "ambient air" only by coincidence, by circumstantial evidence, and by reconstructing the submerged relation between the Image, technology, and the phantom in Pound's poetics. Faced with a similar problem of absent witnesses, Avital Ronell makes the following observation about her cryptological analysis of Goethe and Freud: "Any gamble on a type of intertextuality that would deal with telepathic channels involves a risk, of course; for example, when one aims to exceed Freud's own calculations, the calculation at which one arrives could amount to a seemingly extravagant reliance on coincidence and chance" (*Dictations* 5). The risk, "of course," is that an investigation may prove to be interminable: "The calculation which takes into account some apparent coincidences in order to unmask them might turn out to be inexhaustible" (5).

The Imagist movement springs from a desire to *eliminate* the dangers of uncertainty and excess. Generally, Pound associates these dangers with passivity, or susceptibility to the pleasures of the grave: ghosts, materiality, sentiment. In spite of the powerful taboos against such dangers that Pound enunciates in the name of the Image, his poetry frequently manages to circumvent these prohibitions without actually violating them. His translations from the Noh theater, following the example of his early crypt poems, allow the poet to yield to the enchantment of the grave without abandoning the principles of Imagism. Under these circumstances the Image becomes an emblem of what I will call "magical realism" (borrowing a phrase from Ernst Jünger).[32] The tensions inherent in the concept of magical realism culminate in the radio broadcasts, where the poet upholds the prohibition against passively receiving the Image in the guise of a phantom, even as he occupies the place of the phantom and therefore carries out the work of a dictator (the one who does the talking, who gives dictation, instead of receiving it). Like a somnambulist, the poet speaking over the air walks a tightrope between technology and unreason, science and mimetic enchantment, action and passivity.

Most critics take at face value Pound's insistence on action and will power in poetry as well as politics (a posture which takes shape in the context of Imagism). Jean-Michel Rabaté, however, argues that "passivity is at work behind Pound's often vehement praise of active, i.e., creative personalities."[33] Rabaté views the structure of the ideogrammic Image as inherently passive: "Pound's ideogrammic procedure of 'heaping up' the components of thought" presupposes "the profound passivity of the subject as he writes, which allows him to be the recipient of quotations and other discourses" (*Language, Sexuality, and Ideology* 9). Rabaté's articulation of passivity is essentially a theory of ghosts, which sees the poet as inhabited by "other" discourses, or by language itself. Combining elements of Heideggerian and Lacanian thought, Rabaté characterizes the speaking subject of the *Cantos* as "a discontinuity in the real, a fading presence" (20), whose susceptibility to other voices derives from the passivity of the "ideogrammic method," which depends on the reception of fragments charged with "subconscious energies."

Pound's resistance to passivity (a danger that is analogous to the "power of putrefaction") travels through a chain of figures that stand for the most conventional trope of the Image: the mirror. Pound targets the mirror through various figures of enchantment, including

---

32. For a discussion of the origins of the term "magical realism," see Matthias Eberle, *World War I and the Weimar Artists* (New Haven: Yale University Press, 1985), p. 128.
33. Jean-Michel Rabaté, *Language, Sexuality, and Ideology in Ezra Pound's Cantos* (Albany: SUNY Press, 1986), p. 10.

mimesis, the phantom, and technology, only to find that these figures haunt his own conception of the Image. The mirror is a commonplace trope for mimesis, but it may also be understood as a crude but compelling form of visual technology. In addition, we learn from an early poem, "Und Drang," that Pound conceives of the phantom as a mirror:

> If thou hast seen my shade sans character
> If thou hast seen that mirror of all moments,
> That glass to all things that o'ershadow it,
> Call not that mirror me, for I have slipped
> Your grasp, I have eluded. (*CEP* 172)

The association between ghost and mirror is not surprising, since a ghost is a shade, a shadow—an Image of the dead. The passivity and enchantment associated with the mirror are aspects of the Image that Pound could accommodate in his poetry only surreptitiously. The tensions underlying this duplicity culminate in apocalyptic fashion in the radio broadcasts, where Pound disappears into the "acoustic mirror" of radio and assumes the place of the phantom.[34] He thus resolves his aversion to the specular properties of the Image by becoming an Image, or a shade, himself: a disembodied voice that is visited upon his listeners. He makes the distance between the living and the dead absolute by eliminating it through the transmission of his own posthumized voice.

Pound says that the Image heralds "a revival of the sense of realism" (*GB* 113), yet has nothing to do with mimesis. We should not confuse realism and mimesis, he warns. Mimetic art is mechanistic and passive: "Works of art attract by a resembling unlikeness. Colloquial poetry is to the real art as the barber's wax dummy is to sculpture" (*SP* 43–44). The Imagist poet, on the other hand, "should *depend,* of course, on the creative, not the mimetic or representational part in his work" (*GB* 86). In his work on the Japanese Noh theater—an important arena for Imagist poetics—Pound discovers what he believes to be a strongly antimimetic bias: "The common theater, the place of mimicry

---

[34]. The phrase "acoustic mirror" is from Kaja Silverman's account of the posthumized voice in the cinema. See Silverman, *The Acoustic Mirror: The Female Voice in Psychoanalysis and Cinema* (Bloomington: Indiana University Press, 1988).

and direct imitation of life, has always been looked down upon in Japan" (*T* 219). Furthermore, "The merely mimetic stage has been despised . . . The Noh holds up a mirror to nature in a manner very different from the Western convention" (*T* 221). Even more emphatically, with regard to the state of affairs in London before the first World War, Pound declares, "In every art I can think of we are clogged and dammed by the mimetic" (*SP* 42). According to the explicit aims of his agenda, this statement suggests that mimetic values are blocking the flow of new art. Yet another sort of blockage may be occurring under the guise of mimesis. It is not, perhaps, a new wave of poetry but the pressure of the supernatural that has accumulated behind the wall of mimesis. Mimesis, according to Adorno, is a reservoir of enchantment: "The immediate sensuous presence of art's enchanting quality, which is a vestige of the magical stage of history, is constantly being repudiated by the demystification of the real world without being entirely erased. It is this enchanting quality which preserves the mimetic moment in art."[35] If Adorno is right, what Pound senses behind the wall of mimesis is a horde of ghosts, a residue of the enchanted world that appears in his early poetry. The figure of mimesis itself becomes a crypt harboring ghosts that will later be released through the radio broadcasts.

The power of passivity is almost always present as a subtext in Pound's discussions of the Image, which are generally critical of "a fashion of passivity that has held since the romantic movement" (*LE* 433–434). The epigraph to the original edition of the memoir, which appears on the same unnumbered page as the foreword, is attributed to Machiavelli: "Gli uomini vivono in pochi e gli altri son pecorelle" ("Men live through the existence of the few; the rest are sheep"). This citation transmits a disdain for passivity that is both defensive and readily convertible to its opposite by the time Pound commences the radio broadcasts. It compares the majority of people to sheep who blindly follow the members of an elite ("gli pochi"). The statement also implies a kind of mental displacement or transference, a passivity that allows the minds of many to be controlled, secretly, by the minds of a few. Pound, of course, identifies himself as a member of the elect.

---

35. Theodor W. Adorno, *Aesthetic Theory*, trans. C. Lenhardt (London: Routledge Kegan Paul, 1984), p. 86.

Although Machiavelli's (and Pound's) scorn for the masses is evident, there is no indication that reform is either possible or desirable. The radio broadcasts, however, which also express disdain and condemnation of "the herd," are intent on altering the docile habits of the public. The sheep that Machiavelli refers to become, in the radio broadcasts, "Goyim or cattle" who are "milked, skinned alive, hog tied, sent out to slaughter, or drowned like blind mice in the steerage" (*RB* 339). Pound's zeal to reform his listeners springs from his discovery of a counter-elite that challenges the hegemony of his own artistic-intellectual cadre: the Jews, he believes, now secretly control the lives of the herd. In the case of Machiavelli's statement, Pound condones the relation of shepherd and beast because he considers himself to be one of the elite. In the case of the supposed Jewish domination of the West, he deplores such influence. The vicious anti-Semitism of many of the broadcasts does not seem to be affected, however, by Pound's recognition that he and the Jews share a common role in relation to the herd. "The yidd," Pound declares, "is a stimulant, and the goyim are cattle in gt/proportion and go to saleable slaughter with the maximum of docility" (*C* 74: 453). Pound, like the Jew, is a "stimulant" or agitator. Both are locked in a struggle for control over the life of the herd. We can therefore explain Pound's anti-Semitism, in part, as an effect of this imagined rivalry.

What is important for our purposes is that Pound associates Jewish domination with control over the media, and over radio in particular. In one speech, he asks, "What chance have the scattered [the artistic and intellectual counter-elite] against the super-Zukor, sub-human transmissions of EVERY radio station in your Jew ridden country?" (*RB* 159). These transmissions, which supposedly emanate from a domain that is both above ("super-Zukor") and below ("sub-human") the condition of most listeners, "paralyz[e] the nucleus of will in the goyim victim" (*RB* 297). When Pound received his first radio set as a gift from Natalie Barney in 1940, he speculated about its effect on listeners: "Blasted friends left a goddam radio here yester. Gift. God damn destructive and dispersive devil of an invention. But got to be faced . . . Anybody who *can* survive *may* strengthen inner life, but mass of apes and worms will be still further rejuiced to passivity. Hell a state of passivity? Or limbo??" (*L* 342). Not only is the radio a source of "sub-human transmissions," but it arrives like an infernal gift from the underworld, transforming the mind of the public into a living hell. The poor animals who listen undergo a kind of shock therapy: subjected to waves of electrical current, they are eventually "rejuiced to passivity." Considering Pound's fears about the association of radio technology with passivity and the underworld, we should not be surprised that he later chooses to install himself in what he believes to be a position of control: he seizes the microphone himself in order to channel the dangerous power of the new medium. By tapping into the tribal magic of radio, however, he puts himself on the receiving end of transmissions emanating from Gaudier's crypt, a place that harbors a death wish transformed into a hungry ghost, a vault of ineffable desire.

Pound views the technical media (radio, cinema, and so on) as dangerous forms of mediation that rob "true" art and its audience of vitality. Indeed, he regards technology in general with profound mistrust. In the radio broadcasts, he attributes the passivity of the goyim (his listeners) in part to a subservient relation to technology: "AND if you are more than cattle? If you rate yourselves above cows and sheep, you will in defense of that rating have to ask YOURSELVES whether men are more important than mere machinery. Whether you intend to be slaves, lifelong slaves, hereditary slaves to machinery and whether you propose to sell your children and your grandchildren into long-lasting slavery to usurers *and* to machinery" (*RB* 49). The insidious power of technology reaches deep into our hereditary past, the realm of the dead, as well as into the future, the realm of the unborn. What's more, Pound's fears about technology coincide with his condemnation of usury.

Pound's uneasiness about the technical media comes to light long before he encounters and finally surrenders to radio. He defines Imagism, for example, in part by contrasting it with the "impressionism" of the cinema. "Imagism is not Impressionism," he declares. "The logical end of impressionism is the cinematograph [the motion picture camera]. The state of mind of the impressionist tends to become cinematographical" (*GB* 85, 89). Elsewhere, he states, "The cinema is not an art ... The cinema is the furthest possible remove from all things which interest one as an art critic" (*EPVA* 79). He concludes his attack on the cinema by remarking, "The cinema is the phonograph of appearance" (*EPVA* 79). A link between phonography and the passivity associated with the "cinematographical" mind appears again in "Hugh Selwyn Mauberley." Deploring the vulgarity of the modern era, the poet complains:

> The "age demanded" chiefly a mould in plaster,
> Made with no loss of time,
> A prose kinema, not, not assuredly, alabaster
> Or the "sculpture" of rhyme. (*P* 188)

Furthermore, he laments, the crude phonographic apparatus of the "pianola" (player piano) replaces the lyre:

> The tea-rose, tea-gown, etc.
> Supplants the mousseline of Cos,
> The pianola "replaces"
> Sappho's barbitos. (*P* 189)

Pound relates the sensibility associated here with the new technical media to the sensibility of kitsch. Moreover, the passivity of the "cinematograph" corresponds in the poem to the "mediumistic" sensibility of the character Mauberley. Thus, Pound's resistance to the technical media, and later to the medium of radio, must be understood as a dimension of his anxiety about kitsch—not only its vulgarity and its mass appeal, but its mythographic potency.

In an article on Arnold Dolmetsch, Pound writes, "Our ears are passive before the onslaught of gramophones and pianolas."[36] A similar sense of the mesmerizing but also degenerative aspect of phonography emerges in a passage of Canto 29:

> (Let us speak of the osmosis of persons)
> The wail of the phonograph has penetrated their marrow
> (Let us . . .
> The wail of the pornograph. . . .). (*C* 29: 134)

These statements suggest that listening to the gramophone, a device related to the "devil box" of the radio, is akin to being mesmerized by the noise of mechanical Sirens or the furious wailing of ghosts. Pound also hated using the telephone, which he once referred to as

36. Pound, *Pavannes and Divisions* (New York: Knopf, 1918), p. 260.

the "gorbloody tHellerfone" (*SC* 415), suggesting that it, too, like the radio and gramophone, forced him to accept what Laurence Rickels calls a "telepathic call from the phantom realm."[37] For Pound, the technical media reopened lines of communication with the dead and the illicit realm of mimetic enchantment. "The cult of the dead in any given culture," Rickels explains, "is coextensive with the media extension of the senses current in that culture" (*Aberrations of Mourning* 297).

It is precisely the supernatural aspect of the technical media that produced a schism in Pound's attitudes about technology. Although he frequently condemned the media, as we have seen, he was also remarkably sensitive and responsive to a number of technological developments. Inspired perhaps by Marinetti's concept of the "wireless imagination," which exploits the telepathic effects of the media, Pound marvels at man's ability to make "electricity carry language through air" (*ABC* 19). As early as 1913, he shows an interest in Marconi's invention of "the wireless telegraph" (*LE* 47), and imagines radio technology from the standpoint of a medieval mind: "A medieval 'natural philosopher' would find this modern world full of enchantments, not only the light in the electric bulb, but the thought of the current hidden in air and in wire would give him a mind full of forms" (*LE* 154–155). More important, Pound projects his fascination with hidden currents of energy and with telecommunication into a psychological model where "the charged surface is produced between the predominant natural poles of two human mechanisms" (*SR* 94). He compares consciousness to "a great telephone central"[38] or a telegraphic device: "Man is—the sensitive part of him—a mechanism, for the purposes of our further discussion, a mechanism rather like an electric appliance, switches, wires, etc. . . . In the telegraph we have a charged surface attracting to it, or registering movements in the invisible ether" (*SR* 92–93).

One of the remarkable things about Pound's electromechanical conceptions of the body is their close relation to what he calls the

37. Laurence A. Rickels, *Aberrations of Mourning: Writings on German Crypts* (Detroit: Wayne State University Press, 1989), p. 4.
38. Pound, cited in Max Nänny, *Ezra Pound: Poetics for an Electric Age* (Bern: Francke, 1973), p. 20.

"mediumistic artist," a figure he usually associates with kitsch and the despised regime of passivity. Pound constructs the poetics of Imagism—at least ostensibly—in opposition to this figure: "There are, as often has been said, two sorts of artists: the artist who moves through his art, to whom it is truly a 'medium,' or a means of expression; and secondly, there is the mediumistic artist, the one who can only exist in his art, who is passive to impulse, who approaches more or less nearly to the 'sensitive,' or to the somnambulistic medium" (*GB* 105–106). Alert to the "current hidden in air," the "sensitive" artist moves through the world like a sleepwalker, "registering movements in the invisible ether." Pound also compares practitioners of what he calls "automatic painting" to "somnolents or mediumistic persons" (*EPVA* 8). Furthermore, he remarks, "It is not surprising that the human mind in a state of lassitude or passivity should take on the faculties of the unconscious or sub-human energies" (*EPVA* 8). In the context of medieval love poetry, however, the passivity of the medium takes on a visionary quality that overcomes the pernicious effect of passivity alone: "The senses at first seem to project for a few yards beyond the body. Effect of a decent climate where a man leaves his nerve-set open, or allows it to tune into its ambience" (*LE* 152). Pound archaicizes the analogy of the body as a technical medium by projecting it into a pseudo-medieval context: "Did this 'chivalric love,' this exotic, take on mediumistic properties? ... Did it lead to an 'exteriorization of the sensibility'?" (*SR* 94).

Clearly, Pound's "conception of the body as perfect instrument of increasing intelligence" (*LE* 152) must be considered in relation to his thinking about technology. The technical media—especially radio—should therefore be understood, from Pound's perspective, as new organs of the body that extend the perceptual and expressive range of the mediumistic artist. The medium acts as both receiver and transmitter, drawing ghosts from the "ambient air," and translating, in turn, the "movements in invisible ether." These electrosomatic analogies regarding chivalric love and new forms of intelligence anticipate the experience of telepathic mourning that governs the radio broadcasts. Instead of pulling in erotic signals or new signs of life, the radio poet picks up phantom transmissions from a forgotten crypt—thus confirming Laurence Rickels' observation that "every point of contact between a body and its media extensions marks the site of some secret burial" (*Aberrations of Mourning* 360).

Given the historical speculations about radio's relation to spiritualism, we might usefully ask whether Pound's conception of radio doesn't resemble a kind of ventriloquism originating with the dead— a conception that also resembles, of course, his views on translation. The exteriorization and projection of the voice that occurs on the radio has obvious parallels with the act of ventriloquism, as well as with the experience of haunting. Nicolas Abraham observes, "The phantom's periodic and compulsive return lies beyond the scope of symptom-formation in the sense of a return of the repressed; it works like a ventriloquist, like a stranger within the subject's own mental topography" ("Notes on the Phantom" 289–290). The unspoken words of the body are also the inescapable words of an angry ghost who taps into the radio broadcasts, confessing incoherently, "Belated. I am belated. I am not an alarm clock" (*RB* 131). Pound defers the scene of awakening over the air, even as the effects of a death long forgotten signal a *state* of emergency (the fascist State).

The somnambulist eventually finds himself in a chair behind a microphone, making radio broadcasts. Pound's notion of the mediumistic artist prefigures the moment when he himself will occupy the place of the phantom in the radio broadcasts. Spirits haunt the voice of radio, yet it overcomes the dangerous regime of passivity by *transmitting* the interference from beyond and by controlling, in turn, the thoughts of its stupefied listeners. The mediumistic poet, like the voice of radio, is "the one who can only exist in his art, who is passive to impulse" (*GB* 106); that is, he identifies with the dead—the subject and source of his art. The extended sensorium of the medium—the voice inside the radio—mimics the telepathic faculties of the dead, who are able to communicate with the living. When Pound occupies the place of the phantom in the radio broadcasts, his voice departs from his body in a manner that reconstitutes the young poet described by Dorothy Shakespear in 1909: "He has learned to live beside his body. I see him as a double person—just held together by the flesh. His spirit walks beside him, on the left-hand side—He has conquered the needs of the flesh—He can starve; nay, is willing, to starve that his spirit may bring forth the 'highest of arts'—poetry" (*P/S* 5). The-disappearance of the body through starvation presents a phantasmic spectacle among the living.[39] The poet who becomes a phantom over the radio brings to completion his life's work as a "hunger artist."

Magical Realism

> How strange! That place, which seemed like a grave, is now lighted up from within, and has become like a human dwelling, where people are talking, and setting up looms for spinning, and painted sticks. It must be an illusion.
>
> —From *Nishikigi*, a Noh drama by Motokiyo, translated by Ezra Pound

Pound's resistance to the technical media provides the essential ground of his belated but enthusiastic participation in radio broadcasting. He surrenders for what are apparently pragmatic reasons, such as his desire to communicate directly with as many people as possible through the radio broadcasts (an impulse we can view as a revival of his interest in crowd psychology), but he also, more importantly, surrenders to the variety of enchantment encrypted in the media. He defuses the threat of hyperrationality associated with the media (which is also secretly attractive) by exploiting their atavistic spell. Taking a cue from his earliest speculations about "radiant" Images, Pound incorporates reason into the telepathic effects of radio. Hence, technology, like the figure of the Image, becomes an occasion for the reconciliation of reason and irrationality, science and the supernatural, action and passivity. More specifically, as I mentioned earlier, Pound views the antithetical medium of radio as either the essence of fascism or the instrument of a Jewish "plague," as the last refuge of free speech or a menace to full speech. In this regard, Pound's contradictory views on radio are symptomatic of Jeffrey Herf's conception of "reactionary modernism," which establishes a framework for the "reconciliation of technology and unreason."[40]

---

39. See William R. La Fleur, "Hungry Ghosts and Hungry People: Somaticity and Rationality in Medieval Japan," *Zone: Fragments for a History of the Human Body*, Part 1 (1989): 270–303.

40. Jeffrey Herf, *Reactionary Modernism: Technology, Culture, and Politics in Weimar and the Third Reich* (Cambridge: Cambridge University Press, 1984), p. 2.

Herf devotes considerable attention to Ernst Jünger, whose vision of technology's role in society focuses on the concept of what he calls "magical realism." In 1927 Jünger describes the rise of German nationalism in the following terms: "It is the view which manifests itself in our time in those images of magical realism in whose spaces every line of the outer world is recorded with the precision of a mathematical formula, and whose coldness, although in a fashion that is both inexplicable and transparent, illuminates and warms a magical background" (Herf, *Reactionary Modernism* 83). Jünger's strategy calls for the use of oxymorons such as "magical realism" to naturalize the integration of technology and unreason in fascist ideology. He declares, for example, that the photographic camera produces images of "mathematical demonism" (99)—a variation of the oxymoron "magical realism." Jünger's rhetoric is designed to awaken the public to the supernatural effects of the media (thereby defusing the threat of hyperrationality), even as it requires submission to the "realistic" images produced by the media. To this end, Herf argues, Jünger "advocated a 'heroic' affirmation of passivity" (84). Thus, it is Jünger's protofascist conception of technology that effectively surmounts the antinomy of heroism and passivity.

According to Herf, magical realism synthesizes "precision and passion, rationality and magic, outer form and hidden will" (83). As we have discovered, the qualities that Pound attributes to radio embody similar dichotomies. Radio allows one to speak openly, directly, without the intervention of "secret controls." In other words, radio is the only medium where "realism" is still possible. As for the medium of print, Pound warns, "The press, your press, is a machine for destroying the memory, the public memory" (*RB* 339). Thus, by contrast, Pound implicates the medium of radio in the art of "public memory"—though it also serves as a channel for personal memories, thereby associating the mnemonic effects of radio with the occluded origins of Imagism. Moreover, the radio is a "devil box," a source of "sub-human transmissions." Radio's memory broadcasts direct from the underworld. Yet Pound occupies the place of the phantom in order to speak frankly, to expose the reality of economic and cultural bondage. The realism of radio is truly magical.

By reversing the historical projection of the radio phantom (which moves forward in time), the incongruous features of magical realism can be traced backward from Pound's position on technology to the inception of the Image. As an account of his torturous embrace of the media, magical realism informs a constellation of terms that Pound used to inflect the Image toward its spectral (and occluded) origins: "phantastikon," "phanopoeia," and "phantasmagoria." Pound's use of these terms in relation to Imagism anticipates the reconciliation between action and passivity, reason and irrationality, that eventually allows him to *practice* the medium of radio. All three words derive from the Greek verb *fainō*, meaning, in its active form, to bring to light, to make to appear, to disclose, to reveal, or to give light. In its passive form, the verb means to come to light, to be seen, to appear, or to come into being. "Phantastikon" is the term Pound chooses to denote the Image-making faculty, which he claims extends several feet beyond the body, enveloping it "like a soap-bubble reflecting sundry patches of the macrocosmos" (*SR* 92). As Pound sees it, the phantastikon anticipates historically the "new organs" of the technical media, which extend the perceptual and expressive range of the poet's body.

Although Pound insists that the concept of the phantastikon is relevant to the principles of Imagism (with its emphasis on the active production of Images), the Greek term has distinctly passive connotations. Liddell and Scott define "phantastikon" as "the faculty of being deluded by images," while Ruthven has it meaning "receptive of Images."[41] When Pound describes the term to Harriet Monroe, he writes, "It has to do with the seeing of visions" (Ruthven, *Pound's Personae* 56). In this sense, the phantastikon is a faculty that belongs properly to the "mediumistic artist" who is "passive to impulse" and susceptible to the presence of ghosts. By retaining the term "phantasktikon," Pound inserts a phantasmatic term, an element of the irrational, into the otherwise "realistic" orientation of Imagism.

A similar dichotomy animates the term "phanopoeia," which Pound uses as a synonym for Imagism. He defines "phanopoeia" as "a casting of Images upon the visual imagination" (*LE* 25), and adds, "In *Phanopoeia* we find the greatest drive toward utter precision of word" (*LE* 26). "Phanopoeia" thus denotes the aspect of Imagist poetics that is

41. K. K. Ruthven, *A Guide to Pound's "Personae" (1926)* (Berkeley: University of California Press, 1969), p. 55.

most familiar to readers—a concern with economy, precision, and accuracy of representation. It is remarkable therefore to find that in 1918 Pound published a poem titled "Phanopoeia," which depicts visionary experience in a manner that recalls his earliest poetry (*P* 169–170). Moreover, reviewing the *Others* anthology in 1917, he links the realist poetic of Imagism to "phantasmagoria" (a term that includes the Greek word for ghost, *phantasma*). He makes reference to "Imagism, or poetry wherein the feelings of painting or sculpture are predominant (certain men move in phantasmagoria; the images of their gods, whole countrysides, stretches of hill, land, and forest, travel with them)" (*SP* 424). According to this statement, Imagism synthesizes precise definition and magic, reason and the supernatural. This view is echoed by Richard Aldington, who called Imagism "an accurate mystery."[42] In a passage from the essay "Psychology and Troubadours" (which uses the term "psychology" in its archaic sense, as the study of the soul-image), Pound explains, "In the Trecento the Tuscans are busy with their *phantastikon*" (*SR* 93). Later he adds, "The Tuscan poetry is, however, of a time when the seeing of visions was considered respectable, and the poet takes delight in definite portrayal of his visions" (*SR* 105).[43] Pound implies here that his own age is one in which the seeing of visions is not respectable (thus explaining, in part, his disavowal of his early poetry, which is crowded with apparitions). If the contemporary poet insists on representing such experience, he must find some means to "screen himself from persecution" (*SR* 92). One way of doing this is to emphasize the "*definite portrayal* of his visions." To some extent, the poet can legitimate the supernatural or magical character of his subject by giving it a realistic "look": the ghost must appear to be real, and the landscape is precisely rendered. The poet fortifies the

42. Aldington, cited in Marianne Moore, " 'New' Poetry since 1912," *The Complete Prose of Marianne Moore*, ed. Patricia C. Willis (New York: Viking, 1986), p. 120.
43. The notion that "the poet takes delight in definite portrayal of his visions" finds its strongest proponent in Marianne Moore, who urges poets to become "literalists of the imagination" and to "present for inspection 'imaginary gardens with real toads in them.' " This advice appears in her poem "Poetry." *The Complete Poems of Marianne Moore* (New York: Viking, 1967), p. 267. Regarding Pound's influence on her writing, Moore once wrote, "I have learned more from Ezra Pound about writing than from anyone else—more that I value." This statement appears in a blurb for *The Letters of Ezra Pound, 1907–1941*, ed. D. D. Paige (London: Faber and Faber, 1951).

rationality of his vision, and masks its phantasmatic origins, by emphasizing technique. This scenario not only accounts for the emergence of magical realism in Pound's career; it describes how his early poetry, which is haunted by the spirits of the dead, evolved into the rationalized vision of Imagism.

During the years 1913–1915, Pound spent three winters with William Butler Yeats at Stone Cottage, and became immersed, through Yeats's influence, in the occult. It was during this period that Pound formulated the occult "Doctrine of the Image," based in part on his exposure to spiritualism. I have argued that Pound's interest in ghosts and the occult during these years should be read not as a new phenomenon, but rather as a revival of interests that played a major role in his early poetry. The poem "Redondillas," for example, written in 1910, reveals a familiarity with states of enchantment that not only antedates his personal relationship with Yeats but looks ahead to the psychology of the radio broadcasts:

> I sing devils, thrones and dominions
> At work in the air round about us,
> Of powers ready to enter
> And thrust our own being from us. (*CEP* 219)

Four years later, having spent his second winter with Yeats at Stone Cottage, Pound translates his early infatuation with the dead into a Vorticist polemic: "We turn back, we artists, to the powers of the air, to the djinn who were our allies aforetime, to the spirits of our ancestors" (*EPVA* 182). Twenty-five years later, Pound's use of the radio and his conception of the technical media are still captive to the "powers of the air"—a phrase that he borrows, probably through the influence of Yeats, from William Blake.[44]

Pound's letters during the period of his residence with Yeats reveal that his reading material included works such as *Le Comte de Gablais, ou entretiens sur les sciences secrètes* (Paris, 1670), a work that deals with "Rosicrucian philosophy" (*P/S* 293), and that served as the basis of Alexander Pope's system of gnomes and sylphs in *The Rape of the*

---

44. William Blake, "The Marriage of Heaven and Hell," in *The Poetry and Prose of William Blake*, ed. David V. Erdman, commentary by Harold Bloom (New York: Doubleday, 1965), p. 40.

Lock. Pound also makes reference to Robert Kirk's book *The Secret Commonwealth of Elves, Fauns, and Fairies: A Study in Folklore and Psychical Research* (*P/S* 277), as well as to Joseph Ennemosor's *History of Magic, to Which is Added an Appendix of the Most Remarkable and Best Authenticated Stories of Apparitions, Dreams, Second Sight, Somnambulism, Predictions, Divinations, Witchcraft, Vampires, Fairies, Table-Turning, and Spirit-Rapping* (*P/S* 303).[45] Moreover, as I noted in Chapter 3, Pound wrote to his father during the winter of 1913–1914 asking him to send a copy of *De Daemonialitate, et Incubus et Succubus* (a work whose subject, the incubation of ghosts, has an important bearing on the disturbed pattern of mourning that emerged in Pound's work with the death of Gaudier in 1915).

Dorothy Shakespear's letters of the period reveal that she, too, was taken with the idea of ghosts and may have drawn Pound even deeper into the realm of spiritualism. In 1910, several months after meeting him, she writes to Ezra, "we are both thin gray veils, having nothing in common with humanity (or its physical properties)" (*P/S* 25). Three years later, writing to him at Stone Cottage, she complains, "I have heard a genuine story down here about a ghostly bloodstained floor: The old woman said she couldn't get it out—although she scrubbed and scrubbed—and even had the carpenter in to plane the boards" (*P/S* 108). Finally, growing more concerned about such incidents, she asks, "Please glean any thing you can for the suppression of ghosts, or else the fear of them" (*P/S* 275). Pound responds by letter almost immediately: " 'Intellectual Vision' is, acc. Wm. Blake & others, the surest cure for ghosts. You'd better begin by seeing fire, or else by doing that visualization of points that I recommended. Fix a point, colour it, or light it as you like, start it moving, multiply it, etc. Make patterns, colours, pictures, whatever you like. You'll end up as a great magician and a prize exorcist" (*P/S* 276).

Pound's use of the phrase "intellectual vision," which he first encountered in Yeats's essays on Blake in *Ideas of Good and Evil*, is a remarkable and fruitful misreading of Blake. By "intellectual vision," Blake means prophetic or imaginative vision, in contrast to the outward gaze of "the mortal perishing organ of sight" (Blake, *Poetry and*

---

45. In Canto 83, Pound recalls reading "Ennemosor on Witches" with Yeats (*C* 83: 548).

Radioactivity

Prose 532). Pound, on the other hand, conceives of intellectual vision as an antidote to a more terrifying, irrational form of vision (a visitation from a ghost). Both are forms of internalized, visionary experience, but "intellectual vision" is self-induced and tempered by rationality. (Note the emphasis on geometric patterns and points of light.) For Pound, intellectual vision is a *technique*, a form of exorcism, a means of defusing the irrational power of visionary experience while retaining some measure of enchantment. In this sense, intellectual vision is an oxymoron that synthesizes the intellectual and the irrational in a manner similar to that of magical realism. Not only does Pound alter the terms of Blake's dialectic (internal versus external vision), but he condenses the opposition of rational and irrational into a single phrase. Pound and Blake do, however, agree on an important aspect of magical realism: supernatural vision is always capable of greater precision and "density" than the vision of the "Corporeal or Vegetative Eye." Blake declares, "A Spirit and a Vision are not, as the modern philosophy supposes, a cloudy vapour or a nothing; they are organized and minutely articulated beyond all that the mortal and perishing nature can produce" (532).

During the same period in which Pound was working closely with Yeats (1913–1915), he began to translate "ghost plays" from the Japanese Noh theater, a project that had an important impact on his conception of the Image. It is important to emphasize that Pound produced his adaptations of Chinese poems (published in *Cathay*) *after* he had "translated" the Japanese plays (which, like the poems in *Cathay*, were drawn from Fenollosa's papers).[46] Moreover, the amount of material he translated from the Japanese is considerably larger than his collection of Chinese poems—an indication, I believe, of the special relevance of the "ghost plays" to Pound's evolving sense of the Image.[47] Whereas the Chinese written character emerged as an

46. The priority of the Japanese adaptations in terms of execution is belied by the order of publication. *Cathay* (1915) appeared prior to the volumes containing Pound's Noh translations. Four of his adaptations of Noh dramas appeared in *Certain Noble Plays of Japan: From the Manuscripts of Ernest Fenollosa, Chosen and Finished by Ezra Pound*, introd. W. B. Yeats (Churchtown: Cuola Press, 1916). These four plays, along with eleven others, appeared a year later in Ezra Pound and Ernest Fenollosa, *"Noh" or Accomplishment: A Study of the Classical Stage of Japan* (London: Macmillan, 1917).

47. Regarding the priority of Pound's Japanese adaptations in the earliest formulations

important emblem of the ideogrammic method in poetry and criticism, the mediumistic qualities of the Noh dramas helped preserve (by disguising) the Decadent features of Imagism.

Indeed, Pound's quest for a rationalized form of visionary experience (which is essentially a rationalized belief in ghosts) comes upon fertile ground in the Japanese Noh theater. The remarkable thing about the Noh dramas, from Pound's standpoint, is their relevance to both aspects of Imagism: the public concern with form and technique, and the occult theory of the Image as an instance of possession, as a psychological "complex." In an introduction to his translations of the Noh, Pound writes: "The Noh has its unity in emotion. It also has what we may call Unity of Image . . . This intensification of the Image, this manner of construction, is very interesting to me personally as an Imagiste, for we Imagistes knew nothing of these plays when we set out in our own manner. These plays are also an answer to the question that has several times been put to me: 'Could one do a long Imagiste poem?' " (*T* 237). A footnote in the memoir of Gaudier-Brzeska reiterates Pound's belief in the relevance of the Noh structure to Vorticism and the Image: "In the best Noh the whole play may consist of one Image. I mean it is gathered about one Image. Its unity consists in one Image, enforced by movement and music. I see nothing against a long vorticist poem" (*GB* 94).[48] Moreover, as an extended "complex," as an instance of form magnetized by subliminal "energies," the Noh Image migrates toward the supernatural, the phantasmic. The crossover between material and spectral images in the Noh occurs somewhat enigmatically in the uncertain space between "indefiniteness" and definition: "One must read or 'examine' these texts 'as if one were listening to music.' One must build out of their indefiniteness a definite Image. The plays are, at best, I think an Image; that is

---

of the Image, Marianne Moore once observed of Imagism: "The 'new' poetry seemed to justify itself as a more robust form of Japanese poetry . . . although a specific and more lasting interest in Chinese poetry came later." Moore, " 'New' Poetry since 1912," p. 120.

48. A recently discovered and unpublished essay by Pound elaborates his views on the relation between Imagism and the Noh. The essay, titled "The 'Image' and the Japanese Classical Stage," was apparently written as part of the "Affirmations" series, published in *New Age* in 1915. The essay, with comments by Earl Miner and Walton Litz, appears in *Princeton University Library Chronicle* 52, no. 1 (Autumn 1991): 17–30.

to say their unity lies in the Image—they are built up about it as the Greek plays are built up about a single moral conviction . . . The Greek plays are troubled and solved by the gods; the Japanese are abounding in ghosts and spirits" (*T* 247). As Pound describes it here, the manner of constructing a Noh Image bears a strong resemblance to the dialectic of magical realism: the poet builds a definite Image out of a reservoir of indefiniteness; precise definition is reconciled with a state of enchantment, reason with unreason.

It is important to bear in mind that Pound became absorbed in the Noh theater at precisely the same time he was exploring various aspects of the occult with Yeats at Stone Cottage. Both of these projects, in turn, influenced his conception of the Image, which also took shape during this period. Although Pound found the Noh to be a useful analogy for the formal properties of the Image, it is the "psychology," or the ghostly aspects of the plays, which made the greatest impression on him. Working from Fenollosa's notes, Pound writes, for example, "The most striking thing about these plays is their marvelously complete grasp of spiritual being. They deal more with heroes, or even we might say ghosts, than with men clothed in flesh. Their creators were great psychologists. In no other drama, does the supernatural play so great, so intimate a part" (*T* 280). Concerning a particular drama, Pound remarks, "*Tsunemasa* is gentle and melancholy. It is all at high tension, but it is a psychological tension, the tension of the séance . . . The spirit is invoked and appears" (*T* 265). The tension of the séance, which captures the appeal of a Noh drama, is a tension between the desire to see the apparition and the need to verify its authenticity or truthfulness. Discussing the play *Nishikigi,* Pound singles out the character of a priest who "only wants to see how things happened":

> Let it be a dream, or a vision,
> Or what you will, I care not.
> Only show me the old times over-past and snowed under;
> Now, soon, while the night lasts. (*PMN* 24)

Yet the priest also has "a passion for realism, he is anxious about the facts" (*PMN* 23). Pound himself is deeply familiar with the tension between a desire to surrender himself to the spirits of the dead and a desire to know "the facts."

The Noh drama appeals to Pound because it offers a dignified means of capturing the "tension of the séance," which he scorns in its vulgar or popular form. The most important feature of the Noh, according to Pound, is its capacity to convey "a *sense* of past time in the present."[49] The Noh may be said to provide a means of rationalizing and legitimating his belief in ghosts, his desire to revive the dead. Pound's admiration of the "ghost psychology" of the Noh plays is built on a spurious rejection of "spiritist doctrines": "The lover of the stage and the lover of drama and of poetry will find his chief interest in the psychological pieces, or Plays of the Spirits . . . These plays are full of ghosts and the ghost psychology is amazing. The parallels with Western spiritist doctrines are very curious. This is, however, an irrelevant or extraneous interest, and one might set it aside if it were not bound up with a dramatic and poetic interest of the very highest order" (*T* 222). Pound's rejection of spiritualism is disingenuous because it masks the sublimating effect of the Noh on his own personal cult of the dead. Explaining his position further, he writes, "Some will be annoyed at a form of psychology which is, in the West, relegated to spiritistic séances. There is, however, no doubt that such psychology exists. All through the winter of 1914–15 I watched Mr. Yeats correlating folk-lore . . . and data of these occult writers, with the habits of the charlatans of Bond Street. If the Japanese authors had not combined the psychology of such matters with what is to me a very fine sort of poetry, I would not bother with it" (*T* 236). Once again Pound's rejection of spiritualism cannot be taken at face value, since he is attracted to the Noh plays precisely because they rationalize and legitimate his own infatuation with ghosts. By associating his personal cult of the dead with the sublime tradition of the Noh theater, he masks the sentimental and irrational character of his beliefs.

Following the publication of his Japanese translations (with an introduction by Yeats) in 1916, Pound was inspired to write several plays modeled on the Noh. One of the "ghost plays," entitled *De*

49. This phrase occurs in the introduction to Pound's translation of a Noh drama entitled *Takasago*. The translation and its brief introduction were recently discovered in the papers of Alice Corbin Henderson, to whom Pound had sent the play in 1915. Pound characterizes the play as "the very core of the 'Noh' " and, in a latter to Harriet Monroe, claims that his theme for the *Cantos* is "roughly the theme of 'Takasago.' " See *The Letters of Ezra Pound to Alice Corbin Henderson,* ed. Ira B. Nadel (Austin: University of Texas Press, 1993), pp. xxii–xxiii, 110.

Musset's 'A Supper at the House of Mademoiselle Rachel' (May 29, 1839), takes its inspiration from a celebrated account of supernatural experience published in 1911 by Anne Moberly. (Is her name the source of the more famous "Mauberley"?) In the brief introduction to *De Musset,* Pound quietly establishes a dichotomy between ghosts and rationality, as he jokes with his readers: "Ah no, you would not complain about my giving you Japanese emotion, you would call it European emotion. And then the rational continent always says you English are mad about ghosts" (*PMN* 23). Pound also spells out his debt to the Noh and indicates that his miniature plays, like their more exalted models, depend on the contradictory impulses that engender the "tension of the séance." He advises his readers, "You will have to be pilgrims, or something of that sort. These scenes can only be real for those who desire to see them" (*PMN* 23). While realism depends, apparently, on the *desire* to see, it also requires that one know "exactly or almost exactly what happened": "You might well ask, why I have chosen my subject. I wished to show for an instant an illusion. Yet *an illusion that should be not quite an illusion* [emphasis added]. It so happens that we really can know, in this case, exactly or almost exactly what happened" (*PMN* 24). At the heart of this brief apology for a play about ghosts, Pound discloses the object of magical realism: "an illusion that should be not quite an illusion"; a state of enchantment that is mediated by historical or critical intelligence; an instance of "intellectual vision."

Among the four plays modeled after the Noh is a six-page piece titled *Tristan,* written in 1916 and based on the play *Nishikigi.* The main protagonist is a "keen-eyed" Sculptor who encounters the apparitions of Tristan and Yseult on a walking tour of Cornwall, England. The character of the Sculptor brings to mind Pound's friend Gaudier-Brzeska, who had recently been killed in the war. On this basis, *Tristan* also bears a resemblance to the play *Tsunemasa,* which Pound describes as follows: "As to the quality of poetry in this work: there is the favored youth, slain; the uneasy-bloodstained and thoughtless spirit" (*T* 264). Gaudier, like the Sculptor in *Tristan,* had once taken a walking tour of southern England, which Pound refers to in his memoir of the sculptor (*GB* 76).[50] The most remarkable develop-

---

50. Horace Brodzky's account of this trip includes several details that also appear in

ment of Pound's play occurs when Tristan begins to speak to Yseult in the voice of the Sculptor (*PMN* 36). Eventually the Sculptor displaces Tristan entirely in the affection of Yseult. Thus, the Sculptor, who is alive in the play, functions as a phantasmic presence who taps into and eventually submerges the voice of the central character. For all intents and purposes, the young Sculptor becomes the ghost of Tristan, a figure in a troubled love story. Given the secret identity of the Sculptor (Gaudier), the play can be read as the first sign of Pound's aberrant mourning for Gaudier—and the first transmission of Gaudier's phantom. The final lines of the play, spoken by the young Sculptor, may be understood as a veiled warning to Pound himself: "Knowing you and not knowing you, / There is too much between us" (*PMN* 38.)

A year after writing the plays modeled on the Noh, Pound published the first drafts of an "endless poem" combining dreamlike visions and history, phantasmagoria and fact. Following the opening address to Robert Browning, the narrator of the first canto declares, "Ghosts move about me / Patched with histories."[51] Grafting historical fact onto the enchanted personae of the dead, Pound carries the aesthetic of magical realism into its final phase of development—a process that ends catastrophically in the historical delusions of the radio broadcasts.

Erotic Casualties

> And as for the love-grave, dyed like the leaves of maple with the tokens of by-gone passion, and like the orchids and chrysanthemums which hide the mouth of a fox-hole, they have slipped into the shadow of the cave; this brave couple has vanished into the love-grave.
>
> —From *Nishikigi*, a Noh drama by Motokiyo, translated by Ezra Pound

A ghost, according to primitive or popular beliefs, is a dead person whose death resulted from some form of violence (murder, for

---

Pound's play. See Brodzky, *Henri Gaudier-Brzeska, 1891–1915* (London: Faber and Faber, 1938), p. 22.

51. Pound, "Three Cantos: I," *Poetry* 11 (June 1917): 116. The final version of the *Cantos* opens with a séance, an invocation of spirits: Odysseus/Pound journeys to the underworld to converse with the dead.

example), or a dead person who has been neglected in some fashion through improper burial or mourning. A soldier lost in battle, for instance, is a perennial source of psychic disturbance. Freud, applying a psychoanalytic viewpoint to anthropological researches, remarks upon these traditional beliefs: among primitive peoples, certain categories of the dead are said to have "a particular right to feel resentment."[52] Yet dead persons who have not, ostensibly, been mistreated in any way may also become phantoms. Freud accounts for this anomaly by invoking what he calls "the omnipotence of thoughts," whereby "things become less important than ideas of things: whatever is done to the latter will inevitably also occur to the former. Relations which hold between the ideas of things are assumed to hold equally between things themselves" (*Totem* 85). In other words, in the psychic realm of mourning, one need not actually murder someone; one has only to wish a death for it to come true. Nor is it necessary that the death wish be openly acknowledged: an unconscious wish may be as powerful and effective as an open desire to see harm come to a person. Furthermore, "according to primitive ideas a person only dies if he is killed—by magic if not by force—and such a death naturally tends to make the soul revengeful and ill-tempered" (59). Hence, all deaths are a result of foul play, whether physical or supernatural.

Freud argues that the principle of the omnipotence of thoughts (which is the basis of telepathy) is necessary for understanding not only the thought of primitive peoples, but the psychic operation of mourning in general. The loss of a loved one can produce phantasmic effects that differ only superficially from the experience of primitive peoples. All relationships, Freud holds, are characterized by ambivalence: "In almost every case where there is an intense emotional attachment to a particular person we find that behind the tender love there is a concealed hostility in the unconscious" (*Totem* 60). Observing the effect of ambivalence on a woman who had recently lost her husband, he states, "There was something in her—a wish that was unconscious to herself—which would not have been dissatisfied by the occurrence of death and which might have actually brought it about if it had had the power. And after the death *has* occurred, it is

---

52. Sigmund Freud, *Totem and Taboo,* trans. James Strachey (New York: Norton, 1950), p. 59.

against this unconscious wish that the reproaches are a reaction" (60). The hostility of the survivor, which cannot be openly acknowledged, is projected onto the dead person, who then transmits the evil wish back to the survivor. "The survivor thus denies that he ever harbored any hostile feelings against the dead loved one; the soul of the dead harbours them instead" (61). As a result of the secret death wish, "a dearly loved relative at the moment of death changes into a demon, from whom his survivors can expect nothing but hostility and against whose evil desires they must protect themselves by all possible means" (58).[53] In general, then, we could say, with Laurence Rickels, that "the death wish gives rise to ghosts" (*Aberrations of Mourning* 360).

Improper burial or mourning, which transforms the benevolent dead person into a vengeful demon, may take the form of simple neglect or an inability to mourn, which masks a secret reservoir of hostility. Deferred mourning involves a period of "incubation" that produces an endless cycle of visitations by the ghost of the deceased. Translating the Noh drama *Kinuta*, Pound learns of the law of repetition that governs the phantom's return:

> The way a ghost returns
> From the shadow of the grass—
> We have heard the stories,
> It is eight thousand times, they say,
> Before regret runs in a smooth-worn grave. (*T* 305)

The period of incubation may also be understood, however, in relation to the figure of the incubus, who begets upon the sleeper a brood of phantoms. Laurence Rickels explains, "The deep sleep that left one pregnant, often with prophecy though most frequently with the actual offspring of phantoms, was called incubation" (*Aberrations of Mourning* 9). Pound's own fascination with the figure of the in-

---

53. Adorno extends Freud's theory of ghosts in a manner that is relevant to Pound's trouble with the dead. Adorno writes, "Freud's theory that belief in ghosts stems from evil thoughts of living people about the dead, and from the memory of old death wishes, is too limited. Hatred of the dead is made up of envy no less than a feeling of guilt." Theodor W. Adorno and Max Horkheimer, *Dialectic of Enlightenment*, trans. John Cumming (New York: Continuum, 1970), p. 215. Pound's envy of the dead, which figures so prominently in his early poetry, may indeed play a role in the disturbed character of his mourning for Gaudier.

cubus—a fascination that produces the early crypt poems and that is also evident from the content of his library—betrays a period of incubation within himself. Engendered by ill will and neglect, the restless occupants of Gaudier's crypt eventually hatch in the radio broadcasts, lending Pound's voice its prophetic tone and crippling it with delusions.

By examining Pound's account of the months leading up to Gaudier-Brzeska's death, we can expose the ground of "the phantasmic consequences of improper burial" (*Aberrations of Mourning* 15). The materials of Chapter 3 establish the basis for such an inquiry, namely that Gaudier stands in relation to Pound as Elpenor does to Odysseus. Elpenor haunts Odysseus as a result of his premature death and the failure of Odysseus to observe his death properly. In addition, as we have seen, the character of Gaudier's death resembles that of an earlier friend in Pound's life, Will Smith, who died at an early age and who was deprived (as a "heretic") of his right to proper burial (according to the title of Pound's first book of poetry, *A Lume Spento*). These analogies invite us to examine more closely the circumstances of Gaudier's death, Pound's response to the event, and his role in shaping the public response to it.

The telepathic character of Pound's relation to Gaudier-Brzeska after the sculptor's death actually emerged long before the event took place. Indeed, soon after their first meeting, Pound began to take control of Gaudier's death. One could even go so far as to say that Pound staged, telepathically, Gaudier's death. The two men first met a year before Gaudier enlisted in the French army in July 1914. Pound's record of their first rendezvous at Gaudier's studio is entirely candid about his attraction to the young sculptor: "I was interested and I was determined that he should be" (*GB* 45). Yet Pound also reveals that his meeting with Gaudier aroused feelings that have little to do with affection: "I knew that many things would bore or disgust him, particularly my rather middle-aged point of view, my intellectual tiredness and exhaustion, my general scepticism, and quietness, and I therefore opened fire with 'Altaforte' and 'Piere Vidal,' and such poems as I had written when about his age" (*GB* 45). At the time of this meeting, Pound was twenty-nine and Gaudier twenty-one. The passage reveals, as I noted in Chapter 3, Pound's concern with growing older and a sense that his own youth is behind him; it suggests a loss of vitality. Meeting Gaudier brought Pound face to face with his own mortality, an experience that would inevitably produce ambivalent feelings. Pound's words suggest that he views Gaudier as an image of his own youth, but also, more importantly, as a rival. Hoping to establish some kind of authority over the younger man, Pound "opens fire" with two poems that celebrate a passion for soldiering and the violence of war—a demonstration, apparently, of the older poet's once vigorous youth. The poem "Sestina: Altaforte," which portrays the soldier-poet Bertans de Born, contains passages such as the following:

> The man who fears war and squats opposing
> My words for stour, hath no blood of crimson
> But is fit only to rot in womanish peace . . .
> For the death of such sluts I go rejoicing;
> Yea, I fill the air with my music. (*CEP* 109)

Addressed to a youth of twenty-one in a milieu that was becoming increasingly aware of the possibility of war (London in 1913), this poem can be interpreted as an oblique call to the younger man to prove his virility (and his artistic integrity) by going to war. The figure of "opening fire" must be taken seriously: by aiming these words at Gaudier, Pound launches a death wish that culminates, from the standpoint of the primitive mind, in Gaudier's actual death.[54] It is entirely possible that in retrospect Pound believed unconsciously that his readings had encouraged Gaudier to go to the front and were thus obliquely responsible for his death. The event of his death precipitated in Pound a psychological and political crisis in which he claimed some measure of responsibility for the death.

The projection of hostility through the "Altaforte" reading is only one point of access to a larger command structure that controls Gaudier's death from afar. In the memoir, for example, Pound reveals that Gaudier anticipated his own death long before it occurred: "His sister

54. The ambivalence that would give rise to such a wish may have played a greater role in Pound's relationship with Gaudier than he allows in the memoir. According to Jacob Epstein, Gaudier once rebuked Pound in an argument over Pound's views of modern sculpture, telling him, "Shut up, you understand nothing!" Jacob Epstein, *Let There Be Sculpture* (London, 1940), p. 70.

tells me that years ago in Paris, when the war was undreamed of, he insisted that he would die in the war" (*GB* 64). Pound's telecommand to go to war reactivates this early premonition and brings it to fulfillment. On July 5, 1914, Gaudier made out his will before joining the French forces. Ezra and Dorothy Pound were present to witness and sign the will.[55] Thus, Pound formally documented his control over Gaudier's possible death, and the overt effects of his death, by acting as signatory to his will. Witness to the possibility of Gaudier's death, Pound also participated in what amounts to a public presentiment of the death (an event that coincides precisely with Pound's disengagement from the Imagist movement in July 1914). It was not yet clear to Pound, however, that his signature also bound him to a lifetime of phantasmic consequences.

Once he arrived at the front, Gaudier indicated in a letter to Dorothy that the reading of "Altaforte" continued to shape his perceptions of the war: "We shall pursue the boches [the Germans], it will be hot but rather agreeable, same temperament as 'Altaforte'" (*GB* 67). Ultimately, Pound's reading of "Altaforte" cast a spell over Gaudier's life that was destined to be broken only on June 5, 1915, the day he was killed in battle.[56] In the meantime, Pound ventured deeper into the business of making Gaudier's death his own by continuing to send him war poems at the front. From among his Chinese translations, Pound sent Gaudier "Song of the Bowmen of Shu" and "Lament of the Frontier Guard." Seeing the war through Pound's eyes, Gaudier was guided from afar through his final days by these apparently benevolent but elegiac transmissions from London. Gaudier writes back, "The poems depict our situation in a wonderful way" (*GB* 58). ("Wonderful" because the distance between sixth-century China and twentieth-century Europe, between Pound's mind and his own, vanishes in the act of "translation"?)

55. Roger Cole notes this detail in *Burning to Speak: The Life and Art of Henri Gaudier-Brzeska* (Oxford: Phaidon, 1978), p. 40.

56. An early poem by Pound, "Mesmerism," deals with the experience of hypnotic suggestion. It exemplifies a moment when the poet is inhabited by the voice and thoughts of another (Robert Browning, in this case). From this poem, we can infer that the *art* of hypnosis has its place in Pound's thinking about poetry, as well as his relation to Gaudier (*CEP* 17–18).

As Gaudier's time at the front dragged on, intimations of his fate began to arrive with greater frequency, advancing the premonition noted by his sister and confirming the inadmissible portent of his last will and testament. Uneasy about his role in prompting Gaudier's exposure to harm, Pound was sensitive to the slightest hint of mortality in Gaudier's letters. He notes, for example, Gaudier's description of the hellish landscape of the trenches as "a sight worthy of Dante" (*GB* 59; another instance of viewing the prospect of death through Pound's eyes). Pound also cites a letter from Gaudier which describes an incident on the battlefield where Gaudier gave his comrades a scare by feigning death and then miraculously coming back to life. The morbid cast of trench humor is evident in Gaudier's comment about his mock death: "I have had the greatest fun this night of all my life" (*GB* 57). Sifting Gaudier's final letters for portents of his demise, Pound discovered what he believed to be a "premonition of death": "His premonition of a head wound is curious, for this letter was written I believe only two days before his death. His sister tells me that years ago in Paris, when the war was undreamed of, he insisted that he would die in the war" (*GB* 64). By juxtaposing the final premonition of death with the earliest one, Pound hints at the efficacy of such forebodings, and hence at the efficacy of his own telepathic intervention in Gaudier's life. ("Telepathy" means literally "pain at a distance," a secret suffering.)

The cumulative effect of these forebodings brought Pound to speculate publicly about the possibility of Gaudier's death in an article in *New Age* in February 1915. Moreover, in early June 1915, several days before Gaudier was killed in battle, Pound writes cryptically to his mother, "Gaudier is getting tired of the trenches, it's time someone came in and hurried matters" (*SC* 279). Pound's response to the actual death is curiously nonchalant: "Brzeska has been killed, which is pretty disgusting, though I suppose it is a marvel it hasn't happened before" (*SC* 279). According to Carpenter, "This letter to his father, written just after he had heard the news, continues with mere gossip." In Pound's letter the phrase "pretty disgusting" has a false ring about it, suggesting that he is unable to acknowledge, or disclose, the full spectrum of his response to Gaudier's death.

Indeed, Pound's statements about the war in general have an air of detachment that does little to mask their eccentricity. He refers, for example, to the war effort in England as "a very fine sight," and displays a similar nonchalance (and perhaps a note of defiance) when he observes, "The arrival of Zeppelins seems to have filled London with a quiet contentment."[57] James Longenbach says otherwise: "Most Londoners were far from contented, but some found Pound's composure talismanic. Violet Hunt and her circle considered Pound's presence to be a charm against German Zeppelins. Hunt kept Gaudier-Brzeska's bust of Pound in her garden, maintaining that the sculpture warded off the airships" (*Stone Cottage* 179). To Pound's friends, his peculiar views on the war suggested—via Gaudier's sculpture of Pound—immunity from, but also an inscrutable relation to, the distant events of the war. By ascribing to Pound these "talismanic" powers, his friends confirmed, inadvertently, the bizarre conditions of his telepathic relation to Gaudier. In spite of the ostensibly benign character of the war (from Pound's perspective), he acknowledges that "the war is eating up all of everybody's subconscious energy. One does nothing but buy newspapers" (107). It is not merely a question of being starved for information about an event that is unimaginable to most people (as Pound seems to suggest); rather, his own "subconscious energy" is being devoured by a medium (the press) and by a phantom that he cannot yet acknowledge.

Pound's sympathies in the Great War, which anticipated his treasonous activities during World War II, disclosed yet another "telepathic" link to the front: "I feel strangely enough most for the young Germans who are now being killed. These spectacled, dreamy faces, or so I picture them, remind me more of men that I have known than the strong-bodied young English football players" (Longenbach, *Stone Cottage* 117). The "spectacled, dreamy faces" of the enemy call to mind Pound's conception of the sensitive "mediumistic artist," whom he alternately abhorred and admired. More important, however, the young Germans who were about to die at the front should be understood as displaced images of Gaudier's fate—restless ghosts who visited Pound and rehearsed the deadly scenario that he had set in motion with an aberrant wish.

57. James Longenbach, *Stone Cottage: Pound, Yeats, and Modernism* (New York: Oxford University Press, 1988), pp. 106, 179.

Pound's fanciful resistance to the war and to Gaudier's death secretly describes a period of incubation that aims the death drive of the Image in the direction of politics. The literal deferral of Pound's mourning for Gaudier, which was prefigured by the shadowy presence of death in the poetics of Imagism, spawned a brood of hungry ghosts that eventually, during the 1930s, devoured his poetic faculties and held him hostage, on fascist radio, to the political afterlife of the Image. As soon as he began to acknowledge the impact of Gaudier's death, it is obvious he had waited too long: the dead man had already been transformed into a phantom. In his memoir of the young sculptor, Pound often describes Gaudier in terms of a supernatural presence. He writes of "the daemon of energy that possessed him" (*GB* 39), and recalls from their first meeting "a voice speaking with the gentlest fury in the world" (44). Later, after speaking briefly with Pound, Gaudier "disappeared like a Greek god in a vision" (44).

Pound's susceptibility to the ghosts of young soldiers killed in battle is also evident from his response to several poems that Joyce and Yeats wrote during this period. He praises, for example, what he calls the "phantom vision" of a poem by Joyce (which appeared in the anthology *Des Imagistes*):

> I hear an army charging upon the land,
> And the thunder of their horses plunging . . .
> They cry unto the night their battle name;
> I moan in sleep when I hear afar their whirling laughter;
> They cleave the gloom of dreams, a blinding flame,
> Clanging, clanging upon the heart as upon an anvil. (*LE* 414–415)

He also praises Yeats's rendering of the spectral ranks of "the Magi" (who resemble ill-tempered ghosts) as a superb example of *imagisme*:

> . . . the pale unsatisfied ones
> Appear and disappear in the blue depth of the sky
> With all their ancient faces like rain-beaten stones,
> And all their helms of silver hovering side by side. (*LE* 380)

These martial images remind us of how many of the artists and writers associated with Imagism actually became soldiers: Aldington, Flint, Hulme, Gaudier-Brzeska. It may be wise, indeed, as Robert von Hallberg suggests, to begin to speak of "soldier-Imagists." Furthermore, the motif of phantom soldiers, which secretly depicts Pound's grief over the inhabitants of Gaudier's crypt, reappears later in the radio broadcasts (*RB* 137).

In addition to describing Gaudier in terms that suggest the presence of a ghost, Pound portrayed him as primitive, atavistic. Gaudier, he recalls, liked "to feel as independent as the savage" (*GB* 40). He was "like a well-made young wolf or some soft-moving, bright-eyed wild thing" (*GB* 44). During the late 1930s Pound liked to trace his interest in Leo Frobenius and primitive culture (though he acknowledged he couldn't be sure of this source) to Gaudier-Brzeska (*GB* 142). If it is indeed true that Pound first learned of Frobenius through Gaudier prior to 1915, or thought he did, then it is perhaps not coincidental that Gaudier's ghost begins to show signs of restlessness—after a long period of dormancy—about the time that Frobenius takes center stage in Pound's cultural criticism. Furthermore, Pound is not alone in associating Gaudier with a sense of primitive or archaic potency, both physical and spiritual. Indeed, his characterization of Gaudier as a savage echoes a chorus of infatuated responses to Gaudier's death. H. S. Ede, for example, published a biography of Gaudier titled *Savage Messiah*—an epithet that gives some idea of the hysterical and inflationary aspects of the cult surrounding his death.[58] Horace Brodzky's description of Gaudier resembles Pound's in many respects: "Henri Gaudier-Brzeska was a faun, a clown, and a demon for work" (*Henri Gaudier-Brzeska* 55); he "moved like an animal, quick and alert" (56). One reviewer cited by Brodzky calls Gaudier "a wild, unkempt barbarian" (74), while he himself observes, "Brzeska preferred not to shave, as he considered it expensive and a waste of valuable time. He preferred to be a savage" (74). Even Ford Madox Ford fell under the sway of the death cult (whose members were exclusively male), claiming that Gaudier possessed "great personal beauty" (74).

Once Pound surrendered himself to the visitations of Gaudier's spirit (by compiling the materials of the memoir), there was no question of the impact on Pound of Gaudier's death. In a letter of 1915

58. H. S. Ede, *Savage Messiah* (New York: Literary Guild, 1931). Ken Russell's 1972 film *Savage Messiah* (which takes its title from Ede's biography), is the latest installment of Gaudier's thriving (and manifestly homoerotic) afterlife. See also Gordon Daviot's 1934 play *The Laughing Woman*.

to Felix Schelling, he writes, "The arts will incur no worse loss from the war than this is. One is rather obsessed with it" (*L* 61); to Alice Henderson he observes, "Brzeska has been killed, so sculpture will stick where it is for another half century."[59] Indeed, with the passage of time, Pound became more rather than less preoccupied with the death as a turning point in his thinking and his career. Three years later, he writes of Gaudier's death as "the gravest individual loss which the arts have suffered during the war" (*GB* 136). And in 1934: "For eighteen years the death of Henri Gaudier has been unremedied. The work of two or three years remains, but the uncreated went with him. There is no reason to pardon this either to the central powers or to the allies or to ourselves" (*GB* 140). The significance of Pound's taking some measure of personal responsibility for the death remains open to question. The phrasing of his sentiments suggests, however, that his response to Gaudier's death reenacts his grief over the loss of Will Smith twenty-five years earlier. Of Gaudier he writes, "For eighteen years after Gaudier's death no one has shown the least chance in succeeding him" (*GB* 143). This sounds very much like a letter he wrote to William Carlos Williams in 1921 on the death of Will Smith: "Thirteen years are gone; I haven't replaced him and shan't and no longer hope to" (*L* 167).

People who knew Pound noted the importance he assigned to Gaudier's death in the development of his political and economic interests. After speaking with Pound in 1946, Charles Olson wondered whether "Gaudier's death is the source of his hate for contemporary England and America," and whether "in 1915 his attack on democracy got mixed up with Gaudier's death, and all his turn since has been revenge for the boy's death."[60] In a letter to Wyndham Lewis in 1949, Pound confirms the gist of Olson's speculation: "serious curiosity startin' @ death of Gaudier re: why" (*P/L* 250). What Pound calls "serious curiosity" led eventually, of course, to his commitment to fascism and to the inflammation of his anti-Semitic views. Indeed, his "curiosity" over Gaudier's death gives rise, in the end, to the vengeful phantom of the radio speeches.

59. *Letters of Ezra Pound to Alice Corbin Henderson*, p. 110.
60. Charles Olson, *Charles Olson and Ezra Pound: An Encounter at St. Elizabeths*, ed. Catherine Seelye (New York: Viking, 1975), p. 45.

Dictation and Oblivion

> I don't think it has been sufficiently observed, if it has been observed, how much his work is a structure of mnemonics raised on a reed, nostalgia . . . I'm not sure that, precisely because of the use he has put nostalgia to, and the way he has used himself, he has not made himself the ultimate image of the end of the West.
> —Charles Olson, *Charles Olson and Ezra Pound: An Encounter at St. Elizabeths*

The aim of the translator, according to Pound, is to "bring a dead man to life" (*L* 149), "to resurrect the damaged shade of the author" (*SR* 182). Moreover, as I indicated in Chapter 5, the *impossibility* of translation marks all translation as telegraphic, as an event that is nothing short of miraculous. Translation, like telegraphy, conjures *words at a distance*. This view of translation subscribes, implicitly, to an archaic usage of the verb "to translate," meaning to "transport" spiritually: "to convey or remove from one condition or place to another."[61] Indeed, Pound's theory of translation may owe something explicitly to spiritualist doctrines that commonly use the verb "to translate" in this fashion. More specifically, Pound would have been familiar with this usage from his association with Yeats and from his wife Dorothy's interest in spiritualism.[62]

The idea that translation entails transporting a dead man into the present, or being transported by words to the place of the dead, does not originate with Pound, and he is not alone in holding such a view. Heidegger, for example, whose theory of language has been compared to Pound's, says of translation: "We let ourselves be transported by the poet to the distant shore of the matter spoken here."[63] The translator's destination is a "distant shore" of meaning—the place of

---

61. The *Oxford English Dictionary* also offers a more technical meaning of the verb "to translate": "To carry or convey to heaven without death, also, in later use, said of the death of the righteous."

62. Dorothy uses the verb "to translate" in this manner in a letter to Ezra in 1913: "Georgie [Georgie Hyde-Lees, future wife of W. B. Yeats] had an amusing dream about you two nights ago. You were hanging to the top of a very straight pine tree—all stem-and-a-burst-of-branches-at-the-top kind and had not climbed it—but got there by 'translation' as she says." Cited in Longenbach, *Stone Cottage*, p. 5.

63. Martin Heidegger, "The Anaximander Fragment," *Early Greek Thinking*, p. 32. On the relation between Heidegger's theories and Pound's conception of language, see Rabaté, *Language, Sexuality, and Ideology in Ezra Pound's Cantos*, pp. 1–11.

death—yet he can only reach his destination "by questioning from within the matter" ("Anaximander Fragment" 43). Thus, to attain the place where language and death intersect, the place of the other, the translator must remain behind, subject to a voice from the "distant shore." Heidegger explains the manner in which one word "speaks for" another: "The translation of τό κρεών as 'usage' has not resulted from a preoccupation with etymologies and dictionary meanings . . . The word 'usage' is *dictated* to thinking in the experience of Being's *oblivion*" (54; emphasis added). The translation or "transport" of meaning is undertaken by means of "dictation," yet a form of dictation whose source is "oblivion."

What does Heidegger mean by "dictation" in this context? To begin with, the mode of dictation stands in contrast to a "preoccupation . . . with dictionary meanings," with what he believes to be the calculating, reductive system of lexicography. Thus, "dictation" presupposes a rejection of meaning in a conventional sense; it is, indeed, a mode of translation founded upon the impossibility of translation. What is received through "dictation" therefore discloses a meaning that is unverifiable, yet more authoritative than the definitions offered by a dictionary. Moreover, the fact that the appropriate meaning is "dictated" suggests that translation is part of a larger command structure, a means of thinking, or controlling thought, from a distant shore. There is, in fact, as the phenomenon of dictatorial power suggests, no choice in the matter: the word received is absolute, ineluctable. Yet the source of authority—oblivion—is not only remote but unfathomable. By "oblivion," Heidegger surely intends to convey the idea of forgetfulness: the source of dictation lies in what is long forgotten. Evoking the "experience of Being's oblivion," the word also points to a catastrophic loss that is sequestered in time yet which comes forward in translation.

Avital Ronell's theory of "haunted writing" reiterates the essential features of Heidegger's understanding of translation as dictation received from oblivion. Ronell's idea of "dictation" accounts for "the writing couple whose sustained encounter takes place on the grounds of a catastrophe" (*Dictations* xv). Furthermore, "this writing takes as its point of departure the remoteness of the original author, the incalculable distance of the one who dictates. The resulting texts are bound to assume the function of a double" (*Dictations* xvi). In addition, she notes, "one discerns the playing out of a struggle and a shattering effect that disfigures at once the origin and the copy" (xvi).

Pound's radio speeches, like Ronell's examples of haunted writing, display a "shattering effect." Under pressure of dictation, the inhabitant of Gaudier's crypt, personifying the "radiant" Image, becomes a "savage messiah" that takes possession of Pound's voice over the air. Although the actual Gaudier bears a *distant* resemblance to the legend that flourished after his death (which finds outlet in the radio broadcasts), and although we may detect familiar traces of Pound's "character" in the broadcasts, the effect of dictation on both figures is grotesque. Both are distorted nearly beyond recognition in the course of their extended encounter in the subliminal echo chamber of radio. But this mutilation of character (both linguistic and psychological) is precisely the mark of authentic translation and of the transport of the soul (in the sense that extreme literalness produces "monstrosities" of translation). In the greater economy of Pound's poetics, his radio broadcasts must therefore be understood as "translations" in a Heideggerian sense, as instances of haunted writing. More specifically, these garbled transmissions from the burial site of the Image emanate from Gaudier's crypt. The improbable origin of these transmissions—the image-crypt—confirms Ronell's insistence on "the incalculable distance of the one who dictates."

If we are correct in viewing the radio broadcasts as a "translation" of Gaudier's phantom (and of the poetics of Imagism), we should have no trouble identifying the catastrophic basis of the "writing couple," or, in this case, the radio couple. The specter of mass death rising from the battlefields of World War I (not to mention Gaudier's descriptions of the physical carnage) certainly provided a threshold adequate to the devastation that was destined to occur between the beloved, a dead sculptor, and the poet who had delivered him to a missing grave. It is Gaudier's individual death, however, that discloses the erotic, political, and economic grounds of the catastrophe. Although Pound often failed to recognize the phantasmic consequences of Gaudier's death, he did acknowledge years later that it marked a turning point in his career. Ultimately, as Ronell argues, the "apparition exceeds a notion of the other's anxious receptivity, but is something of a trauma, a mark of devastation that is particularly visible" (*Dictations* xv). The loss of Gaudier is an erotic casualty that marks the origin of Pound's political extremism.

The figure of the Image supplies a link between Pound's politics and the submerged erotics of his early poetry (his love for the dead, which extends eventually to Gaudier). The experience of being haunted by the inhabitants of Gaudier's missing grave, which culminated in the hysteria of the radio broadcasts, may appear at first glance to be simply a biographical or psychological formation. A closer look, however, reveals the interdependence of Pound's belated mourning for Gaudier and his fascination with the Image, which he originally conceived as a means of legitimating or disguising his Decadent infatuation with the dead in his early poetry. Thus, as I noted in Chapter 3, Pound's mourning for Gaudier (which is recorded in the memoir) should be viewed as a vivid and perilous staging of the poetics of Imagism. While Gaudier, in Pound's view, embodied the essential values of the avant-garde Imagist, his death precipitated his *metamorphosis into an archaic figure of the Image*—an exquisite corpse, a vengeful phantom that had to be slain repeatedly. When Pound appeared to relinquish his grief over the loss of Gaudier following World War I, he also accomplished the "final" interment of the Image in his poetics. Similarly, the translation of Gaudier's "damaged shade" into Pound's radio personality constituted a revival of the Image in the context of Pound's idolatrous regard for fascism. The fact that the Image returned to life as a disembodied voice alludes not only to the "radiant" spectrum of the Image, but to the rivalry of verbal and visual values that gave rise to the figure of the Image in the first place. Just as the proximity of the dead originally forced Pound to encrypt the verbal excess of his early poetry in the poetics of Imagism, so the ideogrammic method produced a mythological and radiant substance called meaning, which was eventually transformed by the visitation of ghosts into the posthumous voice of the radio broadcasts.

Freud's essay on mourning and melancholia helps explain the puzzling relation between the resurgence of the Image, Pound's aberrant mourning, and the demonic fulfillment of his racial and political doctrines in the radio speeches. Freud writes, "The most remarkable characteristic of melancholia [a condition associated with mourning], and the one in most need of explanation, is its tendency to change round into mania—a state which is the opposite of it in its symptoms."[64] In contrast to the torpor and inactivity of melancholia, mania is characterized "by high spirits, by the signs of discharge of joyful emotion and by increased readiness for all kinds of action" (254). Nevertheless, Freud observes, "the content of mania is no different from that of melancholia . . . both disorders are wrestling with the same 'complex' " (254). Mania is thus the flip side of melancholia. Triggered by an unknown mechanism, mania discharges the bounded energy of mourning. The *Oxford English Dictionary* adds that mania is characterized by delusions and intense hallucination—that is, by what may be described as a *discharge of images*. This recalls not only Freud's account of mania, but Pound's theory of Images and "new organs" erupting from the surface of the body. Pound's figure of the Image as a vortex also calls to mind the frenzied, boundless energy of mania. In the context of his prolonged yet often submerged mourning for Gaudier—which must be understood as an allegory of the poetics of Imagism—the recurrent activity of the phantom would represent an imagistic disturbance that is characteristic of mania. The erotic, political, or aesthetic energies tied up in repression of hostility or forbidden desires for the dead are suddenly released in the form of a vengeful ghost or *imago*. The survivor escapes persecution by assuming the place of the phantom, by succumbing to what Pound calls "the more difficult art in which we are half media and half creators" (*P/S* 76). The vengeful ghost erupts therefore like an Image from the cryptic body of the one who remains behind, preserver and destroyer of the undead.

In Pound's case, the manic Image erupting from his stubborn, embittered grief falls under a technological spell—what Marshall McLuhan will later call the "tribal magic" of radio. Desperate for access to the airwaves after the fall of Rome in 1943, Pound exclaimed to the station manager of Salò Radio, "Give me a bed, a bowl of soup, and a microphone" (*SC* 633). Yet long before he had become "the Shadow" in his own radio drama, Pound equated the work of the "serious artist" with Marconi's theory of radio waves: "The serious

---

64. Sigmund Freud, *The Standard Edition of the Complete Psychological Works*, ed. James Strachey (London: Hogarth, 1960), vol. 14, p. 253.

artist is usually, or is often as far from the *aegrum vulgus* as is the serious scientist. Nobody has heard of the abstract mathematicians who worked out the determinants that Marconi made use of in his computations for the wireless telegraph" (*LE* 47). Looking back on the period when this essay was written, Pound claims that Western civilization was "by 1918 entering the radio phase" (*GK* 258), a chronology whose only justification may be that it coincides with the disappearance of the Image and Gaudier's memory from Pound's work. Elsewhere, he describes the modern era as "the age of Marconi."[65]

Pound's fascination with radio technology comes to light even earlier, as we have discovered, in the critical writings of *The Spirit of Romance*. His conception of the "mediumistic artist," whose faculties are extended by the technical media, is based on the analogy of a radio set. It is possible, in fact, to trace Pound's fascination with undetected beams or signals to a childhood nickname and, ultimately, to a phantasmic relation with a dead relative. As a child, Pound was called "Ra" (pronounced "Ray") by his family, and occasionally signed his letters "X-ray."[66] Young Ezra's personal identification with radio images, and with a "radiant" energy capable of imaging hidden regions of the body, may help explain his memory of a story about an eccentric family relation: "A sixteenth cousin named Loomis was said to have sent an 'electric signal' between ships, without wires, in the 1860s and was thought to be crazy" (Stock, *Life of Ezra Pound* 2). In the mind of the young Pound, radio communication would therefore have been associated with a distant, deceased relative whose name he shares. (Pound's middle name is Loomis.) Indeed, throughout his career Pound liked to think that he maintained what can only be described as a telepathic relation to certain ancestors. Through pseudonyms and various theoretical channels, Pound established contact with the dead, a process that later found literary expression in his theory of translation. His first published poem, for example, was published under the pseudonym "Weston Llewmys," which evokes his relation to his distant cousin by mutilating their common name. Thus, Pound not only communicates with the dead through this pseudonym but "trans-

65. Pound, *Polite Essays* (London: Faber and Faber, 1937), p. 106.
66. Noel Stock, *The Life of Ezra Pound* (San Francisco: North Point, 1982), p. 9.

lates" his own identity into that of a phantom.⁶⁷ The fact that radio communication and madness are linked in the figure of his ancestor suggests an ominous relation to Pound's wartime activities. Just as Pound viewed the eccentric political career of his grandfather Thaddeus as anticipating his own economic radicalism (*SC* 466), so the figure of his cousin Loomis should be seen as a harbinger of the poet possessed by the spirit of radio and later incarcerated as a madman.

Believing that technology had realized the "ancient dream of flight and sejunct communication" (*SP* 361), Pound associated the modern medium of radio with an archaic dimension of thought or experience, and notes this correspondence in *Guide to Kulchur,* his most comprehensive formulation of fascist culture: "In our time the wireless telegraph has produced a new outbreak of ancient speculations" (*GK* 75). The idea that radio is a "magical transformer" with the power "to retribalize mankind" comes to mind more readily as a component of Marshall McLuhan's widely influential theory of media.⁶⁸ The similarity between Pound's ideas and McLuhan's is no coincidence. McLuhan began his career as a student of modern literature and, more important, as an enthusiastic and perceptive reader of Pound's work. His earliest publications, which attempt to link the work of writers such as Joyce and Pound to the effects of the modern technical media, disclose the literary basis of his later theorizing about the media.⁶⁹ Moreover, in his mature speculations on the technical media, McLuhan argues that the manner of thinking fostered by the media "revolution" is specifically *ideogrammic* (*Understanding Media* vi, 18, 83). Indeed, so substantial is his debt to the ideogrammic model

67. A variation of this pseudonym, "Weston St. Llewmys," appears as the signatory of the epigraph to Pound's second volume of poems, *A Quinzaine for This Yule* (1908). The epigraph refers to the awakening character of the artist as "a figure in the mist," a phantom that secretly alludes to Pound's dead relation (*CEP* 58).

68. Marshall McLuhan, *Understanding Media: The Extensions of Man* (New York: McGraw-Hill, 1964), p. 304.

69. In 1954, for example, McLuhan published an article titled "Sight, Sound, and Fury," in which he argues, "The reader who approaches Pound, Eliot, and Joyce alike as exploiters of the cinematic aspects of language will arrive at appreciation more quickly than the one who unconsciously tries to make sense of them by reducing their use of the new media of communications to the abstract linear forms of the book page." In *Ideas in Process,* ed. C. M. Babcock (Port Washington: Kennikat, 1971), p. 406.

that I think it is useful, and even necessary, to view his "understanding" of the media as reinscribing certain basic principles of Imagism.

Pound, as I have already indicated, views the medium of radio as a kind of "public memory," which is the site of an "outbreak of ancient speculations." McLuhan holds similar views: "Radio is a profound, archaic force, a time bond with the most ancient past and long-forgotten experience" (*Understanding Media* 301). Indeed, radio evokes "archaic tribal ghosts of the most vigorous brand" (301). Pound views radio as a technological effect of "tradition," whereas McLuhan, more provocatively, conceives of "tradition" as an effect of radio: "Tradition, in a word, is the sense of the total past as *now*. Its awakening is a natural result of radio impact" (301). The notion of radio *as* tradition, as a technologized art of memory, helps explain Pound's view that the ideogrammic technique of the first thirty Cantos produces an effect akin to that of radio: "I anticipated the damn thing in first third of Cantos," he remarks about radio in 1940 (*L* 343). In this observation, Pound emphasizes the portion of the *Cantos* which appeared *prior* to the emergence of public broadcasting in the mid-1920s. Indeed, I think it is possible to argue, based on comments that Pound made in 1937 about the Vorticist writings of Wyndham Lewis, that he views radio not only as the technological realization of Vorticism but more specifically as the ideal medium of the *Cantos*. Concerning Lewis' Vorticist play, *The Enemy of the Stars,* Pound writes,

> Here before the B.B.C. murmured at every fire-side WAS and IS (mehercule) the RADIO DRAMA. Written, printed 1914, impossible of presentation by any medium save the human voice, carried through the black air: a DRAMA. The play has awaited a technique for its presentation. Cocteau has evolved the technique . . . Cocteau in his fumoir with his discs and his radio, with his oracle that speaks pure cipher, unsurpassable trouvaille; cleaving-stroke of the spirit, moving as no human voice. (*SP* 454)

Mediated by an idiosyncratic debt to Cocteau and Surrealism, Pound's panegyric to the "impossible" techniques of Vorticism ends by evoking an "oracle that speaks pure cipher"—that is, by evoking the radiophonic ghostland of the *Cantos*. In all probability, McLuhan's favorite analogy for radio—the tribal drum—is borrowed from Pound, whose interest in primitive "drumming languages" develops in relation to the ideogrammic method. Discussing in 1934 the impact of technology on forms of consciousness, Pound states, "Printed word or drum telegraph are neither without bearing on the aggregate life of the folk. As language becomes the most powerful instrument of perfidy, so language alone can riddle and cut through the meshes" (*LE* 77). This analogy, which addresses the correlation between technology and the perversion (or redemption) of language (as well as a link between modernity and the primitive mind), appears again three years later in *Guide to Kulchur:*

> "Gorgias debunks the logical process."—Headline on Athenian bill-board.
> All knowledge is built up from a rain of factual atoms such as:
> Frobenius forgets his notebook, ten miles from camp he remembers it. Special African feast on, and no means of sketching for the records. No time to return to camp. No matter. Black starts drumming. Drum telegraph works and sketching materials arrive in time for the beano.
> Culture possessed and forgotten. (*GK* 98)

In this ideogrammic passage, Pound associates the "drum telegraph" (a precursor of radio) not only with primitive culture and the demystification of logic, but with the materiality of knowledge and a strategy to counteract a failure of memory. Indeed, the ideogrammic method, which accounts for the paratactic structure of this passage, must be viewed as an extension of the "drumming language" that fulfills the ancient dream of telepathy. Later, Pound would claim that the modern incarnation of the tribal drum—radio—exerts spellbinding control over the minds of its listeners.

McLuhan, following the example of Pound, seizes on the figure of the tribal drum to emphasize the relation between radio and primitive mentality. Yet he also gives this figure a specific political identity by linking the emergence of radio to the rise of fascism. He claims that the "tribal magic" of radio "began to resonate once more with the note of fascism" (*Understanding Media* 297). Describing those who listened to Hitler's radio speeches, he writes, "They danced entranced to the tribal drum of the radio that extended their central nervous system" (298). This passage not only situates the figure of the "drum telegraph" in a specific political context, but calls to mind Pound's conception of the mediumistic artist whose senses are extended by the technical media. Indeed, Pound's famous dictum "Artists are the antennae of the race" (*LE* 297) provides the basis for McLuhan's notion of the artist as a kind of high priest of technology: "The serious artist is the only person able to encounter technology with impunity, just because he is an expert aware of the changes in sense perception" (*Understanding Media* 18). McLuhan underscores the psychological and radiophonic properties of the "drum telegraph" when he describes radio as "a subliminal echo chamber of magical power to touch remote and forgotten chords" (302). This passage calls to mind a number of associations which have an important bearing on the crypt effects of Pound's radio broadcasts. First, the reference to radio's "magical power" evokes the equation of technology and unreason that underwrites the fascist ideology of magical realism. In addition, the idea that radio elicits and broadcasts "subliminal echoes" corroborates the need to locate a "remote" and improbable source for the phantasmic bearing of Pound's "on-air" personality. Finally, McLuhan's speculation insists on radio's fundamental association with memory and oblivion. Indeed, the "magical power" of radio derives precisely from its capacity to "touch" and to expose that which has been long forgotten, to evoke the "archaic tribal ghosts" of our past.

Whereas McLuhan's theorizing about radio is essentially a rationalized account of superstitious attitudes, Pound makes no effort to abstract or qualify his superstitious feelings about the new medium. As I noted earlier, these superstitions are fully exposed in a letter of 1940 describing his early impressions of radio: "Blasted friends left a goddam radio here yester. Gift. God damn destructive and dispersive devil of an invention" (*L* 342). In the same letter, Pound calls the radio a "devil box" and compares it to a devouring serpent (*L* 342). Several years later, in one of the radio broadcasts, he repeats the story, emphasizing the memory of his first radio set as a mysterious gift "planted" in his home by friends with malevolent intent: "Two friends determined to break down my antipathy to radio had planted, that is given me, a small sized medium wave apparatus, and then fled the village" (*RB* 236). Although there is a trace of irony in this recollection, Pound was entirely serious when in 1940 he called radio "the cold, evil voice of mendacity and needless excitement" (*SC* 581).

The irony stems from Pound's acknowledgment (in the same letter in which he calls the radio a "devil box") that the ideogrammic technique of the *Cantos* somehow anticipated the new medium, that his poetry is itself a kind of radiological ghostland (*L* 343). Nevertheless, he regards the "devil box" as a cacophonous assortment of voices and music that is riddled with falsehood and delusions—a view that pertains not so much to the medium of radio as to the haunted space of the *Cantos*. The only benefit to those listening would be the development of "a faculty for picking the fake in the voices," a capacity to detect the lie or the secret intent of a familiar voice (*L* 343).

In his radio speeches, Pound links the "fake in the voices" to a network of malevolent forces that infiltrate society (and Pound's own mind) through radio (*RB* 326). According to Robert Casillo, "Pound compares the effects of the radio, in his time *the* instrument of mass communication, with those of infectious diseases; like radio waves, germs travel on the air and work their greatest effects on crowds."[70] Just as Pound remembers his first radio (the "devil box") being "planted" in his home by friends, so he describes "how far the evil is brought in by carriers. Unconscious agents, that bring an *Anschauung*, an attitude towards life, poisonous as the germs of bubonic plague" (*RB* 238). Phantoms, like germs, are "unconscious agents" that plague the living. Indeed, the contamination spread through radio ("a dispersive devil of an invention") is nothing more than a biological account of the phantasmic effects of radio. By overcoming his antipathy to radio and joining the Babel of voices on the air, Pound attempts to "vaccinate" himself against the "unconscious agents" flooding the airwaves. As he does so, however, his own voice is subsumed by "the fake in the voices."

Pound is drawn to the medium of radio because "radio is the only free speech left" (*RB* 182). Yet radio is subject to infection, and to hidden controls, precisely because it is "the ONLY medium still open for free (if you call it free) communication with the outer world" (*RB* 281). The openness of radio provides access for a multiplicity of voices, yet it also makes radio an easy target for manipulation. Pound's views reflect this contradiction: on one hand he extols radio's immunity from

---

70. Robert Casillo, *A Genealogy of Demons: Anti-Semitism, Fascism, and the Myths of Ezra Pound* (Evanston, Ill.: Northwestern University Press, 1988), p. 296.

the evil forces that have infiltrated the medium of print, yet on the other hand he asserts that radio has already fallen under the influence of an insidious power. The threat of *external* control, however, is not the only danger an "open" medium faces; it is also vulnerable to dangerous forces from within. At any given moment, the "free speech" of radio is liable to give way to what Laurence Rickels calls the "primal medium of rumor" (*Aberrations of Mourning* 269), a contagion of speech that mimics the effects of the phantom in Pound's radio broadcasts.[71] Rumor spreads irresistibly, uncontrollably, because it thrives on secrecy and because it is steeped in fantasy. The source of a rumor, like that of the phantom who plagues the radio broadcasts, is shrouded in uncertainty. Thus, the open medium of radio is vulnerable not only to hidden controls from without but to the rumored voices of ghosts from within. Indeed, in Pound's radio broadcasts it is impossible to distinguish between the phantasmic effects of rumor and the hidden forces that control and disrupt the speaker's voice.

According to Pound, the "fake in the voices" originates in the most exotic—and improbable—locations. In one speech, for example, he informs his listeners, "You might remember that during my last broadcasts I was guided from within America" (*RB* 246). On another occasion, he describes the effect of "4 to 8 million invaders, all part of a widely distributed RACE, that has a radio out by San Diego or somewhere" (*RB* 100). The unnamed race of "invaders" is the Jews, who are seeking, Pound believes, to gain control over the technical media: "All the means of intercommunication pass into the hands of the secret and largely Semitic control" (*RB* 172). The trail of secret controls also leads, however, to an unlikely source in Pound's early career. Aestheticism—an amalgam of Decadence and the incipient avant-garde—is implicated, it turns out, in the history of secret controls. Pound suggests that there is an ominous link between the Decadent orientation of his early poetry, which haunts the rhetoric of the Image, and the peril that faces Europe during the time of the broadcasts: "The aesthetic angle, that my whole generation grew up in, all LOOKING harmless, so HARMLESS" (*RB* 75). The hidden danger of aestheticism—indeed, of the category of the aesthetic—concerns specifically his involvement with the group of artists and writers that formed the

---

71. Rumor, according to Rickels, follows a "double trajectory charted by telepathic prediction and advance surveillance." *Aberrations of Mourning*, p. 289.

basis of the Imagist and Vorticist movements. In an early broadcast, Pound remembers,

> Twenty-five, 26, 27 years ago night life, or night dance clubs started in London. Looked diverting, nobody wondered WHY? Ole Frida started the cave of the calf, nobody thought evil. Possibly a little espionage, probably not even that. Wake up one morning and find the spirit of England, immortal spirit of England's May Day, chained in a brothel. Just another hat trick, undermining, cutting away. Where did she get the money to do it? (*RB* 57–58)

Pound is thinking about the Cave of the Golden Calf, London's first avant-garde night club, opened by Frida Strindberg (the third wife of the playwright) in 1912.[72] The club was not only a favorite haunt of the Rebel Art Centre crowd (which included Gaudier-Brzeska), but was decorated with murals by Wyndham Lewis, Jacob Epstein, and other members of the group. The reference to the figure of the golden calf, an emblem of idolatry, reminds us of the dangers inherent in Pound's theorization of the Image during this period. Moreover, he suggests that the cultural plague disseminated by radio, and the "secret controls" that go along with it, may be linked genealogically to the milieu of the Cave of the Golden Calf, a cryptic place that is associated not only with "night life" and the Image, but with the "romance" of London—including Pound's acquaintance with Gaudier-Brzeska. Ultimately, then, one must conclude that the crypt effects of Pound's fascist radio broadcasts derive from the historical translation of Decadence into the cultural poetics of an incipient avant-garde.

In Pound's mind, the events of this period in his life are mysteriously linked to a scene of devastation in the future, as he reveals in a comment about the magazine *Blast*:

> And the magazine or manifesto was in its way a harbinger. (I am never quite sure about that word harbinger, but it does seem to be generally accepted as meaning a sign of something to come.) Well

---

72. The brochure for the new club declared, "Our aims have the simplicity of a need: We want a gaiety that does not have to count with midnight. We want surroundings, which after the reality of daily life, reveal the reality of the unreal." Cited in Richard Cork, "The Cave of the Golden Calf," *Artforum* (December 1982): 56–68.

> the other war came and prevented its being a periodical or annual publication, got out a second number in 1915 and that ended it, Gaudier-Brzeska the sculptor havin' been killed in the interim. (*RB* 107)

The fact that Pound stumbles over the meaning of the word "harbinger" in a speech that refers to Gaudier's death signals a wave of interference emanating from Gaudier's crypt. Indeed, whenever Pound mentions Gaudier in the broadcasts we are sure to find evidence of historical disarray and garbled memories—evidence of the pressure exerted by the phantom. In one speech, for example, Pound alludes to Gaudier's death and remembers rescuing his drawings from a bombed-out studio in Genoa (*RB* 293). Apparently, the inhabitant of Gaudier's crypt has come forward in the radio broadcasts and lodged himself in a scene of devastation that rehearses the legacy of improper burial: Pound recounts a belated attempt to salvage Gaudier's artistic remains.

This phantasmic disturbance only confirms what Pound had learned many years earlier from the "ghost psychology" of the Noh plays. Shortly after Gaudier's death, Pound observes, "There is nothing like a ghost for holding to an idée fixe" (*T* 226). A phantom never lets go; its sorrow, its anger, are inconsolable. In the broadcast of May 18, 1942, Pound all but acknowledges the constant presence of ghosts in his radio speeches and their link to the earliest features of his poetic development. By constructing a demonology for others, he reveals the demons caged in his own mind. "With Phantoms" is the title of the broadcast. It assails "the phantom that the Anglo-Jew world is fighting," a phantom "built out of lies" (*RB* 137). At the beginning of the speech, Pound quotes a line from Tennyson's "Idylls of the King" (which gives the speech its title): "Shall come to fight with phantoms and to fall." This citation anchors the broadcast in Pound's earliest poetic tastes: a weak spot for Tennysonian "rhetoric" coincides, we should recall, with his illegitimate affection for the dead. In addition, the line evokes certain poems that Pound associated with World War I and his commitment to Imagism: the poem by James Joyce that begins with an image of a phantom army in the sky, and Yeats's poem "The Magi." Regarding Tennyson's line, Pound urges his listeners, "Take it as a prophecy," meaning we should expect the

German phantom to triumph over the delusions of the "Anglo-Jew" (*RB* 137). We also have reason, however, to read Tennyson's line as prophetic of the outcome of Pound's own struggle with the phantasmic Image in Gaudier's crypt.

Throughout the broadcasts, Pound worries about the intelligibility of his speeches, on a variety of different levels. From the standpoint of technology, for example, he is concerned about the clarity of the signal and the receptivity of the apparatus. After listening to one of his speeches over the radio (they were prerecorded in batches of four or five at a time), he comments, "Excellent delivery last night. Voice absolutely clear and every word 'visible,' except for a few ORful KRRumpzzz! of static or atmospheric or whatever BLITZED out a few phrases" (*SC* 592). In this report, we find Pound worrying that "atmospheric" disturbance, or perhaps other signals—conceived as a "BLITZ"—might obscure his delivery (a concern that touches the basic problem of unknown or hostile sources of interference in the broadcasts). It also reveals that he conceives of his broadcast voice in visual terms, viewing it as an image projected through the radio, an image that recalls the poetic Image of 1913 in its intangible, and thus highly unstable, clarity. We should therefore understand the "acoustic mirror" of his voice as an expression of the dominant analogy between Image and phantom. The elision of voice and Image in the radio broadcasts creates "a special medium for expressing emotion," which Pound first discovered in the ghost plays of the Noh theater (*T* 241).

Pound's concern about the clarity of the signal verges on the more troubling question of whether or not anyone was listening—a fear that he expressed repeatedly. Writing to William Joyce, a British citizen who broadcast for the Nazis under the pseudonym "Lord Haw Haw" (and who was executed after the war), he complains, "I go it blind, I have no idea if anyone listens" (*SC* 594). Once again, Pound mixes verbal and visual elements in describing the sense of isolation that he felt as he surrendered to the "tribal ghosts" of radio. Even as late as 1945, Pound still wondered if anybody had been listening: "What I am in absolute ignorance of is: whether anyone actually heard my broadcasts" (*SC* 590). What are we to make of this sense of isolation? If it is true that Pound occupied the place of the phantom by speaking on the radio, that he was broadcasting—according to the cryptic economy of the Image—from the realm of the dead, then his fears are not at all surprising; for the dead are jealous spirits, eager for the solicitations of the living. Pound was troubled by the inattention (or nonexistence) of his listeners just as the dead are embittered by the neglect—the ill-will—of the living. Indeed, he communicated the grievances of the dead because he had become one of them: radio offered the means to realize his dream of the "mediumistic artist," whose senses the technical media extend to the realm of the dead. His words issue from oblivion, from the Cave of the Golden Calf, the underground "scene" that preserves and conceals the Image.

Pound's fear that no one was listening coincided with a deeper fear that his speeches were incoherent, riddled by interference from beyond the grave. In either case, he risked being cut off from the world, sealed in a crypt that evoked the prehistory of the Image—a fate conjured by the medium of radio. At one point he says, "Sometimes I try to tell you too much. I suspect I talk in a what is called incoherent manner: 'cause I can't (and I reckon nobody could) tell where to begin . . . I was wonderin' if anybody listened to what I said on Rome Radio" (*RB* 227). Pound's concern about where to begin, where to enter the maze of the past, echoes throughout the broadcasts: "And after a hundred broadcasts it is still hard to know where to begin" (*RB* 192). What is it that he finds so daunting? The idea that he was giving voice to the unspeakable (as Abraham suggests) may help explain the massive case of stage fright that gripped the whole undertaking. It may also be that he found radio disturbing because it revealed, inexorably, the shattering effect of the *Cantos:* his voice, on the air, was continually being interrupted, disguised, and disfigured by other voices. Usually he found himself in the *middle* of a "conversation," as he says of one of his speeches (RB 367).

The impassioned voices of the dead simply won't let him get a word in edgewise. At one point, utterly distraught by the flood of words and thoughts being *dictated* to him out of "NECESSITY," he exclaims, "I am held up, enraged, by the delay needed to change a typing ribbon, so much is there that OUGHT to be put into the young American head. Don't know which, what to put down, can't write two scripts at once. NECESSARY FACTS, ideas, come in pell-mell. I try to get too much into ten minutes" (*RB* 192). The fact that Pound is trying to transcribe "two scripts at once" reveals the effects of "dictation" and the presence of the phantom in the broadcasts. On another occasion, he makes reference to a double source of speech that eludes him: "Had I tongue of men and angels I should be unable to make sure that even the most faithful listeners would be able to hear and grasp the whole of a series of my talks" (*RB* 190). In fact, Pound conversed throughout the broadcasts in the "tongue of men and angels," a torn, hybrid speech forced upon the living by the dead. His indecipherable instructions to the "nobodies" who were listening corroborates Gregory Whitehead's observation that "radio is a medium voiced by multiple personalities, perfect for pillow talk, useful as an antidepressant, but also deployable as guiding beam for missile systems" ("Out of the Dark" 257). In a lucid moment, Pound acknowledges, "I am perfectly aware that I might as well be writing Greek or talking Chinese with a foreign accent, so far as making this statement clear to the hearer or reader is concerned" (*RB* 262). By his own admission, Pound was speaking "in tongues" to his listeners, performing a "translation" of the Image and Gaudier's phantom into the mythography of fascism. The transmissions remain necessarily garbled because they convey, even as they resist, the mutilated hopes and achievements of Pound's youth in London. Indeed, the opacity of his translation is the mark of its fidelity.

The accusations that Pound leveled against his listeners during the broadcasts offer the most telling portrait of his state of mind. The ultimate target of the following indictment, for example, is Pound himself: "You are in black darkness and confusion. You have been hugger-muggered, and carom-shotted into a war, and you know NOTHING about it. You know NOTHING about the forces that caused it" (*RB* 202). These words paint a portrait of a mind baffled and piloted by sinister forces—a mind, like Pound's, that is ignorant of the forces controlling it. At other times, the voice in the broadcasts displays an astonishing, almost clairvoyant sense of the rivalry (between word and Image, the living and the dead) that animated the broadcasts: "An assault on mortal man, an assault on the exaggerated privileges accorded to the whims and greeds of the dead was NEEDED. It came" (*RB* 197). This pronouncement, uttered by the phantom, is largely incoherent; yet it conveys with perfect fidelity the catastrophic logic that underlies the magical realism of the broadcasts. It suggests not only that mortal man and the dead are identical, but that the radio broadcasts are the site of a monumental conflict between the living dead and an unnamed race of immortals (who are led by the prophet Ezra). Ultimately, the devastation recorded by the broadcasts extends to events awaiting the prophet in the future: "Whom God would destroy, he first sends to the bughouse" (*RB* 27).

It is poetic justice, if nothing else, that requires us to judge Pound's radio speeches either as the product of madness or as a record of treason. Although he pleaded insanity at his trial, the guise of madness only conceals the hidden grounds of treason. The word "treason" derives from the same Latin verb that gives us the word "tradition": *tradere*. Hence, the traitor is necessarily bound to the past, to the substance of what he betrays. Conversely, the fascist art of memory that Pound practiced on the air inevitably risked the obliteration of "natural" memory, of history: it was indeed a "science of forgetting" that became indistinguishable from the medium of radio. The treachery of Pound's behavior over the radio therefore revealed, but also disfigured, what spoke through him—a submerged "tradition" of idolatry and illicit affection for the dead. Through the "devil box"—the new medium of radio—Pound fully realized the political aesthetic of magical realism, which he first discovered in the ghost plays of the Noh theater. The Image encrypted in Gaudier's missing grave came forward in the radio broadcasts as an emanation from the past, a "radiant" substance that synthesized voice and image, rationality and magic, technology and unreason. Through the medium of radio, the Image cast a political shadow that encompassed not only Pound's commitment to fascism but the hyperaesthetic qualities of his earliest poems.

Acknowledgments / Index

Acknowledgments

"Every representation of death is a misrepresentation." This statement does not, of course, excuse the blurry vision that plagues this book. Rather, it permits me to state what is obvious, but also inscrutable: this book is itself a crypt, sustained by negation. As a crypt, it is "the very tombstone of the illicit, and marks the spot of an extreme pleasure, a pleasure entirely real though walled up, buried alive in its own prohibition." As a crypt, this book is stored with images that do not properly belong to its subject, death. These images serve, and serve to encrypt, a pleasure denied the author (except in translation) and inaccessible to the reader. A book such as this is misleading, and worse: it is the wrong book, a red herring. What can be acknowledged must only help to conceal and preserve, at any cost, the unnameable word-thing sealed in the tomb of this book.

It is also true, however, that the place of the excluded word-thing looms as a monument—to artifice, to meaning, and, most surprisingly, to tradition. The fanfare of resistance and negativity that sustains my reading of Pound's necrophilia is not only indebted, it is insolvent. The tools of negation, however enigmatic, are acquired, and I am happy to have the chance to give some small idea of my dependence on other writers and scholars. This will be obvious from the text, but my book could not have been written without the superb textual criticism produced by generations of Pound scholars. In a more immediate context, the problem of the image in general cannot be separated, in my mind, from the groundbreaking work of W. J. T. Mitchell

Acknowledgments

or from his generous guidance and support of this project. His remarkable ability to unveil the dialectical features of visual culture remains for me a model of critical thinking. I must also admit that my poor judgment regarding the limits of speculative criticism would be even more obvious than it already is had I not learned a thing or two from Robert von Hallberg. Namely: facts can't hurt; indeed, as Marx reminds us, they have their own spectral qualities.

There are many other people who have contributed directly to this book, by reading portions of it, or indirectly, by their support or example. My thanks is small repayment indeed for the gifts of these friends, colleagues, and mentors: Leo Braudy, Ron Gottesman, James Kincaid, Peter Manning, Françoise Meltzer, Carol Muske, Laurence Rickels, Paul Ricoeur, Avital Ronell, and David St. John. In addition, I could not have completed this book without the financial support of the Mrs. Giles Whiting Foundation and the Zumberge Research and Innovation Fund at the University of Southern California. I also wish to thank Lindsay Waters for his editorial insight and Maria Ascher for her vital adjustments and corrections of the text. Finally, I am deeply grateful to Elaine Armour and Nancy Worth Tiffany, whose long support and encouragement have helped guard this work from irrelevance and estrangement.

Index

Abraham, Nicolas, 54, 75, 106, 110, 112, 139, 159, 161, 187n, 240, 288
Adorno, Theodor, 14n, 183, 244, 264n
Agamben, Giorgio, 54n, 78n, 94n, 204n
Agassiz, Louis, 165
Alchemy, 158–159. *See also* Sublimation
Aldington, Richard, 118, 129, 139, 254, 270
Anaximander, 194
Anderson, David, 188, 202, 203
Angulo, Jaime de, 146n
Antheil, George, 112, 231, 232–233
Anti-Semitism, 168–170, 173–174, 221, 236, 239–240, 244, 251, 272, 284
Apollinaire, Guillaume, 112
Aquinas, Thomas, 95
Aristotle, 97
Arnheim, Rudolf, 223n
Atkins, John, 212
Avant-garde. *See* Vorticism

Bachelard, Gaston, 63–64
Bacigalupo, Massimo, 195
Bacon, Francis, 16, 63
Barney, Natalie, 245
Bass, Alan, 216
Bassnet-McGuire, Susan, 193
Bataille, Georges, 78, 153n, 161, 171, 172, 187
Baudelaire, Charles, 127–128, 165, 188n
Beddoes, Thomas Lovell, 123

Bell, Ian F. A., 28n, 223n
Benda, Julien, 22
Benjamin, Walter, 6, 12, 66–67, 69, 186, 192, 215, 223
Bergson, Henri, 89, 224n
Berman, Antoine, 178–179, 180, 181, 185–186, 206n, 215
Berman, Louis, 166
Berman, Russell A., 24
Binyon, Laurence, 198
Blackmur, R. P., 39
Blake, William, 198, 255, 256–257
Blanchot, Maurice, 1, 4–5, 7–9, 29, 65, 106, 133, 143
Blindness. *See* Negation; Visuality, modern conceptions of
Body. *See* Corporeality; Materiality
Bonnefoy, Yves, 177, 180
Borges, Jorge Luis, 218
Born, Bertrand de, 117, 266
Bosman, Willem, 212
Boym, Svetlana, 67
Brancusi, Constantin, 199
Brodzky, Horace, 261n, 271
Bronfen, Elisabeth, 66, 148n, 150–151
Brooks, Louise, 232n
Brown, Norman O., 150
Browning, Robert, 168, 169, 215, 262, 266n
Brzeska, Sophie, 109–110, 113
Bullock, Marcus Paul, 15n, 74n
Burke, Kenneth, 65

Index

Burne-Jones, Edward, 29, 135, 138
Bush, Ronald, 40
Buss, Kate, 33n

Cadaver. *See* Corporeality; Corpse; Materiality
Camoëns, Luis Vaz de, 134
Carpenter, Humphrey, 120, 268
Carr, Arthur J., 82
Cartwright, Lisa, 16–18
Casillo, Robert, 113n, 173n, 283
Castiglione, Baldassarre, 107
Catullus, 188n
Cavalcanti, Guido, 26, 55, 90, 91, 92–93, 105, 140, 187, 190, 193, 196, 198, 202–208, 209, 210, 214, 215, 216, 217–220, 224. *See also* Pound, Ezra, translations
Céline, Louis-Ferdinand, 168
Chamberlain, Lori, 186n, 215n
Champollion, Jean-François, 180
Chase, Cynthia, 214
Christ, Carol T., 82
Cicero, 94, 96
Cimabue, 198
Cinema, 31, 42, 246–247
Coburn, Alvin Langdon, 30, 33, 34
Cocteau, Jean, 231, 280
Cole, Roger, 267
Coleridge, Samuel Taylor, 81
Cookes, Sir William, 224n
Cork, Richard, 285n
Corporeality, 16, 18–20, 31, 35–36, 119–120, 130, 131–133, 137–139, 143, 150–151, 156, 159–174, 248–250, 253, 277. *See also* Materiality; Monstrosity
Corpse, 1, 4–12, 15, 20, 21, 25, 36, 53, 54, 62, 71, 84, 122, 124, 125, 126, 127–129, 131, 135, 136, 140, 142, 147–148, 152, 156, 159, 169, 173, 184–186, 210, 216, 222, 228. *See also* Corporeality; Materiality
Cory, Mark E., 230n
Crary, Jonathan, 15–19, 35–36
Cros, Charles, 233
Crowds, modern theories of, 48, 63, 235, 283

Crypt, 11, 12, 20, 30, 36, 42, 46, 53, 54, 56–59, 62, 70, 75, 77, 80, 89, 94, 96, 97, 100, 110, 112–113, 125, 139, 141–143, 145–146, 156, 159, 161, 166, 179, 210, 237, 238, 241–242, 246, 249, 275, 285–286. *See also* Fetishism; Medium; Memory; Mourning; Negation; Places (topoi), theory of
Cryptology, 230. *See also* Crypt; Hieroglyphics
Curie, Marie, 224n

Dali, Salvidor, 232n
Daniel, Arnaut, 202
Dante Alighieri, 33, 68, 82, 105, 134, 191, 198, 199, 268
Daston, Lorraine, 13–15, 27, 30, 226–227
Davie, Donald, 24, 87, 111
Daviot, Gordon, 271n
Decadence, 20, 26, 49, 70, 73, 81–82, 84, 114, 115, 121, 124, 126, 131, 132, 147, 149, 151, 152, 156, 258, 276, 284, 285. *See also* Necrophilia
DeLanda, Manuel, 230n
Dembo, L. S., 195
Derrida, Jacques, 10–11, 12, 19, 161, 178, 179, 189, 190, 193, 195, 200, 214–215
Descartes, René, 16, 172
Dolmetsch, Arnold, 247
Douglas, Mary, 114, 153–155, 160
Dowson, Ernest, 88, 115, 121, 148
Dryden, John, 176, 184
Duchamps, Marcel, 232n
Duplessis, Rachel Blau, 43

Eakins, Thomas, 169
Eberle, Mattias, 242n
Ede, H. S., 271
Edison, Thomas Alva, 233–234
Elegy, poetic, 22, 81–85, 188–189, 197. *See also* mourning
Eliot, T. S., 22, 39, 82, 166, 172–173, 279n
Epstein, Jacob, 266n, 285
Exchange value. *See* Fetishism

Index

Fascism, 17, 20, 24, 25, 36, 39, 45, 48, 52, 61, 63, 64, 73, 146, 168, 222, 223, 224–225, 228, 230, 233, 234, 235–236, 251, 252, 270, 276, 279, 281, 282, 287, 289, 290
Feminization of the male poet, 43, 102, 109, 110–111, 112, 129–131, 134, 136–139, 140, 143, 144. *See also* Monstrosity
Fenollosa, Ernest, 55, 130, 225–226, 257, 259
Fetishism: visuality and, 5–6, 9, 14, 17, 21–22, 26, 54, 75, 77, 96, 110 (*see also* Phantom); material culture and, 4, 5–7, 9, 10, 17, 36, 48, 60, 62–63, 64, 70, 74–80, 125, 137, 148–149, 159, 181–182, 193–194, 201, 211–213 (*see also* Materiality); exchange and, 6, 26, 77–80, 175, 180–184, 187, 214, 223 (*see also* Translation); sexual, 6, 63, 74–75, 78, 137, 213, 216–217, 219n. *See also* Marx, Karl
Flint, F. S., 45–46, 270
Fontenelle, M. de, 123
Ford, Ford Madox, 32, 81n, 233n, 271
Foucault, Michel, 17
Freud, Sigmund, 6, 62, 74–75, 112, 145, 150, 184, 189, 190n, 213, 216, 219n, 224n, 241, 263–264, 276–277
Fried, Michael, 169–170
Friedman, Susan Stanford, 43
Frobenius, Leo, 230, 271, 281

Galison, Peter, 13–15, 27, 30, 226–227
Gaudier-Brzeska, Henri, 26, 32, 34, 45, 49, 53, 54, 86–91, 102, 104, 106–113, 114, 119, 130, 140, 145, 167, 232–233, 236–241, 256, 261–262, 264n, 265–278, 285–287, 289, 290
Giotto, 198, 199
Goethe, Johann Wolfgang von, 241
Gombrich, E. H., 223n, 235n
Goodwin, Sarah Webster, 66, 148n, 150–151
Gorgias, 281
Gould, George Milbry, 164
Gourmont, Rémy de, 35–36, 130, 131–132, 157, 162, 170

Goux, Jean-Joseph, 70
Grey, E. C., 139
Grivel, Charles, 236

H.D., 41–43, 47, 92, 129–130, 138, 139n, 146
Hardy, Thomas, 22
Hart, Bernard, 89
Heidegger, Martin, 194–195, 273–274
Henderson, Alice, 32, 49n, 260n, 272
Herf, Jeffrey, 251–252
Hermeneutics, 42, 43, 46, 52, 60–63, 66, 70, 80, 125, 165–166, 178, 180, 230
Hertz, Heinrich, 224n
Hieroglyphics, 42, 43n, 180–181, 229. *See also* Hermeneutics
Hirsh, Elizabeth A., 42–43
Hitler, Adolf, 221, 235, 281
Hölderlin, Friedrich, 186, 215
Homer, 90, 92n, 95, 100, 102–104, 123, 187, 190, 209, 218, 265. *See also* Pound, Ezra, translations
Homoeroticism, 43, 54, 81, 88, 103, 105, 109, 112–113, 119, 120, 130, 131, 138, 141, 232–233, 262, 271, 275–276. *See also* Gaudier-Brzeska, Henri
Hooley, Daniel, 191–192
Horkheimer, Max, 14n, 183
Hough, Graham, 38n
Hulme, T. E., 89, 132, 270
Hunt, Violet, 269
Hyde-Lees, Georgie, 273

Ideogram, image conceived as, 23, 41, 44, 51, 52, 61, 62, 90, 94, 150, 156, 197, 201, 207, 208, 225–226, 229, 230, 234, 236, 242, 276, 279–281, 283
Incubus, figure of, 141–142, 193, 256, 264–265. *See also* Phantom
Invisibility. *See* Negation; Phantom; Radioactivity; Visuality, modern conceptions of

Jacobs, Carol, 215n
Jakobson, Roman, 177

Index

James, William, 224n
Jameson, Fredric, 66, 67
Jay, Martin, 2n, 16n, 20, 23
Johnson, Lionel, 115, 121, 148
Joyce, James, 33, 52, 117, 124, 163, 164, 270, 279, 286
Joyce, William, 287
Jung, Carl, 224n
Jünger, Ernst, 223, 242, 252

Kahn, Douglas, 229–230
Kant, Immanuel, 9–10, 19
Kaplan, Alice Yaeger, 73n, 115n, 225, 235, 240
Kayman, Martin, 47, 223n
Keenan, Thomas, 6n, 181, 182, 183
Kenner, Hugh, 39–40, 48, 101, 187–188, 197
Kincaid, James R., 82n
Kittler, Friedrich, 69, 178, 180, 181
Kristeva, Julia, 11–12, 150, 153–154, 160, 166, 168, 174

La Fleur, William R., 25n
Landor, Walter Savage, 123
LeBon, Gustave, 22, 48, 235
Leibiz, Gottfried, 63, 230
Lenin, V. I., 25n
Leopardi, Giacomo, 135
Lewis, Phillip, 214
Lewis, Wyndham, 84–85, 112, 120, 122, 124–125, 129, 272, 280, 285
Litz, A. Walton, 82
Lodge, Sir Oliver, 224n
Longenbach, James, 47, 269, 273n
Lowell, Amy, 48, 50, 86, 88n
Lycanthropy, 144–146. *See also* Monstrosity
Lyotard, Jean-François, 45

Machiavelli, Niccolò, 244, 245
MacKenna, Stephen, 213
Malatesta, Sigismundo, 68, 135
Mania, 277
Mann, Paul, 69–70, 176
Manning, Frederic, 116
Marconi, Guglielmo, 248, 277, 278

Marinetti, F. T., 221, 248
Martin, Wallace, 89
Marx, Karl, 5–9, 17, 29, 62, 67, 69, 74–80, 96, 180–184, 213
Materiality, 4–8, 12, 13, 18–19, 25–26, 35, 45, 54, 62–63, 70, 76, 84, 115, 120, 122, 143–144, 147–160, 167, 168, 169–170, 209, 211, 222. *See also* Corporeality; Radioactivity
Mathematics, 23, 28–29, 41, 44, 94, 156
Mathews, Jackson, 197
Maxim, Hudson, 28n
McLuhan, Marshall, 84n, 277, 279–282
Media, technical, 2, 15, 16–17, 20–21, 25, 28, 30, 42, 83, 171, 179, 221–236, 238, 242, 246–248, 249, 251, 253, 278–280, 282, 287
Medium, concept of, 14–15, 18, 21, 23, 25, 30, 48, 49, 58, 68–69, 129, 147, 171, 175, 188, 217, 222, 225, 227–230, 232, 236, 242, 249, 250, 253, 273–275, 277, 280, 284, 287. *See also* Fetishism; Translation
Mehlman, Jeffrey, 223n
Meltzer, Françoise, 149
Melville, Herman, 2–4, 29
Memory, 44, 54, 56, 77, 87–88, 91–99, 100–101, 107–108, 175, 184, 187, 190, 196, 213–214, 220, 226, 232, 233, 234, 252, 280, 290. *See also* Mourning; Places (topoi), theory of
Mesmerism, 267n
Metamorphosis. *See* Feminization of the male poet; Fetishism and exchange; Monstrosity; Translation
Milton, John, 151, 164
Miró, Joan, 198
Mitchell, W. J. T., 2n, 21, 76, 137, 149n, 184, 211n, 227
Moholy-Nagy, László, 229
Monroe, Harriet, 32, 57, 119, 260n
Monstrosity, 144–146, 166, 170–174, 214, 215, 275. *See also* Corporeality
Moore, Marianne, 37, 55, 254n, 258n
Mortality. *See* Necrophilia; Translation
Mourning, 11, 22, 26–27, 43, 53, 81, 83, 87–88, 90, 92, 103, 106, 111–

112, 129–131, 134–135, 137, 142–144, 145–146, 156, 188–189, 237–238, 249, 256, 262, 263, 264–265, 267, 270–272, 275–277. *See also* Memory; Phantom

Nabokov, Vladimir, 185
Nagy, N. Christoph de, 196n
Necrophilia, 10, 15, 22, 26, 44, 48, 49, 53, 54, 56–59, 63, 67, 68, 69, 73, 77, 81–85, 114, 115–121, 123–124, 127–129, 134–135, 144–145, 147, 150, 155, 196, 205, 214–215, 248, 276, 278, 290. *See also* Decadence; Mourning; Negation
Negation, 1–5, 9, 10–12, 14–16, 19, 25, 27, 35, 36, 38–39, 42, 49, 59, 66–67, 98, 99, 110, 125, 126, 132, 150–151, 153–154, 156, 161, 226–227. *See also* Necrophilia; Objectivity; Visuality
Nelson, Lowry, 204n
Nietzsche, Friedrich, 1, 175
Nilsson, Nils Ake, 30n
Nostalgia. *See* Memory; Mourning; Necrophilia
Nougé, Paul, 231
Novalis, 180
Nye, Robert A., 235

Oates, Caroline, 145n
Objectivity, discourse of, 5, 9, 11, 12, 15, 19, 20, 21, 27–29, 30–31, 34, 36, 42, 49, 50, 55, 56, 58, 63, 124, 125, 147–148, 149, 150, 156, 199–200, 201–202, 217, 222, 226–227. *See also* Negation
Oblivion. *See* Fetishism; Memory
Olson, Charles, 167, 272, 273
Ophthalmology, 164–165, 166
Ortega y Gasset, José, 175, 177, 179
Ovid, 168, 169

Passivity, 241–242, 244–246, 247, 249, 250, 251, 252, 253. *See also* Feminization of the male poet
Paz, Octavio, 177
Perkins, David, 37n

Phantom, 5, 6, 8, 9, 12, 17, 18, 20, 21, 26, 41, 46, 47, 53, 56–57, 77, 84, 85, 88–89, 90–91, 95, 100–101, 104, 106, 129, 140–143, 157–158, 183, 186, 219–220, 230, 237–241, 242, 243, 244, 248, 250, 254–265, 270–271, 273–277, 282, 283–284, 286–289. *See also* Fetishism; Medium; Mourning; Radio
Phonography, 226, 229–230, 233–234, 235, 240, 247. *See also* Radio
Photography, 15–16, 30–31, 33–35, 108, 198, 203, 252. *See also* Cinema
Picabia, Francis, 231
Pietz, William, 5n, 63, 181–182, 201, 211n, 212
Pineal eye, 171–172
Places (topoi), theory of, 93–102, 125, 160, 226, 250. *See also* Crypt; Memory
Pleynet, Marcelin, 45
Po, Li, 117, 216
Polke, Sigmar, 16
Pondrom, Cyrena N., 42–43
Pope, Alexander, 255
Positivism, 12, 13, 21, 42, 43, 50, 60, 62, 63, 70, 125, 148, 165, 178, 223, 230. *See also* Objectivity, discourse of
Pound, Ezra
    Poems: "And Thus in Nineveh," 118; "Anima Sola," 118; "Apparuit," 56; *Cantos* as a whole, 40, 52, 55, 68, 84n, 102, 112, 123, 135, 159, 187, 201, 236, 242, 260n, 262, 280, 283, 288; Canto 1, 100, 103, 123, 209; Canto 3, 134; Canto 4, 157; Canto 9, 135; Canto 10, 135; Canto 16, 155; Canto 29, 247; Canto 30, 134; Canto 36, 90, 93; Canto 70, 100n; Canto 74, 90, 91, 100; Canto 76, 135; Canto 77, 105; Canto 83, 256n; "Canzon: The Vision," 121; "Canzon: The Yearly Slain," 116; Capilupus Sends Greetings to Grotus," 158; "Dance Figure," 58, 142; "Doria," 56;

Index

Pound, Ezra, poems (*continued*)
"Epilogue," 117, 209; "For Italico Brass," 114; "Histrion," 117, 191; "Hugh Selwyn Mauberley," 51, 52, 55, 90, 104, 111–112, 120, 122, 133–134, 247, 261; "I Wait," 141, 143; "Ikon," 139–140; "In a Station of the Metro," 49, 101, 112, 120, 156–158, 197; "La Fraisne," 105, 141; "La Nuvoletta," 134; "Laudantes Decem Pulchritudinis Johannae Templi," 157–158; "Lord of Shalott," 141; "Mesmerism," 267n; "Middle-Aged," 58, 119–120, 142; "Of Jacopo Sellaio," 136; "Phanopoeia," 254; "Piere Vidal Old," 107, 144, 265; "Redivivus," 118; "Redondillas," 116, 255; "Religio," 116; "Revolt against the Crepuscular Spirit in Modern Poetry," 126; "Sage Homme," 172–174; "Sestina: Altaforte," 107, 117, 265, 266–267; "Silet," 57, 156; "Sub Mare," 57; "Surgit Fama," 58; "The Alchemist," 140, 158; "The Picture," 135–136; "The Return," 56; "The Tomb at Akr Çaar," 58, 118, 142–143, 145; "The Tree," 130; "Threnos," 116; "To E.B.B.," 117; "Und Drang," 117, 243; "Villanelle: The Psychological Hour," 145; "Yeux Glauques," 135, 136, 138, 144;

Translations: Book XI of the *Odyssey*, 90, 95, 100, 102–104, 123, 187, 209; *Cathay*, 55, 59, 194–195, 197, 202, 206, 207, 208, 216, 257–258, 267; Chinese adaptations, 56n; Confucius, 215; *Dialogues des morts* (Fontenelle), 123; "Donna mi prega" (Cavalcanti), 90, 91, 92–93, 99, 206, 220; "Four Poems of Departure," 59; "Her Monument, the Image Cut Thereon" (Leopardi), 135; "Homage to Sextus Propertius," 116, 118, 130, 189, 192, 200–201, 202, 207, 219; "Lament of the Frontier Guard," 59, 267; "Le Vampire" (Baudelaire), 127–128; *Natural Philosophy of Love* (Gourmont), 36, 131, 162, 170–171; Noh plays, 55–56, 243–244, 251, 257–262, 264, 287, 290; "Song of the Bowman of Shu," 59, 267; *Sonnets and Ballate of Guido Cavalcanti*, 26, 55, 92, 187, 190, 198, 202–208, 210, 214, 215, 216, 217–219, 224; "The River Merchant's Wife," 143; "The Seafarer," 55, 207n, 208–211, 214, 218; "Werewolf in Selvage," 146n

Primitivism, 48, 234, 263, 271, 280–281
Propertius, Sextus, 116, 117, 118, 130, 189, 192, 201, 202, 207, 219. *See also* Pound, Ezra, translations

Quinn, John, 31
Quintilian, 94, 98

Rabaté, Jean-Michel, 74n, 242, 273n
Radiation. *See* Radioactivity
Radio, 20–21, 25, 28, 45, 146, 221–222, 223, 225, 228, 230, 232, 234–236, 237, 238, 240–241, 242, 245–246, 250, 251, 252, 265, 270, 271, 272, 275–276, 277, 279–290. *See also* Medium; Phantom
Radioactivity, 16n, 21, 25–26, 148, 222–228, 234, 276, 290. *See also* Materiality
Rainey, Lawrence, 68
Rand, Nicholas, 46
Ray, Man, 232n
Realism, magical, 242, 252–255, 257, 259, 261, 262, 282, 290
Rebatet, Lucien, 235
Redman, Tim, 25n
Reynolds, Joshua, 199

Index

Rickels, Laurence, 99n, 189n, 248, 249–250, 264, 265, 284
Roentgen, Wilhelm Konrad, 226
Romains, Jules, 48, 235
Ronell, Avital, 196, 239, 241, 274–276
Roosevelt, Franklin D., 240
Rossetti, Dante Gabriel, 135, 163, 191, 193, 202, 218
Ruskin, John, 135
Russell, Ken, 271n
Ruthven, K. K., 111, 156–157, 210, 253

Salò, Italian Fascist Republic of, 241, 277
Sappho, 142–143, 188n
Scarry, Elaine, 9, 25n, 71–74, 211
Schelling, Felix, 272
Schiff, Christopher, 232n
Schlegel, Friedrich, 181
Schleiermacher, Friedrich, 185
Schneidau, Herbert, 21n
Schopenhauer, Arthur, 177, 178, 184–185
Science. *See* Objectivity, discourse of; Positivism
Sellaio, Jacopo del, 135–136
Shakespear, Dorothy, 136, 137, 141, 250, 256, 266, 273
Shaviro, Steven, 6
Shelley, Percy Bysshe, 175
Sherry, Vincent, 22–23, 24
Sieburth, Richard, 148, 231n
Silverman, Kaja, 243n
Simonides, 93–94, 96, 97
Simpson, David, 4n
Sinclair, May, 27n, 31
Singleton, Charles, 106
Smirnoff, Victor, 217
Smith, William Brooke, 90, 104–106, 112, 238, 265, 272
Sophocles, 186
Sorel, Georges, 22
Spector, Jack J., 213
Spender, Stephen, 38
Stafford, Barbara, 18n
Steiner, George, 176n, 194
Stock, Noel, 278
Strindberg, Frida, 285

Sublimation, 149–151, 155–156, 158–159, 162, 166. *See also* Fetishism and exchange; Materiality
Surgery, 167–170, 172–174. *See also* Corporeality
Surrealism, 231–233, 280
Swinburne, Algernon, 88, 135, 148, 163, 188n, 191
Symons, Arthur, 115, 121, 152

Tarde, Gabriel de, 48
Taupin, René, 50
Taussig, Michael, 6, 12n, 234
Telegraphy. *See* Media, technical; Radio; Translation
Tennyson, Alfred, 82–84, 141, 286–287
Terrell, Carroll F., 103
Thompson, Sir J. J., 224n
Tolchin, Neal, 137n
Torok, Maria, 54, 75, 110, 139, 159, 161, 187n
Translation, 26, 55, 69, 98, 129, 139, 147, 157–158, 159, 175–220, 223, 234, 237, 250, 267, 273–275, 278–279, 289. *See also* Fetishism and exchange; Medium

Upward, Allen, 122

Valéry, Paul, 185
Valla, Lorenzo, 107
Vega, Lope de, 188
Ventriloquism, 162–163, 234, 250. *See also* Translation
Villon, François, 111, 219
Virilio, Paul, 103n
Visuality, modern conceptions of, 1–9, 12, 14, 15–20, 21–25, 26, 29–36, 99, 125, 135–136, 147, 157, 165, 170–172, 200, 204–206, 222, 223–228, 232. *See also* Fetishism; Medium; Negation; Objectivity
Volkan, Vamik, 131
Voltaire, 162
von Hallberg, Robert, 24, 38n, 270
Vortex, image conceived as, 23, 32, 44, 46, 90, 132, 208, 277
Vorticism, 22, 23, 30–31, 32–34, 50,

Index

Vorticism (*continued*)
 52, 68, 86, 87, 124–125, 232, 255, 280, 285

Wachhorst, Wyn, 234n
Warren, Rosanna, 188
Wellbery, David, 69, 70
Whistler, James McNeill, 29
Whitehead, Gregory, 225, 228, 289
Wilde, Oscar, 168
Williams, William Carlos, 104, 115, 165, 272
Witemeyer, Hugh, 116, 120

Wittgenstein, Ludwig, 50, 81, 147, 223, 229
Wolfson, Louis, 180n

X-ray images, 16, 226–227, 278. *See also* Radioactivity
Xie, Ming, 59, 197

Yates, Frances A., 94–99
Yeats, William Butler, 47, 112, 141, 219, 223n, 255–257, 259, 260, 270, 273, 286